Bev Morrissey-Merriman was born in 1947 in Toronto, Canada. She lives in Richmond Hill, Ontario, with her husband, Dave. They have two sons, one daughter and four grandchildren.

Bev has travelled extensively which has included over 250,000 miles of motorcycling across Canada, the United States and West Africa.

Having retired from a senior administrative position at York University, Bev is now a certified master personal trainer and alpine ski instructor.

Clinically obese, Bev first opened a gym door at the age of 60 and never looked back. Within 19 months, she was physically fit, down 40 pounds and with a healthy 23% body fat percentage. But, more importantly, at 72, she continues to maintain her physical fitness and lift weights.

This book is dedicated to my husband, Dave; our sons, Brent and Kurt; our daughter, Jill; our daughters-in-law, Jess and Katie; and our four wonderful grandchildren: Paige (eight), Penny (six), Madison (five) and Benjamin (three). Their parents, Brent and Jess, and Kurt and Katie, have been relentlessly careful with their children's dietary choices and none of these delightful creatures are overweight. They are happy, healthy, and physically active with downhill skiing, gymnastics, swimming, dance (gotta love those recitals), skating, tobogganing, bicycling and many other fun activities.

Bev Morrissey-Merriman

ARE YOU FAT-MAKING OR CALORIE-BURNING?

How to successfully shift your metabolic engine into a higher gear.

AUSTIN MACAULEY PUBLISHERS™

LONDON * CAMBRIDGE * NEW YORK * SHARJAH

Copyright © Bev Morrissey-Merriman (2021)

Ordering Information
Quantity sales: Special discounts are available on quantity purchases by corporations, associations, and others. For details, contact the publisher at the address below.

Publisher's Cataloging-in-Publication data
Morrissey-Merriman, Bev
Are You Fat-Making or Calorie-Burning?

ISBN 9781647500382 (Paperback)
ISBN 9781647500375 (Hardback)
ISBN 9781647500399 (ePub e-book)

Library of Congress Control Number: 2020915710

www.austinmacauley.com/us

First Published (2021)
Austin Macauley Publishers LLC
40 Wall Street, 33rd Floor, Suite 3302
New York, NY 10005
USA

mail-usa@austinmacauley.com
+1 (646) 5125767

I want to thank my patient book draft readers, all of whom helped me make this book relevant and readable: my dear sweet husband, Dave; my wonderful son, Kurt (reading in-between firefighting calls); my brother, Mike Morrissey (devoting some recuperation time from quadruple bypass surgery); my downhill ski-buddy, Anne Eaton; my bingo-pal, Janet Walker, who is also a nurse (give me a break, bingo dabbers are fun!); my incredibly knowledgeable former personal trainer, Dave Frieday; and my brilliant neighbor, Karen Chiykowski (reading in-between teaching at York University's Schulich School of Business, her English literature degree courses and working out at the gym – wowie, how'd she find the time?).

Table of Contents

This book will give you the tools to change your body's metabolism along with the explanation on why they work for <u>every</u> body including yours. These tools work for men too; nevertheless, I'm appealing to women because I know what it's like to feel the societal pressures to look perfect all the time, regardless of age.

In our contemporary society, it's unfortunate that many people are seeking some sort of magic pill or prescribed approach to quick weight loss. These methods seem to suggest that there's something wrong in your body and that once you correct it with some type of expensive device or nutritional program or weird supplement or unusual exercise prgram, all will be good in a relatively short time. This is simply not the case. There's nothing inherently wrong with your highly versatile body. It's beautifully programed to adapt to a wide range of conditions – good *or bad* – and it can use multiple fuel sources (body fat or muscle or carbohydrates) to meet various energy challenges, it can also repair itself and even reprogram itself when needed.

This book will help you understand how to lose weight <u>*and*</u> become more physically fit within the context of your body's pre-programed biochemical certainties. Certainties that you simply can't alter. When you realize the *type of food* you're eating may not be what you think it is and you understand how physical exercise causes your body to make important fat and muscle *tissue adaptations*, you'll appreciate that all is never lost in the fat war.

Read this book to become empowered with the information you need in order to turn your body from a fat-making engine into a calorie-burning engine. Learn how to understand your body's biology in a way that allows you to outmaneuver it without sending it into an innate biochemical and hormonal panic mode. Learn how chronic stress and sleep deprivation affect your hormones and inhibit fat-loss. Understand how weight-gain is a combination of realities including the facts that your body wants to hold on to its reserves and that for you to change your overall weight, you must engage in a battle of biology between you and your very clever hormonally driven body. Biochemistry explores the chemistry of living organisms. It's the chemical foundation for the understanding of all biological processes, including the regulation of proteins, fats, acids, vitamins and hormones. It can even explain the cause of some diseases and suggest ways they may be treated. Your biochemistry is *extremely powerful* and you should learn how to use it to benefit your goals.

When you finish reading this book, you will understand why I say the following to my personal training clients:

"You are not eating enough food to lose weight!"

"Did you know that drinking zero-calorie flavored water or soda pop make you fatter?"

"Eating fat does not make you fat!"

"Eating fat-free foods does not mean they are not fattening!"

"Dieting without exercising or exercising without dieting will never work."

"How you exercise and what you eat directly affects your hormones."

"Food is the most powerful drug you can ingest, and it can become addictive."

"It's really hard to lose fat by heavily restricting calories!"

"The biochemical effects to your body of the food you eat can't be changed!"

"Doing a lot of 'cardio' exercise when you're physically unfit will increase your body fat percentage!"

I do apologize at the outset about the inordinate amount of food industry bashing in the book. Nevertheless, I want you to fully understand that some of the reasons supporting your body fat are not all attributable to you and, these involve how and why the food industry creates its concoctions. Of course I understand that it needs to create foods that don't cost too much and it needs to address the issue of extended shelf-life; I just want you to be able to recognize what you're eating and how it'll affect your biochemical body. I want you to be able to make more informed healthy choices, choices that will move you away from fat-making or fat-maintenance, and closer to calorie-burning.

You'll also begin to appreciate why countries boasting the highest standard of living also have the highest percentage of clinically obese[1] people. I was one of those individuals before I started my journey to better health and weight 12 years ago at the ripe old age of 60!

Through this book, I'm aiming to explain <u>why</u> exercise, controlled stress and sleep are critical as well as <u>how to learn</u>, or maybe I should say *relearn*, how to eat in a way that meets your body's nutritional needs while avoiding the downsides of ill-informed food selection.

---

[1] To be considered "obese" you'd have a body-fat percentage of at least 35% for women and 25% for men. Your body-fat percentage is really a good indication of how healthy you are. And if you're at least 100 pounds overweight, you'd be considered "morbidly obese" and probably have a body-fat percentage over 40%!

Preface

The information and recommendations in this book are based upon my experiential history as one who hired a certified personal trainer to lose weight and get healthier, my subsequent experiences as a professional one-on-one certified personal trainer in a gym, and my extensive research.

Yes, some of the information in this book can be technical but knowledge is very powerful. You may as well appreciate how and why your body, a biological entity, reacts the way it does and why you can't make it do anything it doesn't want to no matter how hard you try or how long you pray to the fat-loss gods. It has innate systems and it'll only abide by them and not by your fanciful I-gotta-lose-weight-fast wishes.

My intent is not to give medical advice or to recommend the taking of or lowering of any medically prescribed medications. I would suggest that you talk with your medical doctor, your pharmacist and perhaps a certified nutritionist if you have any questions or worries. That said, there's a good chance your medications will probably change if you improve your physical fitness and diet (e.g., you'll lower your blood pressure and you'll sleep a heck of a lot better).

The material in this book is meant to provide information on weight-loss, nutrition and exercise in the most succinct and informative way possible. You'll find some of it a bit technical, but your body is not a simple unit, so I just couldn't ignore its complex systems while explaining what you should or should not do *and why*. I encourage you to read all of the chapters (and footnotes!), even those that are a bit heavy going. It'll only add to your knowledge base and who doesn't want to do that?

I've tried to be accurate by compiling information through research; however, there are always many different opinions on these subjects. Indeed, some of those opinions are confusing and often contradictory.

Writing a book on anything to do with health is always fraught with differences of opinion. Some of the views you may have heard or already read about are fully supported by authentic scientific research with substantial test groups, some not so much. Other suggestions are solely supported by industry-controlled research (research that tends to lean toward what the food industry wants you to believe). I'm not a practicing scientist, though I do have a Physics Degree, and I certainly don't work for the food industry. This is why, should you have any questions or doubts, I suggest always consulting a licensed medical practitioner in any of the specialties that could apply to your goals.

But really, do you actually think that the food industry has *our* best interests in mind? I sure don't!!! Put simply, food is your health so you must be ever vigilant about what you put into your mouth. This book will assist you in understanding how the food industry has hidden some of the negative sides of food choices. That said, there are reasonable rationales for what the food industry does with and to some of its foods. People want to buy time-efficient foods (e.g., bottled pasta sauce) simultaneously demanding that they don't have any preservatives or additives. Is that a reasonable request when those foods have to be able to sit on the counter for months without going rancid? I think not.

Now, back to you. You can hope for short-term weight-loss with some magic bullet promised by some sort of crazy diet or whatever, but when you have completed this book, I hope that you'll fully appreciate that your food consumption, your daily energy expenditure, your stress and your sleep patterns are ALL part of a highly integrated bunch of interacting biochemical pathways and circuits.

You just can't trick millions of years of evolution. Your body is adept and will never fail to save you. It will, for example, very efficiently adapt its metabolic "engine" to any nutritional situation it's placed in – good (nutritionally dense foods) or bad (starvation dieting). Put simply, that's its job and it's really really good at it!!!

When you persistently interfere with any of your normal bodily circuits and inter-related hormonal rhythms such as with unresolved stress or constant crazy dieting or poor sleep patterns or habitual sedentariness, then your body will always follow a built-in *counter hormonal response* and you'll ultimately fail at any long-term healthy maintainable weight-loss.

As the author, I encourage you to share anything in this book with your doctor, pharmacist, nutritionist, personal trainer, work colleagues, family and/or friends. Better yet, go to the library and do your own research. Knowledge is an incredibly powerful beast and it can keep you on the right weight-loss path.

Introduction

Who Am I And Why Am I Writing This Book?

I'm a 72-year-old woman who was quite typical in raising a family. I finished my meals and then proceeded to clean off the kids' plates *directly into my mouth*. Did I gain? You betcha. Then during menopause (in my 50s) I ballooned again. Just shy of 5'3", I weighed 165 pounds at the age of 59, even though I was an avid downhill ski instructor, an adventure motorcyclist and wasn't experiencing any major health issues.

Puffing my way to work from the parking lot, not liking my body and with three kids in their 20s, I knew I could <u>and should</u> put the time to myself – a concept often foreign to mothers. You know the joke – I had four children to take care of, three kids and my husband, and I believe I did a great job at it. No one complained about my weight. But quietly inside I was crying. I needed to do something. It was difficult finding clothes that fit well. When you have a tummy nothing looks very good does it? Saggy shapeless arms made tank tops a no-go. And let's face it, self-image is tied up with our weight and how we look. You may not agree with that premise on an intellectual level; nonetheless, I'll bet you do on an honest more personal level.

I was on two different blood pressure pills, water pills to make those work, cholesterol pills, osteopenia pills and still gaining weight. I'd tried all sorts of crazy diets to no long-term avail. I was unhappy and frustrated.

In 2007 I was completely fed up with myself, so I joined a gym at the age of 60, got myself a personal trainer and a sexy muscular young thing he was. Yup, I followed him all over the gym floor and did what I was told! I ate differently[2], took up resistance/weight-training for the first time, and over a period of 19 months dropped my weight from 165 to 125 pounds, dropped my body-fat percentage from a clinically obese 35% to a healthy 23%, looked great, loved myself again, could buy any type of clothing I wanted, and most importantly regained my self-esteem. I've never looked back. I continue to be a permanent gym fixture (AKA a "gym-rat") and watch how I eat. Indeed, in an effort to inspire older women, I became a professionally certified Personal Trainer just prior to retirement in 2012. Currently, I'm a certified Master Personal Trainer.

You too can do it if you understand *why and how* to achieve these results. I've had clients who have been successful. And I've had clients who were not successful. That is, those who paid for training but simply didn't follow some simple rules hence they gained back all the excess fat and weight. There just isn't any way around the fact that there are absolutely <u>no shortcuts</u>, you simply have to put in the time and the work! To reach your weight goals, you must sign-up for a biochemically *robust marathon,* not a biochemically *shocking sprint.*

I've invested a lot of time into reaching my goals, a lot of time reading reference books, and a heck of a lot of time in the gym. I wanted to create a book that synthesized what I've learned. And I wanted to answer many of the questions I've been asked as a personal trainer. I wanted an easy-to-read yet informative book, not one that glossed over the facts or one that promised results without dedication and resolve.

Why do you want to lose weight? To look better, to gain self-confidence, to be healthier, to get attention, for a big upcoming event, for a relationship, for an upcoming surgery, to get a new job, to be better at sports, to look younger, to look good in a bathing suit, to buy new clothes, to win a bet, tired of being nagged at, to make an EX sorry for the decision, etc. You must know what is driving you to want to undertake this journey. *Never forget that reason.*

---

[2] My trainer told me I wasn't eating enough to lose weight. I thought that was a weird concept but decided to listen and follow that advice, indeed advice I had never heard before. All my earlier attempts just involved trying to eat fewer calories and fewer carbohydrates or avoiding all fats.

You're going to go on a *long* journey[3]. It'll be difficult at the beginning, but as you travel along in time and make changes, your journey will become easier and it'll have been well worth the time and effort.

Your weight is the sum of all your past *and* your current choices. This book will arm you with the self-knowledge that can provide control over your choices, your health, your weight, your energy and even your aging process. When you are fit, you'll enjoy a better quality of life, a stronger immune system and a decreased risk of developing chronic diseases.

Another interesting benefit to looking aesthetically better is purely psychological. An improved appearance, as shallow as you may think that goal is (when compared to better health), will benefit your entire life. You'll be more fun to be with. You'll feel more productive at work. You'll glow with confidence. You'll have reduced stress in your life and you'll be sleeping a lot better. I could go on and on, but you get the rosy picture.

I should mention that you'll see a lot of obvious rules and suggestions near the end of the book; but did you ever really understand WHY those rules are repeated over and over and over??? And I bet you didn't even know about all of the rules mentioned? This book will agree with those diet and exercise foundations, *but it'll also give you the knowledge base* to fully appreciate *why* they work and *how* they work. It'll show you how to move your body from being a *fat-making engine* into a *calorie-burning engine*. And isn't that what you want?

Take a look at the following chart. This book will deal with the *question marks* you see. You may need to change one or more of the *four control points* over which you have power; specifically, the food choices you make, your exercise approach, your sleep patterns and/or your reactions to the stress in your life. If you want to control your overall weight and the amount of body fat you're carrying around, these are the ***only inputs*** you have! In response to those inputs, your body controls hormonal reactions, biochemical adaptations

---

[3] Of course, I should add that you can take the *shorter* journey and go for liposuction or maybe a tummy-tuck, but just keep in mind that although liposuction will remove a lot of body-fat, if you make no other changes in terms of exercise and diet, that fat will just return and it'll go elsewhere on your body. For example, if you have a tummy-tuck, that new fat may end up on your butt or upper arms. It has to go somewhere!!! Also, the cost of such surgeries probably would be higher than the cost of hiring of a personal trainer for one to two years.

and metabolic alterations all of which ultimately determine whether you have a *physically fit calorie-burning body* or an *inefficient fat-making body*.

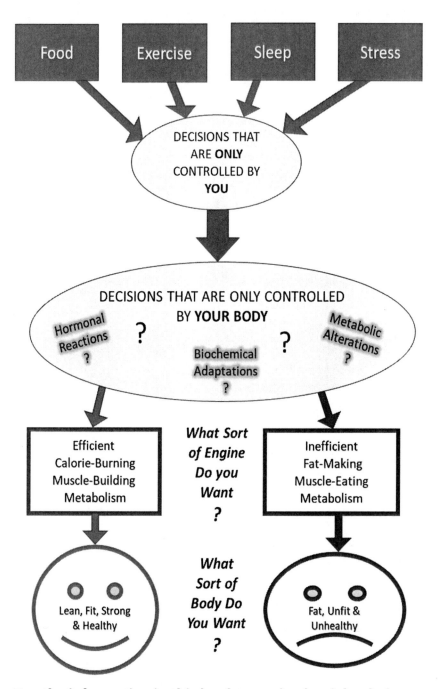

Use the information in this book to make the right choices.

I hate measuring food quantities and I don't like counting every meal's calories. When you finish reading this book, you'll not be doing either! Analyze yourself. How much do you want this? Read on. Be serious.

Individuals who achieve sustainable-weight-loss are a testament to the power of their resolve and their commitment and to the fact that all bodies are innately programmed to be metabolically efficient. *Metabolic efficiency is a measurement of how well your body uses its fuel sources*. Although fats are more slowly converted into energy when compared to carbohydrates, you can *always* improve your fat-burning efficiency through better nutrition, more exercise, more sleep and less stress.

Are you willing to travel along and endure the journey? I say "endure" because it isn't easy. There is no quick fix. There'll be a lot of temptations. It takes time and effort. Be patient and you too can be a **"Before and After."**

What have you got to lose?

I bet it's only that extra weight!!!

<u>Drink this WILLPOWER TONIC throughout your weight-loss days</u>
1 cup "I-need-to-do-this"!
1 quart "I'm-going-to-do-this!"
2 tbsps. "distilled-common-sense"
4 tbsps. "stick-to-it-ness"
2 cups "knowledge-from-this-book"
½ cup "raw-energy"

And while you're at it, check out my YouTube and Instagram videos.

YT = *are you fat making or calorie burning?*

IN = *calorieburningat72*

Book Overview

Why do we all try so many different ways to lose weight, yet never reach or stay at our goal weight for the long-term? When you read on, you may discover that you have actually trained your body to store fat! Or, as weird as it may sound, you have dieted your body into obesity!

To attain a healthy calorie-burning body you need to maintain long-term commitment. I haven't devoted a separate unit to the need for commitment. We know what that is, and we know you <u>have to have it</u> to be successful. Isn't it obvious? Dream on if you think that reading an exercise magazine, driving by a gym[4], eating a lot of junk-food, avoiding all carbohydrates, or not getting enough sleep will be great tactics.

In essence there are four interrelated factors to juggle simultaneously: your daily nutrition, your physical fitness level, your stress level and your sleep patterns. If you don't concentrate on <u>every one</u> of these aspects, you'll always be doomed to perpetual failure at sustained healthy weight-loss. Your body has its own biochemistry and you can't alter that fact. But you can try to understand how your body works hormonally and what you can do to get a lean toned and sexy body. You have to appreciate clean eating[5], be consistent with your exercise[6] and maintain long-term commitment[7]. If you can't change the way you eat, if you won't exercise with weights (either at home or in a gym) and if you simply refuse to commit yourself to an important long-term goal then you

---

[4] I have a lovely T-shirt that says, "Does running out of wine count as cardio??"

[5] "Clean" eating simply means eating *whole nutrient-dense and minimally processed foods*. It's really only about giving your body the nutrients it requires for your optimal health and overall wellness.

[6] Aerobic/cardio-training *and* anaerobic/weight-lifting training.

[7] If you are heavy, I'd say one-two years will be needed for true success at changing your lifestyle and keeping that weight off.

will **NEVER** be successful attaining sustainable weight-loss and a healthy lifestyle.

My favorite "failure" response is this: "But I already know what to do and how to eat! I've been doing that already." Hmmm, then why are you so heavy? Maybe you've been listening to the wrong people or reading the wrong information or exercising the wrong way. In fact, maybe you are failing because you've been educated to eat in a way that promotes both fat-storage and hormone resistance, specifically upsetting your leptin (appetite-regulating) and insulin (fat-producing) hormonal levels just by your food choices (ones that you may even think are healthy). Maybe you're exercising in a way that increases your body fat percentage and exacerbates your saggy skin.

Everything discussed and presented in this book will assist you in understanding how to reach your goal of *long-term* weight-loss and a healthier *more efficient* body. That said, do keep in mind that although this book will talk about the impact of food on your body and some different ways of exercising, it's *not* intended to be a "diet" book nor an "exercise" book. My strategy is to teach you how to focus on the natural ways to increase your body's ability to reduce your body fat, increase your muscle size, lose some weight, and speed up your ability to burn calories and fully process the food you eat into energy (i.e., your infamous metabolism).

Clients and people at work asked me a lot of questions, and indeed those questions form the chapter titles, but the *most asked question* I got was, "how did you do it?" Well, there really aren't any hidden surprises! I had to figure out my optimal calorie consumption[8], use effective eating strategies, and undertake the appropriate weight-training exercises in order to speed up my metabolism[9] so that I could use the calories I ate more effectively (i.e., *build more lean muscle and store less body fat*).

---

[8] Remember that energy comes only from the fuel of calories and fuel comes only from the food you eat. This means that you must eat, and you must eat regularly. But of course, you have to supply your body with the right nutritional food fuel at the right eating intervals and in support of your exercise level. And those choices should reflect your goals to gain, maintain or lose weight.

[9] Put another way, metabolism is the main factor defining your body tissue composition and this composition will include your body-fat percentage and your lean muscle tissue percentage.

I had to change how I ate. I had to go to the gym. I had to be committed and I had to be consistent. I had to think long-term. If you take 25-30 years to put on an extra 40 pounds, you're most certainly NOT going to lose it in 10 weeks. That belief is simply unrealistic. I wasn't in a hurry. It took me almost two full years to do it. I wanted it. I persisted. I accepted that it would not be a short-term time commitment. I was totally committed to change. I put the time and effort into myself. And I looked forward, never backward.

I looked upon it as the outset of a journey, my journey-to-fitness. When you first start on such a journey many of the people you see at the gym may make you feel intimidated as they look buff, lean and sexy. But remember that they're all on their own journeys albeit farther along. I can't emphasize enough how exciting it is to see someone on the gym floor who starts that journey and, after a while, you see them begin to change their body. I always admire them and tell them how well they're doing – after all, it isn't an easy thing to do. It takes time, hard work and dedicated persistence to keep moving forward.

To be honest, building a healthy lean and toned body isn't for the faint of heart. I remember when I hit 142 pounds (down from 165), I just sat there for weeks. It was horribly frustrating. I just wanted to get to 139 as my next achievement and it seemed to be taking forever. But I *never* gave up on my journey (or myself!) and eventually my body began to drop again and I started into the 130s. Now that was exciting. My patience got rewarded.

Being a baby-boomer, I think that my initial failures were because I had bought the contemporary wisdom of my time…hook, line, and sinker; propaganda that convinced women who wanted to lose weight, that they had to:

- eat fewer calories,
- eat less food; and,
- exercise more (albeit discouraging them from lifting weights like muscle-bound men). In fact, there weren't many gyms around in those days. We just assumed that only the Arnold Schwarzenegger-types went there and that was it!

Some further advice – don't read this book if:

- you can't change your approach to eating;
- you can never commit to change;
- you're run by the eating decisions of others;
- you know that you'll quit exercising after a few weeks; or,
- you believe those magazines claiming that you can "get washboard abs in 11 weeks!" *Such a ridiculous idea!*

And certainly, don't bother reading this book if you're a "know-it-all" type who simply won't be open to different avenues, that is a person who has *already decided* the best way to lose weight (e.g., crash dieting, drinking tons of water, and running hard on the treadmill daily).

In sum, if you're not willing to change anything in your life, then DON'T read any more of this book. You'll just be wasting your time.

Those New Year's resolution people that the gyms love to hook in early January pay lots of money for an annual membership and typically quit going after February! The gym gets to keep their money and not have them at the gym clogging up the cable machines, free weights and "cardio" machines. Don't burn up your money that way.

You'll see that the book is divided into distinct Units. At the outset of each Unit chapter you'll read an *inspirational quote*. All of these are attributed to Albert Einstein, a German-born theoretical physicist who was born March 14, 1879 and died on April 18, 1955. Obviously, some of his quotes might be challenged when viewed through today's societal filters, nevertheless he was a highly original thinker and *should only be judged historically*. I love these quotes, from a true renaissance man.

I wonder if Albert was thinking of us when he said that "we can't solve problems by using the same thinking we used when we created them".

Also, within the chapters you'll find some highlighted tips related to *"Fat-Making"* and *"Calorie-Burning."* These are biochemical facts and significant information in terms of changing your metabolic fat-making body into a lean calorie-burning body.

And you'll see a lot of detailed footnotes. You certainly don't have to read them, but for those of you who like to understand the whole comprehensive and scientific background supporting the chapter's suggestions or discussions, they're really quite interesting. And many share personal anecdotes.

As you read, you'll, at least I hope you will, discover how diet and exercise actually *overlap themselves* as far as your biochemical body is concerned. To undertake one without the other will *always* lead to failure in your fat war. And why is that? Well frankly, if you're not fully committed to both sides of the battle *simultaneously*, your body will adjust accordingly and your body *just isn't* programmed any differently than the bodies of the rest of those exercisers at the gym. And seriously, if others at the gym are changing their bodies and you aren't, then you <u>are</u> doing something wrong.

Proper training at the gym can take weight off and it can also keep new weight from appearing, but it can't get rid of <u>all the body fat</u> you built up over many years of inactivity and poor food choices. As you'll discover while reading this book, you'll also have to eat properly and endeavor to get better sleep and less stress to do that.

If you gain some understanding about the food industry, quit making excuses, accept some self-responsibility for your weight and be perfectly *honest* with yourself, you <u>*can*</u> get the healthy fit and toned body you want. Accept and arm yourself with the food product knowledge and physiological information provided in this book.

I'm assuming that if you bought this book, you're not a teenager. What is a year *or two* out of your life to get that healthy gorgeous body that you want? If you were 15 years old, maybe a year or two would sound like a lifetime. But, for you, it just isn't that long.

> ***Think of your diet as a way to control your <u>overall weight</u>***
> ***but think of exercise as a way to control your <u>inches</u>.***
> ***And aren't you after BOTH???***

Every calorie you eat has three potential outcomes and *<u>only you</u>* can help to steer your body's biochemical choice for that calorie.

- <u>You can burn it</u> meaning that your insulin level is kept in check, you won't gain weight and your metabolism won't get screwed up (exercise anybody?);

29

- <u>You can store it</u> meaning that your insulin level goes up, you gain weight and you slow down your calorie-burning metabolism (highly processed foods anybody?); or,
- <u>You can dump it</u> through your urine, causing kidney damage, liver stress (via ultra-low carbohydrate diets and high ketone output), while screwing up your metabolic rate (starvation diets anybody?).

And don't think that the food industry or the government is going to monitor you. There are no top-down answers for you. It's strictly a bottom-up approach that will work. You have to understand your body and its *biochemical* adaptations. **You** have to do the work. **You** have to be invested. **You** have to be in it for the long haul.

OK, let's figure out how to start burning some calories!

Unit 1

The Human Body Is a Beautiful System

What is involved in losing, gaining or maintaining body weight?
    When women choose a diet that promises
    an incredibly fast weight-loss,
    they typically <u>credit the diet</u> with for their results,
    but they'll never blame the diet for the quick weight-gain
    once they are off that diet.
    They'll <u>blame themselves</u> for the return of those unwanted pounds.

    Read on and you may discover that the diet you chose
    is the real culprit for putting that weight back on!

    Your body is just an engine and every engine needs fuel.
    Your biochemical body's engine is called your "metabolism" and it uses
"calories" for fuel.

    **Make any engine work harder and it'll always need more fuel.
    It doesn't matter whether that engine operates your gas-guzzling car
    or whether it runs your calorie-eating body.**

    Makes sense, doesn't it???

1.1 What Are the Main Body Organs Involved in Weight Control?

"Once you stop learning, you start dying." – A.E.

The main organs involved in weight-control are your liver, your gallbladder, your pancreas and your thyroid. An understanding of these organs is vitally important because of their direct relationship with your calorie-burning ability and with your fat-storage efficiency. Let's check each organ and its impact on your weight- and fat-loss goals.

Main Organs that affect your weight-loss and weight-gain.

Thyroid – controls metabolism and calorie-burning.

Liver – metabolizes food and regulates hormonal balance.

Pancreas – influences fat-storing and fat-burning enzymes.

Gallbladder – stores bile for digestion and absorbs fat.

What does your liver do?

While reading, you'll see how much I feel sorry for our livers. Livers are the responsible custodians for so many of your bodily functions and they really work hard to complete normal regulatory and storage functions[10]. Unfortunately, livers are often asked to take on other responsibilities due to our poor eating habits! Because your liver is the primary organ or gland for weight-control, you obviously want a properly functioning one. Your liver filters the blood coming from your digestive tract (including any toxic by-products from your foods) and regulates your hormonal balance. You can choose to help your liver like I did.

Your liver produces about a quart of yellowish-green bile daily, stores it in your gallbladder, and subsequently transports it to your intestines on an as-needed basis during digestion. Bile emulsifies[11] as it breaks down and absorbs dietary fats in your small intestine. If your liver does not produce sufficient bile, then your dietary fat cannot be emulsified. You may think this is great, but it isn't. You need fatty acids; they have many important roles including the transportation of oxygen throughout your body. They also affect bodily inflammation and this includes the *OK-for-your-body* kind of inflammation caused by challenging and fatiguing your muscles at the gym, as well as the *bad-for-your-body* kind of inflammation caused by eating a lot of heavily refined non-nutritive high-calorie carbohydrates.

If you have a muffin-roll, you may well have a "fatty liver." Your liver will have stopped processing the fat that you eat and will now be storing it! Even though it may have stopped processing dietary fat, your liver *will* continue to deal with the protein and carbohydrate you have eaten. It'll convert glucose

---

[10] Your hardworking liver converts carbohydrate glucose into glycogen, breaks down fats, removes excess amino-acids from your blood, synthesizes vitamins, produces bile and blood-clotting factors and removes damaged red blood cells and various toxic waste by-products. Yup, it's busy and you shouldn't be bothering it with tasks normally handled elsewhere!

[11] Emulsion is important because it mixes two things together wherein one does not actually dissolve into the other. In the case above, the bile has a detergent action on dietary fat particles and this causes the fat to breakdown or be emulsified into microscopic droplets.

sugar from carbohydrates, fructose sugar from fruits (also carbohydrates) and galactose sugar from milk products into glycogen. As a form of *stored* carbohydrate, glycogen is the primary fuel that's stored in either your muscle tissues or in your liver.

Whenever your blood sugar level drops (e.g., while sleeping), your liver will efficiently convert some of its stored glycogen back into glucose sugar and release it into your bloodstream. Your body *always* needs fuel and its most preferred fuel is glucose (from dietary carbohydrate). It doesn't like to use amino-acids (from dietary protein) or fatty-acids (from dietary fat) for fuel. If your diet is regularly low in carbohydrates, your liver will be forced to convert protein and fat into glucose in order to maintain your blood sugar levels (inefficient processes) and it'll create toxic and acidic waste by-products while doing that. You may think this is OK but read on through the book and you'll discover that converting either fat or protein into glucose fuel is highly problematic for your hardworking liver.

What does your gallbladder do?

Your gallbladder squirts the liver-made bile into your duodenum (the first part of your small intestine, just beyond your stomach) to digest food, in fact, mainly the fats that you eat. If your bile thickens too much, it can make gallstones which can leave your gallbladder inflamed, particularly after a really fatty meal. Most people in this thick-bile category are already obese. It's interesting to note that the continual thickening of bile, making it more difficult to get distributed, is also a pre-diabetes condition. And if you decrease the amount of bile available to metabolize and burn your body fat, then you're obviously going to get fatter.

If you've had your gallbladder removed, you probably will have trouble digesting fat as well as experience some temporary diarrhea or constipation. To avoid this, you'll have to avoid fatty foods such as: pizza, butter, creamy soups, gravies, chocolate, high-fat cheese, ice cream and whole milk, as well as French fries and potato chips. Fortunately, those are examples of foods we should all avoid, so don't start feeling sorry for yourself.

What does your pancreas do?

Your pancreas secretes both insulin and glucagon, which are *opposing hormones* that regulate your blood sugar level primarily through glycogen/carbohydrate storage. They are opposing because one, insulin, increases fat-storage while the other, glucagon, increases fat burning. Of course, you need both, but you just don't want your fat-making insulin overly predominant. Your pancreas also produces enzymes to help digest your food. Actually, all of your biochemical processes are run by enzymes which work as catalysts to efficiently speed up the various chemical cell reactions in your body. An example would be your digestion. Your pancreas can make both fat-storing enzymes (which are influenced by the number of insulin hormones kicking around in your bloodstream) and fat-burning enzymes (which are influenced by the amount of glucagon hormones you have).

What does your thyroid gland do?

Your thyroid gland controls your metabolism by regulating your body's energy use; hence it controls your ability to burn calories. If your thyroid hormone levels drop then your body's processes slow down and change, and this can cause weight gain due to a slower metabolism. Frankly slowing down your ability to burn calories doesn't sound very good at all if you're trying to lose weight! Furthermore, severe calorie restriction dieting will always cause your body to <u>hold onto body fat</u> as it automatically moves into starvation mode. It tries to store whatever food it gets for future energy by converting calories into body fat stores that can be broken down later to produce any necessary fuel. As I said earlier, your body prefers to use glucose (from carbohydrate) as fuel. If forced, for example through starvation, it'll breakdown your building-block amino-acids stored in muscle tissue and it'll also look in your fatty tissue[12].

---

[12] Unfortunately, not as much body-fat is converted into glucose fuel when there is an improper mix of insulin and fat. When you aren't eating much carbohydrate (glucose), then you won't be producing much insulin. This very important concept will be discussed later in the book.

Other thyroid related issues include sleep deprivation and high stress. Both lead to increased cortisol hormone production which is never good for calorie-burning.

In addition to these four main organs noted above and their impacts upon your body composition, I have to mention that most of the weight-loss resulting from poor dieting is actually from water loss and muscle-wasting. This can never be helpful for your long-term weight-loss. Starving yourself will decrease your lean muscle-mass and increase your body fat percentage. Not what you're aiming for, right?

You simply can't lose more than about 1% of your overall body weight per week (usually 1-2 pounds for the average person) and it's genetically[13] impossible to lose more than *1-1 ½ pounds of body fat* per week. If you lose more than 2 pounds per week, you can be guaranteed that it'll be primarily water and a lot of muscle mass.

Severe dieting and calorie restriction makes
you gain weight after you
start eating normally because you've made your metabolism slower.
It also causes muscle-wasting and a stronger ability to hold onto fat.

I don't want to get you down about losing weight, but have you ever noticed how much more difficult it is for women to lose fat when compared to men? Guess what; women have larger fat cells[14] than men, women's fat cells contain more fat-storing enzymes; and women's fat cells contain fewer fat-burning enzymes. Men have a much higher percentage of calorie-eating

---

[13] To lose one pound of overall weight in one week, you would have to have a 3,500-calorie *deficit* or 500 fewer calories per day. For a loss of two pounds in a week, you would have to eat *1,000 fewer calories per day*. That is not much food unless you're morbidly obese at 300-500 pounds and eating 5,000+ calories daily. But for you, it would translate into starvation and your body will dump water and muscle before it seriously considers its fat stores. You'd never be able to drop 1 ½ pounds of only fat tissue in a week! A 1% loss for morbidly obese people could be 3-5 pounds weekly.

[14] A cell is a discrete membrane-bound part of all living matter. In fact, it's the smallest unit capable of independent existence. All living organisms, with the exception of viruses, have at least one cell.

muscles than do women (almost 40% more), more muscle-building fat-burning testosterone hormones, and a lot more fat-releasing/burning enzymes than women. And to make matters even more unfair, when our fat-making estrogen declines such as during menopause we have a parallel increase in fat-storing enzymes. In the mid-30's a woman's body begins to shift estrogen production, so bye-bye curvy figure.

Compared to men, now you can understand why it'll be a lot *easier* for women to put on weight and a lot *harder* to lose it. Evolution's survival priorities were a lot kinder to men. Geezzz, give me a break!!! Although we just can't seem to win, get over it!

Sure, it's *terribly unfair*; but it can't be changed so quit complaining about it, accept the facts and move on. The truth is that we can still get around that reality. We can still lose weight if we do it the right way and we're not in some ridiculous hurry. That agreed upon, let's face it…we women do have many other amazing attributes.

1.2 How Does Digestion Work?

"A human being is part of a whole called by us the universe." – A.E.

The digestion of food is very interesting. Put simply, digestion covers all the actions of your body while breaking down foods into their simpler components and the *longer* that takes (or more *inefficient* that process is) the less weight you'll put on. It's simple to put on a lot of weight if the carbohydrates you are eating (all the sugars and starches) are *heavily processed* and, therefore, are absorbed into your bloodstream too fast for your body to cope with. And similarly, if you eat a ton of fats (saturated or unsaturated), many more than your body needs and can use, you'll put on weight.

But *how* you prepare or eat a food can also be important in terms of digestion. Many vegetables, for example broccoli and cauliflower, can be eaten either raw or cooked. If raw, your body will have to work a lot harder to break them down into glucose fuel. If you cook those raw crunchy vegetables which are covered with a layer of fiber, some of the work your body would have to do has already been accomplished by the cooking process – the fiber although still there will have been softened. You'll have actually helped your stomach digest those vegetables by cooking them until they're soft. It's just another example of the "processing" of foods before your body starts to digest them. I'm not suggesting that you never cook vegetables, I just wanted to explain why raw food is better for you. Just try not to overcook your vegetables. Leave *some* of the work for your body.

To slow down your digestion and to get as much fiber as possible, a good rule to remember is that *whole/intact food* is better than *chopped/sliced* food. Chopped is better than *diced*, which is better than *mashed*, and of course hugely better than *juiced*! Get the drift? Also, both dietary fat and dietary protein will slow down the arrival of any consumed carbohydrate sugar into your bloodstream[15].

Now let's get back to your digestive system. This system, chiefly the alimentary canal which runs from your mouth to your anus, is very complex. Whenever you eat something, your body will immediately use chemicals to breakdown the food in many different ways. It starts with chewing which

---

[15] Whenever I ate restaurant bread, I used to think it was better to eat it plain; but now I know that putting some olive oil on it or some butter is actually better.

breaks the food into smaller pieces so that those chemical reactions can happen over *more surface area.*

Enzymes are the catalysts that speed up the breakdown of all the food you eat and, depending on what you eat, they can be fat-burning or fat-making
(protease for protein, lipase for fat, amylase for carbohydrate.)

Your saliva has an enzyme[16] which facilitates the breakdown of carbohydrates and another enzyme which tackles fats. Proteins get wet and churned up, though they won't be broken down until they reach your stomach, where a third enzyme tackles them.

The chewed food that reaches your stomach is called a "bolus" and it gets digested more when it hits your stomach juices. The further breakdown of the carbohydrate and fat, as well as protein breakdown takes place in your bolus. The food could be in your stomach for as little as 2 hours or for as long as 4 hours, depending upon what you ate, even though there isn't much nutrient absorption taking place.

Once the bolus is churned up, it gets passed to your small intestine and is then called a "chyme." Your small intestine, which can be between 20 and 23 feet in length, is where *most* nutrient absorption actually takes place. The food you ate is further reduced into its tiniest cell-size pieces and this is where important decisions are made in terms of various and sundry food intolerances and allergies.

The small intestine has villi and microvilli finger-like projections on its internal walls which increase its surface area. Wherever your body has increased its surface area[17], it can always have greater absorption and more biochemical reaction. Your body uses its digestive enzymes to get all of the

---

[16] Enzymes are very efficient complex protein catalysts that significantly speed up specific biochemical reactions in both your digestion and metabolism. They work by reducing the activation energy required to start a reaction and this of course means it can happen faster. Enzymes will help both your digestion and your overall metabolic rate.

[17] Individuals with celiac disease or Crohn's disease have a reduced small intestine and damaged villi surface area, hence they can suffer from nutrient deficiencies.

nutrients that it can absorb from all foods. Depending of course on what you actually ate[18], this part of the digestive process can take about 3 hours. It's here where, once the food is *completely* digested, it becomes small enough to pass through your intestinal walls (as sugar/glucose molecules from carbohydrates, amino-acids from protein, and fatty-acids from fat).

At this point there *isn't any difference* to your body from where the food came. Are you surprised about this fact? It could be sugar molecules[19] from an apple or a potato or a candy, amino-acids from egg white or beef, or fatty-acids from canola oil, almonds, a hunk of butter or ice cream. These resulting little bits are absorbed by tiny blood vessels and finally carried by your bloodstream throughout your body. Job done!

Whatever remains gets moved into your large intestine, where its name changes yet again and it gets called your "stool" or "feces." More commonly, we non-medical types just call it our "poop." Your large intestine is a bit wider and much shorter than your small intestine, at about five feet and doesn't have the surface villi found in your small intestine simply because there aren't many remaining nutrients to absorb into your bloodstream. But it's here where water gets absorbed and your stool is compacted and formed into the shape and consistency of "poop." Without enough water, get ready for some seriously uncomfortable constipation!

The enzymes in your digestive system and probiotic bacteria in your gut are *crucial* for optimal digestion and efficient nutrient absorption. When you don't eat properly, or healthily, your body will become more and more acidic, and then your enzymes will be *delayed* from speeding up your biochemical reactions. This in turn will slow down your metabolic ability to burn calories. Yup, you're going to get a lot fatter.

-----

[18] Carbohydrates, including fruits and vegetables, will move through your digestive system more quickly than either protein or fat.

[19] You will discover while reading this book that all carbohydrates make glucose sugar in your body. When you eat sugar-sugar, the molecules are *simple chains* and we call them sugars. When you eat a potato, the molecules are linked to form more *complex chains* and we call them starches. Regardless, to your body, sugar and starch are both turned into *sugar* molecules by your digestive enzymes. The reason the complex vegetable starch is better than the simple fruit sugar is only because it takes a longer time to be converted into those sugar molecules (and this is why vegetables don't taste as sweet as fruit or sugar).

Just remember that the moment you swallow any food, you have lost ALL control over it. Your body will take over and you have absolutely NO input into any biochemical pathway decisions that will be made.

Ever heard of the expression – "You are what you eat." Yup, truer words were ne'er spoke!!!

1.3 Why Don't "Crash" Diets Work in the Long Run?

"The difference between stupidity and genius is that genius has its limits." – A.E.

The word "diet" comes from the Greek word "diaita" which means a "way of life" or "mode of living." In reality, what you eat and your lifestyle are fundamentally linked, including a healthy body and mind. That's why a proper "diet" has to be *sustainable* which simply means it should be maintainable over the long haul. And lifestyle includes how much sleep you get, whether you can control your reaction to stress-induced situations and how physically active you are.

I'll bet you've tried some crazy "crash" diets; that is, diets that provide strict weight-loss eating rules with the aim of very rapid results. I say these are crazy, but most dieters believe their promises of incredibly quick weight-loss. Indeed, many people don't care how they lose weight; they just want it off and they want it off as quickly as possible. These dieters only care about the number on their scales. I hope this book will convince you how silly and unsuccessful such a measurement is for fat-attack in the long term.

Some of these popular diets say no fat, others say no carbohydrates. Some are heavy fasting or starvation diets where you only eat once a day, or you can only ingest 600 daily calories, or you can't eat any carbohydrates, or maybe you only eat certain foods on certain days, or worse you can't eat solid foods. Other examples include eat all-meat, only cabbage soup, ultra-low carbs, eat no meat, etc. None of these popular diets are sustainable. Why? Because they all fight our natural genetic makeup. They simply go completely against the way your body is intended to use the food it receives. Your body has been designed over millions of years. In fact, your genes (which control *every* bodily function) have also evolved over millions of years and they have shaped your need for specific nutrients. Why would you believe that you can change this in two months???

Put another way; any diet that's based upon some sort of *deprivation* is always based upon a "temporary" status situation. It'll *always* have an expiration date simply due to the impossible-to-sustain factor. These deprivation approaches will never keep the weight off for very long and isn't that what you really want?

When you don't provide your body with enough essential nutrients, it's not forced to burn more body fat. Rather, it takes the easiest path and burns fewer calories because it just isn't getting enough of them. And it'll produce more of those nasty fat-storing enzymes.

Your body knows how to protect itself during both ends of the spectrum – a big feast or a lengthy famine. Crazy crash diets may take of some pounds of overall weight off you, but most will leave your body in a far worse condition then if you hadn't dieted at all. You'll have screwed up the enzymes that are important for the *storage* of fat (lipogenic enzymes which are influenced by your insulin hormones) and for the *release* of fat (lipolytic enzymes which are directly influenced by your glucagon hormones). Remember your pancreas; when you don't eat enough your body will begin to produce more and more fat-storing enzymes. So not only do you *lose calorie-burning muscle*[20] tissue, you also *create more fat-storing* ability! Women always laugh at me when I say, "you're not eating enough food to lose weight!" This always appears to be contradictory to the idea of fat loss!

When you have a lot of excess weight, it'll be coupled with a diminishing ability of your insulin hormone to process energy, fats and sugars. This is a condition often called insulin-resistance, and this results in more fat-storage especially in your midsection. Put more simply, the insulin just *can't* get itself into your cells.

You must eat a balanced and nutritional diet; one that includes all three macronutrients (protein, carbohydrate and fat). Micronutrients such as vitamins and minerals are also a necessity, as well as drinking *plain* water. About the only thing that most eating plans and diets correctly agree on is to *avoid all sugars and highly processed foods*. So, if you do nothing else, at least do that!

You might think that eating less will automatically lead to dropping body fat, but this is not actually correct. When you don't provide your body with enough vital nutrients (vitamins, minerals, glucose, essential fatty-acids and amino-acids), your body is *not* forced to burn more fat. Your body will simply burn *fewer* calories when you eat less. Let's face it, your body does have a few

---

[20] Muscle is the prime tissue for burning calories/energy <u>and</u> body-fat. Suffice it to say that the more muscle you have, the greater your metabolism, and therefore the greater your ability to burn calories and lose body-fat.

choices when faced with too little nutrition. And it *will always take the easiest route* when it's desperate for caloric energy and there's very little around. I think Star Trek's Spock would say that it's just illogical to believe that your body will burn <u>more</u> calories when there are so few around!

With too few nutrients, your body will be forced to make the decision between the process of grabbing calories from body fat or just slowing itself down so that it doesn't need as many calories. And guess which route is the easiest? Yes, it's easier to slow down biochemically than to work off those body fat reserves for glucose energy. If your body is low on energy (and if you've ever tried low-carb diets you'll know how that feels), it'll *also* cannibalize your muscles, to get the necessary energy from its stored carbohydrate (glycogen) – its favorite go-to fuel. It makes sense to your body to dump muscle when you don't eat enough. Why the heck maintain metabolically active tissues that aren't being fed? And don't try to tell me that your body is any different than anyone else's! Starvation causes all bodies to do the very same thing out of sheer desperation. Keeping a lot of your body's fat and dumping a bunch of your calorie-eating muscle is sort of a double negative whammy to your fat-loss goal. Do you really want to lose muscle? I sure don't.

Because crash dieting is highly stressful on your body, it also leads to the production of by-products considered to be toxic poisons by your body. Toxins increase your rate of aging and compromise your ability to lose weight. Did you know that free radicals[21] are toxic to your body? If you eat a lot of fried foods, get a lot of ultraviolet light, smoke or drink a lot, you'll be producing a whack of toxic free radicals. When you produce too many toxins to be expelled by your body, they'll be stored in your body fat cells making them grow bigger and, if necessary, more plentiful.

During starvation, if you don't have enough fat cells in which to store extra toxic poisons, your body will resort to *increasing* its number of fat cells in an

---

[21] Everybody talks about free radicals, but do they really know what they are? I doubt it. A free radical is very *unstable*. Remember your old high school chemistry classes? When a molecule is stable it doesn't have a negative or positive charge. Negatively charged electrons, which orbit the nucleus, are what glues atoms together to form molecules through the sharing of electrons. A free radical will try *to steal an electron* from the nearest molecule making that molecule very unstable thus creating a chain reaction. The final result is the disruption of a living cell!

effort to keep the poisons away from your healthy tissues. Nope, not something you want to force your body to do. Also, your fat cells are responsible for producing your "I'm full" leptin hormones; and it's leptin that tells your brain when you need to burn body fat for energy. The toxic chemicals created by poor dieting cause the release of chemicals that result in damage to your leptin receptors. This is detailed later in the book, but it's called leptin-resistance and it usually leads to obesity.

Let's now take an example of why crazy starvation diets don't work and why they lead to yo-yo[22] results. We'll take a woman who weighs 165 lbs. and is 35% body fat (actually this was me when I finally decided to commence weight-training in a gym). At 35% body fat, she (me!) is carrying a lot of *bulky fat* up and down stairs, trying to fit into clothes, walking. It makes me tired thinking about it.

Let's see what happens *inside* her body when she chooses a starvation diet. I'm sure you've seen someone do this. She does get much smaller, her friends hardly recognize her and everyone is congratulating her. She's just so darn proud of herself. But she simply can't continue starving herself and so the next time you see her maybe months later, she's fat again and looks even *more* obese. She's despondent, commenting that she's back to the same weight of 165 lbs. and you're thinking, "no way, she looks a lot heavier than she used to!" Yes, she has put her body into a *fat super-accumulation mode*. Surprisingly, fat super-accumulation does *not* require her to eat very much at all!!! Why is that? It's because she *has* changed her body though not in the way she hoped. She has changed her metabolism and along the way, she's created a body that's a bit *resistant* to leptin! Then when she stopped crash dieting her body wanted/needed to store more body fat so that she was protected from her ongoing yo-yo dieting approach.

Starvation will turn your body into a fat super-accumulator and will slow down your metabolism, making it much more difficult to lose weight.

Even though she returned to her initial weight, let's detail what actually happened to her on the *inside*. At the outset 165 pounds and 35% body fat, she

---

[22] "Yo-yo" dieting is sometimes referred to as "weight cycling." Put simply, it refers to the cyclical loss and gain of overall body weight while on various crazy diets; sort of like a yo-yo moving up and down, up and down.

had about 107 ¼ pounds of lean tissue (and organs) and about 57 ¾ lbs. of body fat. Her body is just a biological machine – no more, no less. It wants to survive, and it'll do *anything* to survive. She has starved herself "smaller." Her body for all intents and purposes thought it must be on Starvation Island and it began to *eat itself for energy*. From where does it get that energy? You'll probably say it'll be body fat. Well that isn't entirely correct. It'll eat itself skinny by eating _both_ *muscle and fat*. Think about it – your body doesn't want to burn calories when you aren't eating enough of them. Therefore, to protect its ability to store energy, it'll get rid of tissues that always demand caloric energy – yup, muscles.

Fat tissue may have a lot of stored energy, but your body wants to save that energy for as long as it can for Starvation Island, indeed your body will try to store *more* fat. Muscle tissue and fat tissue are *completely different tissues*. You can't change muscle into fat and you sure can't change fat into muscle no matter how you try or what you do. These are ridiculous myths. It takes a lot of specific dedication to build lean muscle. Unfortunately, it only takes a few poor eating decisions to lose it and to easily regain fat. You don't want to lose that muscle!

So back to our test subject; this woman's body *is* starving. After several weeks or months (depending on how long she can tolerate starving herself), she reaches her goal weight and is so excited about her weight-loss. And she's happy that people are complimenting her. She has probably dropped from about 35% body fat to maybe 30% body fat. Eventually she begins to fall off the diet and to eat as she did before the starvation diet. She feels that she deserves to eat again and frankly no one can starve themselves forever. After a while she finds herself back to her pre-starvation weight and believes she's back where she was. But inside her body this is *far* from the truth. She's actually far more *unhealthy* at these 165 pounds than she was at the outset of the starvation diet. She has moved into that *fat super-accumulation mode*.

Remember I said her body was eating both muscle and fat during her Starvation Island visit? Well, her body remembers that Island as she begins to eat again. It has a healthy memory. What if it ends up on that Island again? It wants to survive, so it plans on *more _needed_ fat* and *less fuel-dependent muscle*. Fat-storage provides more potential energy; muscle is for movement and she's not much of an exerciser. Her body decides to store more fat rather than all that lost muscle tissue so in effect her new body may be the same 165 pounds, but it now sits at *40% body fat.* This is 5% higher than before she stared her initial crash diet! Indeed, she has gained 8 1/4 pounds of fat and lost 8 1/4 pounds of muscle. A pound of bulky fatty tissue takes up a lot more physical space than a pound of lean dense muscle tissue![23] Wow, no wonder she looks bigger even though she weighs in at the same 165 pounds. She was really trying to get her weight down and lose body fat, but it seems that her body just didn't get the memo.

If we were to put this more succinctly, her biochemical body adapted by changing its metabolic engine. Her metabolic rate measures how efficient she is at burning calories. The crash diet slowed her metabolism so that her body could store more body fat while on Starvation Island hence she didn't need as much fuel and so now, she's just not burning as many calories. And she's eating as she used to before the diet.

When starving, your body will always choose to get rid of muscle, your only calorie-burning tissue.

Here are her statistics before and after Starvation Island.

	Body Weight	Fat Tissue Percentage	Lean Tissue (and organs)	Overview *vs* Initial Weight Statistics
Initial Statistics	165 lbs. *Before diet*	35% = 57 ¾ lbs.	107 ¼ lbs.	N/A
Reaches "goal"	140 lbs. *During diet*	30% = 42 lbs.	98 lbs.	**Loss of Fat = 15 ¾ lbs. Loss of Lean = 9 ¼ lbs.**
Final Statistics	165 lbs. *After diet*	40% = 66 lbs.	99 lbs.	**Gain of Fat = 8 ¼ lbs. Loss of Lean = 8 ¼ lbs.**

---

[23] You often hear the expression that "muscle weighs more than fat." No, it doesn't but it's lean and, pound by pound, it takes up *much less physical space* than fat.

If our test subject was eating 1,700 calories daily from whatever her normal food selection was <u>before</u> the diet, she might have been burning all of it and staying at her 165 lbs. If she returns to her normal eating habits at 1,700 daily calories with a *slower* metabolism, she may only be burning 1,200 calories a day, hence 500 calories will move straight to body fat! Indeed, because her main concern was only the number on her scales, she actually ended up making her body less physically fit (i.e., less metabolically efficient with any available calories). To make matters worse, I'll bet this woman returns to the Island to lose the weight yet again. Unfortunately, during the second diet cycle (even if on the same diet) it'll take her even *longer to lose the same 25 pounds*, followed by a <u>much shorter time to gain it all back</u>. Wow and who said metabolism doesn't rule???

Let's chart it wherein metabolism A is the starting point, metabolism B is after the end of the first Starvation Island round, and metabolism C is at the end of the second Starvation Island round. Both trips last about 10 months. These are hypothetical numbers, used merely to illustrate the yo-yo effects.

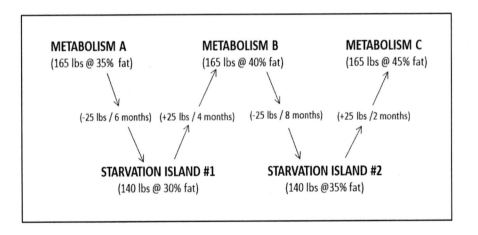

Her body has adapted by SLOWING DOWN ITS METABOLISM. She took less time to put the weight back on during the second round, because her body adapted by decreasing its calorie-burning rate and increasing its fat-making rate. Indeed, metabolism A is faster than B, and B is faster than C. So she got a lot bulkier, but in a lot less time. Check out the timelines in the second visit to the Island.

If you want to lose weight and be healthy, you *must speed up your metabolism*. That is the *complete opposite* of her crash diet.

1.4 Are Low-Carbohydrate, High-Protein Diets Good?

"A man should look for what is, and not for what he thinks should be." – A.E.

If you want to lose bulky mass and lose weight, a low- (or no-) carbohydrate high-protein diet is a very *poor* strategy. The truth of the matter is that these sorts of diets fail to address your hormones, and hormones always dictate what your body will do with food. If you're not eating enough carbohydrate and you're restricting calories to lose weight, your body will use the protein from your diet to meet its energy needs. This of course reduces the amount of protein available for the physiological functions that <u>only</u> protein can perform. Think muscle-building here. You'd be making your body do something it doesn't normally want to do.

When protein has to be used for energy there isn't sufficient protein to build lean muscle tissue hence more muscle is lost. And muscle tissue weight-loss always causes a *reduced* calorie-burning metabolic rate. You need <u>carbohydrate</u> *along with protein* to maintain muscle mass. To drive fat-burning and reduce muscle-loss, the better strategy is to <u>slightly decrease</u> your carbohydrate intake, and <u>slightly build-up</u> your protein intake. This sort of balanced eating is also a more sustainable strategy.

Low carbohydrate diets do not build strength, always slow down your metabolism, and make it difficult to sustainably lose weight.
With too few carbohydrates, your body will be forced to use protein for energy.
This will always negatively affect muscle-building and calorie-burning.

High-protein diets that omit or drastically reduce carbohydrates always promise quick weight-loss. Often these diets are quite high in fat and low in fiber. Without enough bulky fiber, your digestive system will slow down, and this can lead to chronic constipation. Most high-protein diets are dehydrating as well, another constipating factor to consider.

You may see a *drastic* weight-loss in the first few weeks, but it'll be a lot of water as well as some of your vital calorie-eating muscle mass. Oh no, not that problem again! As soon as you go off the diet and eat carbohydrates, water comes back into your tissues and you quickly regain any lost weight. Muscle is composed of about 75% water, while fat is only about 10% water. So, when you lose weight too quickly, it'll be mostly water, and it'll have been swiped from your muscles given their high-water content. The result? Yes, you'll look smaller but it's a loss of muscle water and not a lot of body fat!

You should devote about 30-40% of your daily caloric intake to protein (all dependent upon your goals); but don't eat it all in one meal. Doing that will overload your body's capacity to use it all. In fact, because protein stimulates the production of the glucagon fat-burning hormone, the amount of the opposing insulin fat-storing hormone will be affected as well. These are two hormones[24] that your pancreas tries to keep balanced. Another consideration is the fact that if you eat all your protein in one meal, you would not be having protein with the other meals. And protein is a nutrient that will slow down and help counteract the rapid release of glucose caused by some carbohydrates. Spread protein out over the day and across many meals.

When attempting to lose weight, you should focus not only protein but, rather, on a *balance* of macronutrients (protein, carbohydrate and fat). A proper diet to lose weight would be to eat *a bit less* carbohydrate and *a bit more* protein, along with some healthy unsaturated fats. You need to eat *all three* macronutrients but you can change the percentage of each *slightly* to attain your goal.

Track your daily macronutrient intake (in % of calories) until you get accustomed to portion sizes (on your plate). In subsequent chapters I'll explore macronutrient percentages and various alterations, dependent upon differing goals, and why any percentage changes shouldn't be too drastic. The charts below may look odd because the size of the three sections of each pie-chart look different. That's because we're talking only about calorie percentages in the top chart and plate-size percentages in the bottom chart. Macronutrients have different caloric values per gram of weight. For example fat, at 9 cals/gram, is much more calorie intensive than protein or carbohydrate at only 4 cals/gram; hence, if we were to chart these macronutrients by "actual size" or space taken up on your plate, you'd see the fat "pie" portion on your plate is much smaller than either of the protein or carbohydrate portions even though fat will represent almost 1/3 of your daily caloric intake.

---

[24] Hormones tend to work in pairs. And, like a good marriage, they work hard to support each other in maintaining your body's biochemical balance regardless of the environment.

MACRONUTRIENT DAILY CALORIE PERCENTAGES

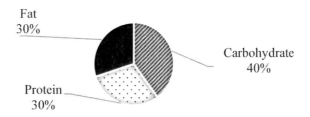

Fat
30%

Carbohydrate
40%

Protein
30%

MACRONUTRIENT PLATE SIZE PERCENTAGES

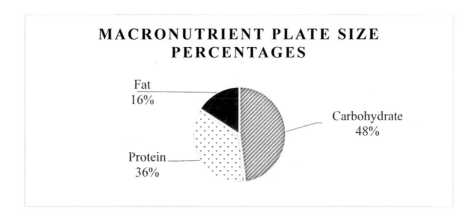

Fat
16%

Carbohydrate
48%

Protein
36%

1.5 Can I Lose Weight During or After Menopause?

"You have to learn the rules of the game. And then you have to play better than anyone else." – A.E.

We all know that our hormones change during the move through menopause[25]. We all age and we're all on the same road and though some of us are further along, we all have to travel the same route. It's nothing to be afraid of. It's a normal and expected reality of growing older, in fact it's the

---

[25] The ceasing of menstruation signals the end of fertility and the child-bearing years. By the way, when I hit 70, I discovered a plus; no more pap smears! Apparently, you're not expected to have multiple partners at that age. My husband thought this was an unnecessary footnote, but then again, he's never had a pap smear test!!!

natural progression of a woman's reproductive life and usually begins between 48 and 55 years of age.

Unfortunately, there can be weight-gain during menopause and I won't lie to you, it can be very difficult to get rid of. Why is that? Obviously, you need to eat food in order to live. Your body had to *evolve* its biological systems over zillions of years in order to control how it actually deals with that food. It also evolved to deal with periods of famine and this is where your hormones come into effect. And guess what? Your weight is largely controlled by your hormones and hormones are masterful adjusters of your metabolism!

Why are hormones so important and why does age affect them?

Hormones are *regulatory substances* that are produced by various glands in response to any imbalances in your body as well as *in direct reaction* to the foods you eat. Hormones exist in order to ensure that your body maintains or moves back to its preferred biochemical balance. They're a type of chemical signal that becomes a communication line between your cells. Hormones, usually working in pairs, regulate quite a variety of biological, behavioral and emotional processes as well. Even your brain relies on a proper hormonal balance in order to appropriately function. Beat up on one hormone and another will come to its rescue.

*Your hormones will change during menopause
and that can cause weight gain.*

Hormones influence both your appetite and how much body fat you store. Other than wolfing down a bunch of hormone replacement pills[26], the one hormone you can't really do anything about is estrogen. You probably know that estrogen is the most important female sex hormone and that it's involved in regulating the female reproductive system. Produced by your ovaries, it's responsible for changes in your sexual characteristics as well as your bone

---

[26] I didn't choose this unnatural route. We all age and we should do it gracefully; it wasn't my idea to look 45 my whole life! That can get stressful and you can look ridiculous at 70 after choosing Botox cheeks, fish lips, butt implants and whatnot! Honestly, haven't you noticed that a bunch of women are beginning to resemble each other.

health. Very high *and* very low estrogen levels can also affect your weight-gain. When you're pregnant you tend to gain weight because of *higher* estrogen levels and when menopausal you tend to gain weight because of *lower* estrogen levels, leading to higher fat-storing enzymes. Can't win, right?

You can make lifestyle changes to alleviate this estrogen issue. You can incorporate more dietary fiber, sprinkle *ground* flax seeds on foods[27] and, you can eat more cruciferous or flower-shaped vegetables such as broccoli, brussels sprouts, cauliflower, cabbage, garden cress and bok choy as well as some other green vegetables.

But estrogen isn't the only factor. Weight-gain after menopause is also dependent upon your age, other hormonal factors and your overall state of health.

Most people complain about gaining weight as they age (especially women), and they fully believe that it's just something that happens, something that they have very little control over. *Without* a change in diet or exercise, as you age your caloric-burning rate will decrease (yes, metabolism again) and your weight-gain will probably increase. And of course, this *will* mean that you'll get heavier as you get older.

In fact, by the time you're 50, you'll probably be burning about 15% fewer calories than when you were 20. I'll wager that you were a lot more physically active in your 20s. Just continue eating the same way <u>and</u> being less physically active over the years and you'll gradually gain weight (usually about 10 pounds every decade). You aren't any different than anyone else in this regard! Look around at those that just retired, and I bet most of them are about 30-40 pounds overweight[28].

Here's the reality.

---

[27] Flax seeds must be ground or powdered in order to be broken down and absorbed by your body. You can always get them at any health food store. I sprinkle them on cottage cheese, yogurt and into some home recipes.

[28] Between 50-60 there's a gradual loss of muscle tissue due to decreased physical activity, eating too little protein and the onset of menopause. All of this increases your body-fat percentage which, coupled with increased stress and high calorie processed foods, will always cause weight-gain.

Age (years)	Typical Calorie Intakes (daily)	Average Calorie Needs (daily)	Drop in Metabolic Rate or Caloric Needs (from age 20 onwards)	Pounds of Extra Body fat each decade (from age 20 onwards)
20	2000 – 2500	2000 – 2500		
30	2000 – 2500	1900 – 2375	100-125 calories	10
40	2000 – 2500	1800 – 2250	200-250 calories	20
50	2000 – 2500	1700 – 2125	300-375 calories	30
60	2000 – 2500	1600 – 2000	400-500 calories	40 *(this was me!!!)*
70	2000 – 2500	1500 – 1875	500-625 calories	50

Other than estrogen, what are the other weight-controlling hormones and how can we ensure that they don't add to weight-gain as we age? The main ones we'll consider are insulin, glucagon, leptin, ghrelin, cortisol and the human growth hormone (HGH).

OK, what about the infamous insulin hormone, your main metabolic *fat-storage hormone*?

Insulin is in charge of how you get energy from the food you eat. It clears the glucose from your bloodstream and allows it to get into your cells for energy, but it can also create fat and then store that fat whenever it's over-produced.[29] Produced by your pancreas, insulin interacts with your cells and your brain, determining whether you'll burn fat *or* store fat. It likes to keep your engine full but, just like a gas tank, it can be overfilled and it will run over; but it won't hit the treadmill rubber, it'll hit your fat cells – its proverbial pavement for overfills of all types. Now that's a really powerful metabolic hormone!

---

[29] Remember that opposing hormone pairing is the rule. If your fat-storing insulin is up, then your fat-burning glucagon will be down, causing an imbalance. Your body hates imbalances.

Most people associate insulin with diabetics and assume the insulin hormone simply regulates blood sugar levels. But it does *much much more than that*. It's responsible for getting fatty-acids (from dietary fat) stored in your body fat cells, getting carbohydrate stored in both your liver and muscle cells (as glycogen) and getting amino-acids (from dietary protein) directed toward protein synthesis to build that nice lean toned muscle tissue you crave. All these actions demonstrate why insulin is often called the "storage" hormone. It stores energy in particular places for future use; hence insulin stimulates fat synthesis <u>and</u> promotes fat-storage. Also insulin not only tells your cells to store fat, but it also can *prevent* that fat from being broken down. Obviously, when you're trying to lose weight, fat-storage isn't the best goal to pursue.

Insulin is what allows your cells to absorb and also to use glucose as fuel. When you constantly overeat sugar, refined and processed carbohydrates and fast-food, your insulin levels will increase to a chronic level and eventually your cells will be, for lack of a better work, "stuffed up." When your cells can't absorb any more insulin, such <u>insulin-resistance</u> causes your insulin to remain in your blood far too long meaning that less glucose gets into your cells to be burned for energy. Compounding the problem is the fact that when your cells can't get the insulin, your body thinks that it needs to produce even more insulin to address that deficiency, but the new insulin can't get the glucose into your cells either! Undeterred, your body just keeps making more and more and more insulin.

After many years in this state, your cells become *so filled* with sugar that they simply can't admit any more sugar molecules! Biologically, there's a decrease in the number of "insulin receptor tissues" in your cells. Put another way, insulin-resistance is sort of a *glucose transport disorder* and it'll always lead to obesity. Persistently higher and higher blood sugar and insulin levels, if left unchecked, eventually lead to Type-2 diabetes (that's the kind that requires pills and only sometimes insulin).

Keep in mind that, contrary to the abnormal insulin metabolism described above, a normal insulin response to meals eaten *temporarily* elevates blood sugar levels which then quickly return to normal levels. This process leads to appetite-control and to the metabolic and thermogenic[30] (heat) benefits needed to encourage weight-loss and long-term weight maintenance.

---

[30] I'll detail thermogenesis and its affect on fat-burning in a later chapter.

People with a severe form of insulin-resistance (usually resulting in visceral/abdominal obesity), have bodies which can't efficiently burn much fat thereby becoming *fat-making engines*. Fat-making bodies will produce increasing amounts of insulin after eating carbohydrates. I'll bet you know a bunch of these people; people who have been forewarned by their doctors that they are pre-diabetic and that they must change the way they eat. Like I said, you want to develop yourself into a calorie-burning engine and not stay a fat-making engine.

Controlling your insulin is one of the most powerful anti-aging strategies you can adopt. Follow a low- or no-grain diet and definitely avoid all forms of sugar. This will limit the foods that cause a fast insulin spike. Insulin-resistance is caused by the overconsumption of refined carbohydrates (breads, pastas[31], and sugary and fast/junk-foods), eating too much saturated fat (from animal products), omega-6 fatty-acids (found in most vegetable oils and processed foods) and trans-fatty-acids/trans-fats (found in all foods with hydrogenated or partially hydrogenated oils).

You can normalize your insulin levels by eating healthy unsaturated fats (omega-3 fatty-acids), increasing magnesium (e.g., spinach, nuts, seeds, legumes) and through regular exercise. You can also take daily omega-3 and magnesium supplements.

Unfortunately, many conditions have been attributed to insulin-resistance and high insulin levels: generalized inflammation, weight-gain, poor concentration, fatigue, elevated bad cholesterol, abdominal obesity, high blood pressure/hypertension, elevated blood triglycerides, syndrome X (a combination of the earlier listed conditions), cardiovascular disease, Type-2 diabetes, and even dementia.

Controlling your insulin levels is one of the most powerful anti-aging strategies.

Your metabolic glucagon hormone is your main retrieval hormone and it *strongly opposes* your insulin hormone.

---

[31] Here's a suggestion for those of you who want spaghetti. Use *spaghetti squash* instead; after you bake it (as a whole or cut lengthwise in half), you can scrape out the insides with a fork. It'll look like spaghetti and can replace it in most recipes.

Glucagon plays a critically important role in maintaining your blood glucose balance if you're fasting and when you're exercising. Glucagon is your body's main retrieval hormone and it can raise the concentration of glucose sugar in your blood by breaking down the carbohydrate stored in your body (glycogen) as well as the amino-acid protein and the glycerol fats stored in your liver. And, when necessary, it can also force your insulin into action. This is why insulin and glucagon are called "opposing" or "paired" hormones. You can increase your metabolic glucagon production by eating more protein and by exercising.

And then there's your *main satiety (I'm full)* leptin hormone.

Leptin is a "signaling" hormone which helps regulate your body weight by sending you a signal that makes you feel full thereby reducing your appetite. You may be surprised to know that these "I'm full" signals are only produced by your body fat cells. Put simply, leptin's job is to tell your brain that there's enough fat in storage and no more is needed. This helps to prevent overeating. It makes sense too that if you have insufficient body fat cells, your body won't want to signal a full feeling and so there'll be less leptin production.

When leptin signaling is not working properly (leptin-resistance), the message to stop eating just doesn't reach your brain, so it doesn't realize that you have enough stored energy and you continue to eat as a result regardless of how much body fat you may have.

Obviously, the more fat cells you have then the more leptin you should have in your bloodstream. It sounds contradictory, but with leptin-resistance, even though a fat body has produced a lot of leptin (for the "I'm full" feeling), your brain just can't recognize it! When your leptin receptors aren't working properly, your body can't see your "I'm full" leptin and it thinks it needs *more* food. It'll then create more and more and more insulin (the key to getting glucose/energy into your cells) and this will drive your weight-gain, especially fatty tissue, because your body actually thinks it's starving! You could almost think of leptin and insulin being cousins. Yup, you'll feel fatigued (that's the conservation of energy) and get hungry (that's the need to store more energy). Eeeek, what a hormonal mess.

And weirdly enough, the fat person and the starving person have the same leptin issues. Obese people will have a leptin-resistance (or insensitivity) issue and starving people will have seriously decreased their leptin production. In both cases their biochemistry has tried to regain lost body fat. You can call leptin by two names: the "satiety" hormone or the "starvation" hormone and that's because its main role is energy regulation and calorie expenditure. Your body just wants to save you from either starvation or over-eating! (i.e., eat more OR burn less)

You can normalize your leptin levels and improve leptin-sensitivity by avoiding inflammatory foods such as sugary drinks and trans-fats[32], eating more fatty fish oil, exercising regularly, avoiding restrictive and crash/starvation dieting or heavy fasting, and by getting more sleep. Like your Mom always said, "eat slowly and chew your food." Little did she know that she could have said "give your leptin enough time to signal when you're full."

But we can't forget to consider ghrelin which is your main hunger hormone.

Opposite to leptin's influence, ghrelin's signaling boosts your appetite and tells your body to keep on eating. Whenever your stomach is empty, it releases ghrelin which then sends a message to your brain via your hypothalamus[33] telling you to eat. It would then seem reasonable that ghrelin should be high *before* eating and low *after* you've eaten.

You can improve the function of your ghrelin by avoiding high-fructose corn syrup (HFCS) and sugar-sweetened drinks and by eating protein at <u>every</u>

---

[32] Trans-fats are extremely unhealthy. They're made through the chemical process of the hydrogenation of oils, which solidifies liquid oils to increase the shelf-life of foods that contain them. Basically, trans-fats are made by artificially changing an unsaturated fat with the addition of hydrogen atoms, sort of saturating the empty (or unsaturated) spaces between the carbon atoms with hydrogen atoms. Yup, the food industry wants and then gets that longer shelf-life which will get you that bigger gut. You're supposed to avoid eating a lot of saturated fats, right? Yikes, the food industry has actually taken healthy unsaturated fats (oils) and turned them into unhealthy saturated fats (trans-fats), because they knew that you were avoiding all dietary fats (and "trans-fats" sounds better than "saturated fats")!!! OMG...let's tell the industry to quit trying to help us!

[33] The hypothalamus is the part of your brain that regulates body temperature, a number of metabolic processes and other involuntary activities. Its hormones govern many functions including thirst, hunger, sleep, and even your mood. It's also the primary area in your brain which is affected by the addictive high-satiety high-calorie foods.

meal. Getting more sleep, eating more fiber and eating a number of smaller daily meals will also help.

Cortisol (a catabolic[34] hormone) is your main metabolic *stress hormone.*

As you age and maybe even more so at menopause, your body may be producing more cortisol. Unfortunately, cortisol enables fat retention, especially near your waist. Whenever your body senses stress, it releases cortisol. It's made by your body for survival. If a grizzly bear is chasing you, your cortisol levels will be enormous. If you're nervously awaiting a performance review meeting at work, your cortisol levels will be huge. Your body's adrenal[35] glands cannot decipher between these two stressful situations and will create the *same cortisol* for running away from both. That's great if there's a bear behind you and you need to get moving fast, but not if you're just sitting in a room sweating it out awaiting an interview of some sort!

Stress triggers the production of cortisol, which in turn triggers fat retention in your tummy area.
Sleep deprivation also produces cortisol.

When you experience chronic levels of stress, the amount of cortisol in your body stays elevated and cortisol signals your fat cells *to hold on to* as much fat as they can and to release as little fat as they need to. Cortisol also slows your metabolism (need I mention what that means?) by blocking the effects of other important metabolic hormones *including* the insulin, glucagon, leptin and growth hormones. This also occurs whenever you're over on Starvation Island, due to the resultant biochemical stresses placed upon your body.

Synergistically, hormones can play havoc with your metabolism with the insulin and cortisol effects being perfect examples. Insulin will make you gain weight, while cortisol will jump on the bandwagon and decide where to put that weight and it'll usually be at your belly level.

---

[34] A catabolic hormone is one that stimulates the breakdown of your body tissues to be used as energy.

[35] The adrenal glands (one above each kidney) are endocrine glands that produce a variety of hormones, including adrenaline and cortisol (which regulate metabolism and suppress your immune system).

And so you can see that there are three major issues that will always add difficulty in losing weight and they're especially effective at thwarting your efforts as you get older and begin to experience menopause.

1. A loss of muscle tissue mass: to get amino-acids for conversion into glucose for energy, your body will breakdown muscles, tendons and ligaments and there'll be a simultaneous drop in your metabolic rate which will automatically result in a reduced number of calories burned *throughout* the day and night. Yikes!
2. An increase in blood sugar levels: there'll be a reduction in glucose transportation to your cells, an increase in insulin-resistance and an increase in carbohydrate cravings (e.g., that delicious chocolate bar or that big bowl of hot pasta).
3. An increase in body fat: there'll be an increase in your overall body fat due to overeating, followed by a *redistribution* of that newly accumulated body fat to the abdominal area. Oh no, not there! Yup, those 5,000 daily crunches aren't going to do much at whittling down your belly fat when your biochemistry is in charge.

You must develop some strategies that will better manage stress, thereby reducing your cortisol levels. You can eat a more balanced nutritionally dense diet without cutting calories too extremely. You can practice meditation and other stress reduction techniques. You can listen to soothing relaxing music and you can sleep more.

Go to bed at the same time every night and get up at the same time every morning – regardless of how you feel. Develop normalized sleeping hours by regulating your times. If you're partying one night and you're up quite late, STILL get up at the same time the next morning. You can take one or two 15-minute snoozes during the day to make up for how tired you were when you got up in the morning. The problem with sleeping in is that you end up having more difficulty getting to sleep at the correct time that night and then the sleep cycle gets horribly off for a few days. Just set your alarm and stick to it.

And you can exercise thereby benefitting from those wonderful *I-feel-great* endorphin hormones that the brain and nervous system will give you, the ones that activate your body's opiate-type receptors (oh yah, bring it on!) Be cognizant of what stresses you out and try to avoid those situations as best you can.

Human Growth Hormone (HGH – an anabolic hormone[36]) is your *main metabolic growth* hormone, especially at puberty.

HGH is responsible for increasing muscle mass and decreasing stored body fat by freeing it up as an energy source. It's secreted from your pituitary gland[37], *primarily when you are sleeping*. It's also produced in response to *regular weight-training exercise*. If you subject your body to high intensity weight-training, your body will release HGH and one of the jobs of this very powerful hormone is to repair the microdamage done to your muscle tissues. Because it takes a lot of energy to complete that repair job, energy will have to come from your body fat stores as well.

What do we see here? The need to exercise and to get more sleep. By the age of 40, there will likely have been a huge decline in your HGH production. By the time you retire you may have lost a third of your lean muscle mass and replaced it with body fat as a result of your HGH decline. You can't rollback your age and you can't avoid menopause, but you sure can slow your HGH decline through weight-training at the gym.

In sum, the metabolic and signaling hormones noted above work *together* to increase or decrease your appetite, your resulting fat-storage and your calorie-burning rate. Although not an exhaustive list, for our purposes, these are the main hormones that are impacted by your age and that includes menopause.

Hormones directly influence your appetite, your metabolism and your body fat distribution. Normally you won't be able to "feel" changes in your hormones (e.g., insulin, glucagon, cortisol, HGH) as such changes will be biochemical reactions to your general lifestyle, diet choices, exercise, sleep patterns and daily stress

---

[36] And anabolic hormone stimulates the build-up or construction of your body tissues and uses caloric energy.

[37] Your pituitary gland is located in your brain, just behind your nose actually. Although only the size of a pea, it's the *master* of your endocrine system because it controls so many hormones and directly affects your metabolism and, as a result, your body tissue percentage composition (i.e., fat versus muscle tissue).

and you just won't notice those internal reactions as they take place.
But you <u>should</u> be able to "feel" your <u>signaling</u> hormones (e.g., leptin and
ghrelin).
Babies do! That's why they spit food out when they're full. They still hear
their "I'm full" leptin signals. Please don't force feed them!

The benefits of exercise for a menopausal woman may include less severe hot flashes, less depression, fewer severe night sweats, and a slowing down of osteopenia[38] or osteoporosis. When you exercise, your muscles must move a weight and so they must pull against your tendons and bones. When a force is exerted on your bones, your bone mass *must* increase or grow. Also, coupling calcium and magnesium intakes with exercise will usually have a synergistic effect on your overall bone health.

If you look at the suggestions above there's a theme and it revolves around eating better, exercising regularly, better managing your reaction to daily stress and endeavoring to sleep more. Like I said earlier, there is no magic surprise method to losing weight. It's really just common sense coupled with a bit of biochemical hormone-based knowledge.

Exercise grows muscle and bone, both of which tend to get weakened as you age.

1.6 What Is Thermogenesis?

"The world as we have created it is a process of our thinking. It cannot be changed without changing our thinking." – A.E.

The term thermogenesis refers to the generation of heat: "thermo" means *heat* and "genesis" means *create*. In your body, heat creation comes from the conversion of food into energy and this is good. Heat is simply a by-product of energy metabolism. And so, when you work your muscles hard, you'll also

---

[39] Osteopenia is a condition in which your bone mineral density is lower than normal. Some doctors consider it a precursor to osteoporosis, however not all with osteopenia will develop osteoporosis (wherein the bones are brittle, fragile, and prone to breaking). Think of all those older people with hip fractures! On a side note, older people can also fall because their core is weak and they just can't catch themselves fast enough, especially on slippery surfaces like bathtubs and ice.

generate heat. Everyone is born with a *thermogenesis metabolic mechanism*, although some people are lucky to be born with a faster, more highly effective one. That means that they can get rid of excess weight or maintain their ideal weight more easily.

People with an innately higher thermogenesis tend to have lower levels of body fat and are less likely to store energy as fat. Ok so they're just luckier than the rest of us and they're closer to that calorie-burning side of the continuum. Highly thermogenic people simply burn more calories than the rest of us, creating more heat and carrying less body fat (so they look great and feel good). You can envy them, but you can't get angry with them for their good luck. A lot of people with tall lanky or long-limbed frameworks are like this (i.e., an ectomorph). Ok, if that's not you, then you need to figure out how to increase *your* level of thermogenesis[39].

Dehydration will always reduce your thermogenic ability.

Your average body temperature will affect your metabolism. The lower your body heat, the slower your metabolic rate. Conversely, the higher your overall body heat, the faster your metabolic rate. There are several ways to raise your body temperature. You can eat more <u>and</u> exercise more. Eating more is a necessity *but without exercise* it'll cause you to gain weight because you can't burn off the extra calories. Maybe a better route to boost your thermogenesis would include eating more but with a *better balance* of the right nutritious foods in the right combinations and with reasonable portion-control. Then throw in some exercise.

I can't tell you how many women at the gym eat very little, exercise minimally and gain weight or increase their body fat percentage. Many of them only jump on the treadmill or will use little 5-pound weights on the gym floor after puffing up a storm on that treadmill. I always tell them that they're "not eating enough food to lose weight" and that they also should be lifting "progressively heavier weights." Of course, many never believe me. They don't realize that calorie restriction will <u>always</u> reduce their overall metabolic rate. And we know what Starvation Island mentality translates into; the

---

[39] Ever wonder what shivering is? It's an example of thermogenesis which occurs when your skeletal muscles contract to produce heat.

lowering of their metabolism (fat-making UP) resulting in a far poorer ability to burn very many calories (calorie-burning DOWN).

To dramatically increase your thermogenesis mechanisms, you must control your cortisol (yes, that powerful stress hormone again) and blood sugar levels, keeping them within normal ranges and you have to eat a balanced diet with protein, fat and carbohydrate. Protein is the key nutrient in this thermogenic equation given its nitrogen-carrying amino-acids. These allow your body to build and repair muscles, bone, hair, and skin. Protein is also the most inefficiently broken-down macronutrient; hence it'll use up more caloric/thermal energy (yeah) while being digested and provide the best dietary-induced thermogenesis; more so then either carbohydrates or fats. Examples of good high protein foods include eggs, skinless chicken and turkey breast, Greek yogurt, lean beef, quinoa, lentils and fish.

The higher your thermogenesis or heat creation rate,
the more you'll control your cortisol and blood sugar levels.
This will translate into more calorie-burning and less fat-making.

Successful dieters who are better at improving their thermogenesis not only eat lean protein, they also eat complex slow-to-sugar carbohydrates (e.g., vegetables, whole grains[40], whole fruits) and good nutritious dietary fat sources (e.g., egg yolks, seeds, nuts, olive and canola oils). To get to their ideal weight they probably lowered their carbohydrate intake *slightly* and increased their protein intake *slightly*. This approach will not result in a biochemical panic dip in their metabolic calorie-burning rate as their body would not recognize any

---

[40] Whole grains contain all the parts of the grain (endosperm, bran and germ) while refined grains (such as white rice and white flour) have had the bran and germ removed. The industry tries to make the resultant grain whiter with bleaching (!) and then enriches the result with the nutrients they initially removed! Geezzz, what a crazy circuitous route! If you must have rice, go with "wild rice" which contains 30% fewer calories and 40% more protein than brown rice. It also takes longer to digest and will spike a slower introduction of glucose into your bloodstream than will other rice. Did you know that wild rice isn't actually a rice? It's the seed of an aquatic grass. You might wonder why it's even called "rice" when it's a grass; it's because it *looks like* a kernel of long-grain rice. Sort of weird. Why don't we call coyotes "dogs"? They do look like them and they're both canines!

starvation or feel anything too out-of-whack in terms of available energy and body hormonal balances.

On another note, drink a lot of water. Dehydration will always reduce your thermogenic potential. Water is an important catalyst for hastening your weight-loss and it's absolutely *essential* for fat-burning, for the maintenance of muscle mass and for boosting your overall metabolism. There's a lot of detail on these concepts in subsequent chapters.

1.7 How Does Stress Make Me Fat, and How Can I Control It?

"I am happy because I want nothing from anyone." – A.E.

Sadly, we all live in stressful times. Stress can come from the office (remember that performance review?), personal relationships, traffic jams, in-laws, financial problems, kids, deadlines, and maybe even from actual bears[41]. We must try better to *manage* that stress so that we can extend our lives, balance our hormones, maintain a healthy weight, and keep our metabolism running efficiently.

Whenever and however you're stressed you'll burn fewer calories and always store more body fat regardless of your diet. Earlier you read that stress leads to weight-gain via the cortisol hormone. Cortisol is really your body's alarm system and there's just no getting around the fact that chronically elevated levels of cortisol lead to overeating and subsequent weight-gain. And due to your ancestors, that extra stress-related weight will settle in your belly area. Why? Because belly fat breaks down more easily and has a more direct line to your liver, and when you have to hunt that live protein you want your stored energy to be readily available for quick fuel.

Your body will *biochemically and hormonally* adapt to any and all changes it encounters using its metabolism, whether via a diet change or an introduction of weight-training exercise or chronically high stress or terrible sleep patterns. Actually the word "stressed" turns into "desserts" when spelled backwards. Interestingly, stress and desserts are related both with your potential response

---

[41] When camping with the kids one year, we left our cooler outside the tent one night. Although scary (AKA cortisol stressful!) at the time, we now love to display the bear's teeth marks in the corners of the cooler.

action and your body's biochemical reaction! I bet you're more prone to eating a bunch of comfort refined/processed desserts when you're stressed out; lots of high-fat and high-sugar types of foods. And then your body gets more acidic, more inflamed and makes more fat cells for storage of excess toxic waste by-products.

One of the best examples of a metabolic adaptation occurs when you severely cut calories to lose weight. Your resting metabolic rate (RMR) is a measurement of the number of calories your body burns while at rest. Well that makes sense! Obviously, that would mean that when you cut calories, your RMR will *also* drop. All of this is an example of a *metabolic adaptation*; your body is adapting its metabolism by burning fewer calories in direct response to its new reality, fewer consumed calories. Remember those badly informed yo-yo dieters pitching a tent on Starvation Island?

RMR is the number of calories burned while at rest. If you drastically cut calories, your RMR will adapt by dropping as well; and that's your calorie-burning ability – even while sleeping.

This automatic adaptation was perfect for our ancestral hunters and gatherers as they faced famine many times and needed to conserve energy, slow any weight-loss and maintain their body fat reserves. That scenario is simply not true for you and me. We don't have to use much energy to hunt down food in the grocery store and we eat regularly. But unfortunately, to make matters worse, many of us *never* stop eating. We eat all day long starting with breakfast and all the way along to bedtime. Some people even get up in the middle of the night to eat!!! No famine there!

But how can stress make you fat? It's because of the excessive excretion of the catabolic (breakdown) stress hormone cortisol, along with a reduced secretion of key anabolic (build-up) hormones, including the human growth hormone (this stimulates protein synthesis, tissue repair, muscle growth and inflammation control). Just as with menopause, this hormonal combination causes changes in the circulating levels of these hormones, making your body *store fat and lose muscle*. No no, not that again! Your metabolic RMR rate slows and your appetite increases. Overall, you *burn fewer calories*, but surprisingly you're *eating more food*. Also, there's an increase in blood sugar levels which means a reduced transport of glucose into your cells and increased insulin-resistance, coupled with difficult-to-ignore carbohydrate cravings. Egads, things really are getting bad on the inside!

Stress produces more cortisol hormones and fewer growth hormones. This means less muscle, more fat, and a slower metabolism (even when you eat more food). Biochemical regulations are in complete control.

To succeed, you must be smarter than your body's natural metabolic adaptation process. You must avoid the huge changes in your metabolic rate that set off your fat-making with a conservation of energy and the cessation of fat-loss. Don't focus only on factors such as severely restricting overall calorie intake or seeking ridiculously fast weight-loss. When you do, your body will *always* outsmart you by hormonally adapting. It'll fight to retain its fat stores and to eat your muscle, while attempting to keep your weight the same.

Make small changes simultaneously to prevent such adaptation; this will make it far more difficult for your body to figure out what the heck is going on, and then it won't alter its RMR. You need to *outsmart* your body's natural processes, the ones that increase appetite, stimulate fat-storage and reduce calorie-burning, by simultaneously targeting multiple metabolic processes such as your cortisol level, blood sugar glucose following a meal, thermogenesis ability, as well as the serotonin hormones produced by your brain (which can lead to depression and the emotional eating that results in obesity) and the thyroid hormones which regulate your RMR.

Control your blood sugar levels, by balancing the quality and quantity of your daily carbohydrate, protein, fat and fiber intakes and by avoiding processed foods, sugars and trans-fats.
You have to outsmart your metabolism by making only small dietary changes, thereby avoiding fat-making adaptations.

If you have a lot of stress in your life, try eating 6 smaller daily meals: breakfast, snack, lunch, snack, dinner, snack. This will better regulate your blood sugar levels and cortisol responses to food. Such an approach will also control your appetite, boost your energy, modulate your powerful ruling hormones, and will encourage fat-burning throughout the day by keeping your metabolic engine running efficiently. You get to eat many meals with lots of highly nutritious foods *and* lose weight. Sign me up for that!

To help avoid excess cortisol, you must *balance your daily intake of carbohydrate, fat, protein, and fiber* in a way that considers both quality <u>and</u> quantity. Having all four at every major meal would be great with the caveat that you *never eat carbohydrate without either protein or fat* to slow down the digestion process. Avoid your body's anti-balance foods such as processed carbohydrates, "junk" foods, fried and sugary foods. This will be detailed in the next Unit.

Below is an overview from the inside of your body of the important factors that are directly affected by **chronic high stress levels**. The adaptation results will show the negative effects on your ability to burn calories; the amount of fat you store; the loss of lean tissue mass; your overall metabolic RMR rate; and your overall appetite.

Catabolic Hormones *(e.g., cortisol levels increase)* ⬆	Increasing your catabolic metabolism will *<u>decrease</u> your calorie-burning.*
Anabolic Hormones *(e.g., HGH levels decrease)* ⬇	Decreasing your anabolic metabolism will *<u>decrease</u> your calorie-burning.*
Fat-Storage ⬆	Adding *<u>more body fat</u> around your abdomen.*
Muscle Breakdown ⬆	Losing lean tissue will *<u>decrease</u> your muscle tone and <u>increase</u> your overall body fat percentage.*
Tissue Inflammation ⬆	Increasing inflammation increases the *risk of autoimmune <u>diseases.</u>*
Overall metabolic rate *(i.e., decrease in your RMR)* ⬇	Slowing down your overall resting metabolism will *<u>decrease</u> your calorie-burning and <u>decrease</u> your overall metabolic rate.*
Overall Appetite ⬆	Resulting in *Carbohydrate (glucose-based) <u>cravings.</u>*

Insulin-resistance *(i.e., chronic high blood sugar/glucose levels wherein the excess sugar just can't get into your cells)* ⬆	Increasing and then chronically maintaining insulin-resistance can lead to ***Type-2 diabetes.***
Thermogenesis *(i.e., your body's heat production)* ⬇	Lowering your thermogenic rate will ***decrease your overall calorie-burning metabolic rate and increase your body fat.***

Here are some handy rules for biochemical balance:

1. Whole foods (natural and unprocessed) have a higher nutrient balance factor.
2. Lean protein can balance refined/processed quick-to-sugar carbohydrate. But still try to avoid the refined stuff.
3. Adding good unsaturated fat to every meal can act as a metabolic regulator (fat *as does protein* slows the post-meal rise in blood sugar and controls your appetite).
4. Eat high quality complex carbohydrate. Choosing whole forms of vegetables, fruits and 100% whole grains (unrefined, unprocessed) will meet your fiber needs (fiber slows the release of insulin and the absorption of sugar/carbohydrate).
5. Avoid high fructose corn syrup (HFCS), a sweetener made from corn and which is very high in fructose.[42] Read ingredient labels before purchasing any packaged food.

---

[42] HFCS is preferred by the food industry because it's cheaper and much sweeter tasting than regular sugar/sucrose. The industry can use smaller amounts *and* save money. Fructose is metabolized quite differently from other sugars and over-consumption can result in an altered metabolism, including a disrupted cortisol metabolism in your fat cells that encourages them to store *more* fat in your abdominal fat cells (yuk!). In sum, with fructose and especially with the HFCS in processed foods, you get the calories, you get the signal to store fat, but you never get the "I'm full" signal (which can only come from the leptin in fat cells). You could drink a litre of soda pop and your body wouldn't react properly to the calories, although it would certainly store them as fat on your waistline.

6. Avoid trans-fats (hydrogenated or partially hydrogenated oils.[43]) Non-hydrogenated oils have the same 9 calories/gram as do hydrogenated oils, but it's the *way* they are metabolized in your body that's most important. Trans-fats interfere with the metabolism of cortisol by increasing it. They also increase both your blood glucose as well as body inflammation. A diet high in trans-fats (i.e., processed foods) will signal fat cells to store as much fat as possible and release <u>as little as possible,</u> *even when calories are cut back.* Wow! Trans-fats sure are powerful fat-makers!

And while we're talking about food, don't forget portion-control. Your body has some built-in portion-control devices – they're called *hands*. If you can't hold something in your hand, then the portion is too big to eat. Pasta is a great example. <u>One</u> handful of cooked pasta is reasonable while a full plate of it (as is served at most pasta restaurants) is far too much. Any protein bigger than a clenched fist is too big for one meal. How much fat can you put into an ice cream scoop? Well that's how much fat you can have at any given main meal (e.g., butter, olive oil and nuts).

People have different bone structures. Small people will have small hands while larger people will have larger hands. Obviously smaller people with smaller hands *should* be eating less than larger people! Using this method will have total breakfast or lunch or dinner calories from nutrient-dense real non-processed foods ranging between 300-600 calories/meal for a small person, and between 500-800 calories/meal daily for a larger person (this does not count snack-based calories). This is a good plan for your long-term weight-loss. And I should mention that if you're building lean muscle through weight-training, you <u>can</u> go to the higher number! Yeah.

---

[43] These are liquid vegetable oils that have been chemically modified so that they can become solid or semi-solid. They're called hydrogenated oils or trans-fats or trans-fatty-acids (all of which refers to the change in their chemical structure). The food industry prefers to use solid oils because they add crispiness and longer shelf-life to foods. Yup, less spoilage equals higher profits for the food industry and more fat for you.

1.8 How Does Metabolism Affect the Body?

"We cannot solve our problems with the same thinking we used to create them." – A.E.

Your metabolism is an incredibly complex biochemical process and it affects **every** cell in your body. When your metabolic engine is slow it becomes sluggish and just can't function well; at that point you'll be depositing fat when you eat instead of burning it as fuel. With a higher or faster metabolism, you'll burn calories much faster. Contrary to what you might think, you <u>can</u> change your metabolism *regardless of your age, even if you're experiencing menopause.*

How can you tell if you have a slower metabolism? Place a thermometer by your bed at night. In the morning put it in your armpit and lie quietly for 10 minutes. Record the temperature this way for 10 straight days. Then determine the average. If it's *below 97.8 degrees Fahrenheit[44]*, you probably have an underactive/inefficient metabolism. The lower your average temperature, the slower your metabolism and you guessed it, you'll be burning fewer calories.

As will be underscored *<u>many times</u>* in this book, metabolism is the engine of your calorie-burning ability. You've probably read lots of theories on how to speed up that engine so that you can burn caloric fuel faster or for longer periods of time. Interestingly, metabolism is responsible not only for burning body fat but *also for storing body fat.* Everybody has their own metabolism, and that's why you may know people who seem to eat all the time and yet never put the weight on. Their bodies are simply more efficient and probably always have been from birth, and they'll have a higher thermogenesis going on too. Well, that's great but it probably isn't you; I know it isn't me either. If you're overweight, then you *must* speed up your metabolism so that it's more efficient like those lucky people who were born with highly efficient metabolisms.

---

[44] Normal body temperature is 98.6 Fahrenheit (or 37 degrees Celsius), although some people may be slightly different by as much as 1 degree Fahrenheit or a ½ degree Celsius either way. NO problem. Using your armpit to take your temperature will make it read about 1 degree less in Fahrenheit. You can still chat with your partner.

Cellulite – that dimpled and lumpy skin appearance – is yet another worry for many women; it's the result of lymphatic congestion[45] and slow fluid drainage resulting from excess wastes being generated by an inefficient metabolism. A sluggish and stagnant lymphatic system leads to excess weight and wastes that can accumulate beneath your skin. In effect, fatty cellulite deposits have pushed through the connective tissues that are located just below your skin. This causes that cottage cheese look that you might see on your body. Often, it'll be more obvious on your upper legs and butt.

The faster your metabolic engine, the faster your burn caloric fuel.
Cellulite is the excess waste produced by an inefficient slow metabolism.

Speeding up your metabolism involves *how* you eat, *how* you exercise, *how* you handle stress and *how much* sleep you're getting. All of these factors work together to give you a healthy body, a healthy metabolism and less cellulite.

Let's start with exercise. Why is it so important as a tool to make your metabolism faster? And how does that direct relationship work?

Well firstly, exercise obviously affects your muscles very directly. Your muscles allow movement to take place and they need caloric fuel in order to properly function. The more muscles you have the more calories they'll burn just to maintain themselves. Fat is fat and muscle is muscle. They are completely different types of tissues and they have very different biochemical roles. Muscle is a lean tissue primarily comprised of protein, water and stored glycogen/carbohydrate while fat is a tissue made up of fatty-acid bundles called triglycerides. Yup, different cell tissues for different biochemical needs and for any required hormonal adaptations.

You can make your metabolism more efficient. The more muscle you have,
the faster your metabolism and the more calories you'll burn
– no matter what you're doing, even while sleeping.

---

[45] Lymph vessels help with the maintenance of fluid balance in your body. If your system isn't working properly, it'll cause your tissues to be swollen with fluid and cellulite can be a result (as well as water retention and joint stiffness).

Body "fat" tissue is a loose connective tissue comprised of adipocytes (specialized cells for fat-storage). Its main role is to store energy in the form of body fat. Body "muscle" tissue contains protein filaments of actin and myosin that slide past one another producing contractions which change the length and shape of your muscle cells. Muscles need fuel in order to contract (or shorten) and lengthen while moving your various joints. That's why they are calorie-eating tissues.

There just isn't any way to get around these facts! Your car doesn't run without fuel (gas or electricity) and your muscles don't work without fuel (calories). You can now imagine how the percentage of body fat to body-muscle will directly affect your need for fuel. A higher muscle tissue percentage means more calorie-burning. The higher your fat tissue percentage, the less calorie-burning is going on. You need to prevent any deterioration of muscle tissue. You need to challenge your muscles in order to increase their size, hence improve your calorie-burning ability. *You need to exercise!!!*

There are three different types of muscles. <u>Cardiac</u> muscles contract your heart to get the blood pumping. <u>Smooth</u> muscles form your body's organs and they allow changes to organ shapes in order to meet their bodily functions (for example an overly stuffed stomach has a vastly different shape than an empty one). <u>Skeletal</u> muscles are attached to bones or to connective tissues such as ligaments in order to move your bones into producing the counter force necessary for motion and for the movement of heavy weights. There are over 600 skeletal muscles in your body and these are the ones we're interested in when visiting the gym to weight-train.

Women are always afraid of lifting weights, stating that they don't want to get to get too bulky or muscular and end up "looking like a man." Believe me you can ***never*** look like a man, unless you take anabolic steroids[46]! Men normally have about 40% more muscle mass than women and *10 times more testosterone* anabolic hormones (yes you too have some testosterone kicking about, just not that much), hence men can bulk up their muscles much more than we can. They call it getting "jacked," getting "defined," getting "shredded," getting "cut" or getting "ripped." Well ladies, that's exactly the

---

[46] Anabolic steroids are comprised of testosterone and other synthetic male sex androgens that are structurally related to and have very similar effects as testosterone. If you see a woman who looks like Arnold Schwarzenegger, believe me, she has guzzled a bunch of testosterone supplements.

same as what you refer to as getting "toned." It just means that you can see the outline of the firmer muscle because it isn't buried under layers of fatty tissue. And isn't that what you want? You want to have strongly defined muscles with less fat over them. I guess "toned" has a more feminine sound to it than does "jacked."

The best way to develop lean, active, fat-burning and calorie-eating muscle is to challenge your muscles using free weights (e.g., dumbbells, barbells and weight plates), exercise tubing, cables, and your body weight (as in push-ups). This is called "strength" or "resistance" or "weight" training. In this book, I'll use the term "weight-training" for this type of training as it conjures up the proper vision of the gym floor with cable machines and free weights[47]. All weight-training involves physical exercises which use resistance forces to induce muscular contractions to build the strength, *anaerobic* endurance and the size of your skeletal muscles.

In addition to "strength" training (an anaerobic/non-oxidative system – think of Arnold Schwarzenegger), there are two other types of training: "endurance" training (an aerobic/oxidative system – think of the marathon runner); and, "power" training for the ability to exert the maximal force in as short a time as possible such as accelerating, jumping and throwing something with great speed – think of the MLB baseball pitcher and his incredible 95 mph fastball.

By challenging your muscles to work harder each time you lift weights, they become stimulated to develop by growing bigger to counter their weight-training teardown. Yes, *teardown*. Muscles are made of tiny, microscopic fibers and when you challenge them with weight-training they get torn a bit. Kind of sounds a bit scary – but it's a completely natural body reaction to exercise, any exercise. These torn muscle fibers must then rebuild, and this gives them better endurance and makes them stronger and more powerful. This will mean they'll get bigger and more "ripped" – oops, sorry I meant "toned." Muscles need caloric fuel to do this. Indeed, they'll use calories for the whole length of time it takes to rebuild. This can typically last 24-72 hours after a

---

[47] I don't know about you, but I simply can't exercise at home. I get so distracted; always something else to do. At the gym, I'm not alone and I'm focused. We're all on our journeys to better health. There are tons of varied pieces of expensive equipment to use. Besides I've paid and there's no way I'm not going! Money can be a useful incentive.

strenuous weight-training workout! Wowie, I love that notion of *burning calories <u>while</u> exercising as well as <u>after</u> exercising* – that's the kind of fat-burning efficiency I want!

Often after I complete a strenuous lower body set of exercises, I'll feel my legs working as I climb or descend stairs, frankly they feel sore! Technically this exercise-induced soreness I feel is directly due to something called "delayed onset muscle soreness" which has resulted from those microscopic muscle tissue tears. There's a resulting inflammation[48] which has caused the soreness. But it's an inflammation that my body recognizes, *knows how to deal* with and has the innate ability to rectify. This delayed soreness is so important in the bodybuilding world that it has its own acronym, DOMS. And acronyms always denote importance, right??

DOMS usually occurs on the second or third day following my leg workout. It makes me happy as I know I'm burning calories while my body is rebuilding my quadriceps (front of the upper legs), hamstrings (back of the upper legs), calves (back of the lower legs) and glutes (yup, the butt). Comparatively, you won't get much DOMS after the treadmill, but I'll discuss that idea later in the book.

There's also a kind of a metabolic "<u>afterburn</u>" which occurs following the completion of strenuous exercise and that's because your body's blood is *low on oxygen*. What's happening is that oxygen is needed at a higher rate, therefore energy is needed at a higher rate. Your metabolism doesn't return to normal immediately. Instead, it's involved in aerobic activity caused by that oxygen deficit. In short, this afterburn effect won't allow your metabolism to return to normal immediately. It causes an increase in your metabolism's efficiency and that's definitely a great thing, because of its direct connection to your calorie-burning ability. It too warrants an acronym, EPOC, which means "excess post-exercise oxygen consumption." You don't actually feel EPOC because it's your metabolism that's adapting by speeding up and you can't *feel* your metabolism. The term afterburn is used because of the fact that calories *are being burned after* you finish exercising.

---

[48] Inflammation from poor eating habits is a completely different beast, one that your body metabolically adapts to in a negative fat-making way. Tearing muscle tissues while exercising causes an inflammation that the body recognizes and deals with in a natural way, resulting in positive calorie-burning and an accelerated metabolism.

Metabolic afterburn is a biochemical adaptation and it's a fat-burning plus.

Certainly you'll get body messages, in the form of stiffness and soreness, from DOMS as it repairs your muscles. The only messages EPOC can give you is via your body's built-in metabolic adaptions such as building up muscle (from weight-training) or piling on body fat (from eating highly refined carbohydrates and way too much bad fat). And these messages are given slowly and deliberately. Pay close attention to them. They involve the following: increased breathing rate, cellular oxygen replenishment, energy re-synthesis, lactate mitigation, blood circulation and body temperature regulation. EPOC can last 15 minutes to 48 hours and its duration is solely dependent on the intensity and duration of your exercising.

Your body burns calories during your gym exercises, usually between 300 and 500 per hour depending on how strenuously you worked out; but, more important to your metabolism, is this fact that your body *continues to burn* calories *after* you leave the gym. You always need oxygen in order to burn calories, hence if you experience an oxygen-deprived EPOC time due to strenuous exercise then your body must burn *more calories* to make up for that deficit.

Isn't that great to think that due to an hour of weight-training, you could be burning extra calories for up to two days (depending upon how hard your workout was and how many different muscles you fatigued)! Some argue that it isn't that many calories, but I know when I can feel my sore muscles that they are working hard to overcome the challenge I gave them by making themselves stronger. Gosh gee who cares how many calories, it's still a lot better than just running on the treadmill which will burn calories while you're running with not much DOMS afterward and the resulting afterburn EPOC will only last about 12-24 hours.

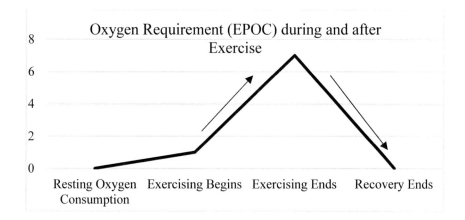

Oxygen Requirement (EPOC) during and after Exercise

In this diagram you can see that your oxygen needs grow (first UP arrow) as you continue to exercise and are at their highest when you finish exercising. At that point, your body must replace the deficit oxygen used while exercising and so you will burn calories while you're recovering (second DOWN arrow) from that oxygen deficit. That's the EPOC zone and weightlifting will greatly enhance your EPOC afterburn, much more than will cardio training. Go for it!

Contrary to what you might think, _both_ progressive[49] weight-training exercises and appropriate cardiovascular exercises (on the stationary bike or stair climber, etc.) _burn oxygen_. They're both aerobic and anaerobic, albeit weight-training is more anaerobic than cardio-training and cardio-training _is supposed to be_ more aerobic than weight-training. I say "supposed to be" because you have to be in a good physically fit condition to keep it aerobic.

Do more weightlifting and less treadmill activity. This will allow your body to continue burning calories long after vacating the gym.

Keep in mind that the number of calories accruing on a treadmill are not necessarily the number _your_ body is actually burning. It's all dependent on how much muscle you have, your physical fitness, how much you weigh, how fast you're running, whether the treadmill is inclined or not, whether you're employing proper posture (i.e., not leaning forward or backward and, in some

---

[49] Increasing the exercise intensity used over time. Always lift what you _should_ lift, not just what you _can_ lift. When I see women lifting 2-3-pound weights, I wonder why they think that is helpful. A newborn grandchild weighs more than that!

cases, whether you're hanging onto handrails or not.) Think about it. How can a physically fit 125-pound woman burn the same treadmill calories as the neighboring obese unfit 190-pound woman??? Their machines may read the same calories, but there's no way they're burning the same number of calories. They simply can't!!! Especially if one of them has relocated to Starvation Island.

That said, if you were walking on the treadmill at about 4-5 miles per hour, you might burn between 150 and 200 calories in an hour. That's not nearly as high as what you would have burned lifting weights for an hour (200-300) and, once you're off that treadmill, you don't *continue* to burn the calories as you would after lifting weights. There just isn't any comparison in terms of energy/caloric consumption.

Metabolism is also very strongly related to your nutritional habits. If you follow a nutritionally balanced diet, it isn't just a lot more enjoyable than those crazy starvation diets, it's also good for revving up your metabolism (contrary to the metabolic result of those crash deprivation diets).

If you eat a lot of protein, this will boost your metabolism and cause you to burn more calories daily. Seem strange? Not really. Protein is made up of amino-acids and these are more challenging for your body to breakdown causing a higher thermogenic effect. The eating of protein makes your body burn more calories than the eating of either carbohydrate or fat, and *especially* more so than processed or refined foods. Some examples of metabolism-revving protein include eggs, cottage cheese, whole oats, quinoa, turkey, wild halibut and salmon, black beans, peas, chickpeas and lentils.

Great news! Protein is hard to breakdown and so your body will use more calories than it would for the breakdown of either carbohydrate or fat.

Processed carbohydrates and sweets are metabolized by your body quite *efficiently* and so they'll *quickly* turn into sugar and increase your insulin hormone which, in turn, will put glucose-based energy into your body cells. If you're not exercising or suffer from insulin-resistance[50], then your

---

[50] Some people have a body that is insulin-resistant which means that glucose is less able to enter their cells. It means that even more insulin is produced as their body tries

extra/unused insulin will make you store more fat *and* slow your metabolic rate. Oops, a doubly bad whammy for your body to contend with.

You already know that both sleep deprivation and chronic stress can also lead to weight-gain by disrupting your hormones, your eating habits **and your metabolism**. High cortisol levels will also make you hungry for sugary and processed carbohydrate foods. In turn, these foods cause your insulin levels to rise, then fall, making you even more hungry. And this rotten cycle can just go around and around and around *with no check point.*

Sugar increases insulin, raises blood sugar and causes more fat-storage.

I'll discuss sleep in the subsequent chapter, including ways to help encourage more restful hours. To overcome stress is a bit more complicated. We all experience emotional or mental or physical stress, and unfortunately much is unavoidable. Don't let stress kill your long-term health and slow your metabolism. You can better control external situations that cause you stress *by changing your reaction to them* through the use of particular strategies. You can also take up weight-training exercise.

This is especially important if you are *chronically* stressed out. Your body will produce the cortisol hormone continually, lower your leptin hormone "I'm full" signaling and encourage more fat-making enzymes. This will drive you to eat those sugary and/or processed "comfort" foods to replenish the energy your body is using simply to cope with the ongoing stressful situation(s). You'll have great difficulty burning off those extra calories and abdominal fat-storage will *always* result. Yet another horrible no-check-point cycle.

---

to get the proper balance of cell glucose. High levels of insulin tend to make a body gain body-fat. Indeed, this is one of the main reasons many people have such difficulty losing weight. One way to counter this is to eat five to six smaller meals daily, each with some lean protein. This will help keep your metabolism from slowing down. When your body gets used to eating every three to four hours, it can keep its paired/opposing hormones nicely balanced and then it stays biochemically balanced. Three examples of opposing hormones are: (1) insulin/glucagon (for blood sugar control); (2) leptin/ghrelin (for appetite control); and, (3) cortisol/HGH (for muscle tissue growth and repair). When one is up, the other is down.

Some useful strategies to avoid too much stress-related cortisol release include the following: ceasing crazy and weird diet obsessions, choosing the right whole foods, developing better time management, reducing chaos in your life (or at least your reaction to it), discussing problems with friends and family, getting more sleep and increasing endorphins[51] through weight-training exercises.

At work, try to remember that whatever situation you may find yourself in, it won't last forever!!! Keeping yourself overly organized at work will help with your things-I've-got-to-get-done-but-I-just-don't-have-enough-time tasks. Keep a trusty "to-do" list, update it daily and check off what you've accomplished that day. Break up large jobs into smaller tasks so that you can check them off as you go. It may sound silly, but in terms of overall stress, it's incredibly rewarding to check stuff off.

Compartmentalize as well. Quit worrying about task #3 while you're working on task #1. Just ensure that you do a bit for all time-sensitive jobs daily, keeping a timeline chart to track your process and to ensure that you meet the boss' deadline(s). If you supervise subordinates who are assigned parts of a job, give them an earlier deadline so that you have a time buffer.

And another simple but *extremely effective* approach that will lower your "desk-stress" is by tidying up your work desk/area/cubicle every couple of days.

1.9 What Are the Real Consequences of Sleep Deprivation?

Did Einstein get much sleep? Yes, he did. He took it very seriously and apparently slept for about 10 hours each night! Wow.

Did Einstein know that sleep was good for his brain? Did he factor in those famous "power-naps" he took as a way to recharge his brain and to help him work those long 10-hour thought-experiment days he put in? Maybe not, but I'll bet that his brain was able to sort out complex theoretical physics

---

[51] These are body chemicals that are produced by your brain and nervous system; they make you feel good and help you relax. Exercise creates the endorphins that give you a morphine-type euphoric feeling without the drugs.

calculations in a deeper way while he was sleeping. I'll bet you didn't know that flies sleep. Check out the website "fliesonly.com" and you'll see that they're like us with light sleep and deep sleep cycles. They sleep most of the night and they sometimes take daytime naps too. Wow, who'd have thought that they might be getting more sleep than some of us? [52]

Sleep is one of the four factors that you need to address in order to better manage your overall weight.

For us, we live in a fast society. Everyone's in a hurry and this affects a lot of our lives in terms of overall stress, sleep patterns, and ultimately our food choices. People work long hours, use a lot of stimulating technology and experience long commuting hours, all of which doesn't lead to great sleeping patterns. Although high stress and lack of sleep are usually connected, let's see how your sleep patterns can affect your overall health and whether it can compromise your ability to shift your metabolism from a fat-making engine and more toward a calorie-burning engine. In other words, let's look at the biochemical outcomes of chronic sleep deprivation. Yes, we're talking hormonal adaptations here.

Firstly, let me say that chronic sleep deprivation *will* age you. You know what you see in the morning mirror when you're not sleeping well; you'll have dark baggy circles under your eyes. That's the result of an increased production of the *cortisol stress hormone*. Cortisol will slow down your production of skin collagen, wreaking havoc on the elasticity of your skin. If you get enough sleep, you'll decrease your overall stress levels as well as your fat-making cortisol production.

Although cortisol is directly connected to stress, it'll still be brought to the forefront in sleep deprivation *regardless* of stress. Because you'll produce more cortisol and more fat-making enzymes with too little sleep, your body is told to retain body fat and to hang on to as much as it can all the while releasing as little as possible. This will in turn slow down your metabolic calorie-burning rate. And cortisol, like insulin, is a *metabolic hormone, that is it affects your calorie-burning ability*. One hormone (insulin) will make you gain weight,

---

[52] I have to say that I can't believe what people study in universities. Do you think that guy got his Ph.D. with this study? Personally, I've never seen a sleeping fly; they always manage to evade my swatter.

while the other hormone (cortisol) will decide where that weight is going (and it'll always make body fat and not lean muscle tissue with it).

Sleep levels will always affect your hormones, just like the food you choose to eat will always affect your hormonal balances. Sufficient sleep increases your human growth hormone (HGH) production and this will always increase your calorie-burning muscle mass and lower your stored body fat by freeing it up as an energy source. You sure don't want to reduce your muscle mass! Unfortunately, by the age of 40, you'll have experienced a huge decline in HGH production and so you'll exacerbate that problem with sleep deprivation!

Sleep deprivation cannot only produce tons of cortisol, with its ability to pack fat onto your waist, but it can also disrupt the hormones that control your eating habits. These are leptin and ghrelin. You'll recall that the leptin hormone is an appetite-regulating "I'm full" signal while the ghrelin hormone sends a difficult-to-ignore "I'm hungry" signal. When you get good sleep, you'll improve both your leptin-sensitivity as well as your ghrelin function.

You must practice good sleeping habits and patterns in order to move through the stages or wave cycles of sleep; the first being alpha waves, then beta waves, then delta waves and finally REM sleep. Yes, cycles because it is normal to have periods of wakefulness intermittently throughout the night as you move through the cycles as many as four to five times a night, although the time spent in each stage may shorten as the cycles repeat themselves throughout the night.

It's obvious how to counter sleep deprivation. Go to bed at the same time each evening and try for *at least 7 hours* a night. And don't give up after a couple of nights. Keep at it until your body responds, and it will. Be persistent. Maybe read a *light* book for 10-15 minutes before turning off the light. And honestly, you'll get no sympathy from me if you have a TV, computer, laptop, I-pad or cell phone in your bedroom. They cause brain stimulations, in fact concussed people are told to lay off these obvious stimulants. Avoid such brain stimulants for at least an hour before bedtime. Some people sleep with a "white noise" machine (with the sounds of a rushing waterfall or wind blowing through trees or heavy rainfall), others meditate before going to bed. Some take melatonin, a natural body hormone secreted from the pineal gland. Many off-the-counter sleep-aids contain antihistamine (also used for allergies) and so the side effects can make you sleepy. Some sleep-aid prescriptions can be addictive; hence they aren't recommended for long term usage.

If you are terribly frustrated when you wake up in the middle of the night, try to get away from the stress of thinking about the fact that you can't sleep by getting up and sitting elsewhere for a while or by reading a light book for 30 minutes. It might help you relax and, in essence, help you to get away from the worry and frustration about not sleeping; sort of like changing the subject.

If you experience a good night's sleep it means that you fell asleep fairly quickly, you didn't fully wake up in the middle of the night (even if you visited the washroom, you returned to bed and fell back asleep relatively quickly) and in the morning, *you woke up refreshed*. For most adults this involves at least seven hours, although some adults are just fine with only four to five hours of sleep. During my work life I worked for a number of university deans, two of whom only needed four hours per night! They were both incredibly productive, healthy and lean. OK, so everybody's different and some are just outliers…but I'll bet that you need seven, like me.

Unit 2

The Nutrition Puzzle

How does food fit into the overall weight picture?

<u>Here are some principles to consider:</u>

- **Obesity** can be partially blamed on a bad diet and huge portion sizes.
- **The food industry** invented convenience foods, and these custom designed foods always make you want more.
- **Consumers have fallen really hard for the seductively palatable tastes** of highly processed salty, fatty, sweet and crunchy foods.
- **Over-consumption of refined/processed carbohydrates, sugars and sweeteners** is responsible for disrupting your body's metabolism.
- **Eating a perfect diet and never exercising** will not give you a toned muscular body.
- Your body needs all three macronutrients for its **primary metabolic functions**: carbohydrates for rapid energy; dietary fats for sustained energy and appetite suppression; and proteins for repairing and rebuilding lean body mass.

**You control what you eat, but your hormones control
all resulting biochemical adaptations and metabolic alterations!!!**

2.1 What Are Macronutrients?

"Education is not the learning of facts, but the training of the mind to think." – A.E.

There are many different ways to classify food. You can count the calories, check to see if it's organic[53], monitor how much processing was used, measure the glycemic load[54] it creates, check the blood pH[55] influence it might have, etc. etc. etc. For me, I found that the most useful and easiest way to classify different foods was by the way a food's chemical compounds breakdown in my body and provide energy. Analyzing your daily macronutrients will accomplish this.

Put simply, macronutrients are the dietary components that you need in order to live, to build lean muscle, and for healthy cell function. They're the sources of your dietary caloric fuel for your metabolic engine. They're called "macro" because you need a relatively large amount of them. Classifying food this way may sound complicated and of course your body is using pretty complicated methods to create energy for itself; nonetheless, macronutrients can be useful as a food classification system, and it's a relatively easy system to follow.

Indeed, by shifting your focus to a food's macronutrient analysis, you can break free from boring, constant and often ineffective calorie-counting. In effect you're moving from a quantity approach to food, to a quality approach to food. And, oh my gosh, who wants to always be measuring, weighing and fixating on the number of calories in and the weight of every single bit of food you eat during a day? Not me! Much too time consuming.

---

[53] Keep in mind that whatever the animal ate, you'll be eating it too. "Pasture-raised" is a great label to look for.

[54] The glycemic load of a food is the average increase of the level of sugar in your blood shortly after you eat that food. It's a key concept for those who are insulin-resistant, pre-diabetic, Type-1 or Type-2 diabetic.

[55] pH simply measures the acidity or basicity of the food you eat. It measures the hydrogen ion concentration in your blood. Your blood should not be too acidic. Too many acid-forming foods will poison your body's hormonal chemistry and that chemistry is what determines how healthy, energetic and pain-free you are.

How you eat and whether you eat *more calorie energy* than you actually use, both play major roles in the amount of body fat you carry around. For the proper functioning of your body organs, to grow, to have energy, to maintain health, and to repair themselves, your body needs dietary **macro**nutrients (protein, carbohydrate, fat), **micro**nutrients (vitamins, minerals), fiber (only found in carbohydrates[56]) and *pure* water.

You need to eat all three macronutrients and essential micronutrients and drink sufficient water for the proper functioning of your organs.

Macronutrients provide energy for your body and the energy in all food is measured in caloric units. Although micronutrients and water do not provide *energy*, they remain critical to your good health. Micronutrients are "micro" because they're only needed in relatively small amounts to support your health and biochemical functions.

The essential micronutrient vitamins in human nutrition are: A, D, B-complex, E, C, Niacin and Folic Acid. The essential micronutrient minerals include calcium, magnesium and iron. "Essential" simply refers to the fact that your body can never produce these vitamins or minerals on its own. I won't recommend how much of what you should take. You should consult your physician and/or pharmacist, or a certified nutritionist with all your questions. That said, you can of course get all essential vitamins from a *nutritionally balanced* diet.

There are categories within these three macronutrients (some good, some not so good, others really bad) about which you should be aware.

1. Fats can be ***unsaturated***, ***saturated*** or ***trans***.
2. Protein can be ***lean*** or ***fat***; and,
3. Carbohydrates can be ***complex***, ***simple*** *or* ***processed.***

As soon as you eat fats, proteins or carbohydrates, your body will turn them into fatty-acids, amino-acids or glucose, respectively. All respond to the different needs of your body and this is an example of why not all calories are considered the same to your body.

---

[56] No-carbohydrate diets have no fibre. Constipation anyone?

Of course, most of the foods we eat are percentage combinations of various macronutrients. Examples are beef (protein and fat), seafood (protein and fat), legumes (protein and carbohydrate) and peanut butter (protein and fat). For our purposes I'll categorize macronutrients according to how your body uses them in terms of *overall percentage of calories* coming from different macronutrients. For example, seafood may have both protein and fat, but it has a higher percentage of protein to fat in composition hence we consider it to be a protein. Seeds and nuts are both protein and fat, but the highest percentage is fat. Peanut butter therefore is considered a fat, a pork chop is considered a protein, and bacon is a fat, etc. Legumes are mostly slow-to-sugar "complex" carbohydrates; fruits are mostly quick-to-sugar "simple" carbohydrates. So don't be fooled into thinking vegetables and fruits are anything but carbohydrates to your body.

As a macronutrient, milk is really interesting. All milk[57] contains the nine essential nutrients, whether it's whole, fat-reduced or skim. That is, all similar-sized glasses of milk contain the same grams of both protein and carbohydrates, although the <u>calories</u> coming from fat grams will be quite different. For example whole milk is mostly fat, while skim milk has almost zero fat. Ok, so whole milk is considered to be mostly fat to your body!!! Because skim milk has had most of the fat content removed, it's mostly carbohydrate with some protein; hence, it'll be mostly recognized as a carbohydrate by your body and should be counted as such. Are you surprised? Did you know that milk is mostly water? Hence, when we talk about grams and calories we're actually talking about a <u>very small *volume*</u> of milk. Just remember that when milk is labelled 3.25%, it does NOT mean it only has 3.25% fat content! It means that the milk fat constitutes 3.25% of *the total*

---

[57] There are industrially created products that call themselves "milk," but let's face it, do you think there's any "cow milk" in "almond milk" or of all things "cashew milk"?? How gullible are you? Almonds and cashews aren't even lactating beasts! Almond "milk" for example, has water, almonds, a few vitamins and minerals, and sea salt; but it can also include flavourings, locust bean gum, gellan gum (which has glucose sugar), carrageenan (can cause inflammation), or xanthan gum (which can cause bloating and flatulence), etc. I don't understand how they get away with calling it "milk." Indeed, lately I've noticed that the "milk" word has been disappearing from some of these products. I'll bet that was forced by the milk industry (can't say I disagree with that).

weight of that milk (which of course must include the water weight). I'll go into great detail on this important distinction in the subsequent milk chapter.

I often have women saying "I can't understand why I don't lose weight? For snacks I eat tons of fresh fruit and I put lots of peanut butter or cheese on my celery sticks." You need to understand food and how it's recognized and subsequently used by your biochemical body. To your body fruits *are* "simple" carbohydrates (quick-to-sugar conversion), peanut butter *is* a fat (often paired with added or hidden sugars making it even worse) and your body considers cheese a fat as well (at about 75% fat, 25% protein with no carbohydrate at all)!!! Those snacks are sure going to add up.

And how would you calculate the amount of each macronutrient that you should eat on a daily basis? Well, it depends upon your goals. How much of each type of macronutrient you'll need on a daily basis is dependent upon whether you want to gain lean muscle, lose body fat, lose overall weight or maintain weight, your level of training, your physical fitness and your infamous metabolic engine.

Although you should consult a certified nutritionist, I would normally suggest that a daily diet consisting of about 40% carbohydrates, 30% protein and 30% fat would maintain your weight. During my health journey, I *gradually* altered these percentages as I *evolved my goals* from losing overall weight to gaining more muscle mass as follows:

Your Goal	% calories complex carbohydrate	% calories lean protein	% calories unsaturated fat
Maintain current weight *(at an appropriate number of daily calories based upon your weight)*	40%	30%	30%
Lose overall weight *(would also lower overall daily calories)*	30%	35%	35%
Build more muscle and lose fat *(would also increase overall daily calories)*	35%	40%	25%
Lose fat and build leaner muscle *(would simultaneously eat a lot more calories to bulk-up on muscles)*	25%	45%	30%

For me, my normal goal is to build more muscle and to look lean (but NOT skinny). If someone comes up to me and says "Wow, you look so great, so skinny!" I know they mean well, but I hate being called "skinny." What an insult!!! I'm NOT skinny! I'm LEAN and I worked really hard to get that way. I have a great muscle-to-fat tissue ratio, contrary to the "skinny" gals.

I know that the weight of my muscle tissue mass will increase with added muscle, but I also know that the weight of my fatty tissue mass will decrease while I simultaneously lose body fat. That means that by adhering to the 35% carbohydrates, 40% protein and 25% fat ratios, I'll have increased my lean body tissue percentage and decreased my body fat percentage as I get more fit. Changing those percentages to the 25%/45%/30% as shown above, would allow me to get even leaner and more defined. Moving between these percentages should always be gradual, so that you never shock your body into hormonal panic-ville.

By not changing the percentages drastically, my body will never think it's on Starvation Island. I don't want to make my metabolic rate inefficient. I want to burn calories (by eating nutrient-dense foods) and not store them due to panic-based biochemical and hormonal adaptations.

I guess you could argue that this is a form of calorie-counting, but in reality, the macronutrient approach differs from more traditional calorie-counting because you are focusing on where the calories are coming from. Straight calorie-counting is just that, no more, no less. But by stressing *quality over quantity* in terms of calories, you'll be nourishing your body by giving it what it needs to be biochemically healthy. You couldn't possibly believe that 2 pieces of pizza at about 500-600 calories is the same to your body as eating 500-600 calories from a nutritious meal with a 6 oz. salmon, a baked medium sweet potato, 1 cup cooked broccoli, and a large green salad with tomatoes and carrots and sunflower seeds, drizzled with 2-3 tbsp. of Italian dressing!!!

A diet that includes lean protein, complex carbohydrate, lots of fiber and healthy sources of unsaturated fat will help your body reach *and maintain* a healthy weight. And you'll feel fuller for much longer.

2.2 How Does the Fat Macronutrient Work in My Body?

"Time is an illusion." – A.E.

Although you probably worry about both fat *and* carbohydrates when you're trying to meet your weight- and fat-loss goals, I'll bet you never worry about tracking your protein intake. The truth is, you need dietary *protein, carbohydrates and fat* all in particular combinations, depending upon your goals. Indeed, you may think that by eating fat you'll necessarily get fat. This is simply not true. Yes, fat has more than double the calories per gram than either carbohydrate or protein, and maybe this is why you think you should focus on cutting fat from your diet. But, contrary to what you may believe, calories aren't the most important thing to your body when you're trying to lose weight.

Put simply, not all fats are created equal. Some are healthy, others are not. You have to know which fats are good for you and which should be avoided. Eating the proper amount of *unsaturated fats* does not make you fat! In fact, it's essential to include such fats in your diet, just like complex slow-to-sugar carbohydrates and lean protein are both critical to a healthy diet.

Eating healthy unsaturated fat does not make you fat. Your body doesn't store much good dietary fat as body fat. Most obesity is the result of storing excess sugary and refined/processed carbohydrates as body fat.

Contrary to what low-fat diets tend to suggest, eating fat does *not* make you fat. Through evolution, your body has become much more complex than that and you simply can't trick it into doing something it was *never designed* to do. Your body recognizes dietary fat as a necessary caloric fuel and among other important needs, it also will use it for long-term energy storage.

Although the main role of dietary fat is to provide a major fuel source because of its high concentration of calories (at 9 calories/gram) relative to either protein or carbohydrate (at only 4 calories/gram each), your body has a lot of other very important biochemical uses for dietary fat other than for fuel storage. Fat is incorporated into all of your organs, including your brain which is actually the fattiest organ in your body at about 60% fat. Fat protects your nerve endings with a protective coating. You simply can't send electrical signals through your nerves without the *protection* of fat! Unfortunately, your body is not able to make all the important fat that it needs. Hence, dietary fat has many purposes *other than body fat storage*! Examples include the manufacturing of cell membranes as well as many hormones and the provision of essential fatty-acids for your cell membranes. Your body also uses fat for the production of vitamins (A, D, E, K)[58] subsequently transporting these fat-soluble vitamins around your body – vitamins that promote healthy skin and hair. Fat insulates your body and maintains a proper body temperature which affects your metabolic rate as well (you'll discover when you lose weight, you'll feel cooler weather more so…it's a nice trade-off). These outcomes seem pretty important to me. Did you think that fat is only stored by your body? Nope. Not true at all. You definitely need to eat fat.

Hmmm…then how the heck do you get a lot of body fat??? Most really heavy or obese people are storing *excess carbohydrate as body fat*. It's much easier for your body to store excess dietary carbohydrate as fat than it is to do so with dietary fat. Interesting, eh? Just remember that <u>your body prefers to use carbohydrate/glucose for energy</u>, not fat and certainly not protein! It'll use carbohydrate as its go-to energy (an easy and direct one-step process) until you eat *far too much of it* (usually via processed quick-to-glucose processed/refined foods and sugar) and then with no other recourse, your body stores all the **excess** carbohydrate as body fat.

For you to store dietary fat as body fat, you'd have to eat a heck of a lot of it. And if that fat is from junk-foods, that'll definitely help you to remain in a fat-storing mode regardless of the quantity eaten. And all of this occurs without the fat-storing insulin hormone response, that you'd get from dietary carbohydrates! I believe that obese individuals get as much as 60-70% of their daily calories from carbohydrates, most of them non-fibrous and highly processed.

Eating too much fat (especially saturated fats and trans-fats) produces
many more fatty acids than are needed by your body.
The excess unused ones will always form body fat.

---

[58] These four vitamins are called fat-soluble because they cannot be absorbed without first being surrounded by fat. Other vitamins, which cannot be stored in fat, are called water-soluble vitamins (e.g., B-complex and C).

Dietary fat is a long chain of carbon atoms bound together with hydrogen atoms, which in turn are attached to each carbon atom with one on the top and one on the bottom. The more *hydrogen vacancies* on a carbon chain, then the *more biologically active* that dietary fat will be. So, this is good. This means it can go to places in your body *other than your fat cells*! Depending upon how many spots or spaces are filled will determine whether that dietary fat is saturated (the chain is filled with hydrogen) or unsaturated (some of the spaces remain). Think of two trains, one with no empty seats (saturated), the other will some empty seats (unsaturated).

You should appreciate that dietary fats can come in many different packages. They can be called either fats <u>or</u> oils which are **both "lipids"** or what we call **"fatty-acids."** The only difference is that fats are *solid* at room temperature while oils are *liquid* at room temperature.

There are three types of fatty-acids and these are named according to their carbon chain structures: saturated, monounsaturated and polyunsaturated.

<u>A saturated fat</u> (dairy and meat products) is a dietary fat with no "vacancies" or spaces; it means that the single carbon chain is carrying the maximum number of hydrogen atoms and can't take any more – this train is full! Saturated fats are easily stacked together into a solid mass and so they're just *not a biologically active fat*; think of a stick of butter. They're *molecularly straight* in structure and that allows them to access your fat cells *very easily*.

<u>An unsaturated fat</u> (oils[59], nuts and seeds) is a dietary fat with some vacancies on its carbon chain – you can get a train ticket; these can be **mono**unsaturated (two carbon atoms bonded together without hydrogen partners such as extra virgin olive oil) or **poly**unsaturated fats (which have more than one carbon bond without hydrogen atoms such as flax seed oil). Unsaturated fats are *less stable* than saturated fats and so they're *more biologically active* and can be used for multiple purposes *other than* for energy storage body fat.

You should limit your consumption of saturated fats (butter, cream, lard, and beef) and eat *moderate* amounts of unsaturated fats such as olive oil, flax seed oil, canola oil, cashew nuts, walnuts, seeds, tofu, soybeans, ground flax seeds (also great for fiber intake), wild salmon, trout and albacore tuna.

---

[59] Oil lipids are better than solid fat lipids because at normal body (or room) temperature they remain as oils and don't turn into a sticky lard-type mess in your arteries.

<u>You may be wondering about the three different omega fatty-acids (3,6,9) and in particular, which are good and which are bad.</u>

Firstly, let's see where those numbers come from. Omega fats have multiple double bonds; omega-3 has the first one appearing on the third carbon atom; omega-6 on the sixth carbon atom, and omega-9 on the ninth carbon atom. Omega-3 and omega-6 are both healthy <u>poly</u>unsaturated fats while omega-9 is a healthy <u>mono</u>unsaturated fat. Your body prefers to maintain a **balance** of all three fatty-acids; any chronic deficiencies in one or another <u>will</u> cause health issues. So, rather than think that one is worse than the other for you, it's just a matter of *balancing* them.

Bear with me. This section is heavy-going but extremely important for the understanding of the fact that dietary fat is not necessarily making you fat.[60] Omega-6 and omega-3 fatty-acids are considered *essential* fatty-acids because they can't be made by your body. They supply important building blocks for various body structures such as your cell membranes and together they'll increase your body's metabolic rate and insulin efficiency. This is all good. Omega-9 fatty-acids[61] can be made by your body, so you don't have to worry so much about eating those. So, how do you keep these three all nicely balanced when there is a *terrible over-abundance* of omega-6 in typical North American diets coupled with *very little* omega-3?

To maintain an omega-3/6/9-fat balance, you should avoid the high levels of omega-6s found in sugary foods, as well as in fatty meats and cured/salted/smoked meats[62]. Peanut butter is also high in omega-6 fatty-acids as are cereals. Many vegetable oils are *over 50%* omega-6 fats! Processed foods tend to be very high in omega-6 fats because of the types of cheap

---

[60] My husband admitted to falling asleep 3 times while trying to "get through" this section, then again, he is 72 and has been prone to afternoon naps!!!

[61] Omega-9 fats, which can be made by your body if need be, are non-essential unsaturated fats though you can eat them. Some examples of foods with omega-9 fats include hazelnuts, macadamia nuts, canola oil, almond butter and extra virgin olive oil.

[62] You may not know this but 99% of the meats in the deli area of your grocery store are processed *regardless* of how real they may appear or what they're called. If you want the real stuff, go get a little chicken or beef cut and roast it in your oven, then slice it up for sandwiches and freeze it in packages.

vegetable oils used. You'll have to scrutinize food labels and do be cognizant that they can be very very deceptive (yup, it's that food industry again). Lots of omega-6 can also be found in vegetable oil-based concoctions such as salad dressings, margarine, "mayochup"[63], mayonnaise and various and sundry spreads. Deep fried foods are usually coated with a very thick layer of omega-6 fats! Go for it if you want lots of inflammation, high body acidity and the propensity for a fat-making metabolic engine. And remember that the food industry is serving you "fried" foods when it calls them "crispy"; it's just a nicer sounding adjective. Ask for "grilled" instead.

This high omega-6 problem is actually the result of the modern vegetable oil industry's use of hydrogenated oils in most processed foods as well as the increased use of cereal grains (high in omega-6) in the cattle feedlots (i.e., it changed the fatty-acid profile of the meat we now eat[64].) Certainly you can consume omega-9 fatty-acids if you want, but you really should concentrate on increasing your omega-3 fatty-acids through your diet and/or by taking a daily omega-3 supplement. Omega-3 fatty-acids will help reduce tissue inflammation[65] and acidity, and lower acidity *always helps* with fat-burning. Omega-6 fatty-acids are inflammatory and if your harmonic balance of omega-3 to omega-6 gets chronically off, you'll definitely develop unhealthy inflammation.

We all need to use oils once in a while so, here are some vegetable oil samples showing their amounts of omega-3 and omega-6 fatty-acids *from best*[66] *to worst*. And remember that none of these unsaturated oils are necessarily bad, it's just that some provide relatively more essential omega-3

---

[63] OMG, gotta love that name! I'm embarrassed to mention that I only bought it because I loved the name and wanted to parade it around at backyard BBQs.

[64] For example, cows don't normally eat grains. They should be grass-fed; that's why they are ruminants with four stomach compartments. But when they hit those "finishing" feedlots, they are fed corn and soy, both of which are high in inflammation causing omega-6 fatty-acids.

[65] Our daughter, while recuperating from her concussion, was told to supplement with omega-3. This is because an underlying factor in concussed brains is tissue inflammation.

[66] Extra virgin olive oil (known as EVOO in the industry) is high in omega-9 but contains very little omega-3 or omega-6 fatty-acids. Don't fry with olive oil as it doesn't do well with the high temperature (I use canola oil).

fatty-acid content than others. Here are some approximations for popular oils, compared to fish.

- Whole wild fish has 100% omega-3 fatty-acids
- Flax seed oil has 57% omega-3, 14% omega-6
- Canola oil has 9% omega-3, 20% omega-6
- Peanut oil has 0% omega-3, 32% omega-6
- Walnut oil has 10% omega-3, 52% omega-6
- Soybean oil has 7% omega-3, 51% omega-6
- Sesame oil has 0% omega-3, 42% omega-6
- Corn oil has 0% omega-3, 54% omega-6
- Sunflower oil has 0% omega-3, 65% omega-6
- Safflower oil has 0% omega-3, 75% omega-6

Keep in mind that vegetable oils are always refined and processed, which means their nutrients have been greatly diminished. That said, in addition to extra virgin olive oil, I do use canola oil (made from a type of low-acid rapeseed plant)[67], as it contains both monounsaturated and polyunsaturated fats and it also tends to have the lowest amount of saturated fats. Many of you hear that coconut oil is better but consider this – it's about *85% saturated fat which is almost double that of butter* – and because that percentage is so high it just doesn't have much unsaturated fat content (with only 6% monounsaturated and 2% polyunsaturated fats.) Now you can see that coconut oil's *8% unsaturated fat* content when compared to canola oil's 29% or flax seed oil's 71% is woefully low. I avoid flax seed oil because I just don't like the taste of it, but to each their own.

Omega-3 fatty-acids, in terms of weight-training challenges, will help your body recover from exercise-induced inflammation (a type of inflammation your body knows how to deal with). It's the non-exercise-induced tissue inflammation that we want to avoid because it has been associated with many diseases. Some of these include cardiovascular disease, Type-2 diabetes, obesity, irritable bowel syndrome, rheumatoid arthritis, asthma, and chronic autoimmune diseases such as lupus, rheumatoid arthritis, psoriasis, and celiac

---

[67] The name "canola" comes from "Canada" and "ola" (meaning oil). Canada was the country that first developed canola oil and it's still the biggest single producer of it.

disease. I'm not going to go into the detailed research on these connections. You can certainly hit the library on your own.

Suffice it to say that omega-3 fatty-acids have benefits that touch virtually *every cell* in your body, regardless of your age. Their ability to help has to do with the composition of your cell membranes. These cell membranes draw on omega-3 and omega-6 fatty-acids to stimulate hormonal signaling functions and you know how important those signals are for a healthy biochemistry. These bits of membrane fats give your cells the ability to address physical activities like weight-training as well as maintaining a healthy heart muscle. And so, yes, when you lift weights, you'll be freeing up some fatty-acids and you want to do that, right??? Once they're free, you may as well kill them off with some subsequent "cardio" exercise.

Omega-3s are found in canola oil, walnuts, almonds, leafy green vegetables, flax seed oil, as well as in cold-water fatty fish[68] such as Atlantic mackerel, cod, haddock, mahi mahi, herring, wild salmon[69], oysters, trout, anchovies and sardines[70]. Dietary examples of omega-9 fatty-acids are the

---

[68] You want fish low in mercury, so don't buy tilapia, Chilean seabass, grouper or halibut. Remember that the larger the fish the greater the chance for it to have accumulated toxic mercury during its lifetime. If you buy canned fish of any type, read the labels very carefully. Avoid soy oils, broths, and odd junk (e.g., mustard, olive or tomato sauces). If you want to, you can add your own flavouring at home. But I do admit to buying canned water-packed albacore tuna as a quick lunch protein.

[69] There's a difference between "wild" and "farmed" salmon. Actually, most of the salmon you see will be "farmed." Farmed salmon has almost *double the fat* content of wild salmon, almost 20% more saturated fat, and a lot more bad omega-6s (which can lead to higher inflammation and more fat-making acidity). Final decision: go for "wild" over "farmed" salmon. If it isn't labeled, it'll be farmed.

[70] Sort of a weird footnote here. When I was writing this paragraph, I suddenly remembered something from my distant past (actually from my late 20s). Being in my 70s, I find that I have tons of memories, though I can't remember them all until I get some sort of trigger. As they say, "it sucks to get old!" Anyhow, I was a secondary school science and math teacher for a couple of years in Gboko, Nigeria, in the mid-70s and I had a pet cat. We used to share food. I loved Nigerian bread; it had a heavy consistency and of course was made with non-altered basic ingredients – no big-time food industry there. I got it from the local open-air market – and it was good with everything. Anyway, back to the cat and me…I would buy a loaf of bread, open up a

monounsaturated fats found in extra virgin olive oil, macadamia nuts/oil, sesame oil, olives and avocados.

Improve your fat-burning ability by increasing your omega-3 fatty-acid
intake and avoiding partially hydrogenated oils
(with their saturated trans-fats).

And finally, what about those infamous "trans-fats"?

Everyone hears about trans-fats and most people know that are not good for your body. Processed and heavily refined foods such as crackers and store-bought baked goods often contain *trans-fats* which should be completely avoided in your diet. In short, I think of trans-fats as dietary enemy #1. But what are they?

Trans-fats are a saturated "fatty-acid" molecule. Although trans-fats can be found naturally in small amounts in some meats and dairy products, the majority of them in the North American diet are *unnatural and artificially created*. They were created by the food industry when people were told to avoid saturated fats. This is so weird because trans-fats ARE saturated fats!

They've been chemically altered through heat and a hydrogenation process. Yup, great for the food industry's money-making business sheet, but really really bad for your health. In fact, they're considered *far worse* for your health than the saturated fats they were trying to replace! Why? Because the altering of these fats has made them more easily brought into your cell membranes causing a biochemical confusion that ultimately causes your body to metabolically adapt by closing down your fat-burning ability. And guess what? The food industry doesn't give a hoot about your fat-burning abilities.

If you see the ingredient *"partially hydrogenated oil"* on a box, then it automatically means it contains industrially produced trans-fats and high omega-6 fatty-acids! Hydrogenation, as argued by the food industry, solidifies liquid oils thereby increasing shelf-life and flavor stability. Yes, I agree, it certainly does. And they're proud of that, even though such oils, and processed foods with them embedded, are terribly unhealthy.

---

can of oily sardines, mix the sardines and oil with a bunch of bread, split in it half and the cat and I would enjoy our lunch together!!! Little did I know how much my cells and hers would enjoy those omega-3s.

Sure, there's a need to extend the shelf-life of processed foods; no one wants to buy rancid food products from their local grocery store. This hydrogenation process is widely used industrially for hard margarine, snack foods, store-bought and packaged baked goods and cookies, crackers (my personal nemesis), fried and fast foods, etc. Yup, all that bad-for-you-but-so-tasty stuff, much of which can sit in your kitchen cupboard for weeks and weeks! Some foods can actually sit on your grocery shelfs for months or even years! Gosh, bet your great-gramma would never have believed that would be possible.

In an effort to eat less fat, you may actually be eating more sugar (much of it hidden in grocery shelf foods) and refined carbohydrates than eaten by your parents and grandparents – and need I add your ancient ancestors, those healthy hunter-gatherers? The food industry is well-known for playing with salt, fat and sugar. Take one of those away and the industry just *increases one or both of the others* in order to maintain an appealing flavor (in terms of sugar and salt) or mouth feel (in terms of fat).

You've probably heard that the typical "Mediterranean" diet is beneficial for weight control and heart health. Yes, you're absolutely correct. A Mediterranean diet is rich in fish, eggs, legumes, fruits, vegetables, nuts, olive oil and unprocessed/unrefined high-fiber grains. But did you know that it's actually high in total dietary fat? Up to 35-40% (!!!) of its calories come from monounsaturated and polyunsaturated fats, and yet it doesn't pack on a bunch of body fat. Indeed, it's highly crammed with unrefined, fiber-rich sources of complex slow-to-sugar carbohydrates with comparatively modest amounts of lean protein. You just don't see the cheap highly refined carbohydrates that're dispersed throughout the North American diet!!!

Quit being a dietary fat phobic. Such a path could have unintended consequences to your longer-term weight-loss/maintenance and health. If you see a food product that is labelled "no-fat" or "low-fat," don't automatically assume it's healthy. Remember that if the industry removes the fat, it'll have to replace it with something else. It'll be either salt or sugar, both of which pose direct consequences to your bloodstream chemistry. And remember that the "I'm full" leptin hormone is made and released *only* by your fat cells. When you don't eat enough fatty-acids or you've canoed over to camp out on Starvation Island, you'll never get that full signal and you'll be growing more fat-storage potential. You can eat good unsaturated fats in your diet OR you can make bad fats in your liver. Here's a quick-n-dirty on various dietary fats and their value to your health. I'll go from the best to the worst.

Dietary Fats	Some example sources	Biochemical Results	Comments
Omega-3 fatty-acids (a polyunsaturated fat)	-Wild fish -Green vegetables -Flax seed oil	**-Anti-inflammatory** **-Repairs cell membranes** **-Increases good cholesterol** **-Reduces triglyceride fat**	Omega-3 intake should be higher than Omega-6 intake
Omega-9 fatty-acids (a monounsaturated fat)	-Olive oil -Avocados and olives -Almonds, pecans and sunflower seeds (not sunflower oil!)	**-Reduces blood pressure** **-Helps burn fat** **-Decreases free radicals** **-Decreases bad cholesterol**	Can supplement omega-9 made by your body
Saturated fatty-acids	-Animal meats and dairy products	**-Raises bad cholesterol**	Should limit amounts
Omega-6 fatty-acids (a polyunsaturated fat)	-Junk-foods -Sugary foods -Smoked meats -Sesame, Corn, Sunflower and Safflower oils	**-Promotes insulin-resistance** **-Pro-inflammatory** **-Promotes body acidity/toxins** **-Feeds fat cells**	Omega-6 intake should be lower than Omega-3 intake
Trans-fats (synthetically produced saturated fats)	-Hydrogenated oils and highly processed foods	**-Promotes fatty-liver disease** **-Lowers fat-burning**	Avoid at all costs

2.3 Why Does My Body Need Fat?

"A person who never made a mistake has never tried anything new."
– A.E.

OK, so we know how dietary fat is used by your body and we know the types of fat preferred and we know that they're essential for good health. That said, we have to consider that the amount of daily fat consumed by people is often far in excess of the amount needed. If you want to lose weight, be mindful of how much fat you're eating and whether it's a heathy unsaturated fat. Eating good fats *in the proper daily quantity* does **not** make you fat. Just like eating the right kind of complex slow-to-sugar carbohydrates in the proper quantity does **not** make you fat either!

Unfortunately the average North American daily diet includes about 40% calories from highly processed and refined foods with unhealthy fats and way too much sugar, as well as depleted vitamins, minerals and essential omega-3 fatty-acids and only about 15% of daily calories coming from protein. And as said earlier, when you choose those *processed* "no-fat" and "low-fat" foods because you're worried about the amount of dietary fat you're consuming, those too are not necessarily good for you. OK, then what the heck should you do?

You already know that fat, like protein and contrary to carbohydrate, *does not produce* an insulin response from your body. This is why a Type-1 diabetic on a "glucose low" is better off to drink orange juice (pure high-sugar carbohydrate with no fat and no protein) or a sugar-sweetened soda pop (both are liquid sugars which don't require much digestion and both make blood glucose *really fast*) than to eat a candy bar which *has fat* in it as well sugar. That candy bar will take a longer time to make blood glucose than will either the sole-carb juice or pop. Bottom line for you – don't be drinking juices or sodas none of which have any protein or fat. No non-diabetic person needs that kind of sugar rush!

Only fat sends the "full" signal, and like protein, fat slows down the breakdown of carbohydrate, and lowers both its glycemic effect and fat-producing insulin production.
Inflammation can increase leptin-resistance.

***Increasing your omega-3 fatty-acids will support your leptin hormone
levels and will counteract body inflammation.***

Your body tells your brain when it has had enough to eat and it only uses fat to send that message to your brain by creating hormones. The satiety "I'm full" feeling is only stimulated by the cholecystokinin (short-term)[71] and leptin (long-term) hormonal signals, and these hormones are used to help your body breakdown fat. No matter how much processed quick-to-glucose carbohydrates you choose to eat, they'll *never activate* your "I'm full" mechanism because those foods will never trigger the production of the "I'm full" hormones as does dietary fat.

If you're on one of those crazy *low-fat diets*, you can end up over-eating because of the absence of that "full" signal. Just think about it. Let's take the example of pasta and beef; if you fill a large plate with pasta and another with the same volume of beef, you'd be able to eat all the pasta but not all of the beef. That's because the beef has fat in it and that fat will automatically signal your brain to tell you that you're full – not with that pasta dish, it's all carbohydrate. The only signal you'll get is physical and it's when your stomach is stretched out so darn far that it hurts a bit and you think "I'm too stuffed to eat another bite!" If you insist on eating pasta, a handful is the most you should eat. I can't believe the amount of pasta served at restaurants and the fact that people actually eat *all of it*. Well, I know *why* they eat it – it does taste great. Carbs and fat always taste great when combined. Potato chips anyone???

On a hot summer day when you're allowing yourself a cheat-eat, maybe you should enjoy some ice cream and not that low-fat frozen yogurt as you'll eat far less of the ice cream (with its fat) than you would the yogurt. Sherbet does contain a little bit of milk fat, but sorbet only contains sugar (in the form of fruit puree, water and sugar).[72] So maybe now you can better appreciate that your body is more interested in *what types of macronutrients are actually providing caloric fuel rather than only the overall number of calories.*

---

[71] Cholecystokinin is a gastrointestinal hormone that's secreted by cells in your duodenum (first part of your small intestine just beyond your stomach) and which stimulates the digestion of fat and protein. It stimulates your gallbladder to release bile for digestion and your pancreas to kick out those let's-get-it-done enzymes.

[72] 1 cup of sorbet can contain as much as 30-40 grams of sugar or about 7-10 spoons of sugar! Whoa.

Eating fat helps you to burn fat; while low-fat diets can cause over-eating. Processed "no-fat" and "low-fat" foods often have a lot of added sugars. Read all labels very carefully.

Without enough fat in your diet it becomes extremely difficult for your body to burn fat. Put simply, fats increase the overall amount of *oxygen* used by your cells when they're creating energy. So, the more oxygen your body can transport to your cells, then the faster you'll burn your body fat.

As an aside, the physically fit person who is eating a proper balance of daily macronutrients can stay oxidative on the treadmill. They'll definitely find it easier to burn body fat than the Starvation Island treadmiller, the one who is avoiding fats and who is eating their calorie-burning muscle tissues to get the required glycogen energy. And think about the biochemical adaptations resulting from yo-yo dieting.

Now you can better appreciate why you shouldn't forget that *you do need to eat good fats* such as extra virgin olive oil (omega-9 fatty-acid) and fish oils (omega-3 fatty-acid). Also, these two fats have an *anti-inflammatory* effect that's very healing to your gastrointestinal tract. Omega-6 fatty-acids promote inflammation in your intestines and increase your body's acidity, which you know is not great for your weight-loss goal. Interestingly, over-the-counter ibuprofen and aspirin work by reducing the formation of the inflammatory compounds derived from omega-6 fatty-acids. That said, it's just healthier to achieve the same effect by limiting your omega-6 dietary intake.

If you avoid fried foods, packaged snack foods, fast-foods, processed foods and all foods high in saturated fat, you'll notice that you'll very quickly begin to feel a lot better. Or, better yet, how about this – avoid eating these types of foods for about three weeks and *then* eat a bunch. I can 100% <u>guarantee</u> that you'll feel terrible and a bit bloated on top of it. As they say, "you are what you eat!"

Omega-6 fatty-acids promote inflammation and are highly acidic, while omega-3 fatty-acids are anti-inflammatory.

Ok, now for omega-3 fats. What can you eat? Go for fish (wild salmon is great), walnuts, chia seeds, *ground* flax seeds, hemp seeds, egg yolks, green vegetables and wild rice.

And so, can healthy dietary fat help you to burn body fat? Contrary to what you used to think, the answer is yes!!! You probably thought that eating any fat made your body fat! Nope, the answer is NO – that only happens if you eat way too much dietary fat of all types, *good or bad – although especially the bad*!!!

2.4 How Does the Protein Macronutrient Work in My Body?

"The woman who follows the crowd will usually go no further than the crowd. The woman who walks alone is likely to find herself in places no one has ever been before." – A.E.

Protein provides your body with a slow and steady form of energy. It also transports fluids, creates hormones[73] and enzymes, and helps with your immune system. Yes, protein is necessary for life but interestingly it does *not cause* any weight-gain because it doesn't trigger the release of glucose sugar into your bloodstream. So, why would you try to avoid or limit protein or worry that you are eating too much of it?

The major role of protein is to build and repair tissues such as your muscles, tendons and ligaments. *Doesn't that sound important for movement and exercise?* Protein is not the primary source of energy unless you're adhering to a lengthy Starvation Island visit or you're over-exercising/training[74]. These are situations when your body simply can't get enough energy from carbohydrate or body fat stores. Frankly, almost every part of your body needs protein to function properly and is at least partially made up of protein! That's why your body doesn't like to be forced to use protein for fuel. Doing so runs along a long arduous breakdown process. Don't force your body to that that. It'll not be happy at all.

Protein breaks down into amino acids and these repair and build all body tissues. Because protein takes a long time to digest,
it doesn't alter blood sugar levels too fast for your hormonal balance.

---

[73] Hormones, of course, are secreted by various glands and they produce specific effects on cell activity. Frankly, the food you eat will always control your hormones. You could say that your food choices BECOME the hormones floating around your body!!! That's how important your diet is.

[74] Over-training or chronic exertion occurs when your body does not have a healthy biological balance of exercise, rest and nutrition. The results can be very negative and can include a loss of muscle, fatigue, disrupted sleep, more cortisol stress hormone production, and an impacted thyroid gland (the gland that helps regulate your metabolic calorie-burning rate).

Protein also has a long gastrointestinal emptying time, that is it takes a relatively long time to digest when compared to fat or carbohydrate. Eating lean, less fatty, protein is always better when trying to control your weight.

Protein is made up of long chains of different amino-acids and these can be either animal-based (with the most complex mix of amino-acids) or plant-based. Each gram of protein has *4 calories of energy* for your body. You can check online charts and from them calculate how many grams of protein per pound or kilogram of your weight you should be eating, all dependent upon your goals. Just track yourself and you'll soon discover that you're probably not eating nearly enough protein. I would suggest about 0.8 to 1.0 gram protein per pound (1.8 to 2.2 grams per kilogram) of body weight, but you should probably check with a certified nutritionist to see what's best to meet your weight-loss goals and exercise demands.

Examples of lean protein include lean beef, egg whites, veal, lean pork tenderloin, white-meat[75] poultry, fish, whey protein, lentils, soybeans, broad beans, tofu, tempeh, Greek yogurt and shrimp.

Know what your goals are, whether you want to lose weight, maintain your weight, lose body fat or build muscle. And remember that when you're building bigger muscles through weight-training and increasing your protein intake, *you'll be re-sculpting your body's shape* with more muscle and less body fat. Indeed, although you'll look a lot smaller, you may not weigh much less as muscle is much *denser* than fatty tissue, that is a pound of lean muscle tissue takes up much less space than a pound of bulky porous fatty tissue.

Quit being a daily slave to the weight scale and just track how much better your clothes will fit over time.

---

[75] Ever wonder why white turkey/chicken meat is less fatty then the dark meat? White meat is full of fast-twitch muscles that are good for short bursts of intense action; they burn glycogen (stored carbohydrate) and work without respiratory oxygen. White meat also has fewer oxygen-carrying red pigments than red/dark meat. Redder muscle fibers have their own fat supply and, of course, this makes darker meat more flavourful. White meat, with less fat, always translates into fewer calories and a more bland taste. I ordered some grilled chicken at a restaurant the other day and it was called "muscle" chicken; that's going to be "white" meat but I'm guessing they thought it was a much cooler descriptor.

2.5 Why Is Protein So Important in Most Diets?

Ego has a reverse relationship to Knowledge, per A.E.—

"More the knowledge, lesser the ego. Lesser the knowledge, more the ego."

To make or build anything, you need to have some construction materials, right? To build muscles and generate energy, your body's metabolism uses dietary macronutrients (protein, fat and carbohydrate) as its construction and energy materials.

Your body can manufacture many new cells as well as energy from both carbohydrate and fat, but it needs protein from food to *replace and build* new protein. Indeed, protein has a very special place in the hierarchy of dietary nutrients. This is because protein is the *only* macronutrient which contains nitrogen, and nitrogen is required for your body to manufacture *new* amino acids (protein synthesis). Carbohydrate and fat both contain carbon, hydrogen and oxygen atoms in various configurations but no nitrogen. The nitrogen in protein ensures that damaged body protein is regularly replaced with new protein. This keeps your lean muscle mass from dwindling with age. When you lose more protein than what is created, you are in a *catabolic* (breakdown) metabolism state. When you create more protein than is being broken down, your metabolism moves into an *anabolic* (building) state. Proteins are used to form enzymes as well, and these are the molecules that referee all of your biochemical cell reactions including fat-burning *and* fat-storing. And if all of this isn't enough reason to eat protein, the DNA which makes up your genes also contains nitrogen. Better eat up that protein and get to the gym to increase your protein synthesis by lifting some muscle-building weights!

The nitrogen in protein equals muscle damage control. Make the protein you eat work harder for you.

Eating protein throughout the day causes your body to burn *extra calories* because protein stimulates the production of the immunoregulatory proteins that protect you from infection as well as the cell signaling molecules that *regulate* your appetite. One of these is glucagon and it's the "fat-burning" hormone, opposite to the "fat-making" hormone insulin (produced after eating high-sugar carbohydrate foods). Glucagon breaks down and releases your

106

stored fat (triglycerides) into fatty acids for use as fuel by your cells. This process allows your body to function optimally.

Both of the opposing insulin and glucagon hormones are produced by your pancreas. Glucagon (fat-burning) and insulin (fat-making) *need to work together* to keep your blood glucose levels stable and your body will work really hard to keep these two hormones balanced. Hormones are social beasts – they like to work and live together in pairs. If you upset one, you'll just start an angry reaction from the other one. And when these two are out of whack, that angry chain reaction will always put more body fat on your frame!

When you eat a high-protein meal, your glucagon level will rise, your insulin level will not get so elevated and you get more muscle-building amino-acids. That means more fat-burning. Yeah!!! And remember that working muscles are amino-acid-eating. And because amino acids are more difficult for your body to breakdown, you have yet another reason why dietary protein will burn more calories during digestion. I have read that protein is so inefficiently digested in terms of thermal energy needs, that it can use up to 25% of its calories just to get digested.[76]

Eat refined and/or sugary carbs	Insulin **Up**	Glucagon **Down**	Blood sugar **Up**	Fat-storage **Up**	Hunger **Up**	*Fat-burning Down*
Eat lean protein with fiber	Insulin **Down**	Glucagon **Up**	Blood sugar **Down**	Fat-storage **Down**	Hunger **Down**	*Fat-burning Up*

Eating protein with fiber always equals appetite-control and protein drives your fat-burning protease enzymes.

Calories from carbohydrate (both starch and sugar) are *much more efficient* at being converted into body fat than calories from protein. But you simply don't want that kind of efficiency. You actually want calories to be *inefficient*

---

[76] For example, if you eat 400 calories of lean protein, your body will use 100 calories just to break it down and digest it! Carbohydrates and fats are more efficient, using only about 5% of their calories to get digested.

at moving into body fat. This is why you should eat both fiber (which isn't well digested, hence never moved to fat) *and* protein (which uses a lot of thermal energy) at *every meal*. Together they'll ensure that your digestion process remains inefficient. Furthermore, after the protein is digested, any *excess* will be sent to your liver to be converted into glucose (a process called "gluconeogenesis"), causing *more inefficiency* by further slowing the dump of sugar into your bloodstream. Niiiiiice!

Earlier I said that most people aren't eating enough protein and that it's really hard to eat too much protein. That said, keep in mind that eating too much protein *in relation to your activity level* and your lean muscle mass ***while limiting carbohydrate,*** can majorly stress out your liver and kidneys. Severely restricting carbohydrate leads to nutritional deficiencies and lower energy levels, as well as the depletion of your glycogen carbohydrate stores. As you deplete your stored glycogen, you will also lose water (3 grams water for every lost gram of glycogen). This is why people lose a lot of weight relatively quickly when on a high-protein with low-carbohydrate diet. Most of it will be water at the beginning. And to complicate things further, that loss of water can lead to dehydration and eventually to constipation.

> *Eating too much protein without enough carbohydrate can stress out both your liver and your kidneys, and they have too many other important jobs to complete.*

The ideal ratio of protein intake versus carbohydrate intake is never about the number of calories, rather it's about *the amount of protein you eat*. Too much or too little protein is not healthy. It really has to match your body's biological requirements and of course your goals. Too little protein can cause a weakened immune system and the dreaded loss of lean calorie-burning muscle mass, while too much protein (coupled with too few carbohydrates) can actually induce ketosis[77].

If you are eating a moderately high *lean* protein diet (about 30% of your daily calories) and supplementing with healthy *complex non-refined fibrous*

---

[77] Ketosis occurs when your body has insufficient glucose from its primary and preferred carbohydrate energy source. This results in a build-up of ketone acids (a by-product of breaking down body-fat) which have to be eliminated through urine. Chronically high ketone acidic waste levels can poison your body.

carbohydrate (about 40%) and *good unsaturated* fat (about 30%), then you will maintain or lose weight at a *healthy rate* depending upon your diet and exercise commitments. A well-developed and sustainable diet usually has a *similar percentage* of protein to fat. You can play with the percentages *a little bit*, especially if you are weight-training, by taking the protein up just a little and the carbohydrate down just a little if your goal is to lose weight. You'll notice that you still have to keep the *protein-to-fat ratio fairly similar to each other*. For example, instead of the more normal 30% protein, 30% fat and 40% carbohydrate, you could try 35% protein, 35% fat and 30% carbohydrate. Such an approach never shocks your body into over-reacting to an imbalance; hence, it never gets triggered into a hormonal panic mode. It just doesn't see anything too incongruent from its biochemical norm.

If you want to calculate your calories based upon some set of these percentages, here is how you would do it – carbohydrate is <u>4 calories per gram</u>, protein is <u>4 calories per gram</u>, and fat is <u>9 calories per gram</u>. If your daily calorie total is 1600, and if your goal is similar to mine which is *to build a lot of muscle*, you could go a little bit more extreme and calculate the following for daily macronutrient intakes:

Daily Macros	Calories/gm	Day %	Daily Calorie calculate	Daily Cals	Daily Gms
Carbs	4 calories	35	1,600 X .35	**560**	560 / 4 = 140 grams
Protein	4 calories	40	1,600 X .40	**640**	640 / 4 = 160 grams[78]
Fat	9 calories	25	1,600 X .25	**400**	400 / 9 = 44.5 grams
Total Calories		**100%**		**1,600**	

---

[78] Yes, I'm eating a lot of protein but I'm still eating 35% of my daily calories as carbohydrates, hence my liver and kidneys are never stressed out. And I have <u>gradually</u> changed my macronutrient percentages to these levels so that I don't shock my body into some sort of hormonal panic.

You'll see that my protein-to-fat ratio is not similar in this chart; but I have moved toward these percentages very gradually during my two-year journey. Remember that you don't want to surprise your body into reacting drastically in order to correct a perceived hormonal imbalance. Hormones rule! Just don't make them do the wrong reactive thing in terms of body fat.

And recall, a weekly weight loss of 1% of your body weight is healthy. For most people this translates into 1-2 pounds per week. For a morbidly obese person, a healthy weekly loss could be as high as 3-5 pounds. Any higher and you'll be losing mostly water.

It took me almost two years to lose 40 pounds and I've *never* put it back on. I never yo-yoed again. I never revisited Starvation Island. I was in it for the long haul, not the quick fix-it approach (the one that doesn't last).

2.6 How Do I Get Enough Protein if I Don't Eat Meat?

"Look deep into nature, and then you will understand everything better." – A.E.

Both <u>vegetarians</u> and <u>vegans</u> don't eat meat. Vegans, the name of which is the front end attached to the back end of the word "veg"etari"ans," not only avoid meat but, as part of the movement against the exploitation of or cruelty to animals, they're more strict than vegetarians as they eat absolutely NO *animal products* at all. They side-step eggs and dairy for example. So how can these people get enough protein into their diets when they avoid the most plentiful source of amino acids in meats?

You can still build muscle without eating meat as long as you plan the protein in your diet properly. You need to balance your amino-acid intake because they're the nitrogen-based construction blocks needed to build and maintain your muscles.

There are 22 amino acids, all of which *combine* to construct the proteins for the growth and necessary repair of your cell tissues (including muscles). Of these 22, 9 <u>can't be made</u> by your body and so they *must* be provided by the foods in your diet. They're called "essential" amino-acids and foods that contain *all 9* are called *complete proteins*. The nine types of essential amino acids you are looking to combine are: histidine, isoleucine, leucine, lysine, methionine, phenylalanine, threonine, tryptophan, and valine.

Examples of complete proteins include dairy products, cottage cheese, eggs, meat, poultry, fish and other animal sources. Soy is also a complete protein which provides all 9 amino acids.

Complete protein sources will contain all 9 essential amino acids and can be found in animal-based sources and in soy, but not in plant-based foods.

Various plant foods typically provide *incomplete or partial proteins* that either lack or are low in one or more of the 9 essential amino acids. This doesn't mean that plant-based foods are low in protein; rather, it means that you must be cognizant of how to carefully combine their different sets of amino-acids in order to get all of the 9 essential proteins from those plant-based sources *on a daily basis.*

Obviously, vegans will experience much more difficulty balancing their daily amino-acid intake. Indeed, I would venture to add that it's extremely difficult to do. Without dairy and meat, vegans need to consume a lot of nuts, seeds, peanut butter, grains, legumes, tofu and soy milk. I'll flash up my bias card here and add that I believe veganism to be genuinely unhealthy in the long-term. I believe that a pure vegan should always take vitamin and mineral supplements. On the other hand, for vegetarians, eating milk and eggs will contain a protein combination that encompasses all of the 9 essential amino-acids needed for tissue growth, repair and maintenance and I believe this is a more healthy non-meat approach. We all have our biases, right?

To get enough of these essential amino-acids from a vegetarian diet, you must select foods that complement each other's limiting amino-acids. You must mix and match these foods *during meals* so that a food low in one essential amino-acid is eaten with a food high in that amino-acid. The best approach for getting a complete protein meal is to combine grains (e.g., wheat, rice and corn) with leguminous plants (i.e., plants that have seeds in their pods, such as peas, beans, lentils and peanuts[79]).

---

[79] I bet you thought peanuts were nuts; nope, they grow underground and are actually a legume crop. Other nuts, such as walnuts, cashews, almonds and pecans, are produced on trees and are known as "tree" nuts. To be a "nut," it must come from the shell-covered fruit (never found underground) of a plant or tree. Peanuts grow

Grains are usually good sources of phenylalanine, tryptophan, methionine, valine and isoleucine. But they *often lack threonine, leucine and histidine; and they can be low in lysine.* Legumes, on the other hand, are generally good sources lysine, but can be *low in methionine.* So, you can see that a vegetarian has to do a lot of research if they're weightlifting and hoping to build lean strong muscle tissue!

Some fully nutritious protein combinations that will provide the required 9 essential proteins include the following:

- Brown rice and beans
- Legumes and whole grains
- Corn and beans
- Beans and nuts and seeds
- Tofu and quinoa
- Corn tortillas and refried beans
- Pasta[80] and bean soup

Some of the top plant sources of protein (for vegetarians and vegans) include the following: almonds, black beans, chickpeas, garbanzo beans, green peas, hazelnuts, hempseed, kidney beans, lentils, peanut butter, peanuts, pinto beans, quinoa, seitan, soybeans, spelt, split peas, sunflower seeds, tofu and walnuts.

Do be careful with dairy products (milk, cheese, yogurt) as they tend to be very high in saturated fat so try to choose the plain unadulterated dairy products. These can be lower fat if you ensure that the food industry hasn't upped the sugar content, added fillers or fructose-based syrup. You may think this is a contradiction to my earlier comment about avoiding "low-fat" and "no-fat" foods but I was referring to carbohydrate foods. Low- or no-fat carbohydrates tend to have more sugar or salt, while a low-fat dairy product may just mean a higher percentage of natural unprocessed carbohydrates, but

---

underground and have multiple seeds in each legume. Though peanuts are called "ground nuts" in Africa, they aren't nuts.

[80] Beware, pasta is a "*super*-carbohydrate"; a concept which is detailed elsewhere the book.

NOT necessarily useless fat-making sugar. I'll examine this in the milk chapter.

According to developing research regarding non-meat proteins, there can be some destructive inflammation when eating high volumes of grains or legumes. We know that not everyone responds favorably to some legumes and grains (examples include whole grains, beans, lentils, peas, potatoes, chickpeas/hummus and peanuts) and now there's a theory that this is due to their higher concentration of lectins. Lectins are *plant-based proteins* that like to bind with sugar molecules. Research on the negative effects of lectins in terms of toxicity, hormonal activity and blood viscosity is relatively new and remains somewhat controversial. Lectins are also known to promote weight-gain inflammation. Although I occasionally eat popcorn for a snack, I am aware that it's jammed up with lectins. No one is perfect ALL the time, right???

Unfortunately, I must be completely honest with readers who are vegetarians. In my view, the various combinations of foods listed above are examples of protein sources that are *inferior* to those found in diets with meats, chicken, fish, eggs and dairy. The fact is that not all plant sources of protein are available in the same way to your body; for example, some plants have more fiber and this in turn will prevent the digestion or absorption of some of the amino-acids that would normally be used for protein synthesis by your body. Are you getting frustrated?

If you're interested in the bioavailability of plant proteins and the purported effects of plant lectins, then I recommend that you read the book "The Plant Paradox" by Dr. Steven Gundry.

Sorry, but I'm entitled to my personal and positive opinion about eating animal-based proteins. I'm just saying to be extremely careful with your overall meal selections if you're avoiding all meat and poultry.

And finally, if you're going to follow the latest food trend to replace red meat with plant-based meat alternatives in an effort to eat more healthy and/or to reduce your carbon footprint, be very conscious of your choices and read the ingredient labels very carefully. When vegetables are made to look and taste like meat, you better believe that a whack of major food processing has gone on. Many of these new products, perceived by consumers to be healthier alternatives, have a lot of saturated fat, high amounts of salt and/or sugar content! Again, the food industry is just trying to meet the demands of their consumers, and *they'll remove whatever you want removed* (e.g., animal-based protein) but don't automatically assume that these new products are super-great for your health! The industry only has salt, fat, sugar and crunch to play with in terms of taste and successful palatability. No one wants to eat cardboard-tasting food.

2.7 How Does the Carbohydrate Macronutrient Work in My Body?

"If people are good only because they fear punishment, and hope for a reward, then we are a sorry lot indeed." – A.E.

I'm going to show you that in an effort to get fuel, your biochemical body will always try to burn the most efficiently digested macronutrient-to-energy first, and so on; *first carbohydrate, second fat and lastly protein.*

The major powerhouse role of carbohydrate is to provide the *most efficient and quickly accessible energy* for your working muscles, energy boosts for running to the bus, and for your brain and nervous system as well as to help with digestion by providing fiber[81]. Is it any wonder why people on the no-carb beaches of Starvation Island have very little energy and feel tired all the time??? They tend to be chronically constipated too – that's because fiber is *only* found in carbohydrates.

Your body will breakdown all carbohydrate into glucose, which is used to produce your body's energy currency "ATP" (adenosine triphosphate[82]) for cellular energy. I like to refer to ATP as the body's tradeable "currency" because ATP is always either being used by your body or being made by your body, sort of like a biological ATM energy exchange machine. Each gram of carbohydrate or protein has *4 calories of energy* for your body. Even though it has far less caloric energy than a gram of fat at 9 calories/gram, glucose

---

[81] Some people consider fibre to be the fourth macronutrient; but technically it's an undigestible glucide (a type of carbohydrate) found in fruits and vegetables (never in fat or protein). It'll increase the volume of the food you eat and also decrease the amount of time that food spends in your intestines. This'll counter constipation.

[82] ATP is the source of energy for every body cell and it allows for the muscle contractions needed for movement. It's the biochemical way both to store and to use energy and it's absolutely critical to your body.

(carbohydrate) remains the preferred energy as it's the most efficiently synthesized.

So, while 50 grams of dietary fat is a whopping 450 calories and 50 grams of carbohydrates is a modest 200 calories, it's those carbohydrates that'll be producing your fat-making insulin hormone and not that high-calorie fat! Are you surprised? Like I said, your body doesn't just concern itself with calories so don't make them the basis of how you eat.

All carbohydrates are built out of sugar molecules. These sugar molecules can exist in single sugar units called <u>monosaccharides</u> or they can be joined together to form double/twin sugars called <u>disaccharides</u>. When many sugars are connected in long chains, they're then called <u>polysaccharides</u>. Just to explain the terms "simple" and "complex" when applied to carbohydrates, think of the single and double sugars as "simple" and the long chains of sugars as "complex." Fruits are examples of "simple" disaccharide carbohydrate chains, while vegetables are "complex" polysaccharide carbohydrate chains.

Another key point to remember when thinking about dietary carbohydrates is that "fiber" is indigestible and can never be absorbed by your body. Your intestinal enzymes just can't break up the extremely strong bonds that link the complex *glucose <u>polysaccharide chains</u>* into the fiber. Hence, fiber can never be changed into glucose sugar. And fiber, which is never absorbed by your body, can even help to clear poisonous and acidic toxins from your body!

"Simple" or quick-to-sugar carbohydrates (e.g., fruit juice, milk and refined sugary foods) will create blood sugar much more quickly than "complex" carbohydrates (slow-to-sugar starch with its higher fiber) because there just isn't much fiber to slow it down!

***Avoid simple carbohydrates, especially the refined ones,
which are the most efficient (fastest) at raising blood sugar levels.
Unsaturated fat and lean protein will slow that absorption.***

Let's talk about the methods your body uses for getting energy. Why does your body like to use carbohydrates as fuel, with fat and protein as its second and third choice? If you force it to pick fat and/or protein, you'll have to do it with some sort of low- or non-carbohydrate diet. It won't get you those toned arms, but maybe you're only interested in losing a whack of scale weight quickly??? Maybe you aren't worried about your overall health or whether you have toned skin or not. Again, choices have to be weighed against goals.

The conversion of protein into caloric fuel is not natural for your body. Suffice it to say that amino-acids are *not efficiently converted* into bloodstream glucose and when they are converted (which can occur due to ill-advised avoid-all-carbohydrate visits to Starvation Island), they too need insulin in order to be stored as body fat. Hence, proteins aren't stored, they're used – because with no insulin, the sugar/glucose can't be transported to your cells. Think of that fast-shrinking undiagnosed Type-1 diabetic who eats a ton of food, including lots of carbohydrates, yet continues to lose overall weight[83].

Protein demands a very inefficient *five different steps* in order to be converted into blood sugar glucose:

1. conversion to amino acids;
2. conversion to glucose;
3. finding insulin;
4. transforming into fatty acids; and finally,
5. meeting up with glycerol-3-phosphate.

Wow, now that's a lot of work for your body and at worst you could call your body lazy. It really wants the *easiest pathway to meet its energy needs*. It wants that really quick carbohydrate glucose – a nice simple 1-step conversion-to-glucose process which, in the healthy person, will automatically produce the right amount of insulin.

Fat on the other hand, must undergo *two steps* to make it into your bloodstream as glucose blood sugar:

1. conversion to fatty acids; and,
2. meeting up with glycerol-3-phosphate.

If you want to lose weight in a more healthy fashion, you must choose your carbohydrates very very carefully. It's better to choose complex carbohydrates which are high in fiber as well as lower in sugar. Unfortunately, this can end

_____

[83] These individuals must take daily insulin injections in order to convert dietary carbohydrates into glucose energy, otherwise they're eating themselves. Prior to Banting & Best, that meant they got skinnier and skinnier and then they just died.

up being very confusing. Why is one carbohydrate better to choose than another? Carbohydrates affect your blood sugar levels much more than either protein or fat, obviously because it's the *only macronutrient that triggers glucose and insulin*. That's why Type-1 diabetics who have to inject the right amount of synthetic insulin to match any ingested carbohydrates, must manage their carbohydrate intakes and their daily exercise so carefully. When a non-Type-1 individual, presumably you, eats carbohydrate, your body automatically produces the right amount of insulin to break it down into your primary glucose energy source.

In order to store glucose as body fat, you *must have* the insulin hormone. This is why an undiagnosed Type-1 diabetic with no ability to produce the insulin needed to get at the glucose, will drastically lose weight and it'll be *both muscle and fat*. They simply can't digest <u>any</u> carbohydrate (unhealthy refined/processed or healthy whole/fresh), regardless of how much they may be eating. So their bloodstream gets higher and higher in blood sugar level. Even their breath begins to smell sweet. They actually move into a *hyper*glycemic state. Their urine is full of ketone by-products[84] due to their desperate need for energy by breaking down fat (and muscle). Their poor liver is working non-stop. But yes, sorry I digressed. I guess I go to diabetic responses because they always provide the extremes and they can be informative. But, back to you; if you eat too many carbohydrates per your physical sedentary lifestyle[85], then your body will automatically store all of the excess carbohydrates *as body fat*. This will especially be true if those carbohydrates are either sugar or highly processed simple quick-to-sugar carbohydrate foods.

---

[84] Normally, when your cells get enough glucose energy, there are miniscule ketones in the urine. Their high presence indicates that your body is using a lot of fat rather than carbohydrate for energy (an avenue it prefers to avoid). Some diet plans make your body create ketones in an effort to burn body-fat. Of course, these diets say that the ketone levels in urine should be tested and not go too high. Do you think people who jump on the current "fad" Keto carb-deprivation diet or go on other starvation diets are getting healthier? Nah, don't think so!!! Though they'll probably like what they see on the scales.

[85] You know what type of person this is; they sit a lot, watch a lot of TV or sit reading a lot, are hunched over a computer all day, and are in general very inactive. And many have poor posture too.

Because *complex carbohydrates* have both high-fiber and low sugar; they can help you *reduce* your blood sugars, lose some weight and increase your energy levels. Complex carbohydrates, which we call starch[86], can be thousands of long sugar-chains all locked in with fiber. As a direct result, it takes much longer for your body to breakdown complex carbohydrates into blood glucose and this means a slower release of glucose, all of which is good for controlling your weight. Remember that we're seeking an *inefficiency* here in terms of flooding your body with blood sugar glucose.

Examples of such starches include sweet potatoes, brown and wild rice, barley, couscous, buckwheat, beans, hummus, edamame, lentils, *100% whole grains*, winter squash, *non-processed* oatmeal and fresh peas. Also, think of any vegetables that you could eat raw (not that you must eat them raw), like those generally found in fresh salads, and you can be certain these are examples of some very low-sugar *complex carbohydrate* vegetables that are great for you at any time of the day.

Simple carbohydrates contain very little or no fiber and are much higher in sugar content than "complex" starch; hence, they're converted to blood sugar very quickly, usually far too quickly for your body (pancreas and liver) to deal with. They're extremely efficient at creating blood glucose, not an efficiency you should be seeking. They're not "starch" carbohydrates, they're "sugar" carbohydrates.

Examples include the following: breads, pasta, milk and milk products, fresh fruit, fruit juice, table sugar, syrup, soda beverages, sweetened iced tea and lemonade, the seemingly healthy "vitamin water"[87], sweetened coffee drinks and flavored milk. Milk and whole fresh fruit aren't *all* bad; they do contain vitamins, minerals, antioxidants and some fiber but as simple

---

[86] Starch is to the plant what glycogen is to your body, simply a storage form of v=carbohydrate which will supply glucose energy to the plant whenever needed.

[87] When the sugary soda pop makers discovered that people weren't drinking as much carbonated pop (even with artificial sweeteners), they decided to keep their sales profits up by producing vitamin waters. Well guess what? Just look the nutrition labels and you'll see that each 590 ml bottle contains over 30 grams of sugar! Did you know that 4 grams of sugar is the equivalent of ONE teaspoon of white sugar? Geezzz, that vitamin water has about 7.5 teaspoons of sugar (30 divided by 4). Doesn't sound very healthy to me! May as well drink a sweetened bottle of soda pop – same amount of sugar.

carbohydrates they still need to be portion-controlled. The others have little or no nutritional value and should be avoided altogether.

Your body does not treat fruits (simple quick-to-sugar carbohydrates) and vegetables (complex slow-to-sugar carbohydrates) as the same food group.

As with most food groupings and as difficult as this might for you to hear, *not all fruits are created equal.* Some fruits contain a healthier ratio of nutrients to sugar (berries, oranges, grapefruits) than do some others (apples, bananas, grapes). And remember that although they're both carbohydrates, fruits and vegetables are not interchangeable. They're used in completely different ways by your body! Just think about it logically. You could eat 10 servings of starchy-type vegetables[88] daily and it'll make you healthier and leaner. This is never true of fruits, due directly to their relatively high concentration of sugar. Indeed, some fruits contain 15-20 times *more sugar* than the same weight in some vegetables.

Just remember that if you're eating a fruit, eat only one portion and stick to the smaller size, where "small" would be the size of a tennis ball or at the most a "medium" size which would be the size of an MLB baseball.

The more I think about it; I really can't understand why food guides[89] put out by federal governments to model a healthy diet classify *vegetables and fruits* as one food group. They are radically different to your biological body! Indeed, your body will never be able to read a food pyramid or guide. It has its own biochemical "hormonal guide" which was established eons ago!

Refined or processed carbohydrates cause big blood sugar glucose spikes and they have absolutely *no* nutritional value. This is because during

---

[88] Some "starch" vegetables (e.g., broccoli, bell peppers, kale) contain a lower amount of carbohydrate and fewer calories than do other "starch" vegetables (e.g., potatoes, corn, peas). This is the glycemic index (or GI count) of the vegetable, a concept which will be detailed later.

[89] Most food guides list vegetables/fruits, grain products, milk and its alternatives, and meat and its alternatives as the four food groups. And don't get me going on the suggested percentages. I think there's a lot of food industry lobbying going on and as you'll know by the end of this book, I don't trust the food industry at all.

processing the bran and germ of the grain have been removed; hence, they have been *stripped of all fiber*, vitamins, minerals and antioxidants.

Examples of such industrially processed foods include refined grains, most breads, most pastas, rolls, bagels, white rice, muffins, cookies, donuts, croissants, scones, sweetened cereals, crackers, chips, pretzels, sweetened dried fruit, yogurt covered snacks, cake, candy bars, cereal bars, all sugars, corn syrup, fructose, sucrose, dextrose, maltose[90], and fruit juice concentrates. Also, be aware of gluten-free[91] carbohydrate foods as they tend to be much higher in sugar content[92]. Always read the labels on all foods, even if you believe that they're healthy.

2.8 How Much and How Often Should I Eat Carbohydrate When Dieting?

"What is right is not always popular, and what is popular is not always right." – A.E.

Now of course some of you will believe that eating either sugar or starch will always make you fat. Both, of course, *are* carbohydrate. Rather than either protein or fat, it's carbohydrate that tends to create your body fat. But you don't get fat because you're eating too much carbohydrate, but rather because you're eating too much of the WRONG type of carbohydrates. In general, people are eating too many that are refined and highly processed. Immediately this translates into too many non-nutrient calories filling us up, instead of nutrient-dense lean protein, complex carbohydrates and unsaturated fats.

---

[90] Look out for the suffix "ose" in food ingredient labels; it *always* signifies a lurking sugar. In Latin "ose" means "full of" (e.g., the lactose in milk is actually a sugar).

[91] There is no such thing as "gluten-free wheat"; all wheat contains gluten. But there is a wheat starch that is gluten-free; it's made by washing the wheat flour with water in order to remove the gluten. The work "gluten" comes from the Latin word for "glue"; it's the protein in wheat, barley and rye that gives elasticity to baked goods such as bread, cereal and pizza. And, you need special "DPP-IV" non-digestive enzymes to break it down.

[92] Companies play with salt, fat and sugar to make foods tastier to consumers. Take one away and they'll up one or both of the other two. Take a look at the sugar content on gluten-free bread and compare it to the other breads. Egads!!!

Obviously, a lot of the food that you eat, even good unadulterated whole food, does *contain* carbohydrate. These foods will include sugar and starch, for energy, and fiber for a healthy digestive system. We do need to eat carbohydrates. We just don't need to eat the quick-to-sugar carbohydrates that compromise our muscle-building ability and, therefore, our calorie-burning ability.

Carbohydrate molecules are comprised of carbon, hydrogen and oxygen chemical elements. The form in which various carbohydrate molecules combine will determine whether they're <u>sugar</u> carbohydrates (with atoms that are hexagonal or pentagonal *rings* in ones or twos), or whether they're <u>starch</u> carbohydrates (where the rings get combined into unbranched or branched *chains*). Very long *indigestible chains* create dietary fiber. And of course, don't forget that your body will eventually convert <u>both</u> sugar rings and starch chains into glucose[93], albeit at different efficiencies.

Whole, unrefined carbohydrates are great to eat whether they're sugar <u>or</u> starch molecules. But you should remember that there's a maximum amount that your body will stock. Once your liver and your muscles fill up with stored carbohydrate (i.e., glycogen), your liver will *automatically* convert the rest into body fat. This fat is then stored either directly beneath your skin (in your subcutaneous fat tissue, the innermost skin layer) or in other areas of your body (as visceral abdominal fat around internal organs such as your liver, pancreas and intestines). These tendencies are then intensified when you're stressed out or when you've been chronically sleep deprived (more cortisol fat-making production).

Eat whole unrefined carbohydrates to build muscle but be aware of the quantity.
If too much, the liver will always make extra body fat.
Severely restricting carbohydrates leads to depleted glycogen stores.

---

[93] Remember Starvation Island? When you don't eat enough carbohydrate, your liver will begin converting fat, with ketone by-products, and protein into glucose in order to generate energy. Yes, you'll definitely lose weight, but it'll include some of your calorie-burning muscle too. Get ready for a slower metabolic rate and some toneless skin!!!

The amount of muscle glycogen (long strings of glucose molecules linked together) you can store is completely dependent on how much muscle mass you have. The more muscular you are, the more glycogen you can store and the less the need to make more body fat. Makes sense then to build-up muscle, right? You can store several hundred grams of glycogen in both your liver (a maximum of 100-120 grams) and in your skeletal muscle cells (between 300-500 grams). You can see that muscles are able to store the most carbohydrate/glycogen! This is related to the fight-or-flight scenario wherein you always need to have some immediate fuel ready for unforeseen emergencies. For our ancestors who were hunting wild game, this was critical to survival. I have strong big muscles and so I can store a lot of dietary carbohydrate without becoming fat again. I'm chasing gym weights rather than wild game. And I can probably eat a heck of lot more food than you, simply due to the fact that I have a lot more muscle mass.

More muscle will give you a higher glycogen (carbohydrate) storage capacity as well as decrease your ability to make body fat.

To build calorie-eating carbohydrate-storing muscle in the gym, I usually eat about 1.2 grams of carbohydrate per pound (or about 2.6 grams per kilogram) of my body weight *daily*. The amount is completely dependent upon your goals. Again, you can check it out with a certified food nutritionist.

If you want to lose weight and not stress out your hardworking liver, you should appropriately increase your lean protein intake, and only slightly decrease your overall carbohydrate intake BUT eat all three macronutrients at *every* major meal.

2.9 Why Does My Body Need Fiber?

"Look deep into nature, and then you will understand everything better." – A.E.

Fiber is roughage or bulk and it's found in vegetables, fruits, whole grains and legumes – in other words, it's *only* found in carbohydrates. That's why Starvation Islanders who shun **all** carbohydrates will *always* get chronically constipated. Constipation may have a variety of causes but it's often the result of the slow movement of food through your digestive system.

Fiber is both a structural and a storage form of carbohydrate. Although your body doesn't have the ability to breakdown the strong glucose chains that form fiber, your intestinal <u>living</u> *I'm-a-separate-entity-from-you* probiotic bacteria can. Your bacteria subsequently breakdown the fiber in order to use it to meet their own energy needs.

Fiber can be soluble or insoluble. Soluble fiber dissolves in water while insoluble fiber doesn't. You might think that insoluble fiber is a waste of eating, but it's insoluble fiber that increases your stool's bulk and helps prevent constipation. As a "poop" softener, insoluble fiber regularizes your bowel movements both in consistency and in frequency. It also decreases the risk of hemorrhoids[94]. Try to eat more 100% whole grain flour, or bran[95], *ground* flax seeds (these also contain anti-inflammatory omega-3 fatty-acids), as well as fruit *skins*. Insoluble fibers can also be found in seeds, nuts, broccoli, green beans, cabbage, onions, tomatoes, carrots, zucchini and root vegetable skins.

Soluble fiber, like psyllium (made from the husks of the plantago plant) or inulin (a dietary prebiotic fiber extracted from the roots of the chicory plant), absorbs water and becomes a jelly-like slimy mass that'll slow down your digestion, making it less efficient and that's what you want. If you buy either of these to treat constipation, make sure you avoid any that add sweeteners[96], artificial coloring or other "fillers." Soluble fibers will also lower your cholesterol and glucose levels. They can be found in oats, beans, lentils, asparagus, peas, citrus fruits, strawberries, apples, pears, bananas, cucumbers, carrots, barley, garlic and high-fiber[97] cereals.

---

[94] Hemorrhoids, sometimes called "piles," are swollen veins in your rectum and anus. Insoluble fibre and lots of water will help control this uncomfortable affliction.

[95] When you think of a <u>100% *whole*</u> grain kernel, the starch or glucose is on the inside (i.e., the "endosperm") while the bran fibre is on the outside (like a protective "coat"). The whole kernel is an insoluble fibre; but, if the food industry takes away the bran (via processing), then you'll just be left with the starch/glucose and voila, your body must deal with an insulin peak.

[96] Why do they have to be made sweet-tasting when normally, they are relatively tasteless??

[97] The very best high-fibre cereal, in my world, is "Fibre 1 <u>Original</u>." I seldom eat cereal, but this is my go-to when I do. It has a whopping *15 grams* of fibre for every ½ cup. You sure won't see that in many other cereals. Whole Wheat Cheerios, for example, only has *1 ½ grams* of fibre for every ½ cup!

Another way to think about fiber is whether or not it absorbs water. Insoluble fiber doesn't absorb water; but soluble fiber dissolves in water and so it has to absorb water. This process turns it into a jelly-like mass. This means that insoluble fiber will add bulk to your stool while soluble fiber will slow your digestion. Both outcomes are good. Because you can't digest fiber or use any of it for energy, both types of fiber once through your intestines and having met with your probiotics, will eventually be headed to your toilet bowl.

Surprisingly, you may not even know how much fiber you're actually consuming in a given day. This is because it can be added to foods for a number of reasons including the reduction of fat and/or sugar content. Although this isn't normally bad, especially as a replacement for nutritionally useless sugar, you may be eating *too much* of it or eating it *too quickly* and this can cause digestive issues such as bloating and abdominal pain. You might wonder why it's used to replace the fat content in low-fat foods – it's because inulin causes a *creamy mouth-feel* very similar to that of fat. It's also slightly sweet-tasting and so it can reduce some of the sugar normally used in processed foods and some beverages.

For me to stay lean and healthy, I generally aim for about 25 grams of fiber daily (if I was a man, I'd probably go for about 35-38 grams of fiber). How does fiber help with weight-control? Firstly, high-fiber foods are more filling than low-fiber foods, so you'll usually eat less of them and stay satisfied for a longer time. It'll also take you longer to eat a high-fiber food and that lets your body catch up and send leptin's full signal. And so it seems that although high-fiber foods are less energy-dense, meaning that they have *fewer calories*, they still fill you up faster. A stalk of celery is a great example, with 95% water, only 10 calories and about 1 ½ grams of fiber.

The right types of foods are high in fiber and result in a much lower metabolic response. Yeah, no body hormonal panic. High-fiber foods will lower your levels of insulin resulting in a reduced appetite and a much more compromised fat-storage ability. As required for the digestion of dietary protein, your body must use more caloric energy during the digestion and absorption of all high-fiber foods. And lastly, high-fiber diets are always lower in calories helping you to manage your weight in a more natural way.

If you decide that you need to eat much more fiber, increase the levels very gradually as rapid increases can cause digestive pain. If you find you're getting bloated or visiting the bathroom too much, then eat smaller multiple meals that include protein, carbohydrate and fat. Eating frequent smaller meals will give you a timed release of energy while lowering the total amount of fiber eaten at any given meal.

Fiber is roughage or bulk. As an indigestible carbohydrate it can prevent constipation. It takes longer to eat high-fiber foods; they keep you full for longer, compromise your fat-storing ability, are lower in calories and have a lower glycemic index.

When you drink *any* liquid (fruit or vegetable juice, wine, beer, soda pop, etc.), it won't require much digestion and so it'll go directly into your bloodstream as glucose. Such liquids have no fiber at all. That's why you should eat when drinking liquor. If a liquid has <u>any</u> sugar and other than water most do, look out for a sugar rush and a quick burst of your fat-making insulin hormone. Guess what's at the end of each part of the liquid spectrum? Water at one end, the good end, and beer at the other end thanks to its maltose sugar which, by the way, is worse for your body than white table sugar. Forget about heaven...*for your body's sake*, quit drinking your calories – they'll all be non-fiber!!!

Here are some example calculations that will illustrate the effectiveness of fiber in relation to your overall dietary carbohydrate intake – we'll assume that you want to choose the one with the least number of carbohydrates. In this chart, all three foods are comparable. For example, they might be different boxes of crackers or cereal. A funny thing happened on the way to the publisher. A couple of my readers wanted three completely different foods detailed in this chart. At first, I ignored it for the book draft but as the suggestion got repeated, I had to think again about it. In the end, I still wanted my own chart. I wanted you to see what happens when you're faced with different choices for ONE type of food, not three different types of carbohydrates such as oatmeal, lentils and pasta. I want you to appreciate the comparative carbohydrate choices. Oatmeal, lentils and pasta all offer completely different mixes of carbohydrate fibers. I want to compare three of the <u>same kinds of carbohydrate</u> mix and so I picked *wheat-based crackers* as my example. Watch the big impact of the fiber factor and how it directly impacts the carbohydrates in play.

Three types wheat crackers Assume each comparison is for the *same volume* of product.	Total Grams Carbohydrates *(probably ONLY what you look at on the label)*	Total Grams Fiber *(probably what you don't really notice)*	Net Grams Carbohydrates *(the ONLY carbohydrate count you should be concerned with)*
Cracker A	20 total grams	15 grams	**5 net grams**
Cracker B	16 total grams	5 grams	11 net grams
Cracker C	**14 total grams**	0 grams	14 net grams

Now you can more easily see that Cracker A (although having the highest number of carbohydrate grams), actually has *fewer net grams* of available carbohydrates than either Cracker B or Cracker C. If you didn't make this calculation you might *not have chosen Cracker A* though it would be a *significantly better* choice than the other two. Indeed, if you were shopping for lower-carb crackers, you may have chosen Cracker C (the poorest choice in terms of net carbohydrates).

The Harvard Health blog[98] states that many "whole-grain" carbohydrates can be misleading in terms of the fiber content. Their blog indicates that a good ratio of *fiber to carbohydrates* would be 1:10; that is, you should try to ensure that you get *at least* 1 gram fiber for every 10 grams of carbohydrates though they suggest that a 1:5 ratio is much better.

---

[98] www.health.harvard.edu

2.10 Why Do People Avoid All Breads?

"The important thing is to not stop questioning." – A.E.

I am one of those people who avoids _all_ breads most of the time. I just find I can't trust their ingredients. I don't care whether it's white bread or whole wheat bread or rye bread or bagels or pitas. To me they're all bad! Just a lot of calories with very few nutrients. In fact, bread is a sort of _super-carbohydrate[99]_ food in terms of what it does to your blood glucose levels and that's something I'll always try to avoid.

Wheat, rice, barley, and oat grains, for example, naturally grow with _three parts_: the endosperm, the bran and the germ. As such these _whole_ nourishing grains are loaded with fiber, minerals, vitamins and even some protein. But something happens to these grains _after_ they're harvested. Most of their nutritional parts, the bran and germ, are _processed out_ by the food industry and the remaining endosperm (mostly carbohydrate) is then ground into a _refined flour which is mostly calories_. Indeed, many calorie-dense foods are not very nutritious. Even then, the food industry isn't finished. It's highly aware that you're beginning to question what's going on in their kitchens. It knows it has to advertise that their "refined flour" is healthy for you, so that you'll buy it. Hence, it adds some vitamins and minerals and then calls the bread "enriched." The glycemic index[100] (GI) of such refined enriched processed breads is far higher than what you'd find in "100% whole grain" breads because there's a faster rise in blood sugar and the resultant _fat-storage_ insulin hormone.

Of course, you'd have to agree with the food industry on the fact that many additives are used in their commercial breads for a variety of fairly reasonable justifications. The industry wants to avoid costly spoilage by extending a food's shelf-life[101]. It wants to provide the perfect texture, to enhance flavoring and to retain moisture, hence the use of a lot of additives.

---

[99] This is a term I'm using for the most "highly efficient" carbohydrates, those that make blood sugar almost instantly.

[100] The GI of a food is a measurement of how efficiently you get the sugar into your bloodstream. Lower GIs are better.

[101] But, do we really need foods that can last anywhere from 6 months to 4 years!?? Maybe during the atomic bomb threat days…yes, I'm that old that I remember those bomb-shelter days.

Examples of some of the questionable additives to bread (in terms of your health) include the following:

1. <u>Potassium bromate</u> – an oxidizing agent used to strengthen the dough and improve the rising, giving it more volume.

2. <u>Azodicarbonamide (ADA)</u> – a dough conditioner used to improve both the texture and the strength of the bread.

3. <u>Partially hydrogenated oil</u> – a process used to make the unsaturated fats more resistant to oxidation and spoilage; and, it *most certainly* means the product contains those dreaded artificially created trans-fats.

4. <u>Sugar</u> – to produce a sweet taste, help produce a finer more even texture and retain water which makes the bread moister.

5. <u>Monoglycerides and diglycerides</u> – these are emulsifiers, they pull together the water and oil-based ingredients that would *not normally come together at all*. They aren't the worst emulsifiers, but they sure signify that the bread you bought is industrially produced!

6. <u>Butylated hydroxy anisole (BHA)</u> – an antioxidant used as a preservative to prevent rancidity (the deterioration of fats due to exposure to oxygen). OMG!!!

7. <u>Sodium</u>[102] – this is an important component of flavor and texture.

8. <u>Artificial caramel coloring</u> – is commonly used to darken the color of bread, especially in dark wheat or rye breads.

---

[102] Sodium and potassium have opposite effects on your heart health. High sodium intake raises your blood pressure, while potassium intake relaxes/decreases your blood pressure. If you must use salt, try the healthier Himalayan pink salt which is iron rich and has more potassium than sodium. It can assist with reducing muscle cramps, promote better blood sugar levels and healthier lower cell acidity. Also, in terms of weight management, salt causes an increase in water retention/weight and it'll make you feel bloated.

9   High fructose corn syrup (HFCS)[103] – this sweetener is made from *genetically modified corn*[104]. The industry prefers this to sucrose (sugar made from sugar cane or sugar beets) simply because fructose is cheaper and much sweeter than sucrose; hence, less is needed and so again the industry saves money. This product has excess fructose which can lead to higher triglycerides (body fat).

10 Soy – can be called either soybean oil or soy lecithin in bread ingredient listings and is usually from *genetically modified* soybeans. It's another emulsifier, keeping water and oil from separating and it prevents rancidity as well. If it's partially hydrogenated, it'll be adding those terrible trans-fats to your diet.

Try your very best to avoid most, if not all, of the above 10 ingredients! Unfortunately, you'll quickly discover that it'll be really difficult to do this when choosing bread. *And that's why I very rarely eat bread!*

If you were to make your own bread, you might use food-based egg yolks and milk as emulsifiers (and these provide nutrients as well). That said, I can't be bothered making bread, so I just don't eat it. Maybe if my kitchen counter was bigger and I bought a bread-making machine, it would be a possibility. I really do love bread and I admit a major weakness when restaurants insist on putting a breadbasket in front of me.

When I was young, most of the neighborhood moms, including my mom, made their own bread and they used just four quite simple ingredients: water, flour, dry yeast and a bit of salt. Some added a bit of sugar or shortening, but

---

103 You will discover that the terrible effects of HFCS on your body are commented upon in many other book chapters. Some consider HFCS fructose to be the #1 enemy of good health, other choose "trans-fats." AVOID both!

104 When a food is "genetically" modified, the *DNA of that food* has been altered by using a genetic engineering method to change the plant in some way that simply does not normally or naturally occur. If you want to avoid GMOs (genetically modified organisms) then only buy "100% organic" food. You'll read confusing information regarding organic foods. Some say they're *more* nutritious, others say not. But at the least, you can be sure that the animals are treated more humanely and the soil for plants is not chemically altered. These are two bonuses. One of our sons says that GMO foods are OK, because we need to feed more people on the planet and getting plants to grow bigger or faster ultimately helps that altruistic goal. Hmmm…OK, true for the globe!

not much. Others used egg yolks and milk. And wow, I can still smell that delicious bread hot out of the oven. Today's bread is a comparatively weirdly concocted beast indeed. It has tons of preservatives along with some bleaching. Basically, it has simply become another form of simple sugar to your body.

If you're one of those people who simply can't give up all bread, what bread ingredients should you look for? You could go for superior "sprouted" or "100% whole" grains, both of which use the entire grain, are more nutritious and have fewer inflammatory plant-based lectin proteins. Or you could try for "cultured" flour. This will be an all-natural off-white powder containing short-chain organic acids and other *natural* fermentation-derived metabolites[105] that can extend shelf-life. By preventing the growth of unwanted bacteria and molds, "cultured" flour can replace chemical preservatives such as sorbates and benzoates. Another possibility is *real sourdough bread*, a yeasted bread made from a fermented mixture of flour and water. You can make this yourself! Look up some online recipes – you can even make your own "starter" mix.

Most breads are refined fast-to-sugar "simple" carbohydrates with very low nutritional value. "Cultured" bread products are better choices.

If you must eat bread, please ensure that you practice portion-control. Unfortunately, bread can become one of those addictive foods. Do you really need to have two slices at breakfast and another two slices at lunch? Do you really need to eat the whole breadbasket provided by the restaurant?

And try to buy breads that contain at least 2-3 grams of fiber per slice and no more than 1-2 grams of sugar per slice. If the bread has soy flour and ground flax seeds, it'll also contain digestion-slowing protein and fiber as well as anti-inflammatory omega-3 fatty-acids and that would be a much better choice.

That said, I seldom eat any bread.

---

[105] Metabolites are a necessary intermediate product of your metabolism; they're made during the breaking down of foods or even your body's own tissues (e.g., the catabolic process of fat and muscle tissue breakdown).

2.11 Is Wheat Really So Bad?

"Any fool can know. The point is to understand." – A.E.

I'd bet that you probably believe that an organic high-fiber multigrain slice of wheat-based bread is a better selection than a sweet cake dessert; but do you really know what you're eating? The cake is obviously processed and currently we're all told that the multigrain bread is a far better choice (even though it too is industrially produced), so I can understand why you might pick the bread over the cake. But you may view it very differently once we breakdown the actual contents of that bread and what it ultimately does to your body's biochemistry.

Ancient wheat was a far different beast than what our more recent ancestors cooked with and certainly much different than what we have today. 75% of today's wheat carbohydrate is a chain of *branching glucose units* called *amylopectin-A*, which is the *most efficiently digestible* form of amylopectin. It's quickly converted to glucose and sent into your bloodstream, hence modern wheat's strong ability to produce blood sugar spikes or glucose-highs quickly followed by glucose-lows after which you want to eat again. You could even argue that *wheat is an appetite stimulant*! And remember that it really doesn't matter how much or how little processing is involved, whether high-fiber, whole wheat or white, *wheat is basically the same to your body*; that is, your biochemical body deals with the amylopectin-A from all wheat breads **no differently**.

In sum, when compared to all other carbohydrate food whether complex or simple, modern wheat is really a *super-carbohydrate* because of the highly digestible amylopectin-A carbohydrate that's so efficiently converted to blood sugar. You want to eat food that is *inefficiently* digested, meaning it doesn't get converted into blood glucose too quickly for your body to maintain healthy balanced blood sugar levels.

Many non-wheat carbohydrate foods also contain amylopectin, but not the same kind as is found in wheat. Amylopectin-B (found in bananas and potatoes) is only *partly digestible* while amylopectin-C (found in beans) is completely *indigestible*. Hence, it's better for you to eat beans (C) rather than bananas (B), and it's better to eat bananas (B) than wheat bread (A)! Any undigested amylopectin-B and all undigested amylopectin-C will move on to your intestine to be feasted upon by your living probiotic bacteria. This makes

131

those sugars *unavailable* for your digestion but great for your hungry gut bacteria, and you'll recall that they too need some sustenance and they only get what your body can't digest on its own.

The best foods to eat are those that're difficult for your body to digest; ones that keep blood sugar levels even and biochemical hormonal balances more easily regulated. Modern wheat on the other hand is a super-carbohydrate in terms of blood sugar glucose arrival rates. Unfortunately, fiber does not mitigate the negative effects of amylopectin-A in any way.

So let's get back to that slice of multigrain bread and that piece of sweet cake. I'll bet that the desert has fat in it and fat *will always slow down* the breakdown of the carbohydrate into glucose. This means that your blood sugar glucose will rise a bit more slowly resulting in a slower release of the fat-producing insulin hormones that're needed to move that glucose around your bloodstream. Sounds much better for your body and it is. But, of course, this doesn't mean that you should be eating sweet cake whenever you crave a slice of bread. You know that cake doesn't have a lot of nutritional goodness. I'm just making the point that bread is not very good for you. Even if a 100% whole wheat bread slice has a bunch of fiber, regrettably the effect of the bread's amylopectin-A will not be reduced by much at all as the fiber's ability is offset by the quickly converted glucose that will always take place.[106]

On a comparative note, the higher the blood sugar after eating a specific food, the higher the "glycemic index" (GI). The GI of a whole grain bread slice is about 70 while that of a regular-sized chocolate bar is about 40 because its fat content will make the arrival of blood glucose more inefficient. Good grief, who would ever have guessed that? No, don't start eating a chocolate bar as a bread substitute. Obviously, just like the sweet cake argument, calorie-dense chocolate bars are not nutritionally dense and should be avoided if you're trying to control your weight and drop body fat.

---

[106] If I decide to have a sandwich and the waitress says "white" or "brown," I say "you choose" because I know that they're both bad so who cares. If I do choose, I actually go for "white" only because I prefer its taste over the equally bad "brown" and I know they'll always be some; there's never a big run on white bread because people think it's far worse than brown bread.

Interestingly, doctors have noticed that celiac[107] sufferers who change their diets by eliminating bread-based foods, actually experience weight-loss. Well, guess what? Bread-free diets, especially wheat-free ones, are also super-carbohydrate amylopectin-A-free!!!

We've talked about wheat bread a lot but, you might be wondering about the effects of *wheat pasta* on your body. Whole wheat pasta is a bit better than white pasta in terms of GI counts because it has carbohydrates that convert to sugar a little more slowly than those of white pasta (made of highly refined carbohydrates); however, pasta has the weird ability to generate high blood sugars for *4 to 6 hours after consumption*. This capability will send your blood sugars up and keep them elevated for sustained periods of time. This may not be great for *you*, but you can now appreciate why marathon runners like to eat a big breakfast of pasta before running an early morning race! In fact, many endurance athletes for half- and full-marathons will "carb-load" over the weeks prior to the run, in order to maximize their muscle-based glycogen storage. This will allow them to last for more than the approximate 90 minutes it takes to use up the amount of glycogen in their muscles. Somebody running a 5- or 10-km run won't have to carb-load as it takes less than 90 minutes, normally, to run such an event.

If you insist on eating pasta, eat smaller portions or maybe eat it only as a cheat-treat. You could also consider soy pasta[108]. It's very rich in protein; hence, it slows digestion thereby slowing the release of glucose into your bloodstream. Your body doesn't have to produce a big whack of insulin and so it can maintain its blood sugar balance much better. And, for heaven's sake, don't eat that full restaurant plateful! Practice portion-control by only eating what you can imagine holding with one hand.

Also, just a little trick for you. If you want to lower the overall glycemic or blood sugar effect of an upcoming meal, take some psyllium or inulin about 15-20 minutes before you eat. These fibers will make a slimy jelly-like lump

---

[107] Celiac disease is an autoimmune disease that damages the small intestine because of *a gluten-intolerance.* Gluten is a protein found in wheat, rye and barley. During gluten-intolerance, dietary gluten makes your immune system attack your digestive organs – specifically the intestinal villi - hence you can't absorb all nutrients into your system.

[108] Soy is a plant-based estrogen (phytoestrogen), but don't worry, you'd have to eat a heck of a lot of it to affect your estrogen hormone levels enough to cause breast cancer!

which will move right through your alimentary canal, clearing out a bunch of stuff along the way, including potential constipation and high blood sugar. They'll also slow down the speed of your digestion and that's what you want, more inefficiency.

2.12 Am I a Food Addict?

This isn't a quote. Just wanted to mention that the day after Einstein turned 74, in 1953, he agreed to allow his name to be used for the first medical school built in New York City since 1897. It's called the "Albert Einstein College of Medicine" and, interestingly, it currently has an "Addiction Fellowship Program."

You bought this book, so just be honest with yourself! It's just you having a discussion with yourself. Just be truthful with yourself. No one is watching, and certainly no one is listening. Are you addicted to a food?

Are you a food addict???

The typical foods that people can get addicted to include the following foods or ingredients and you'll see that NONE of them are proteins or fats – they're **all** some type of "simple" hyper-palatable carbohydrate[109] and they'll make you hungry by creating new cravings and sugar highs:

- Bread
- Potatoes
- Potato chips
- Pasta
- Rice
- Sugar, candy or licorice
- High fructose corn syrup (found in many highly processed foods)
- Fruit juice
- Soda pop
- Chocolate

---

[109] Nope, I've never heard of anyone having a spinach, celery or fish addiction!

If you're a food addict, you MUST avoid all intense *cravings* for any of the above. Remember that hunger is a *physical sensation* with your stomach muscles and it'll result in a feeling of stomach emptiness. It does NOT involve any particular food or drink. Cravings are quite a different beast. They always involve particular foods and are usually caused by an addiction that was developed by eating the wrong foods or in some cases resulting from depression[110] or boredom or even the time of day, for example. Hunger doesn't go away, and it can get worse. Cravings *will* dissipate, and they can go away or be replaced by a glass of water or an activity.

And remember your signaling hormones, specifically those short-term cholecystokinin and long-term leptin ones? They're supposed to be telling your brain when you just don't need any more food. If you've developed leptin-resistance, I'll bet you just don't get that "I'm full" message at all. Indeed, the lack of these hormones may have contributed to your food addictions.

Particular carbohydrates can cause food addictions.
Distinguish between hunger and cravings – make serious adult decisions.

Be honest. How much do you want to move from your **"before" fat-making** body to an **"after" calorie-burning** healthy gorgeously toned body? Sure, you'll have to practice some self-control. To break a food addiction, you'll have to avoid that food for at least two to four weeks. To be successful, you have to be tough and really stick to your avoidance plan. If your addictions can't be tamed within a month or so, it may be that they're rooted in some sort of previous trauma or abuse or reward system. If this is true, perhaps you should consider some sort of mental health counselling. There isn't anything to be embarrassed about. In fact, it takes a good serving of personal strength to seek out help.

If you can control your food addictions, it'll give you a feeling of exhilaration. My kryptonites are "all-sorts" licorice and "ju-jubes" and, given a bag of either, I would eat the *whole* thing in one sitting – geezzz, my poor busy liver was married to a sugar addict!!! When I realized I had the self-discipline to go into a grocery store and look at the rows of ju-jubes and licorice and walk by, simply imagining and remembering how they tasted, I felt elated

---

[110] Some anti-depressants can potentially cause weight-gain by slowing your metabolism while others are less likely to do so.

not cheated! I suffered none of that "after" guilt and self-loathing; and you all know what I'm talking about. I loved myself instead and I felt empowered.

And funnily enough, when I recall my sugar addiction I think of the Romans and their liking of sweeter foods. Did you know that many ancient Romans (circa 80 A.D., about the time the Coliseum was being built) were actually *poisoned* by lead acetate[111]? They used it as an artificial sweetener because sugar remained a hard found and expensive luxury (I'll bet Roman Emperor Marcus Aurelius chugged some). It wasn't until the industrial revolution, around 1800, and the resultant more widespread wealth, that sugar use started climbing. Wow, interesting indeed! That said, they never ate as much as us and, to make matters worse, we increased our sugar intake significantly with the advent of that very tasty high fructose corn syrup (HFCS) in the 1970s.

The food industry is less than clear regarding the inclusion of HFCS, which has many different names and is included in many packaged processed foods. The industry does its research and it knows that some of you do too, so it's cautious with food ingredient listings, labels and with its marketing in a concerted effort to mislead even the more astutely informed consumer. So if you're a sugar addict like I was, it can be difficult to control it simply because sugar is hidden in so many different foods and it has many many different names too.

Another consideration regarding cravings is that they can be environmentally driven. An example is the movie theatre. Do you just have to get a big bag of buttery popcorn with a super-sized soda pop or a large chocolate bar just to sit down and watch the movie??? You're just giving in to an association that triggers you to eat a particular food (and let's face it, there sure isn't much healthy food at a movie theatre.) You must endeavor to untangle yourself from this very mindless eating habit! Just ask yourself:

- "Why do I want to eat this?"
- "Am I really hungry?"
- "Am I serious about getting rid of my excess body fat?"

---

[111] Lead acetate, made by treating lead oxide with acetic acid, is a white crystalline chemical compound that has a sweet taste. Unfortunately, similar to other lead-based compounds, it's very toxic to your body.

- "Is this a good choice for my weight-loss goal?"
- "Do I have no self-control at all?"
- "Does this chocolate bar trump my fat-loss goal?"
- "How long do I have to exercise to work this off?"

The book "Atomic Habits" by James Clear can offer you some practical and strategic frameworks for dealing with habit formation and behaviors. When you want to get rid of bad eating habits and replace them with good eating habits, read this book as a great resource on how your (food) addictions work, how to break such bad habits and how to adopt some good ones. Frankly lots of little bad eating habits can stack up and create highly impactful weight-loss obstructions. If you need some practical strategies, I highly recommend this book.

Occasionally you'll just want something at some particular time of the day. Go for popcorn, without the butter and caramel of course. Regardless of its lectins, popcorn is a great snack; it's crunchy, easy to eat, it's loaded with fiber, has a low glycemic impact and doesn't normally cause food addiction. You can only stuff so much popcorn into your mouth as it's very filling.

Surprisingly it seems that some of the addictive foods you eat to *satisfy your hunger*, actually make you want to *eat more*! Whaaaaat, some foods you eat can make you hungrier??? It just isn't fair is it? And remember that it takes a *lot more food intake* to resolve the issue of low blood sugar/glucose, than it does to prevent it. That's because of the glucose blood sugar rush and the resulting sugar fall, making you feel hungry very soon after.

Eat food combinations that only gradually increase or decrease your blood sugar levels. Don't surprise your body's built-in chemistry. Don't force it into a fat-making biochemical adaptation!

2.13 What's Up with Breakfast?

"It's not that I'm so smart, it's just that I stay with problems longer."
– A.E.

Well, nothing really. Whatever works for you is OK. You might think that this is a contradiction to other parts of the book, but it's not. Your body doesn't really care *when* you eat, it just wants the nutrients it needs and it doesn't want them all in one meal or in the middle of the night when you should be sleeping.

And remember that "breakfast" is just the very first meal you eat after waking up, hence it will "break" your overnight "fast." You can skip an early morning breakfast, which constitutes a type of "fasting," or you can eat an early morning breakfast. Or you can eat a really late breakfast which in effect extends the fasting time from the time you ate before going to bed to the time you eat that first meal of the day. Some people say that by skipping breakfast (or by eating it much later) they have better weight-loss and weight maintenance; others believe that breakfast is the most important meal of the day. Frankly, the choice is yours.

If you eat breakfast and want to start delaying it a bit, or if you don't eat breakfast and want to start doing so, you have to be willing to give your body the time to catch up to your new choices. Don't try to change your breakfast habit and expect to adjust instantaneously. Give your body time to adjust. Persevere and all will be well. You may find that you don't even need that piece of morning toast. It just depends on your daily activity level.

Some studies say that skipping breakfast or fasting by leaving a longer time between the last meal in the evening and the first meal the next day can lower blood sugar and cholesterol. Others say it'll clear some of the stored glycogen/carbohydrate from your liver and this is good for weight management (I adhere to this second theory).

The problem with eating breakfast lies only in the food choices people tend to make and not with the time of the meal. If you choose cereal, toast, bagel, jam, marmalade, fruit juice, a raisin scone, donut, muffin or some other sort of "simple" carbohydrate, then you'll "crash" in about 2 hours. The result is simple, it's hunger due to your low blood sugar/glucose levels and it's very difficult to fully ignore. Your body is just doing what it's supposed to do with high glucose efficiency meals – manufacture a ton of insulin to deal with such rapidly arriving sugar, frequently way too much. Remember that your dietary nutrients are in complete control over your hormones. Hormones can make you hungry during the day; eat a bunch of quickly metabolized sugar and you'll want more of it – very soon after! This is just that notorious hormonal imbalance.

If you can't go without breakfast, aim for lean protein, a bit of fat and complex carbohydrate. It'll keep you feeling full for longer by triggering your leptin hormones and you'll avoid that awful blood sugar "crash" in the mid-morning. When you eat poorly at breakfast, your hormones get all screwed-up.

These same hormones also promote fat-storage because of excess quick-to-sugar carbohydrates. Remember that eating the proper amount of dietary fat doesn't make body fat, excess refined carbohydrates do!

An example of a reasonable breakfast might be whole eggs (protein and a little saturated fat) or egg whites (protein), cheese (get low-fat) and red or green bell peppers (complex fiber-laden carbohydrates). A nice little get-you-through-the-morning omelet. You can use a little extra virgin olive oil (omega-9 fatty acids) or canola oil (9% anti-inflammatory omega-3 and 29% unsaturated fat) in the skillet, or you can microwave the mixture if in a hurry. Notice, there's no super-carbohydrate amylopectin-A bread here!

This is my usual breakfast. Yes, I know that maybe it's boring to eat the same thing most mornings but, you might be surprised to hear that people who successfully control their weight normally eat similarly each day. It may sound a bit tedious to stick to, but it certainly leaves them with fewer decisions to make and they become less prone to giving into food addictions.

Breakfast is OK as long as it's a balance of lean protein, healthy fat and complex slow-to-sugar carbohydrate.
This will keep you full for longer.
A breakfast with high sugar will make you sluggish in mid-morning (a drop in blood sugar) and hungry as well.

2.14 Are Eggs Good or Bad for Me?

"Learning is experience. Everything else is just information." – A.E.

Eggs have gotten a bad rap over the years, especially with regard to your body cholesterol levels. That said, they're now re-emerging as one of the more perfect nutrient-dense foods around. They provide a healthy balance of proteins (13 grams) and they're nutritionally rich in iron, vitamins, and minerals. They're one of the very few food sources of vitamins D and E (an important antioxidant) and they have the essential omega-3 and omega-6 fatty-acids in their yolks.

Eggs also contain the carotenoids zeaxanthin and lutein, both of which are highly bioavailable antioxidants which help protect your cells from the damage caused by free radicals (those highly reactive molecules with unpaired electrons). When toxic free radicals are whipping around your body, they can cause damage to cell membranes, proteins and to your DNA[112] by stealing electrons via an oxidation process. The aging of your skin can be caused by free radicals damaging your skin's DNA.

OK, so eggs are good to eat. That said, you probably believe that eating too many eggs will raise your blood cholesterol levels. This is simply *not* true. The yellow yolks are certainly dense with cholesterol, but they raise *both* the bad and the good cholesterol, with a ratio of bad to good that is quite acceptable. Also, you might be a bit surprised to know that dietary cholesterol is actually quite minuscule when compared to the amount of cholesterol that is *created by your body*. That said, if you eat a lot of trans-fats, your liver will produce <u>more</u> LDL cholesterol and that's the bad one!

And another weird thing you might believe concerns the color of eggs. People seem to believe that brown eggs are healthier than white eggs. The truth is that the color of an egg does not reflect its nutritional value at all. The color of an egg is only determined by the breed of the hen that produced it. Brown hens produce brown eggs and white hens produce white eggs. The only reason brown eggs may cost more at your grocery store is because brown hens tend to be larger in size and, though they produce about the same number of eggs in a lifetime, it costs more to feed them. The egg farmer will pass along that cost to the food industry, which in turn will pass along the farmer's additional cost *plus* their handling charge to you, the uninformed consumer who believes paying more means a better-quality food! Hey, better for their profit line yet again. Are you feeling duped yet?

> **Eggs are the perfect breakfast, and they don't raise your
> bad blood cholesterol more than your good cholesterol.**

Also, you will see some eggs that boast omega-3 fatty-acid content, the good anti-inflammatory fat. How is this possible? Farmers simply feed flax seed to their hens. You can buy them and yes, these eggs do cost more, but if you really want to increase your omega-3 fatty-acid intake more significantly, then eat more fish. Or, like the hen, eat some flax seeds. The hen is OK with

---

[112] DNA or **d**eoxyribo**n**ucleic **a**cid, is the self-replicating material residing in the centre of *every one* of your body's cells. It's the main constituent of chromosomes and the carrier of your genetic information. Not something to screw up!

flax seeds – just make sure yours are ground for proper digestion. I like to buy the 100% whole sprouted flax seeds that have been powdered. They aren't as crunchy as the ground ones and so they combine smoothly with cottage cheese.

As an aside, try to keep your eggs fresh. The older they get, the poorer their quality. For example, an older egg will have a runnier egg white due to dehydration via the porous eggshell and the membrane around the yolk will be weaker. The best fried or poached eggs are made from really tasty fresh eggs[113].

Do I eat eggs? You betcha. I eat two eggs for breakfast *every day* and that's 7 days a week! Unfortunately, the eggs have to be in cartons as the poor hens are cooped up. I have to check every egg in the carton to see if the thin shell has cracked while being trucked in and stacked on the grocery shelf. For a daily maximum, I don't think you should eat more than 3 whole eggs a day as for some people it *can* increase their LDL to HDL ratio. Many bodybuilders eat only egg white protein and tons of it.

You can buy regular on-sale eggs and these are usually from "caged" hens, hens that never leave their tiny little cage their whole life – indeed some can't even turn around. If, on the other hand, you want to buy eggs from farmers who take a bit of pity on their hens, you can buy "free-run" eggs (from hens that can run free in an open concept barn that has nests and perches, but no cages) or "free-range" eggs (from hens that have the same freedom as the free-run hens but they can *also* roam outdoors if they so choose[114]). The choice is yours. Just remember that nutritionally, eggs are eggs are eggs in North America.

---

[113] Whoops, I just thought of another crazy Nigerian food story and simultaneously, I'm wondering why so many of my memories are tied to food…Hmmm, anyway, while living there, I used to ride my motorcycle down to the local food market stalls and buy some fresh eggs (they weren't cleaned on the outside either – which at first was a bit disconcerting for a North American grocery store shopper). I'd fling them into my saddle bag all bunched together (no packaging provided), and ride back home along the bumpy hard dirt road. Did they break? Never! Those egg-laying hens were running free, eating whatever, just like at my gramma's farm years ago. They had strong tough shells, non-runny whites, orangey coloured yolks and they were stunningly delicious!

[114] Unfortunately many still don't go outside. It's a long way to the exit and hard to get past all their neighbours. It's also scary if you've never been outside!

You can also choose to eat duck eggs which have a similar but far richer
taste than hen eggs. Duck yolks stay fresher longer and are much larger
than hen eggs.
They're higher in omega-3 fatty-acids (anti-inflammatory)
and in protein (building up those fat-burning enzymes),
giving them a higher overall nutritional value <u>per gram</u> than hen eggs.
They're a great alternative if you have an egg-allergy
or have developed an immune-response due to the over-consumption of
hen egg white protein.
Duck egg white contains more protein than hen egg white (at 9 grams vs. 6
grams),
although duck eggs do have over 30% saturated fat content as well,
much more than the approximate 14% in hen eggs.

2.15 Is It True That I Shouldn't Be Drinking Milk?

"I never teach my pupils; I only provide the conditions on which they can learn." – A.E.

Well there are many theories on this and some certainly make for some interesting reading. And don't forget the very active dairy industry lobbyists. Those milk promotors sure wouldn't agree with inserting such a book chapter but I'm not afraid of them.

Suffice it to say that the milk of different mammalian species tends to contain the same nutrients albeit in *different proportions* and that's the interesting issue. Also, cow milk-drinking became widespread relatively late in our biological evolution and for this reason the level of lactase (the enzyme that allows you to digest the lactose sugar in cow milk) *decreases after infancy*. This is why many people simply can't drink and fully digest cow milk.

That said, let's start with the composition of cow milk compared to that of human milk. The dairy industry can't refute that. Cow and human milk are significantly different from each other nutritionally and it has been argued that because of that, cow milk is not well suited for human consumption on a long-term basis.

<u>Some of the **nutritional** content differences between human and cow milk are shown below (I've used 1% cow milk).</u>

1. The **calcium** content of human milk is much *lower*, at only about 26% that of cow milk.
2. The **protein** content is also *lower*, at 28% of cow milk.
3. The **sodium** content is *significantly higher*, at 65% of cow milk.
4. The **phosphorous** is *significantly lower*, at 19% of cow milk.
5. The **carbohydrate** is also *much lower*, at 18% of cow milk.

Now let's look at some of the calories provided by human and cow milk. The percentage of **calories** provided by protein in human milk is only 5% but in cow milk it's a whopping 15-20%. There's a definite relationship between protein content and the number of days required for babies to double their weight. *The slower nature's intended growth of the baby, the lower the percentage of calories provided by protein.* We know that the protein macronutrient is used to build and repair muscles, ligaments and tendons. Yes, we're talking growth and motion here. Is there a difference between the newborn human baby's needs and the baby calf's growth needs? You betcha! A human baby will take about 6 months to double its weight and at least a year to triple its weight. A calf, who has to stand up and start nursing 2 hours after birth, *must double its birth weight* in about 6 weeks which is 4 times faster than that human baby can accomplish along that timeline!

Most certainly, cow milk offers nutrition to humans. It has fat, carbohydrate, protein and calcium. That said, there's no essential nutritional factor in cow milk that can't be found from other healthy foods, foods that may be better suited to human growth patterns. Obviously, I'm a huge advocate for breast-feeding until at least 6-7 months and hopefully for 12 months. That said, if your child is asking for and then pulling your breast out for a drink, personally I think you've been at it far too long. Yes, another one of my biases.

The milk industry promotes cow milk for adults as *the best way* to get calcium; but, let's face the fact, there are many other options for consuming calcium without drinking tons of milk. Although the actual amount of calcium is higher in a cup of cow milk, the *absorption* of calcium is greater from a cup of kale (41% of its 100 mg.) or broccoli (53% of its 50 mg.), then from that cup of cow milk (at only 31% of its 305 mg.) Another option is canned sardines, which provide a whopping 351 mg. of calcium, 37% of which will be available for absorption. Two other beneficial options for seeking calcium elsewhere; (a) calcium-rich non-milk options don't have the saturated fat which can promote cardiovascular diseases and (b) vegetables are never treated with growth hormones. You may have thought growth hormones were a thing of the past, but some farmers do inject their cows with a *synthetic copy* of the natural *bovine* growth hormone in order to boost their milk yields. Obviously, those growth hormones can be passed to you (and to your grandchildren) along the food eating chain. If the cow ate it, you'll be eating it too. Your body can't distinguish between something natural or that same thing synthetically produced. And that's why bodybuilders will ingest anabolic growth steroids as a way of supplementing their naturally produced human growth hormone (HGH).

Another interesting fact to consider is the disproportionate percentage between the magnesium and calcium content in cow milk. One cup (8 ounces) of cow milk has <u>26.8 mg. of magnesium</u> and <u>305 mg. of calcium.</u> I guess it might sound awesome that cow milk has so much calcium; but can you actually use the higher calcium content in cow milk when the magnesium content is so disproportionately low? Because you need magnesium in order in order to *fully absorb and metabolize* calcium, such an imbalance would not be very helpful to your bones. For this reason, if you consume too much calcium and not enough magnesium, your body can't use the excess calcium and that excess can become toxic and you now know that toxicity adds body fat cells. Compounding this issue is the fact that the chemical breakdown of the lactose sugar in cow milk *<u>decreases</u> the absorption of magnesium*, though it doesn't seem to affect the absorption of calcium.

And so, strong bones are not just the result of adequate calcium intake, but rather a *balanced* intake of magnesium as well. Magnesium is a highly plentiful body mineral; it comprises *at least* 50% of your bone content and as much as 40% of your muscle tissues. About half of your calcium minerals reside in your bones with the rest in your teeth. Nope, you don't want to have an out-of-whack calcium-to-magnesium ratio in your bones! If you're taking mineral supplements, try to aim for a 2:1 ratio (e.g., 300 mg. of calcium *and* 150 mg. of magnesium.)

*Your body will steal calcium, potassium and magnesium
from your bones if you're in an acidic state.
This will cause brittle bones.
To help build strong bones, decrease your intake of sugar,
highly refined carbohydrates
and carbonated drinks.*

And if we're considering the drinking of cow milk, what about the array of choices? As I mentioned earlier, don't be confused: "2% milk" is *not 2% fat*. "2% milk" is 98% fat-free <u>by weight</u> but it still gets 36% of its calories from fat. Even "low-fat" 1% milk gets 22% of its calories from fat. And nearly half of the calories in 3.25% cow milk come from fat and that's the same as ice cream!

You might wonder how this is possible. Well remember that I said milk is *mostly water* and that water, depending on the type of milk you choose, can be anywhere between 85-95% of the total volume. The rest is fat, lactose sugar, protein and other vitamin and mineral nutrients and this is where the milk's calorie count comes from – it's certainly not from the water.

Below is a table to help you analyze the approximate macronutrient content and overall calories for different 8-ounce glasses of cow milk. You'll notice that regardless of the type of white milk you buy, you'll still be drinking about the same number of grams (and calories) of both carbohydrate and protein. Chocolate milk adds a bunch of sugar and so the carbohydrate count is always a lot higher. Where your white milk choice differs is strictly in the number of grams of fat you would be consuming. This makes sense given the differences in "milk fat percentage" noted on the milk carton. Because the fat macronutrient is relatively high in calories per gram, it'll obviously affect the total number of consumed calories to the greatest degree.

Looking at this chart will show that "3.25% milk fat by volume" rolls with a whopping 47% of the milk's calories being from FAT (and NOT the 3.25% it may *appear to be*) while skim milk has 58% of its calories from CARBOHYDRATE (still a lot of **_sugar_** that you may not be interested in guzzling).

8-ounces or 1 cup of some milk choices	WHOLE milk (@ 3.25%)	REDUCED-FAT milk (@ 2%)	LOW-FAT milk (@ 1%)	LOW-FAT choc. milk (@ 1%)	SKIM milk (@ .02-.05%)
Approximate **Overall Calories**	152 cals	125 cals	102 cals	170 cals	83 cals
FAT Analysis **(saturated)** (1 fat gram = 9 calories)	8 gms 72 cals **(47% of 152)**	5 gms 45 cals **(36% of 125)**	2 ½ gms 22.5 cals (22% of 102)	2 ½ gms 22.5 cals (13% of 170)	1/3 gm 3 cals (4% of 83)
CARB Analysis **(lactose sugar)** (1 carb gram = 4 calories)	12 gms 48 cals (32% of 152)	12 gms 48 cals **(38% of 125)**	12 gms 48 cals **(47% of 102)**	28 gms 112 cals **(66% of 170)**	12 gms 48 cals **(58% of 83)**
PROTEIN **Analysis** **(amino acids)** (1 protein gram = 4 calories)	8 gms 32 cals (21% of 152)	8 gms 32 cals (26% of 125)	8 gms 32 cals (31% of 102)	9 gms 36 cals (21% of 170)	8 gms 32 cals (38% of 83)

Bottom line: If you are drinking 3.25% milk, count it as fat calories. Count both 1% (white or chocolate) and skim milk as carbohydrate calories.
2% milk can be counted as either fat or carbohydrates, given that both macronutrients offer similar content percentages.

Many people equate strong bones only with high calcium intake, but I haven't found any strong medical proof that the consumption of milk (or dairy products) promotes strong bones better able to prevent osteoporosis (brittle bones). North Americans are one of the highest consumers of dairy products,

146

yet they have one of the highest rates of hip fractures! Weird wouldn't you say?

Strong bones can be built with appropriate and progressive weight-training, but we'll deal with that topic in the subsequent book Unit. Suffice it to say that weight-bearing exercises such as lifting weights and activities such as alpine skiing, hiking, jogging, jumping rope, stair-climbing, and tennis, will all benefit your bone health.

Your body wants to be in a slightly alkaline (non-acidic) state. To buffer acidity, your body needs *alkalinizing* calcium, potassium and magnesium and it'll steal from your bones if it has to. 50% of your magnesium and 20% of your potassium is stored in your bones, while 99% of your calcium is in your bones and teeth. Doing this occasionally is fine, but if your body is constantly trying to balance itself against high acidity, then you're continually weakening your bones. When your bone's mineral content is weakened, your bone mass will begin to fall. Get ready for bone issues over time if you eat a lot of highly acid-forming foods such as: sugar, red meats, processed grains, *carbonated*[115] drinks and other highly processed/refined carbohydrate foods. Care for any hip fractures?

Other than putting some 2% milk (not cream at about 18%) in my coffee, I *never* drink milk. To me it's just added calories and saturated fat and sugar that I really don't need at my age. If I have a high-fiber cereal the odd time, I usually mix it with unflavored plain natural yogurt or cottage cheese, not milk. A ½ cup of 4% cottage cheese has about 40-50 calories of fat, 2% has 20 calories and 1% has 10 calories. It's saturated fat, but it isn't yucky trans-fat and so I'm not really concerned.

---

[115] I've read arguments on both sides; some say that carbonation has no effect on bone health while others say that your bone-mineral content (specifically calcium) is negatively affected by it as is tooth enamel. Honestly, I don't know what study to trust and have done enough reading to imagine the soda pop industry promoting themselves by having paid for any research that solely supports their products. Like my ancient ancestors, I just don't drink anything carbonated.

2.16 How Much Water Should I Drink?

"Reality is just an illusion, albeit a very persistent one." – A.E.

I'm sure you know water is important, but did you know that water is critically important for growth, development and health? You may not have thought of water as a nutrient, but life can't be supported without it and so yes, it's an essential body nutrient. It may not provide your body with fuel, like carbohydrate is able to do, but *it's critical for energy formation*. The best way to continually flush out your body while metabolizing body fat is with continual water input. Just remember that water is one of the *most significant components* of a successful weight-loss routine.

Water is the main solvent for foods, vitamins and minerals; it breaks food into smaller particles for your body to assimilate and it's used as a transporter of all substances in your body. Water increases the efficiency of your red blood cells to collect oxygen from your lungs. Water clears acidic toxins by delivering them to your liver and kidneys (instead of your fat cells) for eventual disposal. Water is used in your spinal discs for absorbing shock. Water lubricates, helping to prevent constipation. Water decreases your blood's viscosity helping to prevent clogged arteries. Water cools your body through sweat. Water is needed by your brain in order to produce hormones (yeah!) Water makes your skin smooth and your eyes shine. Water decreases hot flashes. I could go on and on and on and on. But surely you can understand and much better appreciate the importance of good body hydration.

In terms of your weight-loss goals, water molecules help form the macromolecular structures that contain protein and stored glycogen energy; hence, they're active contributors to all of your body's biochemical, energy and enzyme reactions and these include your sought after fat-burning. In fact, water is the primary fluid[116] in your body and though it will fluctuate daily, it should constitute about 55-65% of your overall weight. It acts as a solvent for minerals, vitamins, amino-acids, glucose and other nutrients. Without water, you *can't* digest, absorb, transport or use any essential nutrients. And you can't

---

[116] Water constitutes about 10% of your fat, 25% of your bones, 75% of your muscles, 75% of your brain, 80% of your blood, and 80% of your lungs. Water is second only to oxygen as the most important ingredient for sustainability because it allows for any biochemical adaptations necessary to maintain or return to a healthy balanced hormonal environment.

get rid of waste either! Constipation isn't very much fun. Get the picture? Water is critical for your good health. You can survive three to four weeks without food (while your body eats itself), but you can <u>only</u> survive three to four days without water!!!

If you're weight conscious, reflect on the fact that your body needs water in order to burn your body fat effectively and *the more the better* as it dilutes the concentration of other substances in your blood. This is called hypo-osmolality (i.e., body fluid levels increase, leaving a lower concentration of other particles).

But do be mindful that fluids and water are not the same. You can obtain water from foods and beverages, but *fluid and water are **never** identical to your body*. Because plain pure natural water is used for the enzyme and chemical reactions required for fat-releasing and subsequent fat-burning, hormones and oxygen will be moved around your body. This makes water the very best beverage for your calorie-burning metabolism. Tap water is fine. I'm not a big proponent of bottled water (too much single-use plastic), unless I'm on a long-distance motorcycle trip and need to have it handy.

> ***Water is essential and constitutes <u>about</u> 60% of your weight.***
> ***When dehydrated your metabolic rate will slow down and you'll burn fewer calories.***
> ***Never allow yourself to get thirsty.***

If you have a day when you're feeling tired and you can't seem to exercise as well, you may actually be dehydrated. Your joints need water as a lubricant and your muscles need water to move your bones by contracting (or shortening) their fibers.

Chronic dehydration is especially difficult on your brain cells even though they only represent 2% of your body weight. Your never-sleeping brain cells need as much as 20% of your total blood circulation[117]. Your liver is your

---

[117] When you increase blood flow to your brain, with exercise, you'll automatically send more blood to your brain through the large carotid arteries in your neck. This will increase the amount of oxygen, glucose energy and other nutrients needed by your brain. Higher brain blood flow will also help flush out waste by-products and this has to be good! And keep in mind that getting drunk can damage your brain's neurons

body's detoxifying center (poor thing) for chemical by-products, as well as the manufacturer of vital fat-burning hormones. Your brain and your liver can't operate effectively without sufficient water. Muscles and joints can also undergo serious damage during chronic dehydration and remember, this will affect your overall strength.

Furthermore, if you're dehydrated your calorie-burning ability will be highly compromised and you know what that results in. More weight! You just won't burn as much body fat nor as many calories. You should probably be drinking 8-10 eight-ounce glasses of water daily. And for heaven's sake, 8 ounces is only one cup of water! If you don't like plain water, squeeze some fresh lemon juice[118] into it. Tea, coffee, and other industrially manufactured beverages do not count as water! It doesn't mean you can't drink these liquids, just don't count them as "water." To your body they're *not* water because they simply don't function the same as water in your body. Yes, they do *contain* water, but they usually also contain dehydrating substances, such as caffeine, that deplete your body of any of the water they're dissolved in.

Whenever you drink *carbonated soda pop*, you'll be making your body more acidic; hence, it'll tend to be more fat-storing. Indeed, the side effects of these phosphoric acid fluids even go beyond your body's acidic balance. In an attempt to rebalance your blood's high acidic level, your body will try to protect itself by drawing upon any available calcium it can add to your blood. This alters your body's physiology as well as your overall bone mineral content since minerals are stored in your bones. To complicate matters further, *diet soda pop* will have an artificial sweetener (a chemically synthesized product) and this creates yet another insulin-related negative impact on your body's biochemical systems. How and why this occurs will be detailed in a subsequent chapter.

There are inexpensive scales that will estimate your body's water percentage by sending a harmless electric current through your body. Because electricity travels more easily through water, the scale will measure the resistance as a percentage to calculate an approximate body water content reading. My bathroom scales measure my weight as well as my water content

---

making it more difficult for them to relay messages to each other. Excessive drinking can even cause permanent neuron damage.

[118] This will help address the inflammatory issues that result from an acidic body as well.

(I must stand in bare feet). It doesn't hurt and it's a nice "quick and dirty" measure, even if it's not a perfect measure, I can still look at it from a relative standpoint.

Just remember to aim for 60% but to at least keep it above 50%. Body fat contains 10% water, while muscle is about 75% water. Now you can really appreciate the necessity of keeping your body sufficiently hydrated. Also, if you see your skin getting that "alligator" crusty look, you can bet on the fact that you're dehydrated. This is because skin cells are made up of a lot of water (20%). Indeed, 80% of that skin cell water is hoarded in the dermis of your skin, and so it lies on top of your subcutaneous fat. If your skin is dehydrated, you'll get that dry flaky skin look and it'll be more prone to wrinkles. Noooooooooo, not those.

Your average water content percentage will depend upon your body's fitness level and overall tissue composition. It may seem strange to think that these factors would affect how much body water you carry around, but muscles are mostly water. By increasing your muscle-to-fat tissue percentage through exercise, you'll have grown bigger muscles and these will need more water to significantly power up their cells in order to meet your weight-lifting challenges.

Some problems might even be helped by drinking a lot of water (e.g., general fatigue, kidney stones[119], colitis pain and joint pain[120].) Bones are about 25% water, so the ability of water to relieve joint pain makes sense to me. If you suffer from such pain, why not drink more water? It can't do any harm. The viscosity of your blood can also be a signal for some diseases. Viscosity measures "thickness"; so, you can imagine that _lowering your blood's viscosity_ would necessarily translate into an environment wherein proteins and those important fat-burning enzymes would swim _more efficiently_ (i.e., swim more easily). I hope that you can now better appreciate the necessity of keeping your body sufficiently hydrated by drinking more plain water.

Even your kidneys depend on water to filter waste products from your body. If they don't have enough water, then they begin leaning on your liver (!!!) for help. One of your liver's many many functions is mobilizing body fat

---

[119] Water dilutes the substances that lead to kidney stones (e.g., uric acid).

[120] Colitis and joint pain are linked to inflammation and inflammation can be exacerbated by dehydration. I do have to mention that the pain in the lower left part of my abdomen DID disappear when I drank a couple of glasses of water every morning.

for fuel. Your poor old over-worked liver, now crying "uncle," can't do its fat-burning job very well if it's always called upon to help your kidneys do their work and so, in a water-starved body, the priority of fat-loss becomes seriously compromised. You want to avoid that, right?

Ghastly to consider is that the average person carries around 10 to 15 pounds of fecal matter in their intestines. The decaying matter in your colon will have a high concentration of toxins which eventually will have to be released into your body in order to be dealt with by your liver (of course). Indeed, it's your private fermenting sewage and waste disposal septic tank.

Are you often or even continually constipated? In my opinion, if you eat three times a day then you should be pooping[121] three times a day. That's what babies do! What the heck happened to us? Incredibly enough, some people only poop every third or fourth day! Yikes, now there's a really screwed up digestive system. And I can only imagine how uncomfortable that would be. The food you eat should come out within 24-48 hours, if not, it's rotting and decaying and is buried in your body. Some people do a colon cleanse to detoxify. I can't comment much on this approach as I've never done one. I'd rather just drink a lot of water. It's a cheaper approach, more private, not invasive, and obviously less prone to potential intestinal cramping or rectal perforations. Oh-em-gee!

When you're low on water, you'll also be low on nutritional electrolyte minerals (sodium, potassium, calcium, magnesium and phosphate). These create electronically charged ions which can be either positively or negatively charged due to the loss or gain of negatively charged electrons. And because electrolytes provide the small electrical currents that are needed by your muscle tissues, when they're low your aerobic/cardio power will be directly compromised. Without sufficient electrolyte levels, you'll experience muscle weakness and can even have severe muscle contractions (i.e., cramps). You'll also need both calcium and magnesium electrolytes for weight-building exercises. Calcium will allow your muscle to contract or shorten while magnesium will allow those same muscles to relax or lengthen. You'll have

---

[121] You'll hear people referring to their early morning poops as their "morning constitutional." This phrase comes from the good ol' days when people had to make an early morning walk to the outhouse; and, a walk certainly can be good for your "constitution" and that's your overall health.

difficulty making sustainable fat-loss progress if you've joined the gym on Starvation Island!

Obviously, marathon runners don't want to have muscle cramps during a competition and so it's critical that they hold on to their electrolytes! In some cases, runners will pre-load electrolytes in order to ensure their bodies can deliver enough fluid to their hardworking muscles. When you watch a marathon or a Tour de France bicycle race, you'll see lots of water stations along the route as well as small packets or drinks with electrolytes for the athletes. I bet you wondered what they were guzzling from those stations or from their "fanny" packs. Not chocolate and certainly not fructose sugar! No athlete wants to experience a crash in blood sugar.

Your thirst mechanism will kick in when you are down by *only 2%* of your body's water weight; but, by that time you are *officially dehydrated*. Yes, I know. You're thinking that 2% isn't that much but for your biochemical functions it's a *huge* loss. If you care about growing lean muscle tissue, then you need to care about the *volume* of your muscle cells, or the *hydration state* of your mostly-water muscle cells. Well hydrated muscle cells *decrease protein breakdown*. Your muscles want those amino-acid building blocks and they don't like to give them up. Remember your body's highly inefficient five-step protein-to-glucose process? Keep yourself well hydrated and your body will thank you in many healthy biochemical ways.

Water also forms the makeup of your synovial fluid, which is the lubricating fluid between your joints and the shock absorbing fluid between your spinal vertebrae. Pretty important indeed. If you want to protect healthy joints and ensure spine maintenance while weight-training, you need water as a protective fluid for optimal performance. Drink a lot of water *while* you are exercising, whether you feel thirsty or not. Always drink water (or a protein amino-acid powder mixed with water), while you're taking that well-deserved rest between exercise sets. And regarding synovial fluid, if you hear some "cracking" or "clicking" in your joints while exercising, it's the "popping" of some nitrogen gas bubbles in your synovial fluid. There's no scientific evidence that this causes issues such as arthritis, but if you're worried or if you experience simultaneous pain or swelling where the "click" is, you should get it checked out by your medical doctor. I sometimes hear it in my shoulder or knee joints, but it's never painful and so I don't worry about it.

Also, as you burn off stored fatty-acids for energy, you'll release the fat-soluble toxins that were stored in your body fat cells. The more water you drink, the more you *dilute* those toxins in your bloodstream, and the more rapidly your body can expel them. Helping out your liver sounds pretty awesome to me!

As stated, adequate water is essential on a regular basis,
not just while you're working out.
And, water is free,
so you really have NO reasonable excuses!!!

Contrary to the mythical belief of some, water can't accumulate and add weight. Of course, if you're a Starvation Islander, you'll lose a bunch of weight at the outset, but it'll be mostly water. But eventually you won't be urinating much of it as your body moves into a dehydrated panic mode. I think this is where people get mixed up. They think because they lose weight when they lose water, then they think they'll gain weight when they drink water, but this is simply not true. Actually, the opposite is true. Insufficient water means that your kidneys *must hang on to water* and store it so that they can continue to process toxic biochemical waste. On the other hand, drinking the right amount of water causes a beautiful flow-through cycle for your body to enjoy.

Now let's talk about the risks of drinking too much water. It's normally very difficult to drink too much water and that's because any excess water won't be stored in your body. Rather, it'll automatically be passed out in your urine. Your kidneys are able to eliminate about 20-24 liters daily, but they can't process more than about *one liter of water per hour*. That said and although *extremely* difficult to do, let's see how someone *could* drink too much water and become *overhydrated*.

Because your body has a one-liter-per-hour water elimination capability, any surplus water will start to dilute your electrolyte levels and this will eventually cause your body's fluids to move *inside* your cells. This notion may seem oddly weird to you, but proper hydration is a very *delicate balance* between fluids and minerals. The concentration of electrolyte minerals in your bloodstream must lie between a very narrow range or it can affect muscle contractions (which would include your heart – don't forget that it's a working muscle too!)

If you take in too much water relative to the number of electrolytes in your body, you'll be *hyperhydrated.* Some people actually call this "water poisoning"! Basically, when there's too much water *outside* your body's cells you'll have a very diluted number of electrolytes on the outside of your cells, compared to those *inside* your cells. Because of this, the fluid outside your cells will move into the fluid inside your cells to *re-balance* the electrolyte concentrations between your cell membranes. Such imbalances can lead to severe headaches (because your brain cells become swollen[122]), muscle weakness, pain, cramping, thirst (surprised?) and sometimes to nausea or vomiting.

In sum, whether you're ***dehydrated or hyperhydrated,*** your levels of electrolytes will never match your fluid levels. It really is yet another biochemical imbalance that your body will try to deal with one way or the other. And, I can say that it certainly won't be good for your weight-control and fat-burning. It's hard to move those fat-burning enzymes when your blood is too viscous or when your fluids are way too diluted!

How can you tell if you are properly hydrated? If you're insufficiently hydrated your urine will be a very dark yellow color (as your body tries to retain precious water), while the urine of a properly hydrated person will be almost clear with only a little hint of yellow. Some medications, prescriptions and vitamins can darken or brighten your urine; examples include some antibiotics, laxatives, muscle relaxants or B2 (riboflavin). *Usually* it's harmless and just related to your body dumping any unneeded amount of the culprit. If you're worried, ask your medical doctor at your next physical.

As your body ages, it's less able to efficiently regulate its water intake, simply because it loses its thirst signals. Good grief, what next for us agers??? Do we not recognize our own gradual dehydration? It's an interesting concept. Some people mistake the thirst sensation as hunger, then they eat solid foods. At some point your body sends a stronger message of thirst as it now needs even *more water* for the digestion of that extra food. Many people drink water during a meal. To separate the thirst sensation from the hunger sensation, it might be better to drink a glass of water *prior* to eating. A side bonus is that you probably won't overeat in terms of quantity either. In case you're wondering, the thirst sensation is separate from your leptin hormone signals

---

[122] Many of those "skinny-fat" treadmill runners drink tons of water and don't eat much. I often hear them complaining about headaches. Now you know why.

(the feeling of fullness created by your body fat cells) and ghrelin hormone signals (which promote fat-storage due to hunger signals).

If, instead of water, you're drinking sweetened drinks of *any type,* they'll be bad for you – and it won't matter whether they're sugar-laced or artificially/synthetically sweetened. Even your gut microbiome, a collection of all of the pre- and probiotic microorganisms that inhabit your body and line your intestine, will be affected by sugary-*tasting* drinks. More inflammation anyone? How about more fat storage while you're at it? Nope, doesn't sound too promising for your overall weight- and fat-loss goals.

We know why sugar is bad but why are these diet *non-calorie* artificially sweetened drinks bad too? Well, firstly they're not plain simple water, hence there will always be an assortment of synthetic chemicals involved. And some drinks are carbonated which means theft of your bone calcium will take place. Osteoporosis anyone? But another more interesting reason is that your body *can't* tell the difference between a sugary drink, fruit juice or an artificially sweetened drink. I'll discuss details regarding this very important biochemical fact later in the book.

<u>Here's what I do to keep properly hydrated:</u>

- I'll drink a glass of water as soon as I get up in the morning (to counter the dehydration built up overnight);
- drink a glass of water before every meal (to ensure I don't overeat);
- drink a glass of water *about ½ an hour* after every meal (to help with food breakdown though delayed a bit so as *not to inhibit* my digestive fat-burning enzymes);
- drink a glass of water before I go to bed (to counter middle-of-the-night dehydration) and another little one if I get up in the middle of the night to urinate (remember my age!);
- always drink a glass of water if I feel hungry (as I'm probably thirsty);
- always drink extra water if I am constipated or experiencing any gut pain (e.g., 2 glasses upon waking up);
- always drink a glass of water for each alcoholic drink being consumed (i.e., a glass of water and a glass of wine on the table sitting side-by-side); and,

-   I'll drink at least 3 cups (750 ml) of plain water (or water mixed with a protein powder) while weight-training.

2.17 Why Do People Worry About Their Ph Level?

"Everything should be made as simple as possible, but not simpler." –
A.E.

By now, you should better appreciate your body as a living biochemical system. It *will always be affected* by chemicals, by diet, by physical and psychological factors; all of which can alter your body's alkaline/acid balance. Remember your old high school chemistry classes where you discussed basic (alkaline) and acidic balances? Well those same numbers will apply to your body. It'll be acidic when your pH is 0.1 – 6.9, be neutral at 7.0, and be basic or have alkalinity when your pH is 7.1 and higher.

Firstly, you need to understand what "alkaline" and "acid" and "pH" mean. And you need to appreciate why alkaline-forming and acid-forming reactions are so important to your body. How can they affect your overall health? How can they be measured? And finally, what would your body's ideal alkaline/acid balance be?

Maybe you weren't listening to your high school chemistry teacher when s/he was discussing whether a substance was alkaline or acidic and that it was completely determined by its "potential hydrogen" or pH level; pH numbers refer to how many hydrogen atoms are present. Technically, pH is actually the measurement of the *electrical resistance* between the positive and negative ions in your body. All of your body's ions have a <u>*net* electrical charge</u> due to the loss or gain of negatively charged electrons. *Negative ions* are alkaline-forming while *positive ions* are acid-forming. pH simply measures how much those different negative and positive ions push against each other. Indeed, you actually have a biochemical system that's a bunch of highly organized electrical reactions! The stronger you are, the better your reactions vibrate. I wonder if that's what your "aura" is.

But why do we care about such vibrations? It's critically important to remember that your body acidity and your body fat are strongly linked. Body fat is your body's primary defense outlet when dealing with your pH balance and you *must maintain* a healthy slightly basic pH (around 7.2-7.4) in order to maintain healthy life processes. If your pH level is chronically acidic, you'll have much greater difficulty losing weight. You also need oxygen to burn body fat and there'll be less oxygen being delivered to your cells when you're more acidic.

As mentioned earlier in the book, normally your body will deal with excess acid (and the resulting toxins) by sweating or urinating or defecating them out. When there are far too many acidic toxins to deal with using those avenues, your body will then resort to disposing of the excess acid by *producing toxic waste cells* for storage. And these will **always** be fat cells[123]. *In other words, if there isn't enough fat cell space to bury that waste, your body will just make more storage fat cells.* Wowie, more fat cells when you're desperately trying to get rid of them. When your body is acidic, it needs, uses and makes more of those body fat cells to get enough storage space in which to keep the excess toxic acids safely separated from any healthy tissues. And keep in mind that fat cells *won't go away* without a huge fight!!! You may not like the extra body fat, but your body needs it and you'll *always* lose that battle if you're chronically acidic. And remember – your body can't be deceived. You can exercise a lot, but if you're highly acidic from eating a lot of processed foods your overall results will be depressingly poor. Blood pH levels also control the efficiency of insulin and surely by now, you know that insulin regulation plays a huge part in controlling your overall body weight and your body fat percentage.

Your body processes minerals from foods and these will always affect your alkaline/acid balance. Certain minerals are "acid-binding" which means they *bind acid toxins* and leave an "alkaline-forming" residue behind. *This is good.* Such alkaline-forming minerals include calcium, magnesium, sodium, potassium, selenium and manganese. Foods that contain these minerals *increase* your body's alkaline level. If you eat too many foods high in phosphorus/phosphoric acid, you'll *decrease* your alkaline level. *This is bad.* Foods that will decrease your alkalinity include meat, dairy, fruits, grains, soda

---

[123] The size of your fatty tissue depends directly on the number of fat cells and their size. Usually the number of fat cells are determined in your early years. Fat cells are like balloons; they can be empty or full, but they love to be filled and hate to be emptied. Unfortunately, this isn't the final line in the fat cell creation story. Yes, you can make a lot of new fat cells by eating poorly as unhealthy diets directly affect your pH acidity and your oxygen levels.

pop, fruit juice and even long-term consumption of ionic iron pills[124]. I'm not suggesting that you don't eat these foods, just that you're careful not to overdo it.

But how does your body manage excess acids? It can store excess acid in your body fat cells, joints, muscles, and arteries. It can excrete excess acid via your colon, kidneys, lungs and skin. But if you're chronically acidic, your body *will also* swipe calcium from your bones. It'll also use other alkaline-forming minerals such as magnesium, potassium, and sodium to shield itself from high body acidity during the search for its favored biochemical balance and pH range. Obviously, you don't want to use up all your mineral reserves!

In terms of your fat-loss goals, if your body can use its mechanisms to deal with excess acid, why does it even matter that your body *stores* excess acid? Put simply, being too acidic *prevents you metabolically from losing weight*. In fact, being highly acidic weakens your body's systems and creates an environment which is far more susceptible to illness and disease. You can catch a viral or bacterial infection from someone else if your body is *chronically acidic*. Viruses and bacteria *love to eat waste* tissue acids. I don't tend to get sick much, even when around someone who is sneezing and carrying a lot of mucous! They're just not very contagious to my slightly alkaline body, though they probably will be for someone who has an acidic imbalance. High body acidity also compromises the ability of your protease (an enzyme catalyst) to breakdown dietary proteins and you need amino-acids for building muscle strength. If you don't want to grow more body fat cells (more fat-making) and if you want to build more lean muscle tissue (more calorie-burning), you'll not want to overtax your body with excess acid.

Your alkaline/acid *balance* will also affect your energy levels. An alkaline-forming reaction energizes your system, while an acid-forming one will decrease your energy levels. Although your diet should include both types of reactions resulting in both types of residues, you still want a proper balance of alkaline-forming and acid-forming reactions.

Post-menopausal women have particular concerns regarding hormonal changes, overall stress and altered sleep patterns. Added to these metabolic

---

[124] Iron pills that are *non-ionic* won't result in the same affliction. That's because your stomach doesn't have to deal with splitting up ions, hence it doesn't have to steal water from elsewhere in order to do so. That'll help with constipation too, an affliction often coupled with ionic iron pill supplements.

predispositions is a diet that's often higher in acidic levels from food choices rich in animal foods (acid-forming), high in sugars (acid-forming), high in omega-6 fatty-acids (acid-forming) and low in vegetables (alkaline-forming). When your body is high in acid, it'll *always steal* alkaline-forming calcium from your bones in an attempt to lower its pH and this can lead to those infamous hip fractures. Suffice it to say that if you're highly acidic, your joints, tissues, muscles, organs and glands will pay the consequences in the longer run.

> *The more acidic your pH level, the less efficient your insulin is*
> *and the more body fat you can accumulate.*
> *Avoid processed foods, omega-6 fatty-acids, HFCS, MSG and trans-fats.*

Remember that some of the toxic (acid-forming) chemical food ingredients that you may be ingesting would include artificial sweeteners, monosodium glutamate (MSG – yes, it's still in any processed foods which contain hydrolyzed plant or vegetable[125] proteins), unhealthy hydrogenated oils (with those ugly trans-fats), high fructose corn syrup (HFCS), food preservatives, and various and sundry industrially processed and highly refined carbohydrate foods.

Some examples of alkaline-forming/acid-binding foods are: apples, bananas, cantaloupe, dates, figs, grapes, grapefruit, lemons, limes, mangos, melons, oranges, pears, pineapple, raisins, raspberries, strawberries, tangerines, watermelons, asparagus, beets, broccoli, Brussel sprouts, cabbage, carrots, cauliflower, sweet corn, eggplant, kale, leeks, lettuce, mushrooms, okra, onions, bell peppers, pickles, potatoes, pumpkin, radishes, sauerkraut[126],

---

[125] Hydrolyzed vegetable protein is produced by boiling the food (e.g., corn, wheat) in hydrochloric acid and then neutralizing the resulting solution with sodium hydroxide. This results in the glutamic amino-acid, which we more commonly know as the sodium salt called MSG. Hence, if you see "hydrolyzed vegetable protein," think MSG! Isn't the food industry super-great at labelling? You gotta give them an A+ grade for that!

[126] Try for non-pasteurized sauerkraut as it has no added sugar and no preservatives. Oh no, here comes another food memory. My now deceased step-dad was a chiropractor and he used to tell me to drink sauerkraut juice (right from the jar) whenever I had an upset stomach. And guess what? It always worked! Now I know

seaweed, swiss chard, tomatoes, turnips, quinoa, lima beans, peas, tofu, string beans, granola, potatoes, almonds, chestnuts, fresh coconut and sesame seeds.

Interestingly, honey (a natural sugar) is alkaline-forming, while white sugar is not. And garlic is fabulously alkaline forming.

Some examples of foods that are neutral or a little alkaline-forming are: almonds, coconut, corn, and canola/olive/soy/sesame oils.

Some minerals are "alkaline-binding," hence they bind the alkaline reserve minerals and leave an "acid-forming" residue behind. *This is bad.* Such acid-forming minerals are phosphorous, sulphur, chlorine, iodine, bromine, fluorine, copper and silicon. Foods that contain these *increase* your body's acidic level. Don't think these minerals themselves are bad; we're talking about a *balance* here, which means you still need *both* alkaline- *and* acid-forming minerals.

Some examples of acid-forming/alkaline-binding foods are: blueberries, cranberries, plums, prunes, watercress, water chestnuts, barley, buckwheat, corn meal, steel cut oats, basmati rice, brown rice, spelt, wheat, most beans (black, broad, kidney, garbanzo, navy, pinto, red), lentils, brans, breads, cereals, crackers, pastries, pastas, popcorn, tapioca, cashews, dried coconut, peanuts, pecans, walnuts, pumpkin seeds, sunflower seeds, all meats and fish. Coffee, white sugar, maple sugar, molasses and artificial sweeteners are also acid-forming.

All liquor, wine, beer, drugs and tobacco are acid-forming. You'll probably find these facts especially disappointing!!! And most high-protein foods (meat, fish) are acid-forming, though they're still important for other essential nutrients.

If you are chronically acidic your body will be prevented from losing weight, especially body fat.

The processing and refining of foods will always *reduce* their alkaline-forming ability. Some surprising examples of food industry meddling that result in creating an acid-forming food from one that normally wouldn't be include the following: fat-free yogurt (which can also contain high sugar) and fat-free cottage cheese! Any refined (i.e., "white" foods), processed, enriched,

---

why…it's fermented (therefore probiotic-friendly) and, as an acid-binding food, it countered any temporary acidity I was experiencing.

chemicalized, or preserved foods, sugars, and salts will be acid-forming. Try to eliminate or at least reduce these from your diet.

Coffee, soda pop, sugar, alcohol, refined/processed carbohydrates, anger, too little sleep and high stress are common acid-creating *dependencies*. All of these can be controlled by you with practice, perseverance and common sense.

Some examples of foods that are neutral or a little acid-forming are: butter, cheese, milk, eggs, whey, and plain natural yogurt.

Although it may sound contradictory, a quick way to deal with gastrointestinal upsets is to alkalize your body by putting one teaspoon of fresh lemon juice into 4 ounces of water. It's the citric acid in the lemon which converts to carbon dioxide and water that results in an alkaline effect!!! It's super safe and very alkalizing. Drink this every morning and you'll soon be feeling super! Maybe brush your teeth before leaving the house just to take the acidity off your teeth enamel. Who'd have thought that lemons would do this? It's not very difficult to buy some whole lemons, store them in the refrigerator and squeeze real lemon juice into your water. The citric acid in limes also have an alkalizing affect and so the limes you might put with your Corona beer or the limes squeezed for your frozen[127] margaritas are nicely acid-binding.

And don't forget, drinking water is also essential for maintaining your electrolyte balance which in turn will help with your acid-alkaline pH balance. Your body has many homeostasis[128] regulating control actions and this is just one of them.

And so when you consider the chapter on the importance of drinking water and then this chapter on the importance of water in order to regulate your blood

---

[127] On one of our motorcycle trips, we ended up on Duvall Street in Key West Florida and discovered a great little ingredient for deliciously decadent margaritas…use lime sherbet! Our BBQ guests always request these. Here's the recipe: 12 ice cubes, 6 tbsps. freshly-squeezed lime juice, ½ cup tequila, 2 tbsp Grand Marnier (or Cointreau), and 1 cup frozen lime sherbet. Mix the first 4 ingredients in a good blender capable of crushing ice and then blend in the sherbet. Enjoy.

[128] This is the body's tendency to seek and maintain a relatively stable and balanced equilibrium within all of its internal physiological processes and systems (even when faced with external changes or challenges). An example would be attempting to keep a constant internal body temperature regardless of the outside environment.

acidic levels, you should consciously endeavor to drink the right amount of daily water spread across the day.

Take your weight in pounds and then divide by two. That will tell you the *minimum* number of ounces of water to drink daily. For example,

Body Weight	Divide by 2	daily 8 oz cups of water[129]
120 lbs./55kg	60 oz.	7.5 = 8 cups minimum
140 lbs./64kg	70 oz.	8.75 = 9 cups minimum
160 lbs./73kg	80 oz.	10 = 10 cups minimum
200 lbs./91kg	100 oz.	12.5 = 13 cups minimum

If you decide to test your alkaline level, remember that a slightly alkaline blood pH of 7.2-7.4 is optimal while that of your saliva or urine will show a much lower pH level of about 6.6-6.8 due to the protein present in the solution. This is fine. You can buy urine and/or saliva sticks that will measure your pH level; kind of like testing swimming pool water (but don't use pool-testing sticks). I found them at a health food store. Also, your medical doctor can order a blood pH test (a normal part of a blood gas test or arterial blood gas test.)

You should try to eat about 75% alkaline-forming foods
and only 25% acid-forming foods.
Always choose your alkaline foods wisely.

2.18 What About Alcohol?

"In the middle of difficulty lies opportunity." – A.E.

You may have heard many different takes on alcohol, for example a glass of red wine is heart healthy or drinking beer is great for replacing fluids and carbohydrates. But don't be fooled. To your body, alcohol is just another *poison* that has to be metabolized by your liver and then filtered out of your body by your kidneys. And alcohol is acid-forming as well.

Aside from all the usual well-known side effects of alcohol, did you know that it *dehydrates* your body? As a dehydrating fluid, alcohol causes your

---

[129] Not greater than 1 litre per hour.

kidneys to flush out some of their precious water reserves, not to mention that your poor over-worked liver (aawww) will have to clear out the poisonous side of the alcohol. And alcohol decreases both your exercise performance and your muscle endurance and contributes to high triglycerides (fat cells) and obesity.

Can you drink alcohol? Sure you can, but as they always say, "in moderation." But what is "moderation"? Obviously, it's highly subjective so what might a reasonable definition for "moderate drinking" be? Is it one drink per day? Is it seven drinks per week and can you consume them all in one evening? What about a maximum of three drinks daily, but for how many days straight? And what's a standard amount for a drink? Is the wine 5 oz. or 8 oz. or 10 oz.??? Haven't you noticed how much bigger wine glasses are getting.

I checked up on Canada's *low-risk alcohol drinking guidelines* and they state the following:

- Maximum of 3 drinks/single occasion for women; 4 for men.
- No more than 10/week for women; 15 for men with the caveat that some days are alcohol free.

But what is alcohol? Well, you might think it's a regular carbohydrate macronutrient. Just think about it. It can't be a fat! It can't be a protein! So, it must be a carbohydrate. That's the only macronutrient choice left and so yes, it is. But alcohol, as a carbohydrate macronutrient, doesn't actually react like other carbohydrates. It travels along different biochemical pathways.

Alcohol is a form of sugar which gets converted into fatty-acids and causes dehydration.
Beer spikes insulin more than super-carbohydrate bread!
Drink a lot of booze and you'll be growing body fat, especially around your belly.

Although a gram of carbohydrate provides 4 calories of energy while a gram of fat provides a whopping 9 calories of energy, due to the sugar and starch that booze is made from, it'll provide energy at a relatively high 7 calories per gram. And it's *just* the alcohol providing all of those calories with *nothing else at all*! Beer has a little more to offer, at least in terms of carbohydrates from grains but still, not much else.

Furthermore, as a type of carbohydrate, alcohol is a bit weird in yet another way. Unlike other carbohydrates, it isn't converted to glucose for energy. Instead it's converted <u>directly into fatty-acids</u> and so it's much more likely to be stored as body fat. If you're tracking calories via the macronutrient system, then you should probably add the wine and liquor calories as fat and maybe the beer calories as carbohydrate. You can't just ignore those calories. You have to account for all of them *somewhere*! If you drink and you train in the gym on the same day, then your fat-burning process is basically put on hold while your liver is hard at work. Hmmm, I guess on Saturdays and Sundays my weight training isn't very effective.

If you're a beer drinker, you actually have two problematic issues going on (compared to the wine or hard liquor drinker).
Beer has that alcohol macronutrient at 7 calories/gram,
but it <u>also has</u> the traditional grain-based carbohydrates (maltose sugar) at 4 calories/gram.
Yet another double whammy in terms of added body fat.
Beer belly anyone???

If you want to lose weight quickly, I would suggest laying off **all** alcohol for a while until you get your weight back on track. I did it and though it was difficult at the beginning, I got used to it. I felt physically great and I began to sleep like a baby. My incentive was our middle son's 2011 wedding (when I was 63) and it was the best I've ever looked. I got asked twice if I was a friend of the bride. Whaaat!

If you drink wine, remember that it *is* a form of sugar to your body. Although much of the fructose (from those grapes) is burned off during the fermenting process, wines do retain a lot of their sugar. Although the "maltose" sugar in beer doesn't contain the dreaded "fructose," it'll still spike your insulin hormone levels which in turn *will* make you fatter. In fact, it <u>spikes higher insulin levels</u> than *super-carbohydrate* breads. Hard liquor has no fructose, but when you mix it with soda pop you will get a big sugar hit. And we also now know that carbonated soda pop steals bone minerals.

Drinking excess amounts of alcohol causes your kidneys to flush out water much much more rapidly than normal. Because of that, alcohol becomes a diuretic. Indeed, the higher the alcohol content of your drink, the greater its diuretic effect. This is because alcohol decreases your body's ability to produce the anti-diuretic hormones (ADHs) that are used to reabsorb water. Usually you'll have to get up to urinate in the middle of the night a few times. When you drink a lot of alcohol, your body will suffer from a fluid imbalance and this can lead to seizures[130]. Drinking water will reduce this dehydrating effect. Like I said earlier, drink water between alcohol drinks. Your body will thank you in multiple biochemical ways.

And a final word of caution; if you drink alcohol, it's best to eat at the same time. Eating will slow the absorption of the alcohol while the water dilutes it. You'll avoid those terribly unpleasant hangovers too – remember how much your brain hates to be dehydrated.

Always drink water and eat some food when drinking alcohol
to prevent dehydration and to slow the sugar dump.

2.19 Why Do I Hear That Not All Calories Are Created Equal?

"Not everything that can be counted counts, and not everything that counts can be counted." – A.E.

A calorie is a *measure of energy*. All foods provide caloric energy and, as you now know, this is true of alcohol as well. Yes, a calorie is a calorie! And every calorie contains 4.184 joules of energy. BUT, to your body not all calories are treated in the same way. For example, if you eat 400 calories from a large industrially processed bran muffin versus eating 400 calories from some grilled wild Pacific salmon, there most certainly IS a difference to your body! How could you possibly think otherwise?

Your body is not a calorie in/calorie out mathematical entity.
Swallowed calories travel along different biochemical pathways in the
body.

_____

[130] Ever read Eric Clapton's autobiography? Three bottles of brandy a day for awhile = a grand mal seizure!!! Mixing lager with vodka was a favorite too. Apparently though, he could still play incredible guitar while horribly high. He's completely sober now.

Diets which base your weight-loss on a low-calorie daily diet are quite misleading at best and very dangerous at worst. That said, most people are always counting calories. And I'll also wager that many are overweight too. Long-term sustainable weight-loss can *never* be solely based on calorie counting.

Yes, I know. You'll lose weight quickly by not eating very many calories, but such Starvation Island visits will only produce a temporary result. Your body will reduce its need for energy (calories provide body fuel) whenever you cheat it of calories. *Eat less and you'll burn less.* Eat more and you'll burn more[131]. Pretty simple result. Changing your daily caloric intake always triggers a very complex *biochemical survival* response and *it'll always* involve your metabolic rate. That's a simple way to underscore why your *metabolism* __is__ *your ability to burn calories.*

As noted, calories are fuel or energy for your highly complex biochemical system. Your body does *not* act only according to the laws of thermodynamics meaning that it *does not deal with energy* in the same way as any other energy-consuming material will. The **First Law** of thermodynamics states that energy can't be created or destroyed in an isolated or closed system (in effect this is the conservation of energy). It specifies that the internal energy (**E**) of a closed system is the amount of heat supplied by that system (**H**) less the amount of work done by that system (**W**).

E = H – W
Thus to maintain your energy balance and body weight (E),
one calorie eaten (H) must be balanced with one calorie burned (W).

Heat and work both either add or subtract energy.

If your body interpreted the First Law the way many calorie-counters believe, it would mean that your body dealt with *every calorie eaten* in the very same way. If you believe that "calories in" *equals* "calories out," it wouldn't matter what type of food you ate. It would mean that your body would be ignoring all your hormones as well as your metabolism. It would mean that your weight-gain is only related to how many calories you eat and whether you

---

[131] Obviously, you have to eat nutrient-dense foods while practicing reasonable portion-control.

eat more than your body wants or less than it needs. It would mean that you could eat either five jelly-filled donuts (at about 300 calories each) *OR* 1,500 calories of nutrient-dense food during the day and still be healthy, and not alter your weight over time. If all fat calories are the very same to your body it would mean that there is no difference to your body between healthy unsaturated fats such as avocados and the saturated fats found in processed salami or, for that matter, even synthetic trans-fats. If all carbohydrate calories are the same, who cares whether you eat 100 calories of candy or 100 calories of fresh vegetables!

Sound ridiculous? Well if you believe that all calories are the same, then this *is* what you believe. Your body is just *not that simple* and you can't make it that simple, no matter what you do, how you do it, when you eat, or how much you pray to those fat-loss gods! Your body has very elaborate built-in processes to regulate its energy balance. Different foods travel via different biochemical pathways. Different macronutrients affect your hormones and ultimately your eating behavior in different ways. This means that simplistic calorie counting, to lose weight and body fat, is really not very effective in the long run. You should be considering calorie *quality* and not quantity.

So, do you get the drift? Maybe it isn't how many calories you're eating but what type of calories they are. Many weight-conscious dieters worry that they are eating too much food and cut back on daily calories, but maybe the problem is completely different. Maybe they're eating too much of the wrong foods and too little of the right foods. Maybe if they ate the right nutrient-dense foods, they could even eat *more* calories! Wow now isn't that an interesting concept.

And again, how could you possibly think that 400 calories from a processed bran muffin would be the same as 400 calories from that hunk of grilled wild salmon? This might be new information for you but it certainly isn't a newsflash for your biochemical body. Your body is a biological unit and it wants to survive your flawed eating habits, so it'll do *whatever it takes* to maintain homeostasis stability over time. You simply can't turn your body into a mathematical equation. You are no different than anyone else. I agree with the expression "you are what you eat." Frankly, if you're overweight, you're most certainly not eating properly, and I doubt you are weight-training effectively either.

How satiated (or full) you are and for how long after eating is a good measure of the *quality* of the food you are eating. Eating a can of drained white albacore[132] tuna (170 grams at about 140 calories) with a large fresh veggie salad[133] (about 100 calories) will keep you full much longer than 1 regular-sized slice of pizza (at about 300 calories). Yes, the fewer calories you need to make you feel full, the more nutritious the food and probably the more fiber it'll have. Furthermore, you're also less likely to overeat. How much a food stretches your stomach and other digestive organs is related to the amount of water and fiber in it. That's why 17 calories in two large fibrous celery stalks is much more filling than the 90 calories in 30 M&M candies or the 263 calories in a 57 gram "Oh Henry's" chocolate bar.

Your body adjusts to the types of calories you eat and use to achieve homeostatic balance both immediately and over the longer term. It'll automatically regulate your insulin and bloodstream glucose levels. When you drink a lot of water, you'll urinate more. When you eat more calories, you'll burn more calories. When you eat fewer calories, you'll burn fewer calories. That's when your metabolic calorie-burning ability, is re-adjusting by *slowing down*. And that's just not something you want!

The best example is sugar. Although I'll go into a lot of detail about sugar in another chapter, let's talk a little bit about it here too. There are many kinds of sugar and there're many chemical compounds that are labelled as "sugar." The two main simple sugars are glucose and fructose, and both are problematic for your body. Sucrose (or "table" sugar), which binds together glucose and fructose molecules, doubles the problems for your body. Fructose alone is a terrible ambush on your busy liver.

Different foods affect your hormones and eating behaviors,
as well as your fat and muscle tissues.
In response to whatever you eat,
your body will always adjust its hormones to maintain biochemical balance.

---

[132] "Albacore" tuna has a relatively high percentage of anti-inflammatory omega-3 fatty-acids when compared to other tuna choices.

[133] With 2 cups lettuce or spinach, ½ cup sliced carrots, 1/2 cup sliced celery, 2/3 cup cherry tomatoes and 2 tbsp. of balsamic dressing.

Glucose and fructose may have the same chemical formula and weight BUT to your body they're metabolized quite differently. Glucose is naturally metabolized by *all of your body's tissues* while fructose can *only be metabolized by your liver.* Normally when you eat natural whole food, like an apple or a whole grain or a real vegetable, glucose is bound to or stuck to the food's cell membranes and mixed up with some fiber. This forces your body to take longer to breakdown the food in order to reach the sought-after glucose. Put more simply, it means that it takes longer for the glucose to hit your bloodstream, maybe even hours depending on the combination of fat and protein and fiber with the other food eaten, and so the pancreas doesn't have to make the fat-producing insulin so quickly. Therefore, it's better to eat an apple than to drink apple juice (which has *no* fiber and causes a *huge* spike in insulin). Indeed, all liquids are absorbed by your body much more quickly than any solid food.

I always cringe when I see people drinking huge glasses of orange juice with their breakfast. Often, they couple that juice with a huge plateful of fresh fruit, also high in immediate sugar to their bodies. I'm certain they actually believe it's a healthy thing to do. Meanwhile, their bodies are desperately trying to deal with the huge sugar rush, as bodies are pre-programmed to do.

Fiber-free fruit juices overload your liver's ability to deal with the high amount of fructose and remember that it's combined with glucose which will also cause your pancreas to produce insulin. Is it any wonder that many heavy fruit juice drinking people become more and more insulin-resistant, unfortunately leading to Type-2 diabetes[134] and to weight-gain.

You know that the ghrelin hormone decreases after you've eaten and the leptin hormone increases after you've eaten. *Non-fruit* fructose[135], which has added sugar and little or no fiber, actually leads to *higher* ghrelin (hunger) levels and *lower* leptin (full) levels hence it creates more hunger than does glucose alone. It's almost as though your body doesn't seem to recognize non-fruit fructose as sugar! Normally eating a bit of natural fruit-based fructose is

---

[134] The one where you have to take pills, usually not insulin injections.

[135] Fructose found in fresh fruit is always combined with some fibre which slows the rate at which it's metabolized by your body. Fruit fructose is also combined with glucose and because those 2 sugars are linked together, they get sent to your intestines to be split up. Thus the arrival of fructose (not used for energy as is glucose) to your liver is slowed down a bit and that's good.

OK because of the fruit's fiber. Canned fruit and fruit juice have absolutely no fiber, hence, get converted into sugar extremely quickly. Indeed, my husband (a Type-1 diabetic) must drink a big glass of orange juice when he's experiencing extremely low blood sugar or is near comatose. My conclusion: don't drink a big glass of orange juice unless you're almost comatose or immobile. Having never been in that state, I never drink the stuff[136] and neither should you!

There's also the thermic or heat effect of food to consider. As mentioned earlier in the book, different foods go through different metabolic pathways in your body. The more efficient a metabolic pathway is, then more of the food's caloric energy is used for work by your body with less dissipated as heat. Protein pathways are far *less efficient* (losing many calories to heat) than those for either carbohydrate or fat. Put another way, protein requires much more heat energy to be metabolized than either carbohydrate or fat. A high-protein diet will boost your calorie-burning ability due to this *metabolic advantage.* So, if you like to eat sandwiches, you're better off eating a sandwich made from 100% whole grain bread, butter, cheddar cheese, lettuce and lean beef or chicken (whole food) than a heavily refined bread sandwich with margarine, processed cheese, sliced processed meat or turkey and a sandwich spread of some sort (again a processed food). You would burn more calories eating the metabolically advantaged first sandwich!

Protein is also the most fulfilling macronutrient, leading of course to a reduced appetite. You'll feel fuller from a protein meal with sweet potatoes, chicken, eggs, and beans than you will from a higher calorie one with pasta, cake and donuts. Protein takes longer than carbohydrate in order to be fully metabolized and, because it influences the brain's "full" hormonal signals, it keeps you feeling full for much longer which leads to less snacking. The nitrogen in protein also helps with protein synthesis.

Calories from healthy foods flow through your body easily as energy, maintaining a wonderful balance in your body. Calories from sugar or highly processed and overly refined foods affect your body's biochemistry by turning to fat in your liver and by keeping too much insulin in your bloodstream. When

---

[136] He was also told that a can of regular cola would do the trick as well. So to your body a can of sweet soda pop is *the very same* as a glass of orange juice in terms of quick blood glucose! 12 ounces of each contain 33 grams of sugar or about 8 (!!!) teaspoons of sugar. Holy cow!

insulin is hanging around you just can't lose weight by burning off body fat. And any new calories arriving just can't be burned off effectively, so you'll just get fatter and fatter and fatter. Guess what? You've become a fat-making engine. Nope, not good at all!!!

Like I said not all calories are equal; to your body a protein calorie is not the same as a carbohydrate calorie or a fat calorie or, for that matter, an alcohol calorie. When you eat, your digestive system completely takes over and *it decides* where the caloric energy will go. Not you, no matter what tricks you may try to employ. <u>You lost your power as soon as you swallowed the food.</u> Your body will decide what will be used for repair, for fueling, and what would be best used to fatten you. Your body's top priority is to rebuild anything that has broken down (yes, let's exercise and tear-down those muscle tissues) with some just used for the fueling of normal daily activity. With nutritious and consistent incoming calories, this will be easy. With little nutrient-dense food intake, your body will automatically resort to swiping energy from muscle and, in fear of starving to death in the future, it'll resort to storing calories as body fat!

Let's look at the potential effect of *moderate* caloric restriction on the percentage loss of both bulky body fat and lean muscle mass.

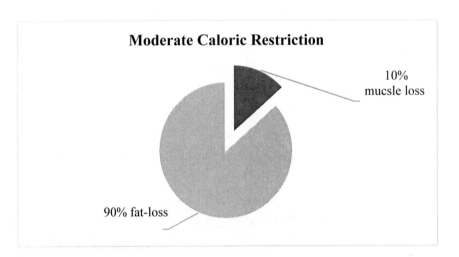

Now how about the woman who resorts to *severe* caloric restriction while camped out on Starvation Island. She'll certainly dump some fat, but she'll also lose a heck of a lot of muscle mass too.

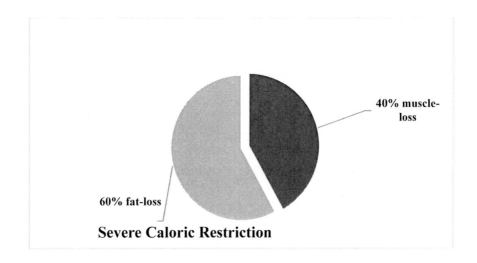

Severe Caloric Restriction

I don't think I want to loss that much muscle. My upper arm skin will be blowing in a high wind. And I'll have hurt my ability to burn calories efficiently by slowing down my metabolic rate. No way, I want muscle tone not muscle loss!!!

Now if your body is quickly bombarded with super-carbohydrate fast-to-glucose high-calorie foods, such as pasta and bread and sugar (think of that gigantic restaurant lasagna choice coupled with a plate of hot garlic bread), a huge pile of carbohydrate hits your body *all at the same time*. When this happens, it's just easier for your body to send it to fat-storage. Remember that your body will *always* take the easier route.

This doesn't mean that you should eat less (your body can always handle a lot of food), it just means that you should eat more nutritious foods – foods that fill you up without dumping glucose into your bloodstream too quickly for your body to deal with – as well as foods that trigger your brain to say, "that's enough food for now!" Your body loves a lot good food – food that allows it to hear its signaling hormones. But it doesn't like *too much* glucose all at once! Hence, your body loves highly nutritious foods and hates overly processed foods.

With highly efficient metabolic pathways
(as with simple quick-to-sugar and super-carbohydrate foods),
far less energy is being dissipated as heat[137].
If you aren't exercising much then get ready for some extra body fat for
storage.
Protein requires a lot of energy to be metabolized
(remember that arduous 5-step process to convert protein into glucose)
and so it's far less efficient than either carbohydrates or fat,
hence, it'll leave you feeling fuller for longer as it's being slowly digested.

Sure, you can say that a calorie burned is a calorie burned, <u>but</u> a calorie eaten sure isn't a calorie eaten! Yup, not all calories are equal to your body.

2.20 What Is Glycogen?

"The distinction between past, present and future is only an illusion, however persistent." – A.E.

Your body gets its energy by burning off the glucose in your bloodstream and using the energy from the stored glucose in your liver and muscle tissues. As mentioned from earlier perspectives, this carbohydrate form of stored energy is called *glycogen*. Starch (stored energy in plants) and glycogen (stored energy in you) are both strings of glucose sugar molecules. When your body needs energy, its stored glycogen can be easily hydrolyzed back into glucose energy. The breaking down of glycogen is a chemical reaction and it needs water to do so; yet another reason to keep yourself well hydrated. *After all of that glycogen depletion and as the next resort*, it'll then burn your body fat.

Your body will burn glycogen for energy before tackling body fat. Drink a lot of alcohol, soda pop or fruit juice and you'll be growing body fat. Eat a

---

[137] You will recall that when you control your thermogenesis (heat production), you'll lower your blood sugars, lower your fat-making tendencies and increase your calorie-burning abilities. Higher thermogenesis also controls your cortisol stress hormone production, hence increasing your thermogenesis will always be good for increasing your metabolic rate and for controlling your overall weight.

lot of quick-to-sugar processed simple carbohydrates and you'll be even more inefficient at burning that body fat.

Because your body always prefers to burn carbohydrates for energy, is desperate to hang on to as much fat as it can, and needs oxygen to create energy, this is precisely why an *unfit treadmiller* will burn up their muscle tissue fast. It's easier for their body to grab that stored glycogen energy from their muscles then it is to breakdown their body fat tissue, and your body will always take the easiest route. It wants to conserve its stores. Keep going down that road and you too will have poor skin tone and little muscle. Just look at those people huffing and puffing on the treadmills and you'll see toneless[138] skin hanging from their arms and saggy skin on their backs[139].

And keep in mind that it's really hard to build up muscle mass, but easy to lose it. And it's easy to accumulate body fat, but really hard to lose it.

When sleeping your body will use stored glycogen for energy, and so when you eat in the morning, you'll top up those depleted glycogen reserves first. I like to exercise *before* eating breakfast in order to use up my liver-based glycogen storage and then move into fat-burning right away by weight-lifting and then jumping on the stair-climber to kill the fatty-acids that were freed up. Some people like to eat breakfast before exercise and then use up that newly formed glycogen while exercising (so that it never goes to body fat storage). Whatever works for you is fine. I'm retired and so I can eat a later breakfast. If you're hitting the gym before work, it might be simpler to eat a healthy breakfast before hitting the weights. Actually, you should try both approaches over a couple of weeks, to see what works best for your timelines, as well as track your fat- and weight-loss.

---

[138] One of my draft book readers complained that I was displaying a major bias against toneless arms…well yah, I didn't want them and I bet you don't either. That's why I'm pointing out what *causes* them and how you can *get rid* of them.

[139] Yes, I know; I'm certain you can see my treadmill bias, but this book's target market isn't the physically fit marathon runner with fabulous endurance and incredible oxidative abilities. Rather, it's written for the physically unfit overweight woman who wants to lose weight, to lose body-fat and to get toned, especially in the arms. Elite marathon runners aren't trying to build muscle and indeed most don't have huge muscles and are quite sinewy; rather, they train for running for a very very long time without stopping. Just imagine running 42 km (26.2 miles) in under 2 hours!!!

2.21 What Is the Glycemic Index?

"Insanity is doing the same thing over and over and expecting different results."

I do have to add that there is some ongoing controversy about whether Einstein actually said this. Regardless, it still is a great quote and it doesn't seem to be attributed to anyone else so I'm leaving it with him – my hero!!!

The glycemic index (GI) of food was actually created as a measurement to help you know how specific foods will affect your blood sugar levels, sort of a measure of the <u>freely available</u> sugar in a food. GI measures how *quickly* foods *raise* your blood sugar and then act like a roller coaster to your body's insulin and blood sugar levels. If a food has a high GI, then it raises your blood sugar level way too quickly, and then crashes it down in an effort to normalize your blood sugar leading to a craving for yet another high GI snack! The lower the GI score on a food, then the slower it gets converted into blood sugar/glucose and the effect on your blood sugar level is much more gradual, hence much more biochemically balanced. And, did you know that the glycemic effect of various foods uses glucose *sugar* as a reference point against which all other foods are compared (i.e., GI of glucose sugar = 100).

The first thing to remember is that all *refined carbohydrate*s are bad! They're always low in fiber. They get digested and absorbed way too quickly. These are the types of foods that always have a high glycemic index (GI). Foods with a high GI index number (70 or higher) should be eaten only occasionally. Foods with a medium GI index number (56-69) should be eaten only moderately. And foods at the lower end of the GI index (55 or lower) can be eaten freely. Obviously, knowing the GI scores of various foods is especially important to diabetics (both Type-1 and Type-2), as well as to pre-diabetics or insulin-resistant people.

A higher GI score normally means there's very little dietary fat or protein to slow down the carbohydrate absorption. A crazy counter-intuitive example is ice cream. Because it has fat in it, it has a GI score like an apple. Who would have guessed that? Because fat doesn't spike insulin or blood sugar levels, then the GI score of full-fat ice cream is kept lower[140]. In actual fact, the fat in the ice cream has slowed the digestion time allowing insulin to be introduced into your bloodstream much more slowly. Of course, I'm not suggesting that you eat an ice cream cone in place of an apple! As usual you have to maintain some common sense when you're eating to lose body fat and/or wanting to gain lean muscle weight/tissue.

> **High GI foods create roller-coaster blood sugar levels,**
> **an insulin increase and more body fat for storage.**

If you're measuring the GI index scores of various foods, obviously all sugars will score very high and should be avoided. All sugars raise your blood glucose rapidly to a level that is *far too high*, and then drop it rapidly to a level that is *far too low*. This upsets your body's balanced biochemical and hormonal states. If you've driven your blood sugars up and then down, your body wants *more food* to bring your blood sugar level back up to normal. And it doesn't care how many calories you've eaten; it's *only* interested in re-balancing its hormonal environment. Again, I'll stress that only you can control your food choices. Be smart and believe your body. Once you swallow any food or drink, you've passed control over to your body and it has very firm decision rules and irrefutable metabolic pathways.

Unfortunately measuring things on the GI scale can become quite frustrating. One of the reasons this is true is because you can't assume that all similar types of foods register the same GI index score! Rice is an interesting example. Based on the availability of particular starches to your body, different types of rice will show a *wide difference* in GI index scores. Basmati rice will score medium (GI 57), soft jasmine rice will score quite high (68-80) and white rice will score extremely high (GI 83). Basmati rice is high in amylose[141]

---

[140] And if you think that the sneaky food industry doesn't know this fact and ultimately use it to advertise some foods as low GI (not mentioning the high-fat content), well like I say in another chapter, I have some great Florida swampland you might like to consider.

[141] Amylose is a form of energy storage, a starch *with linear or straight chain glucose units,* although not as many as with amylopectin.

starch[142], which has less effect on blood sugar than the amylopectin[143] starch found in both jasmine and white rice.

Another troublesome feature is that the GI for some foods can actually be affected by *how* you cook them, strange as that may sound[144]. Let's take a cup of carrots as an example. Carrots have a GI of 16 when raw, dicing the same amount increases their GI to 35 (more surface area to attack) and boiling them further increases their GI to 49! A cup of raw, sliced carrots contain 11.7 grams of carbohydrate, while these same boiled and drained carrots contain 12.8 grams of carbohydrate. This isn't particularly high, but I mention it only to show you that *how* you cook your food affects the GI of the food and your resultant carbohydrate intake. And of course it's harder for your body to digest raw carrots than cooked carrots and this lowers their GI counts. Yeah for inefficiency!

And then there are the red potatoes that I like. When you boil them, their GI is at about 73. But if you take those SAME boiled red potatoes and put them into the refrigerator to cool down (let's say for a potato salad), their GI drops to 56! 73 is in the high GI range, while 56 is in the medium GI range. What the heck happened to these potatoes? How could this occur when the food is exactly the same (except for its temperature)? Well to your body the hot and cold potatoes are not the same when digested. Yup, and here we go again where your body is in control of whatever you decide to eat. When you heat the potatoes, their starch granules absorb water, and this changes the *structure* of the starch making it more efficiently digestible (into sugar). If these same hot boiled potatoes are then cooled, their molecules bond in an *irregular geometry*

---

[142] Starch is a polysaccharide (large polymers with thousands of monosaccharides joined together).

[143] Amylopectin is also a form of energy storage, a starch with *branched chain glucose units – with a higher molecular weight than amylose (having between 2,000 and 200,000 glucose units).* And remember that amylopectin-A is the most highly digestible form of branched chain glucose and it's found in breads (hence my term *super-carbohydrate* bread). Also, white potatoes have almost 80% amylopectin and only about 20% amylose which is why it's better to eat sweet potatoes which have less amylopectin at about 65%. Interestingly, cooked white potatoes that have been cooled also have less amylopectin than the warm just-cooked ones.

[144] European Journal of Clinical Nutrition (2005) 59, 1266-1271.

(i.e., the shape and relative arrangements of molecules change) making them much more difficult for your enzymes to break down.

This means that the cooled molecules are more resistant to quick digestion/absorption. Although all of their molecules and their final nutrients are *still there*, they're simply *bonded* differently. This rationale for the GI change is true for all potatoes, although sweet potatoes and yams have comparatively lower GI counts all round due to lower amylopectin levels. Now, of course, if you decide as a result to only eat potatoes that are in a cold salad, do be careful with the mayonnaise, bacon, etc. when creating a recipe! Try using healthy ingredients such as hard-boiled eggs, plain Greek yogurt, Dijon mustard, olives, radishes, green onions, etc. But on the plus side, when potatoes *are combined* with the right amounts of dietary protein and fat and fiber their GI level will be mitigated for sure. Maybe eat some grilled chicken or shrimp with those high GI potatoes.

Given the many disparate factors that can influence the GI of a particular food, you'll soon discover that it's extremely difficult to calculate an *exact* GI for the meal on your plate, a meal that will probably be a combination of many different foods.

Some rather confusing factors that will always affect the GI of foods include the following:

- the *ripeness* of the fruit (riper = higher GI)
- the *physical form* of the food (applesauce has a 25% higher GI than a raw apple)
- the proportion of *different carbohydrate starches* in a particular food (e.g., amylose, a slowly digested carbohydrate, versus amylopectin, a rapidly digested carbohydrate)
- the *shape* of the food such as pasta (macaroni at GI 68 and spaghetti[145] at GI 45, thick linguine at GI 68 and thin linguini at GI 87)
- the *degree of processing* and the methods used wherein the more processed the higher the GI; highly refined white bread registers 73, while pumpernickel bread is only 46

---

[145] Macaroni is not an extruded pasta, whereas spaghetti is made under an extrusion process and this gives it a lower GI number. During extrusion, the pasta dough is pressed through a sieve instrument using really high pressure.

- *preparation methods* can change GIs (e.g., the amount of heat and water used in cooking, the time of the cooking, the sizes of the chopped food particles before cooking wherein smaller pieces with their increased surface area will cause the GI to rise)
- the *type of sugar* in a food can affect its GI; glucose and corn syrup register 100 (the highest possible), sucrose 65, and polyol (a low-calorie synthetic sweetener) is below 50
- the *fat content* in foods affects GI because fat slows the absorption of carbohydrate; an example is French-fried versus baked potatoes. French-fried potatoes have fat (GI 75), while baked potatoes don't (GI 85) unless you add it after the baking with cheese and sour cream and butter (but of course, the baked potato is certainly better for you in terms of nutrition and for the avoidance of omega-6 acid-forming fatty-acids)
- *acidity* affects GI values; acid, like fat, slows the carbohydrate absorption rate (this is why lemon juice and vinegar are good for you)
- *protein* affects GI values; it delays absorption, which is always great for your over-worked liver
- *fiber* affects GI by slowing digestion and decreasing fast absorption
- and finally, just imagine a *mixed meal?* High glycemic and low glycemic foods mixed on a plate will change the total GI level of the whole meal.

Now you can better appreciate how difficult it is to figure out the actual glycemic index of a meal. There's also a proliferation of mystifying terms used by the food industry for foods and their effects on the amount of absorbed carbohydrate and the resulting effect on your blood sugar/glucose.

Some of these *carbohydrate labels* include the following:

- Glycemic index (between 1-100)
- Glycemic load[146] (between 1 – 20+)

---

[146] The glycemic load (GL) is an alternative to the GI concept. It measures the amount of available carbohydrate grams in a **normal food serving** multiplied by that particular food's GI. This makes the GL of a food directly related to *the weight of the food*. Still,

- Zero (no carbohydrate absorption)
- Net[147] (total grams of carbohydrate *minus* total grams of fiber; that's how important fiber is!!!)
- Slow (amount of carbohydrate absorbed)
- Complex (slow absorption) versus simple (fast absorption)
- Digestible (absorbed) versus undigestible (not absorbed)
- Available (absorbed), bioavailable (absorbed) versus unavailable (not absorbed)

I just find it much simpler and less confusing to eat "complex" carbohydrates (starches) instead of "simple" carbohydrates (sugars). Look for what's sometimes termed "slow" carbohydrate or "net" carbohydrate. That's a very useful measurement. If the package doesn't list it, then you can do your own subtraction – **total carbohydrate grams less fiber grams = "net" carbohydrates**. You'll always see carbohydrate and fiber grams listed.

And here we go again, nothing is simple. Believe it or not M&Ms have a relatively low GI while watermelon has a high GI! This illustrates a major flaw in GI measurements, because certainly you shouldn't be eating a lot of candy and avoiding fruits like watermelon. And let's face it, although cooked carrots have a high GI, you'd have to eat a heck of a lot of them to get a lot of carbohydrate, maybe even 1-2 pounds of them! I doubt you'd ever do that. The problem with the GI measurement is that it doesn't consider realistic serving sizes and that's where the GL or glycemic "load" measurement becomes more useful. Just go to the internet to check out GI, GL and food weights when tracking this sort of thing. When you do this, you'll see examples such as these:

---

as with GI, the lower the GL, then the lower the resulting blood sugar spike. Low GL foods have a GL value of 10 or less; moderate GL foods are between 11-19; and, high GL foods will run 20 or higher. If you're trying to lose weight, the GL measurement is a more accurate way to estimate the effect of any given food on your blood sugar level than is the GI measurement.

[147] This is a good measure as total carbohydrate counts include fibre, but because fibre is not broken down and does not affect your blood sugar level, it should be subtracted.

- pearled barley grain (GI 36 – very low) versus cornmeal (GI 98 – very high)
- whole fat milk (GI 39) versus skim milk (GI 46)
- a pear (GI 38 – fairly low) versus a banana[148] (GI 55 – medium)
- All-Bran (GI 60 – medium) versus shredded wheat (GI 99 – extremely high)
- Fettucine (GI 46) versus brown rice pasta (GI 100 – wowie – who'd thought that?)
- Wheat crackers (GI 90 – very high) versus rice cakes (GI 100 – the highest count)
- Cabbage (GI less than 20 – extremely low) versus sweet corn (GI 78 – quite high)

OK, let's get back to that M&Ms versus fresh watermelon decision. Peanut M&Ms may have a lower GI than watermelons, but they actually have a similar GL. So with that choice, it's watermelon for me. The makers of M&Ms don't tell you that; they say that you can eat a handful of low-GI peanut M&Ms guilt-free but it's really only low because of the low GI of peanuts! Check out this chart and look at some of the differences between GL and GI counts.

FOOD in a reasonable proportion	Glycemic Load GL count	Glycemic Index GI count
Pita (1, 65g)	22 (quite high)	57 (medium)
Jasmine Rice (1 cup, 180g)	42.5 (very high)	109 (really high)
White spaghetti (1 cup, 180g)	52 (very high)	92 (really high)
Full-fat Ice Cream scoop (50g)	6.1 (low)	61 (medium)
Orange (1 med,130g)	4.4 (really low)	44 (low)
Apple (1 med, 150g)	6.8 (low)	39 (low)
Dried dates (5, 40 g.)	27.8 (quite high)	103 (really high)
Watermelon (1 cup, 150g)	5.7 (low)	72 (high)
M&Ms (1 pack, 1.7 oz)	6 (low – due to peanuts)	33 (surprisingly low)

---

[148] Lots of women eat a ton of bananas for the potassium content. That's fine; but for me, I avoid them due to their GI 55 carbohydrate count and their fairly hefty 18 GL count.

Raw Carrots (1/2 cup, 70g)	1.5 (really low)	49 (low-medium)
Honey (1/2 tbsp,10g)	4.6 (low)	58 (medium)
Maltose (2 tsp, 10g)	10.5 (low-medium)	105 (really high)

Clearly all of this can be quite overwhelming. Suffice it to say that if you eat as suggested below, that will work for weight-loss:

- Eat fresh vegetables and fresh fruits, not canned ones or juices.
- Eat more beans, chickpeas, kidney beans and lentils.
- Omit refined (white) and processed foods.
- Make your own salad dressing using extra virgin olive oil, vinegar or lemon juice and mustard.

Better yet, practice common sense with your food choices and portions.

2.22 Is There Anything Good About Fasting?

"If you want to live a happy life, tie it to a goal, not to people or things." – A.E.

I've never suggested anything to my clients nor would I within this book, unless I've tried it out on myself first. Fasting *can work* if your body gets its macronutrients and fiber and you don't end up messing up your metabolic rate with Starvation Island pilgrimages. There are a number of choices for fasting. There's *alternate day fasting* where you eat in an unrestricted way one day and the next day you don't eat at all or you eat very small amounts of what you might normally eat (I've never tried this diet approach and think it doesn't sound healthy or sustainable, at least for me). And then there's *modified fasting or the 5:2 fasting* where you eat normally for five days and then greatly restrict your food intake to as low as 500-600 calories for two days (again never tried it and not up my alley). Or how about "water fasting" – all I can say is OMG!!!

But another type of fasting is a *time-restricted* type of eating wherein you only eat during specific times. I find this approach best matches my arguments for biochemical and hormonal body health. And it was successful for me, though I didn't stay on it longer than a few weeks at a time. It's well described in a book titled "The 8-Hour Diet." This would be a 16:8-hour approach and there's no crazy trips to Starvation Island. Basically, you can eat whatever you want within an 8-hour period, *within reason of course* and in line with your overall weight-loss goals. Obviously, you're not going to maintain a fast metabolism by eating bagels, drinking diet soda pop and eating a lot of fruit.

This way of dieting has you eating real[149] nutrient-dense foods and *as much as you wish*. Such foods fill you up and so you just can't over-eat them such as you can with heavily processed non-nutritious *higher calorie* foods. Real foods are not heavily processed, are not laced with sugar, and are free from additives and other artificially created substances such as trans-fats and HFCS. But you must only eat these foods within a specified 8-hour "eating" window. You can choose the 8 hours that best match your lifestyle. For me I stopped eating at about 7 pm in the evening and started again at about 11 am the next day. I was sleeping for part of the fasting time so that made it easier. I had a morning coffee with some milk when I woke up and then went to the gym, drank branched chain amino-acid proteins (BCAAs)[150] while there, and then kept myself busy until 11 am. This can be reading, food shopping, paper-pushing at the office, watering plants or whatever you normally do in the early morning. My coffee milk and BCAAs are not really allowed outside of the 8-hour eating period on this diet as they broke my fast too early, but I needed my morning coffee and I needed my workout protein/amino-acids.

By 11 am I would have cleared much of the stored glycogen energy from my liver which would help me to start burning fat. Yes, I was hungry by 11 am.; but, let's face it, isn't it great to eat when you actually *are* hungry!

Fasting is also interesting in terms of your hormones. Remember that all of your hormones and their activities are *completely controlled* by what you eat. During the sleeping phase, you are (or should be) fasting. Getting up in the middle of the night to eat is not good for your body as it triggers the fat-making insulin hormone and interrupts protein synthesis, as well as the production of other hormones. For example, your body produces the human growth hormone

---

[149] I heard a funny comment: "If your grandmother doesn't recognize something as food, don't eat it."

[150] Visit a local health food store for a workout powder and make sure it has BCAAs in it. There are many brands and lots of flavourful choices. I also mix some hydrolyzed collagen into my workout drink; it provides low molecular weight protein that's very rapidly absorbed, helping to regulate my metabolism and support muscle repair. BTW, it's the same collagen that is found in bones, joints and cartilage.

(HGH), a hormone that *builds muscle tissue,* only during *deep sleep.* Ever wonder why newborns sleep as much as 16 hours per day?

Normally your body will switch to fat-burning about 2 hours after you go to sleep and it'll stay in that mode for 12 hours if you don't eat or until you eat, and it's great for cell repair and anti-aging as well. This may be why "The 8-hour Diet" works as well as it does. This is another one of the reasons why I don't eat breakfast until after my morning workout, whether I'm on the 16-hour fast or not.

Most people start eating from the moment they rise until the moment they go to bed, with some getting up in the middle of the night to eat! When you *never* give your digestive system a rest, your liver and other organs are over-working. They never get a break to replenish themselves. And we now know that your liver is in desperate need of daily rest periods.

Is fasting the same as a *crash* diet? You may believe that an 8-hour diet will translate into the same result with your body (i.e., your body will store fat in response to periods of starvation). Standard starvation and low-calorie and non-carbohydrate dieting *deprives* your body of the necessary amounts of some nutrients hence, it'll go into major biochemical and hormonal panic. It'll reduce the production of your leptin hormone (which suppresses appetite) and increase the production of the ghrelin hormone (the one that makes you hungry). It'll also slow down your metabolic rate, making it more catabolic or breakdown in nature (versus muscle-building anabolic). You want to eat because your body wants to store fuel. It's your hormonal system that signals hunger[151]. When you give in to that hunger during a crash diet, your body stores the calories as fat because it believes food is scarce and it might be a long time before you eat; hence, it wants to pack you up with *easy-to-store, slow-to-burn body fat.*

Intermittent 8-hour fasting is *not* based on nutrient deprivation! Your body activates plenty of fat-burning on this diet. So, with this approach, you can lower your overall weight simply by *changing your eating schedule.* This sort of intermittent eating still allows your body to burn body fat. "Crash" diets tend to breakdown muscle tissue for energy (to get at the stored glycogen)

---

[151] Real hunger is a signal and that signal will not diminish as will a craving, it'll get stronger. Hunger is a chemical reaction resulting from the fact that your metabolism did not get the amino acids, fatty acids, enzymes and carbohydrates it needs in order to complete its job.

which in turn slows down your metabolic rate, causing you to be fatter after completion of the diet then when you when you started on the diet (i.e., a higher body fat percentage).

That said, I wouldn't suggest staying on this 8-hour diet forever. As with any diet or exercise program, it's always best to *surprise your body* by shaking it up a bit but not enough to cause hormonal panic-ville. Whenever you hit a weight-loss plateau, it's time to try something else (and that notion pertains to exercising as well).

During my years as a personal trainer, the term we used for those women (and it's usually women who do this) who ate very little, drank tons of water and just jumped on the treadmill at the gym was "skinny-fat." Yes, I admired their time commitment but I felt badly because their approach to loosing body fat was just not efficient. Sure, they may not appear "fat" to you but if a personal trainer completed an analysis of their body fat percentage it would be relatively high because they have very little muscle tissue. Look more carefully at these dedicated treadmill runners the next time you're at the gym. Bet you see those jiggly undefined soft upper arms and untoned skin on their backs!!! Then look at the women on the gym floor, the ones using the free weights. They're *not* jiggly. Certainly, they'll do some cardiovascular/aerobic exercise during or after their workout routines, but it'll probably only constitute between 10-15% of their gym time over the week. Some will do 10-15 minutes of cardio after every daily workout; others will devote one workout day only to cardio and they'll do it at a slow-to-medium steady pace for at least an hour. And it usually isn't the treadmill; it'll be the stair-climber, stepper, stationary bike or rowing machine. These all involve compound, multiple-joint movements, hence they also challenge larger muscle groups.

Most of the women I trained were always seeking toned arms, ones that did not sag. Well, of course, as stated elsewhere in this book you can't spot-reduce your arms. I remember when I got myself a personal trainer, I too said I wanted to tone up my arms, then I added that I doubted he could arrange that – after all I was 60! His response, "yes, I <u>can</u> tone up your arms!" And he did, well <u>actually I did</u> while following his workout instructions. Don't give your trainer the kudos for your new body. YOU are using the tools and knowledge base s/he shares with you, but <u>you're the one doing the work</u> and reaping the results. You're the one who should be patted on the back!!!

After training a lot of older women and doing body tissue analyses on them, asking them how they exercised, how they normally ate and how much water they drank, I found that I could actually tell a lot by just looking at their upper arms *before* meeting with them. In general, I found that I could categorize three different types of problems by just visually studying their upper arms before formally conducting any tissue analyses.

If someone had big arms, then it was an indication of *too much fat on them*. Their upper arms were quite wide and they squished *out away* from their body when pushed toward the sides of their body. This usually meant that the woman was overweight and had a really high body fat content. Even though some women with big arms had strong underlying muscles, those muscles just couldn't be seen as they lived beneath many layers of fatty tissue.

If someone had sagging arms, then it was a strong indication of *reduced calorie dieting or fasting without much effective exercising*. The faster the weight-loss, the worse the excess skin and resultant sagging.

If someone had soft arms which were not necessarily big or saggy, but rather, lacked the outline of the arm muscles, it meant that there was no tone, no firmness and no muscle definition[152]. Tone only occurs when you can see the outline of the muscles. These women reside in the "skinny-fat" world and it has a name - sarcopenic obese. Skinny-fat people seem lean and appear slim, but if you touch their skin, you will sink into fat and not feel the firmness of muscle. Usually their overall body weight is OK for their height, but they have *a relatively high percentage of body fat* tissue and have soft muscle tissue. Soft arms (and doughy tummies) are usually the result of *reduced calorie diets or heavy fasting, very little weight/resistance training coupled with an over-reliance on muscle-wasting cardio exercise.*[153]

---

[152] Muscle "definition" is called "toned" by women, and "defined," "jacked," "ripped," "cut" or "shredded" by men. Like I said earlier in the book, maybe tougher words, but with the very same meaning and aesthetically-pleasing outcome!!!

[153] You should be physically fit to use cardio equipment as a fat-burning exercise (and not a muscle-eating exercise). I'll talk a lot about this important concept later on in the book.

When your body gets proper nutrient-dense foods regardless of intermittent fasting,
it will use all of those nutrients
and will be far less likely to store them as body fat.

2.23 What About "Junk" Food and "Fast" Food?

"Stay away from negative people. They have a problem for every solution." – A.E.

What are these foods? And how might they hinder your fat-burning capability? The Oxford Dictionary describes junk-food as "pre-prepared or packaged food that has *low nutritional* value" and fast-food as "easily prepared *processed* foods served in snack bars and restaurants as a quick meal or to be taken away." The Merriam-Webster Dictionary defines junk-food as "food that is not good for your health because it contains *high amounts of fat or sugar*" and fast-food as something "designed for ready availability, use, or consumption and with *little consideration given to quality* or significance."

> *Summary no matter where you look for a definition:*
> *"Junk" = NO nutritional value and with HIGH fat and/or sugar.*
> *"Fast" = PROCESSED and with LITTLE quality.*

None of this sounds good, does it? Let's face the facts, it isn't *real* food if it comes through your car window! Unless you're ordering a salad (and who should be eating that while driving a car?), any "food" passed to you through the window of your car is either junk-food or fast-food. As an example, let's explore those get-'em-from-a-window French fries. Did you know that many fast-food fries have sugar!!! Whaaat? Yup they do and that's why they taste so darn good. The potatoes are par cooked in hot water or steam, which actually removes the excess sugars. But during further processing, a dextrose solution is added in order to give the potatoes a more uniform golden appearance. Now for those of us who actually understand that *dextrose is just another corn-based sugar*, fast-food places would probably say that their fries are OK because dextrose is only about 2/3's as sweet as table sugar! But I say to that, "so what?" Who cares how sweet it is; we don't know how much they use and it's still sugar to your I-can-never-be-fooled body! It's really sort of weird that the food industry decreases the amount of natural sugar, and then ends up adding some. Like I said earlier, **sometimes weight gain isn't all your fault** when you don't actually know what the industry is doing to the foods you choose to eat.

Obviously, the *flavor* in fast-food fries is mostly from potatoes and oil and not from the added sugar. But now I'm wondering *what kind of oil* is being used. You guessed it; some of it is *hydrogenated* soybean oil and this is one of the worst kinds of fat. An industrially produced trans-fat is much worse for your body than is a natural *saturated* fat. And remember that soybean oil is very high in omega-6 inflammation-causing and acid-forming fatty-acids which no one in North America needs more of. And acidity always leads to extra body fat cells, a compromised fat-burning oxidative ability, and the over-production of toxic free radicals. Yikes, what a mess!

But I digress. Let's get back to junk- and fast-foods. Any "food" that has a long shelf-life, like potato chips, is always a very highly processed junk-food. Let's do a quick review of how the food industry produces those potato chips. OK, they do cook the potatoes (and they are potatoes – yeah!), mash and dehydrate them before refining them into a flour. Actually, they may even add some corn and wheat starches, ending up with a mixed flour base. The second stage is to squeeze the resultant flour dough mixture through some differently shaped machine slots with high pressure in order to get the shape of potato chip you want (e.g., with ripples). The chip remains at this point, only partially cooked. These half-cooked chips are then dried and passed through a continuous frying machine to provide a rapid and consistently even cooking. After shaking the cooked potato chips of any excess oil, they're sprayed and sprinkled with fake flavorings[154] and other synthetic additives. Finally, those chips arrive at the packaging area. Believe me, such overly processed foods are almost *always high* in useless calories, sugar and bad trans-fats, not to mention salt, and they're extremely low in nutrients and fibers. Bye-bye calorie-burning, hello fat-making.

---

[154] The food industry even runs contests to get consumers to think up of different flavour combinations for them to apply. Some successful submissions include maple/bacon, poutine, jalapeno, grilled cheese/tomato soup, etc. Do you really think you're eating <u>any</u> real cheese with that last one? No way, it'll be a chemically created flavour.

Any "food" item boasting a long shelf-life will not present a high nutritional value to your very discerning body.

And, if you think you're always eating the real deal, consider that many chain restaurants (and grocery stores) don't really do much of the cooking or baking. Many receive dough ready-made for their ovens, and that's it. I used to get warm "fresh sourdough" bread for special occasions at my grocery store's bakery. Then, only because I asked the guy behind the bakery counter, I learned that the bread dough arrives partially baked and frozen and they just thaw it and fling it into the oven on an as-needed basis. People love to buy warm bread, right? Wow, I was so disappointed, though I suppose I shouldn't have been so surprised.

Another example would be chicken nugget-type food. These are usually processed at some factory plant. That plant will marinate the chicken (yes, of course there will be *some* real chicken there), season it, add "stuff" to it (e.g., corn and other fillers[155], synthetic flavorings, etc.) and then cook it, freeze it and send it off to some distribution warehouse. In turn that frozen-food warehouse will deliver those nuggets to a restaurant or cafeteria or school, where they'll be re-heated and united with some sort of sugary sauce from some *other* industrial processor, placed on a *non-100%* whole grain bun which was *partially baked* in yet another factory. Well I guess we could find *some* positives; at least we've created lots of jobs.

Now the restaurant or pub or cafeteria or bar or school or grocery store "bakery" can say it has "freshly baked" buns, "real chicken" nuggets, etc. But where are the real kitchens and who is actually planning the food? Guess what? It may be industrial factories and big laboratories. Do you really know what you're eating when you step out of your own kitchen? I would suggest not! In fact, for the informed knowledgeable person, eating out can be downright scary! So, you should keep in mind, if you or your unsuspecting grandchild eat at a fast-food chain, you won't just be getting what you thought you ordered. You could also be eating any or all of the following: modified starch, salt,

---

[155] Food fillers are used to help bulk up the weight of a food, and by using less expensive ingredients, then the price to the food industry drops. Examples of fillers include: Monosodium Glutamate (MSG – also called "hydrolyzed vegetable protein"), sodium nitrate, guar gum (a sugar), HFCS (fructose), synthetic sweeteners, carrageenan (causes inflammation) and sodium benzoate.

yeast, wheat starch, synthetic flavorings, dextrose, HFCS, citric acid, sodium phosphates, bleached wheat flour, yellow corn flour, corn oil, hydrogenated soybean oil, trans-fats, etc. All I can say is, *wow*! Your hormones are waiting and they'll make valiant efforts to keep balanced.

When we look at the average North American now compared to those in the 1960s, we see many more overweight and morbidly obese individuals. Even kindergarten children are struggling with obesity! How can a 5-year-old be obese? It's really hard to force feed a child! Even though many of them are less active than years ago, still it just doesn't make any sense to me. How can so many young children become fat-making bodies in such a short time period. When I was young, you hardly ever saw an obese child. They were calorie-burning because they ate unadulterated nutritious foods *and* they were always outside exercising through play. Remember when you were free to play with all your neighborhood friends – using skipping ropes, playing hide-and-seek and riding bicycles all over the place? The only rule was to be back home when the streetlights came on. Even the dogs ran all over without leashes – of course, not on garbage days. Yes, I know that times are different now, but really, do we have to give our children *and ourselves* non-nutritious high-calorie foods so frequently. And should we place them in front of the TV or with an iPad all the time?

There used to be "juvenile" diabetes (where insulin injections are required) and "adult-onset" diabetes (treated orally with pills[156]). Guess what? They had to change the names simply because there were *so many children* who were being diagnosed with adult-onset diabetic metabolic disease! So now we have Type-1 diabetes (treated with insulin) and Type-2 diabetes (normally treated with pills). Children can fall into either group. In fact, rates of Type-2 diabetes in children are continuing to climb, though it wasn't even seen 35 years ago. Type-2 diabetes is the result of an insulin-resistance problem in a body, so my bet is that these children are seldom eating nutrient-dense foods and are probably eating a lot of fast-foods and pre-packaged foods. When you see a

---

[156] What do these pills do? Generally, Type-2 diabetes medications work to improve the sensitivity of body tissues to your insulin hormone so that your body uses that insulin more effectively. Some pills stimulate the production of insulin, while others lower blood glucose levels. Some Type-2s take combinations of pills. I believe that many Type-2s and pre-diabetics can reverse their insulin-resistance direction by changing their diets and by exercising with weights.

pre-school child with upper arms and/or upper legs that are noticeably bigger than the lower parts of their arms/legs and with little muffin tops, they have too much body fat and will be overweight and headed down this path! I just find it so sad.

People don't realize how much sugar they're actually eating or unfortunately
how much they're allowing their kids to eat,
especially when frequenting fast-food restaurants.
There's just too much sugar in everything and this affects insulin-sensitivity.

As I've mentioned, my husband is a "Type-1" diabetic and this makes it really easy to realize that we've eaten a whack of sugar. What we discovered was that we can no longer eat at Asian or Mexican or Thai restaurants, even though they're not traditionally considered *fast-food* places. His sugar levels spiked extremely high after those meals and that can <u>only</u> be the result of hidden sugars. He also has to avoid any sauces or gravies at most restaurants, as they cause glucose/sugar spikes like crazy! It never looks like sugar, and sugar isn't listed on the menu, but those foods are usually full of it in some form or another! Because this is so prevalent, I've devoted a subsequent chapter to the problem of high amounts of "hidden" or "dishonest" sugar in foods. If you want a calorie-burning body, avoid fast-food joints until you reach your fat-loss goal. If you must go for some reason then choose a salad. I have to say that I've always found Wendy's salads to be great.

2.24 What Makes Sugar So Bad for Me?

"The ones who are crazy enough to think they can change the world are the ones who do." – A.E.

Everyone knows sugar isn't the best thing to eat and I'll bet that you try your best to avoid it. Keep in mind that it doesn't matter whether the sugar you eat is organic or not, white or brown, your body still must deal with it and deal with it in the *very same way* it's programmed to do. But why is sugar so bad for your body? And are you *really* that effective at avoiding it?

Because sugar affects your body in a uniquely different way than other carbohydrates do, you really need a better understanding of what happens to sugar in your body. Once you understand how your body makes and stores body fat from the perspective of sugar, then you'll see why you must be ever-vigilant at side-stepping it. Many medical doctors believe that sugar triggers many of the diseases typically associated with obesity, including Type-2 diabetes, as well as stroke and high blood pressure. In fact, some say that sugar slowly kills you and that sounds like a pretty serious indictment to me![157]

Also, when you think of eating sugar, consider the fact that there's *no physiological requirement* for your body to even have sugar. Indeed, all the different nutritional needs of your body can be met with other foods. Even though this is true, just like those Romans we do have a natural liking of sweet-tasting foods.

There's no physiological reason to eat sugar.
It produces unhealthy changes in your cholesterol and triglyceride fat levels.

Why control your blood sugar level? Because if you let it get too high OR too low, it'll dramatically *detract* from your ability to burn body fat and to control your appetite. Both high <u>and</u> low blood sugar will cause your body to say, "eat more" and while you're at it "make sure they're carbohydrates, I'm in a real hurry!" After all, we know that your body prefers to get its energy from carbohydrates and it's now low on glucose because either you ate too much sugar and it cleared its blood glucose to get ready for more sugar or you've been camped out on Starvation Island and are eating very little sugar (i.e., carbohydrates). The biochemical reaction making you *crave carbohydrates*, may be what you would expect from *low* blood sugar but probably the <u>reverse</u> to what you may have thought would happen when you have abnormally *high* blood sugar.

---

[157] Our dog's vet used to remind us that fat dogs kept him in business! I guess medical doctors can't put it that bluntly.

Sugar also produces many other changes in your biochemistry including the increase of both cholesterol[158] and triglyceride[159] fat levels. And some types of sugars (e.g., fructose) work hard at mimicking the insulin hormone, causing your liver to release excess fatty-acids into your bloodstream. You can try to spin it along many diverse hopes but in reality, fat production is *directly related* to your diet and *directly connected* to your liver. In terms of sugar, it really is very simple; eat a lot of it and you'll get a fatty liver.

Sugar can fall into two groups: "natural" sugars which are found in vegetables and fruits (both carbohydrates), and "refined" sugars which are processed by the food industry's laboratories (table sugar, candies, etc.) But sugar is in fact a *really extraordinary* carbohydrate biochemically. And unfortunately, it now accounts for far too many of all the calories North Americans normally eat and, shockingly, it's in 60-70% of all processed, low-fiber and heavily refined foods[160]. The sugar excess that you see in these heavily refined foods arrived with the creation of high fructose corn syrup (HFCS), a carefully built food industry product that has resulted in excessive North American sugar-eaters who unfortunately *don't even know* how much (hidden) sugar they're actually eating. But I still have to add that it's hard to decide whether that insidious HFCS or those horrible trans-fats are public health enemy #1 or #2, but you can be certain they're both in the top two!

***Non-fruit fructose** and the **industrially produced HFCS** both move directly to your liver for processing (not to your intestines as do other sugars).*

---

[158] Cholesterol is an oil or lipid-based fatty substance which does not mix well with your blood (a water-based substance). You need some of it but too much will always result in fatty deposits in your blood vessels.

[159] Triglycerides are a type of fat in your blood. Whenever you eat more than your body actually needs, it'll always convert the unused calories into blood triglycerides and *eventually* store them in your body-fat cells, making new ones if needed. Portion-control is *always* important in weight management.

[160] Of course, dietary sugar can be naturally occurring such as with fruit, vegetables and milk; but it can also have been added to foods and beverages to make them more tasty, etc. Bet you don't even know how much sugar you're eating. Did you know that one can of soda pop can have over 8 teaspoons of sugar!!! Yikes, that's a lot. Just imagine putting 8 spoons of white sugar/sucrose into your coffee…bet you'd gag on the sweetness. Still, you could drink that fructose-based soda pop in a flash!

Neither have any fiber whatsoever.
Most of the fructose sugar just gets moved into body fat cell storage.
It lowers your "I'm full" leptin hormone level and
increases your "I'm hungry" ghrelin hormone level.
Not a very good goal to pursue.

Your liver has lots and lots of options for excess glucose energy including glycogen storage tissues (especially with weight-training and muscle-building) but not much choice at all for excess fructose.

But why does your body treat fructose sugar so differently than either dextrose sugar (from corn) or sucrose sugar (from sugarcane)? Throughout evolution fructose *was always a very rare sugar* found only in natural honey and fresh whole fruits, hence your liver was *never used to getting a lot of it*. It simply never evolved a biochemical understanding of how to efficiently deal with a lot of fructose <u>all at once</u>. Your ancestors ate and enjoyed ripened fruit, with its built-in fiber, though certainly not all the time. Such naturally sweet fructose treats were normally found only in the late summer and early fall, and this timing would probably have helped with winter preparation due to the fat accumulation that resulted. Why do you think bears wolf down about 25,000 berries a day in late August and early September? They need to build-up a ton of body fat prior to hibernation.

Now, however, you can get that sweet fructose taste by consuming foods and drinks that have very little *or even no* nutritional value at all, except of course calories – empty non-nutritive fat-making calories. You can even buy a drink that has a more gorgeous orange color than pure orange juice, has a far stronger sugary taste, is excessively sweet-smelling, has absolutely no fiber, is a lot less expensive to buy than pure 100% orange juice and that probably has <u>absolutely no vitamin C at all</u>! Now wouldn't your ancestors be amazed at that 21st Century outcome!

The food industry also gains your approval by calling their fructose-based sweeteners "natural." Sounds good, right? Yes absolutely, fructose is in fruit, so most people would think it's good. But don't be so easily fooled! Once the industry *removes the fructose from the fibrous fruit* and uses it as a fiber-free sweetener for their processed foods, it's always *extremely bad for you*. When you consider this outcome, it seems that the food industry has taken something normally good for you and made it bad for you! Geezzz, who'd have thought they'd do that?

When you eat *sucrose sugar* it moves to your small intestine where an enzyme splits the sucrose into its two components, glucose and fructose. These molecules are then absorbed into your bloodstream eventually making their way to your liver. Along the road to your liver, glucose is used by any cell that needs a bit of caloric energy and that's good and is what your body wants to do with glucose. So, because the two sugars are *wedded together* and have to go to your intestines before moving to your hardworking liver, at least you don't get the fructose hit so fast. Fructose on its own, <u>*when not coupled with glucose*</u>, completely bypasses your small intestine and arrives *almost completely intact* at your liver. Then it's just processed into body fat. This unique ability of fructose will be intensified through its high concentration in HFCS (the sweetener most used in those tasty highly refined/processed foods).

As I said, people normally don't think of fructose as an enemy because they know that it's found in fresh whole fruits. But because fructose is coupled with fiber when eating those fresh fruits, it's more naturally dealt with by your body because the *fiber slows down the sugar absorption*. Fructose, <u>when not accompanied by fiber</u>, keeps the glycemic index (GI) score low simply because it has bypassed the natural intestinal breakdown process and therefore doesn't directly reach your bloodstream to spike sugar levels. Rather than think that's good, do remember that *fructose without fiber causes fatty issues* in your overworked liver and then it turns the rest of the excess fructose into body fat! And that's not good at all for reaching your fat-burning goal.

Because the food industry adds a lot of fructose sugar to processed foods, it can boast that foods sweetened with fructose have lower GI affects. Voila, buyers (especially people trying to avoid sugar) are happy because they know that their fat-creating insulin level is not immediately affected (though only happy out of pure ignorance about what fructose actually does to their balance circuitry and to their busy livers).

And remember that when you don't have any more space in your fat cells, your body will just make more body fat cells. Egads, you want to reduce the size of those suckers not fatten them up and then add more to the mix! Think about force feeding ducks or geese with large amounts of carbohydrate; they get *extremely* fatty livers. You eat this delicious delicacy, known as foie gras. In a fructose-dominated diet, you're doing the very same thing to your liver.

The feet of such unfortunate birds are nailed to the floor, yours are not! You can get away.

Another fallout of an overly worked fatty liver is the creation of uric acid, a consequence linked to gout and kidney stones. Earlier you read that sugar is an acid-forming "food" (and I use that word loosely), hence you know it compromises your overall ability to burn body fat. So you actually have a double whammy with sugar in terms of fat; it diminishes your fat-burning ability and it makes your liver fatty. Remember, just like the song *your-leg-bone-is-connected-to-your-hipbone*, everything is connected in your biochemical body and you can't change that fact. Eating too much sugar will *always increase* your blood's acidity (i.e., lower your pH) and compromise your fat-burning ability. And while growing more fat cells to store excess toxic waste byproducts, it'll also cause some tissue inflammation along the way.

High dietary sugar makes body acidity, and acidity is <u>always</u> linked to body fat creation.

Because fructose produces lower levels of the "I'm full" leptin hormone and increases the production of the "I'm hungry" ghrelin hormone, you can now better appreciate how people can become obese from eating too many processed foods containing HFCS. Once your liver is "full" of fat from fructose, and don't kid yourself there is a limit, it just stores the remainder. And, with **no** proper hormonal signaling, it **never ever** stops doing that. You've heard of the expression "you are what you eat"? Yes, but this is true because what you eat *always effects your hormones*. An endocrinologist might suggest the more apropos expression ***"your <u>hormones</u> are what you eat."***

When you dump a lot of fructose into your body, your liver becomes highly stressed because it's forced to use up a ton of energy converting the fructose into other molecules leaving it with very little time to cope with its many other normal biochemical functions. This can eventually lead to a greatly diminished glucose tolerance or acceptance (i.e., the pre-diabetic state of hyperglycemia or too much blood sugar) and to potential insulin-resistance (i.e., your cells actually become resistant to insulin), not to mention those high bloodstream triglyceride fats. We all know that many health care specialists have linked high sugar consumption to a number of metabolic diseases[161]. And fructose makes matters even worse as cholesterol fat can interact with triglyceride fat, forming dangerous particles that can clog your arteries leading to chest pain (angina), a heart attack or stroke. If you eat mostly sugar in a meal or a snack the effects are far worse. Your body must absorb a lot of glucose, produce tons of fat-making insulin, all resulting in that infamous *fast fall of blood sugar* as it tries heroically to regain its homeostasis/balance. But guess what? You're hungry again. Weirdly enough, the best anecdote for low blood sugar (glucose) is by avoiding sugar in your diet. Just imagine a bunch of candies on an empty stomach… YIKES say both your liver and pancreas!

Once your liver is full of fructose (hidden in all that processed carbohydrate food),
there's no biochemical signal to tell it to stop storing it as body fat.
Dietary fat doesn't make you fat;
it's all those refined and sugary carbohydrate foods that accomplish that.

Obviously, it isn't only dietary sugar that will alter your blood's glucose levels. Any meal that you eat will always result in an increase in the level of your blood sugar. That's quite a normal-to-the-body process. Ensure that you have protein and/or fat in that meal, then your digestion (or absorption of those nutrients) will be much more inefficient (i.e., slowed down) and your blood glucose levels will be increased much more gradually. This will be much easier on your body. The rise in blood sugar is always temporary as your pancreas will have been stimulated to produce the proper amount of insulin thereby avoiding the up-and-down blood sugar crashes.

Remember that your hormones[162] are fully responsible for what your body does with the food you eat. Do you burn it for energy or do you store it as body

---

[161] Examples include insulin-resistance, hypothyroidism, diabetes, and "syndrome X" or "metabolic syndrome" (a combination of conditions such as high blood pressure, high blood sugar and excess body-fat around the waist).

[162] You probably know some really thin people that seem to eat whatever and not get fat. My guess is that their pancreas always secretes just the right amount of insulin to balance out the amount of glucose in their blood sugar. Great for them, but this just doesn't happen with most of us. Many people have some level of insulin-resistance

fat? If your ability to use insulin isn't working properly such as with insulin-resistance or if you have some glucose-intolerance going on. Then the glucose can't get into your cells very well and so more and more and more glucose ends up circulating in your bloodstream. In effect, your insulin finds your cell doors locked, and no matter how many times or how loudly your insulin rings those doorbells, it just can't get any response. It's almost as if your cells *don't recognize your insulin hormones as friendly neighbors.*

Whenever you eat a ton of *super*-carbohydrate foods such as sugar, bread and pasta, your body's normal biochemical balances are thrown way off. In effect, you have a hormonal imbalance due to eating the wrong foods and, of course potentially worsened, by not exercising enough to build-up sufficient glycogen/carbohydrate storage capacity. Yup, you're getting fatter and fatter and fatter; you've built a fat-making engine and you haven't even eaten that much dietary fat!!! You've just eaten a ton of the wrong types of carbohydrate.

Like I said earlier, it isn't dietary fat that makes you fat (unless you eat way too much of it). It's eating too much "simple" non-complex overly sugary, processed and heavily refined carbohydrate that will always make you fat.

2.25 How Can Sugar Be "Hidden" in Foods?

"Remember your humanity and forget the rest." – A.E.

For the processed food industry, the three juggled money-making gods are *salt, fat and sugar – with crunch as a distant forth.* Sugar is the very best though, because it screws up your appetite-control and can even become addictive by lowering your leptin "I'm full" hormones and increasing your "I'm hungry" hormones. Again, more money for them because you just can't resist your food addictions. Normally if a processed food is advertised as low-fat, then you can be almost guaranteed it'll have higher sugar. If it has low sugar, it'll probably be high in salt *and/or* fat. With processed foods, you just can't win. In fact, the slandering of dietary saturated fat actually led to the creation of both high fructose syrup and those artificial (saturated) trans-fats! Villains #1 and #2. And the truth of the matter is that we want to eat bad stuff because it really does taste good. The industry is just giving us what we want!

---

going on, wherein the insulin produced is both excessive and not well recognized. If this is you, you CAN change that.

When we eat sucrose (glucose and fructose), it's really the sweet taste of the fructose that we like. Fruits probably developed fructose to attract animals that would eat them and subsequently spread their seeds. Indeed, *fructose is about twice as sweet as glucose* and this is why not as much is needed to make a processed food sweet. Yup, if you want something really sweet then bring on that high fructose corn syrup (HFCS)!

Sugar tampers with your appetite control and your body biochemically deals
with all sugar the same way – it creates fast arriving blood glucose.
And your body doesn't give a hoot whether the sugar arrived from
a piece of fruit, a drink of fruit juice, a bowl of pasta, a handful of candy or
some "hidden" sugar carbohydrate industrial product boasting a long
shelf-life.

On another interesting note, the only difference between a sugar addict (getting a lot of fructose along their dietary road) and an alcoholic is *how* they get their sugars. One eats theirs, the other drinks theirs. Both the sugar addict and the alcoholic do equal damage to their bodies. 100% of the fructose goes directly to the sugar-addict's liver (to be metabolized into body fat). For the alcoholic, the alcohol sugar gets converted into fatty-acids, not glucose, and about 80% of its ethanol goes directly to their liver to be broken down (producing some of those age-making free radical toxins along the way). Both individuals will wreak metabolic mayhem, grow risky visceral fat, develop a fatty liver and grow additional body fat cells due to high toxicity. The sugar addict will also grow a bunch of subcutaneous fat, looking fatter than many alcoholics, although that kind of fat isn't as dangerous as the visceral around-your-organs type of fat.

There are <u>hidden</u> sugars in many foods and so it could even be considered *more* difficult to tackle a sugar addiction versus an alcohol addiction. Abstinence becomes difficult if not impossible when you simply *don't know* if there are hidden sugars in the food you're eating. You must become a serious label reading detective. I don't really like it, but I find that I have to take my bifocals to the grocery store. *"Buyer beware"* is my food shopping motto.

You already know that carbohydrates can be categorized into two groups: those that can be absorbed (digestible) and those that can't be absorbed (indigestible). Sugar (simple) and starch (complex) carbohydrates are digestible/available carbohydrates while fiber, a pulp roughage, is an indigestible or unavailable carbohydrate.

Sugar carbohydrates can be further categorized. Some are *mono*saccharides (one molecule) such as glucose and fructose, others are *di*saccharides (two monosaccharide molecules) such as maltose (two glucose units), lactose (one glucose unit and one galactose unit) and sucrose[163] (one glucose unit and one fructose unit). You can see that all sugars will contain some amount of glucose.

The conversion of carbohydrate into glucose is a completely natural process. As long as you don't *surprise* your body into a drastic rebalancing hormonal response by visiting Starvation Island you'll be OK. When you eat *any* starch-based food, glucose will be converted into *poly*saccharide[164] glycogen. Whenever you need some quick energy, your tissues can eventually release that stored glycogen for energy. The challenge is to NOT eat too much sugar all at once.

When you eat <u>sucrose</u>, with its one glucose unit and one fructose unit, your digestion process will create and send equal amounts of glucose and fructose into your bloodstream (i.e., 50% of each). Sucrose is found naturally in sugar cane, sugar beet and most fruits. But you'll also find it in most processed foods. Your body will deal with all sucrose <u>the very same way</u>; it doesn't care whether you are eating fresh whole fruits or a big bowl of hot pasta or eating a chocolate bar. That said, at least the fruit has some pulpy indigestible fiber to slowdown digestion, making the sugar whammy spread out over more time.

When you eat a grain type of starch, you'll be eating <u>maltose</u>, with its two glucose units joined together. These two glucose units will of course be digested as glucose. Maltose, found in germinating seeds, is commonly found in beer. The alcohol in beer will transform into *fatty acids*, while the beer's maltose will be treated as carbohydrate *sugar* by your body. Surely you didn't think it was a protein.

When you drink milk, or eat milk products such as yogurt and cheese, you eat <u>lactose</u> sugar, which has the two monosaccharides glucose and galactose.

---

[163] Sucrose also exerts synergistic effects when combined with table salt; it produces more hypertension than does salt alone. Sweet and salty popcorn anyone? Nah, not a great choice if you already have high blood pressure.

[164] Polysaccharides are made up of many monosaccharide units.

Some people, who have a lactose-intolerance (causing gut distention and pain) and can't drink cow milk, can actually eat cheese. This is because when the cheese is made, the lactose remains in the whey and *dry* cheese has no whey. Whey is the liquid part of the milk that is separated from the solid curds during the process of making cheese. It's rich in lactose sugar. Be careful with your protein workout drinks. If you're using a 100% whey protein shake/drink, get ready for a large release of insulin and for your fat-burning to be put into a holding pattern for a short while – even if it's good for your fatigued muscles.

Whey is actually one of the two types of protein in milk and this may be why some protein drinks like to use whey as a base. The other one is casein (the curds) and though casein and whey both contain the same amino acids, they're absorbed differently. Whey gives a faster amino-acid level, while casein's is slower but lasts a lot longer. Casein can be highly addictive and is potentially inflammatory as well.[165] Do you know any adults addicted to milk casein, adults who drink many glasses each day? I do. That said, large populations are actually *lactose-intolerant*[166] to some degree, in fact it's so widespread *at a global level* that lactose *tolerance* could even be viewed as *abnormal*. Many people across the globe simply can't digest lactose[167].

---

[165] Remember Little Miss Muffat sitting on her tuffet eating her "curds and whey"? Well "curds" are casein milk protein, made by curdling the milk and draining off the whey protein. The more whey that's removed, then the drier the cheese gets. Cottage cheese with have both proteins, but cheddar cheese will only have casein. And so, Miss Muffat was actually eating "cottage cheese" but I guess it just didn't carry the rhyme as well as "curds and whey."

[166] For most people, the enzyme "lactase" (made in the small intestine) declines after weaning, unless milk consumption continues as tends to be the reality in North America. Lactase is needed in order to breakdown the lactose sugar into its two smaller sugars. For people genetically predisposed, the decline of lactase is much slower and so they can continue to digest lactose. If you have an intolerance, the eating of dairy products will cause some discomfort, bloating, abdominal pain, flatulence and even bad diarrhea. If you're *completely* lactose-intolerant you won't be able to eat <u>any</u> diary products. Those only mildly intolerant will be able to tolerate lactose to a limited extent. Lactose-intolerant bodybuilders must buy whey-free powder for workouts.

[167] One of our sons, Brent, became lactose-intolerant when he was about 30. We had seen no indication of it when he was young, but lo and behold, when he was 38, he decided to lose weight (a whopping 45 pounds) and suddenly was no longer lactose-

In case you're discombobulated, here's a summary of the three *mono*saccharide single-molecule sugars and how they lovingly bond together to make the double-molecule *di*saccharide sugars you might more easily recognize.

Glucose + Fructose = Sucrose (typically called "table sugar")
Glucose + Glucose = Maltose (commonly found in beer)
Glucose + Galactose = Lactose (found in milk and milk products)

But let's get back to this villainous fructose and investigate how it can be hidden in foods you would *never* expect to have sugar.

Fructose itself is a natural sugar (found in fruits), but when it's created by the food industry in the form of fructose corn syrup there's nothing "natural" about it! And while you're learning about fructose, keep in mind that *it's **never*** found *alone in nature*.

I'm sure that before reading this book, you were somewhat aware that HFCS had been recognized as one of the *most harmful sweetener additives* on our grocery store shelves and you may have been consciously trying to avoid it. Unfortunately, you may not be as successful at dodging it as you might think.

Regular white table sugar or sucrose is made from sugar cane or sugar beets and, as said above, it is 50% glucose (used for energy by the body and causes the natural need for insulin) and 50% fructose (also found in pure honey and fresh fruits). But did you know that HFCS is made from cornstarch which is *only* glucose molecules? How is it possible for the food industry to create (from *corn-based glucose*) the fructose sugar found in HFCS?

To better their bottom line, the food industry learned via trial and error that rather than only glucose, it could actually create a mixture of glucose *and* fructose from carbohydrate *starch*. This conversion process uses an enzyme called glucose-isomerase which can convert glucose *into* fructose. Holy

---

intolerant! I have no idea why this happened but will surmise that his body was suddenly in a homeostatic state again and no longer highly inflamed. It had balanced all its circuits and biorhythms. He feels wonderful and has tons of energy again. Need I add that he looks a lot younger?

mockers! Yes, after many years of dedicated expensive research and chemical manipulation, the industry happily discovered that it could influence the final *percentage* of glucose converted to fructose (sometimes called "invert[168] sugar"). Indeed, it could get it up higher than 90% fructose!!!! Who would have believed this incredible feat? What has happened? Well the glucose and fructose, *normally bound together* as sucrose, becomes separated which allows the fructose to move even more quickly into your liver. Jeepers, yet more body fat production.

This high fructose syrup (HFS) has been used by the food industry to replace the more expensive ordinary sucrose sugar. Given the fluctuations in the cost of sugar the industry discovered that it can use HFCS/fructose as a sweetener substitute in processed foods/drinks and save a bundle of money. And remember that fructose tastes sweeter than glucose, hence they can use less of it. Great, more profits for them, more corn fields for the farmers to tend and more fat for us. And please recognize that this body fat is *not caused* by eating fat.

HFCS fructose is recognized as the most harmful sweetener additive for your body.

On another note, why people think that "unrefined" sugar is better to eat than "refined" sugar always baffles me. You can call it different things and use different adjectives, but let's face it; sugar is sugar is sugar. There just isn't any way for your body to get around that fact. Sugar is a simple quick-to-glucose carbohydrate and eating too much always translates into more body fat.

The food industry has, of course, discovered that sugar has a wide range of properties which in turn make it a popular and very versatile constituent that can be used in many foods and drinks. Some are obvious (e.g., sweetening beverages, enhancing flavors, preserving candied fruits and jam, and wine fermentation). And I guess I'd have to agree that others are actually *necessary* for some foods (e.g., producing different confectionery textures, depressing

---

[168] A synonym for "invert" is "upset" and that's actually what the industry has done to the sugar percentages!!! That said, you might question the eating of "upset" sugar and not worry about "invert" sugar, right?? Again, some super great labelling going on here!!! Another successful food industry marketing committee meeting for sure.

freezing points for ice cream, caramelizing bread crusts, icing decorations and promoting gelling). That said, all rationales still lead to a terribly high intake of sugar by North Americans.

Aside from HFCS, people eat a lot of other sugar *without realizing it,* thinking that they're eating something very healthy. A perfect example is fruit juice. To your body, fruit and fruit juice are very different beasts indeed. Fruit is a balance of nutrients, fiber and sugar all designed to be *slowly metabolized* by your body. Put simply, it is nature's dessert. Even so, I would suggest no more than two fruits per day keeping in mind that grapes, apples, bananas and pears are all relatively high in fructose, while berries and cherries contain the least amount of fructose.

OK back to juice; a small glass of apple juice is not the equivalent of eating an apple, but it *is* the equivalent of the sugar of about four apples. Bet you can't eat four apples one after the other in the same time it takes to drink a glass of apple juice. You could of course put them in the juicer and drink the result pretty fast. All the fiber will have been stripped out, leaving only the sugary fructose liquid behind and no hormonal signal to tell you when you're full. Instead of eating four whole food apples, you'll be drinking about 80 grams of sugar with very little effort. This would be the equivalent of dumping about *20 spoons of sugar* into your body very quickly. And let's look at that glass of freshly squeezed orange juice that you see health conscious people drinking for breakfast. Sounds pretty good. Lots of people drink it for health, right? A cup (8 oz.) of "unsweetened"[169] orange juice will give you about 21 grams of sugar, or about 5 spoons of sugar! And that's non-fiber sugar you could have avoided. If you're watching your weight, *you'd better cut out all fruit juices.*

Fruit juices are digested into sugar by your body in a rapid 10-15 minutes. And if you drink fruit juice on an empty stomach, it moves so fast through your stomach (maybe 5 minutes) and on to your intestine for conversion to glucose that you could liken it to pouring water from a glass onto the floor ready for immediate mop-up. All I can say is "wow," what efficiency and what a production of fat-making insulin and fat-storing enzymes will result!

---

[169] Who needs to sweeten orange juice?? That said, it's a nice advertisement to get you to think it's healthier for you. What I am saying is that no one would need to sweeten orange juice anyway! I'll bet you've never tasted bitter-tasting orange juice!

The recent fad of "juicing" is really just the removal of fiber from fruits and vegetables in order to make easy-to-drink juices. But beware, juicing removes *the primary controls of fiber.* If you do insist on buying fruit juices[170], remember that most of them are a mixture of fruit juice concentrate[171], water and *synthesized* flavor. These too will flood your liver with the dreaded fiber-free fructose.

Dried fruits have had their water content removed and so their sizes are much smaller; but they still remain very high in fructose albeit they retain their fiber. Take a little box of raisins (maybe 80-90 dried grapes). You can probably eat the whole box. Now try to eat 80-90 grapes. Nope, I don't think so. You'd be lucky to get to about 25 before the water and fiber in the grapes told your brain that you were full (yeah, bring on that leptin "I'm full" hormone)!

Please watch your daily sugar intake; and look out for HFCS and other "hidden" sugars along the way.

2.26 What About Sugar Substitutes and Artificial Sweeteners?

"In order to succeed, your desire for success should be greater than your fear of failure." – A.E.

There are many sugar substitutes and artificial sweeteners (all with fewer calories than sugar) used by the food industry to successfully market products to consumers trying to avoid "sugar." Yes, they want that sale, that money, that profit. And you probably buy them to reduce your daily caloric intake as part of your effort to reduce or control your overall weight and body fat. But do you

---

[170] If you are drinking any type of fruit juice, fruit syrup, fruit concentrate or eating a fruit by-product (e.g., fruit snacks), then you may as well be eating a handful of candy. It's the very same to your body.

[171] Fruit juice concentrate simply means that all the excess water has been removed, yielding a product that's more concentrated than the initial juice. It can be as high as 7 times more concentrated than the original. This may explain the reason why some orange juices, made from concentrate, taste sweeter than some others. It may simply be that that particular manufacturer suggests adding back *less water* than its competitors.

still think one calorie equals another calorie? And are the number of calories you consume over the day all you care about?

Remember that your body is a very complicated biochemical creature and for this reason using sweeteners for controlling weight and body fat may not be quite as simple as you might imagine or hope.

Any perceived sweetness touching your tongue will *automatically stimulate* your pancreas to secrete the fat-storage insulin hormone (even from sugarless gum)! Any sweet taste from any food that does *not* provide glucose confuses your body's sugar handling processes. To your body, sweetness normally means that caloric fuel is entering your body and sweet foods provide the most efficient glucose energy. But if there isn't any real sugar to convert because you just ate a bunch of chemically manufactured *non-sugar*, your body becomes very confused by this *pretend* sugar. Actually, I shouldn't even suggest that! Your body is too smart to be confused. It'll always do what it has been programmed to do. Therefore, *"pretend" sugar* will force a **biochemical adaptation** which will always result in **more insulin and more fat-storage** and that's all there is to it.

So let's see how this works. Because of that lack of real sugar for your newly created insulin, this new where-is-the-sugar insulin will end up promoting weight-gain and fat-storage instead. Your body will *always* follow its built-in programs and still complete its natural biochemical responsibilities, which in this case is to *store* fat. This is because your body, through its taste buds, believes it has eaten enough sugar for your blood circulation. At this point your brain tells your liver not to circulate any more sugar (glucose) but, rather, to *start storing* glucose (thinking that more will be arriving imminently). Lo and behold, there isn't any *real* sugar arriving! At this point you'll get a hunger sensation and want to eat yet again – that's the kicking in of your ghrelin hunger hormones. Remember that your body wants to keep its blood sugar balanced and so by clearing out some of its bloodstream glucose, it's just getting itself ready for *anticipated* glucose from the "food" you just chewed. But unfortunately, there's now a bunch of completely superfluous insulin kicking around your bloodstream with very little blood sugar in sight. This is a form of biochemical imbalance in action. Your body will always do what it was programmed to do, so if you want to help with fat-burning and calorie-burning quit chewing artificially sweetened gum as a way to stop eating!

In terms of homeostasis, your body would be better off if you drank a sugar-based soda pop rather than that artificially sweetened soda pop. That said, you'd be ingesting nutritionally useless sugar (indeed probably fructose-based sugar) and bone-theft carbonation, while increasing your acidity thereby compromising your fat-burning ability. If you're trying to control your weight, I'd most certainly recommend replacing all soda pop and sugar-free gum with plain water. What the heck? It doesn't taste bad, so why avoid it?

So in sum, with *artificial* sweeteners there's no real increase in blood sugar, hence as a direct result there's an increase in hypoglycemia[172] (a deficiency of blood glucose) or you could call it an increase in hyperinsulinemia[173] (excess insulin). When these changes occur, your adrenal glands[174] are taxed. They'll spike your adrenaline and cortisol stress hormones in order to mobilize sugar from other sources (the liver and muscle glycogen[175], or protein, or body tissue) in order to bring your blood glucose level back up to its normal level. Stress hormones are supposed to be in response to a "fight-or-flight" scenario (remember that bear?), not when you're simply eating a meal. Because your body is trying to signal you to eat, you could think of sweeteners leading to *increased* food intake, less weight-loss, more body fat and probable weight-gain! Some of the consequences of excess stress hormones in your body are a suppressed immune system, increased inflammation[176] and lower thyroid function (an organ that directly influences

---

[172] Another way to look at this is when your body produces too much insulin to match your actual blood sugar glucose, then the balance is off with too much insulin and *too little glucose*. This causes "hypo"glycemia and overall fatigue, moving sometimes into chronic fatigue. Indeed, some argue that women are more susceptible to glycemic fluctuations and resulting mood swings. Hmmm…maybe.

[173] Although this is an excess of insulin, the result is the same as hypoglycemia. Both are different nouns for too much (hyper) insulin and too little (hypo) glucose.

[174] Your adrenal endocrine glands increase blood circulation and carbohydrate metabolism.

[175] Yup, you could be eating up a bunch of your calorie-burning muscle tissue.

[176] Inflammation is a normal body process wherein your body's white blood cells protect you from infection such as bacteria and viruses. When your immune system triggers an inflammatory response *when there are no invaders to fight off*, then your body begins to cause damage to its own tissues, thinking they're somehow infected. That's bad.

your metabolic rate). And we know that your metabolic engine affects how efficiently you burn your dietary caloric fuel!

The usual responses of your body to sweet food <u>in small amounts</u> is to produce the correct amount of insulin, to increase energy use and to blunt your appetite later in the day. With substitute sweeteners, <u>none</u> of these *natural biochemical* processes will ever happen.

> *Artificial sweeteners will tax your adrenal glands into producing*
> *the stress hormones adrenaline and cortisol.*
> *Perceived stress by your body can lead to*
> *suppressed immunity, increased inflammation and more body fat.*

Real sugar or sucrose, on the other hand, stimulates your brain chemical serotonin[177] (which may be why some people are addicted to sugar), but real sugar also carries the message that enough sugar has been consumed. Of course, you have to listen to that message as well. Synthesized sweeteners carry no such message and may even carry the opposite message wherein your brain believes that *more sugar* (carbohydrate) is needed.

> *Both real sugars and artificial sweeteners will cause your body to react*
> *as it would normally to sweetness, as it believes glucose will be arriving*
> *imminently.*
> *When blood sugars are artificially lowered through "pretend" sugars,*
> *you can expect weight-gain.*

OK, so what are some of the industrially manufactured sweeteners that you may have heard about or have used?

<u>Sugar polyols (I've seen these on energy bar ingredients' listings)</u>

These non-traditional sugar substitutes are *a group of non-glucose carbohydrates* and can be called "sugar polyols," "polyol sugars," "sugar alcohols," "hexitols," "hexa-hydroxy alcohols" or "hexahydric alcohols." Obviously the "hex" prefix refers to the fact that they're six-sided structures.

---

[177] Serotonin is a neurotransmitter that transmits nerve impulses between your cells. As you've probably heard, it's key to mood regulation. But did you know that it's also involved with the perception of both hunger and fullness/satiety as well as the narrowing of your blood vessels which in turn cause migraine headache pain?

You're probably most familiar with one called "sorbitol" which you might see listed in the ingredients for some "sugar-free" candies, chewing gums, breath mints, mouthwash, processed baked goods and cough drops. These are neither sugar (sucrose) nor alcohol (ethanol) which of course makes the term "sugar alcohol" misleading. They can be made from cornstarch carbohydrate, the stalk residue of sugar cane, birch wood waste (whaaat!?), or whey protein (the watery lactose-rich part of milk that remains after the formation of cheese curds). If you're lactose-intolerant you might be wise to avoid this sugar substitute.

They're also quite a bit different from other carbohydrates because they're absorbed slowly and incompletely into your bloodstream, but they do leave fatty-acids and gases in your intestines. This can cause uncomfortable bloating, embarrassing flatulence, more bowel movements and sometimes bad diarrhea.

Another interesting fact is that although "sugar alcohol" products boast "sugar-free" on their labels, they're *not necessarily* carbohydrate-free! Some candies have a regular and a sugar-free version, but often both versions will actually have the *same number* of carbohydrate grams and some can be higher in fat content as well. This is because the carbohydrates are counted as sugar alcohol instead of sugar on the label! Maybe you should always look at the total carbohydrates and the fat content on food labels as a better gauge.

And don't be a latte fatty. Did you know that a large "skinny" latte made with a sugar-free syrup still has about 15 grams of fat and that's the equivalent of guzzling about 10 slices of bacon? Wow, useless calories all between meals.

Now let's take another example, wherein you might go for the "sugar-free" version in an attempt to avoid eating more sugar. We'll use wafer-type cookies and compare three *regular* vanilla wafers to three *sugar-free* vanilla wafers. Remember when looking at the numbers that all carbohydrates eventually end up as sugar in your body, albeit some take a longer time to become blood sugar. In this example you'll see that the <u>total fat</u> in both is about the same! The reason the <u>total calories</u> are *about the same* is because you're getting your carbohydrate grams/calories as either 88 calories in the 3 "regular" wafers or 72 in the 3 "sugar-free" wafers – and frankly, that's just not much different is it?

For Three Wafers	Sugar Carbohydrate (% total cals.)	Carbohydrate *(in addition to the added sugar)*	Fat (% total cals)	Total Calories
Regular Vanilla (uses sugar)	16 g = 64 cals. (42%)	6 g = 24 cals. (16%)	7 g = 63 cals. (42%)	151 calories
Sugar-free Vanilla (uses sorbitol)	0 g = 0 cals.	18 g = 72 cals. (50%)	8 g = 72 cals. (50%)	144 calories

Stevia

Stevia is *a plant derived sweetener* that comes from plant protein rather than plant carbohydrate. This makes it natural as opposed to synthetic. Green leaf stevia comes from the leaves of annual Stevia shrubs. White stevia is a chemically processed white powder. Now of course you really shouldn't be very surprised about that as *nothing in nature is pure white*. White stevia can be found in some toothpastes. If you have insulin-resistance or Type-2 diabetes, stevia has been shown to increase insulin-sensitivity[178] which would be good. As a non-sugar, stevia doesn't support glycogen energy storage because it obviously doesn't provide your liver with glucose such as honey[179] would do. But, if you *must* use a sweetener, I would say that the best choice would be green leaf stevia.

Saccharin (or Sweet n' Low) and Cyclamate

Both saccharin and cyclamate *are chemical sweeteners* which are synthesized from sodium or calcium salts. Both are sweeter, cheaper and easier to handle than table sugar (nice for the food industry). Again, because blood sugars are lowered, these two sweeteners can be appetite stimulants hence leading to weight-gain.

---

[178] Anton SD, Martin CK, Han H, Coulon S, Cefalu WT, Geiselman P, Williamson DA. Effects of stevia, aspartame, and sucrose on food intake, satiety, and postprandial glucose and insulin levels. Appetite 20120; 55:37-43

[179] As usual, the real stuff is always better for your biochemically driven processes. Just use honey in your tea.

Aspartame (otherwise known as NutraSweet or Equal)

This *is a synthetic sweetener* made of a combination of two commercially produced amino-acids (L-aspartic acid and L-phenylalanine) that provide sweetness with very few calories. Although much sweeter than sucrose, aspartame loses its sweetness if heated unlike either sucrose, saccharin or cyclamate. Still, aspartame is subject to the same weight-gain argument as are other chemically produced sweeteners.

Sucralose (or Splenda)

Sucralose, also *a synthesized sweetener*, is made by chemically altering sucrose through chlorination. It remains stable at high and low temperatures. Most is not absorbed and passes through your intestinal tract unchanged, which is why the industry uses it in low-calorie foods and beverages. These too are subject to the same weight-gain argument. This sweetener does affect your thymus gland[180] which in turn can negatively affect your immune system.

Allulose (or Psicose)

Allulose is a relatively new sweetener. It's a "rare sugar" which is found in small amounts in raisins, figs, molasses and maple syrup.[181] Contrary to most synthetic sweeteners, it's a low-calorie naturally occurring monosaccharide that's actually digested. You might wonder why it isn't listed as "sugar" on ingredient labels; it's because it doesn't cause the same biochemical blood glucose reactions that sugar does.

Unfortunately, there really isn't a lot of long-term research on potential side effects, but certainly it does sound promising as a low-calorie sweetener.

And then the question remains, what's the best choice if you are avoiding sugar? Well, probably none of the above for various negative outcomes and none of them due to the weight-gain argument.

---

[180] The thymus gland is more closely related to your immune system rather than your endocrine system. It's vital in training and developing your T-lymphocytes or T-cells, which are important types of white blood cells.

[181] The food industry makes allulose *from cornstarch* through an enzyme process. On long-distance motorcycle trips down through the States, I used to wonder why there were so many corn fields – now, I'm thinking that I should have put some money into corn commodities! Corn seems to be in everything.

Still, I can't lie; it'll be really difficult for you to go cold-turkey on sugar. If you take sugar in your coffee, maybe try some green leaf stevia and then gradually cut back on the amount used. Another plan for when you just need to eat something sweet would be to have a piece of fresh fruit (which also has some fiber) – it would be a much better choice for your hormones than a chocolate bar or a donut or sugar-free chewing gum!

2.27 What Is the Best Diet to Follow?

"You never fail until you stop trying." – A.E.

This is a question I get asked a lot. Certainly most popular diets will work to drop weight to some degree for some time. Nevertheless, I'm hoping that after reading this book you'll understand why most of them concentrate on lowering your weight quickly with very little consideration to how your body's *I-want-to-survive-your-ill-informed-eating-decisions* biochemistry is actually dealing with your new way of eating.

People make a lot of money developing and selling new diet plans and books. It really is a highly lucrative business. They know that people want a plan, a plan that assures a perfect body in a relatively quick time. They like to suggest their plan is the best one to follow and that it's guaranteed if you follow it religiously. They know that people are in a big hurry to look great and so they like to promise that their approach works really fast. And normally there isn't much thought given to sustainability. Any diet that doesn't have long-term sustainability will never work! I'll bet that you've tried some of them. I know I did.

Indeed, many diets are "fad" diets that try to tap into the avoidance of whatever society has deemed to be the current anti-hero (e.g., saturated fat or carbohydrates or gluten, etc.) Diet-promoters know that people like to have a villain to blame and a simple eating framework to follow. No one likes to blame themselves for the state of their bodies, though they often do following failure – especially after returning from various and sundry Starvation Island diets.

Selling popular diets to a hopeful public is a powerfully lucrative business. Most popular diets concentrate on quick weight- and fat-loss with very little consideration of either bodily needs

or internal biochemical adaptations to drastic change.
The general public seems only interested in achieving lower weight and less
fat,
not necessarily overall health and improved physical fitness.

Unfortunately, people don't know how their biochemistry works though, I suppose, many don't really care either. I *want* you to have long-term fat-loss and muscle-building success. I want you to appreciate your body's adaptations. I want you to understand how and why they work. *And I can promise that eating properly will make you feel absolutely fantastic.*

Example quick-fix approaches that rarely work for sustained fat-loss include the following popular fad diets:

- Low-fat (wherein less than 10% daily caloric intake is from fat)
- Low carbohydrate (with unlimited fat and protein, and severely limited carbohydrate)
- High-protein (usually low-carbohydrate diets in disguise)
- Overall caloric reduction (suggesting that, to your body, one calorie is the same as any other calorie)
- High-fat and extremely low-carbohydrate
- Vegetarian (which excludes all meat products)
- Vegan (which excludes all animal products *and animal-derived* ingredients)
- Non-carbohydrate and high fat[182]
- Paleolithic (eliminates whole grains, legumes and dairy) – AKA the "caveman" diet OKA the "hunter/gatherer" diet

These diets tend to deprive you of all or most of one or more of the three macronutrients in some way that tries to make your body drop overall weight

---

[182] When you completely drop carbohydrates from your diet you'll seriously compromise your fat-burning ability; you'll lose water weight at the beginning (water is a mixture of hydrogen and oxygen) as your body clears its stored glycogen/carbohydrate molecules (which hold three to four molecules of water). Fat molecules are *mostly* carbon and hydrogen. That's why you need oxygen to mobilize and seriously burn your body-fat! Yes, at the molecular and biochemical levels, it's complicated for sure!

and body fat faster than it would normally be able to do. Vegetarians and vegans of course are not necessarily adhering to their strict diet primarily to lose weight, though most are never obese.

Prescriptive diets which deprive you of one or more of the macronutrients
will slow down your metabolism,
your calorie-burning ability.
Once you start eating normally
you'll build-up more body fat because of a compromised metabolic rate.

As an aside I have always believed that a healthy weight-loss would be a maximum of 1% body weight for the non-morbidly obese) or 1 to 2 pounds per week. It took me almost two years to drop 40 pounds. Why? Because I never deprived my body of what it wanted and needed to remain healthy, fit and strong. I wanted to gain muscle *while* I was losing fat. I ate all three macronutrients, watched my micronutrients (vitamins and minerals) with supplements, drank a lot of water and increased my exercise by adding progressive weight-training at the gym. I didn't yo-yo. I never felt like I was starving or hungry. I never went back to being overweight or having an unhealthy internal body. My eating plan was sustainable, filling and delicious.

During my two years of weight-training and clean eating, I *gradually re-sculpted* my body shape, including the loss of my muffin top waist, the loss of the fat on my back (you know the kind that rolls up and into your neck making you appear a bit hunch-backed), and I gained lean toned muscles on my arms and legs. I didn't worry about counting calories. I didn't continually dwell on my overall weight. Rather I just kept enjoying the change in how my clothes fit. The most I ever weighed myself was once a week.

But again, I've digressed; let's get back to those popular diets. How could the removal or high reduction of one or more of the three macronutrients actually make you lose weight in a healthy sustainable way? Remember that your body is a *hormonal machine* and its adaptive biochemistry will always react to <u>any drastic changes</u> in your overall daily nutrient intake. The food you eat will control your hormones and you can't change that fact. Your body wants to survive regardless of what nutrients you deprive it off. Due to this inborn determination to survive, it's kind of your biochemical savior. That's its job and you better believe that it's really good at saving you.

People worried about their weight and their body fat tend to join various and sundry food "camps," stating that they are "paleo" or "keto" or "lemon-detoxers" or "non-carbers" or whatever. Many of these diets are too good to be true and many imply changes to your body chemistry. Hmmm, your biochemical body was developed long before these fad diets and long before the food industry's manipulation of real foods. Your body's *chemistry* isn't changed by HOW you eat, your body's chemistry ADAPTS to what you decide to eat along pre-determined processes. Unfortunately you may not like how it adapts.

As an example, we'll take what I would call the current "fad" diet that a lot of people are talking about; the "keto" or "ketosis" or "ketogenic" diet. This is a high-fat (70% of daily calories), ultra-low-carbohydrate (5%), adequate-protein (25%) diet which claims to load you up with fat and take away carbohydrate, making your liver create ketones to breakdown your stored body fat for use as your body's main fuel. And note that this diet doesn't necessarily consider the nutrient value of the calories either. The only macronutrient that's *somewhat* adjustable is protein which is dependent upon how physically active you are.

Most people who adopt this diet are in a crazy hurry to lose scale weight and many never exercise. They just want the quick-n-dirty result.

The "Keto" diet proports to force your body into *burning fat instead of carbohydrate* (its preferred go-to for energy). Well of course it does! You're not eating enough carbohydrate to burn much of it. This diet limits your carbohydrate intake to between 20 and 30 grams per day (only 80 to 120 calories!) Believe me, that isn't very much at all – only about 1/5 of what I usually eat. Normally, to maintain my calorie-burning, I usually aim for about 150 grams of daily dietary carbohydrate (or about 600 calories).

Let's delve more deeply into what's happening biochemically on this Keto diet. Your liver is really the central boss for your metabolic activity. It's able to store glycogen and release it later whenever you need it (for example when you are sleeping it'll release glycogen energy for your ongoing cell activity). It's true that your muscles also store glycogen, but that glycogen can't be released or shared very easily as it's solely put there for your muscles' use – remember that starving ancestral hunter who needed to run after his live protein. If you go a long time without much carbohydrate, the glycogen in your liver <u>will</u> eventually get completely depleted. When this happens, your liver will then have to begin inefficiently converting both your body's fatty-acids (a 2-step conversion process) from your body fat and eventually amino-acids from your muscles (a 5-step process) to get the necessary glucose energy. Sure you'll lose weight but better get ready for that toneless skin you hate. Severe carbohydrate restriction also raises your cortisol stress hormones and so belly-fat here we come.

Unfortunately, your body fat can't be turned into energy fuel unless there's a proper mix of fat <u>and</u> glucose *all in the presence of oxygen.* With very little dietary carbohydrate available via the Keto diet, you're not able to synthesize much blood glucose energy from your body fat because there just isn't enough insulin to transport it around your body.

On the Keto diet, your liver is unable to fully metabolize all the excess fat you're eating and therefore it's forced to breakdown fat into ketone by-products which are in turn urinated out.

Remember that carbohydrate gets broken down into glucose in an efficient 1-step conversion process. Protein gets broken down in amino acids which are the essential building blocks for all tissues and organs (you want strong muscles[183], right?) Fat gets broken down into fatty acids which are involved in a wide range of biological signaling pathways all contributing to a number of necessary bodily needs such as strong immunity, thermal and electrical insulation, cell membrane formation and transporting fat-soluble vitamins.

So, this diet has fat (that's good) and it has protein (also good) but it deprives you of sufficient carbohydrate (which in my view is not good over

---

[183] Ever wonder why people who starve themselves can have heart attacks? Yup, the heart is a muscle too. Take away its energy to move blood and you too can have cardiovascular issues due to lower heart muscle mass. Back in 1983, the velvety-voiced Karen Carpenter, lead singer for "The Carpenters," sadly died of heart failure. She was only 32(!) but suffered from the compulsive life-threatening anorexia nervosa eating disorder, which is characterized by self-starvation and purging, rapid weight-loss and sometimes coupled with excessive exercising. Her heart muscle just gave up! Imagine exercising like crazy but never eating very much food. You're killing your muscle, but at the same time asking it to work really hard. Individuals who suffer from this disorder sometimes do so because it's the only part of their lives that is completely controlled by them and no one else. So sad.

the long haul). If you have to use protein for sufficient energy, then you simply can't build and repair bodily tissues very well and most certainly *your metabolism will have to change in order to survive*. Without enough blood sugar/glucose you can become hypoglycemic which can lead to confusion, dizziness, headaches, sweating, chronic fatigue and general weakness among other symptoms. You'll also experience a major decrease in body fluids resulting in dehydration, not good if you have any kidney issues. And surprisingly, proponents of this particular diet even warn you about these side-effects in advance!

But what the heck is a "ketone"? It's a chemical substance that your body makes naturally when it doesn't have enough insulin in your blood. This will occasionally happen to anyone when there's too little insulin and that's why a ketone-producing process is biochemically available to your body. That said, when these by-product ketones build-up in your body for *a long __un__natural time*, serious illness can result.

There are a number of stages that a starving body goes through. In the first stage, your body will maintain blood glucose levels by producing glucose from stored glycogen/carbohydrate, as well as the breaking down of both amino- and fatty-acids. When body fat gets broken down, that's when *ketones come into play*. Your body will hang on to its proteins as long as it can. It wants to be able to rebuild old tissues as needed; only in the final starvation stage will your body go to protein for energy. Maybe we evolved this way because when we were starving, we still had to retain the ability, even if diminished, to run after wild game. And so, you see that energy comes first from carbohydrate (your body's preferred energy), secondly from fat (creating ketones) and lastly from protein (not normally used for energy).

You probably know that before the scientists Banting and Best came up with insulin injections, people died when they had Type-1 diabetes (although no one knew what it was at the time). People literally wasted away and starved to death, even though they were eating tons of food!!! Why was this? It was because their pancreas quit producing insulin, hence their bodies didn't digest any dietary carbohydrate and never produced any insulin. At that point, their bodies were forced to rely upon body fat and muscle tissue for energy. That can't go on forever, it's just not sustainable at all. Since insulin also transports any fatty acids from dietary fat, that form of fuel becomes mismanaged as well.

Indeed, you could think of diabetics as experiencing an inability to fully manage their body's fuel supply.

My Type-1 diabetic husband was "spilling ketones" in his urine when first diagnosed. In my opinion, the Keto diet puts your body into *a Type-1 diabetic* mode! Just like Type-1's, you're not getting much dietary carbohydrate! They sure didn't choose that affliction, but if you chose the Keto diet, you're choosing the Type-1 biochemical experience. What does that mean? Your body is a biochemical machine and it wants to help you survive this diet. It can only survive just as an *un*diagnosed Type-1 body survives! It'll eat itself skinny, it'll overdose on ketones (poor liver) while eating your fat and it'll eventually cannibalize your muscle tissues to get at those glycogen energy stores.

Yup, you WILL lose a lot of body weight but you sure won't be healthy and your body will have screwed up your hormones trying to solve its dilemma. The result is very simple; your body will move into starvation mode *and it'll resort to burning something else for fuel (which is what the proponents of this diet actually want to happen).* But remember, there goes your metabolism again. Yes, your ability to burn calories in the future will be negatively compromised and, let's face it, you simply can't stay on this carbohydrate-starvation diet for very long. And frankly, you won't look toned at all. You'll weigh a lot less and if you're only measuring your overall weight as a health indicator, you'll probably be happy, right? Flappy arms anybody?

No dice, not for me! I like my body and I want to help it do what it wants to do and what it should do. I don't want to be toneless and skinny – I want to be a lean toned calorie-burning engine; I don't want a huge and unhealthy metabolic shift in the workings of my body. Most of the women who adopt the Keto approach to weight-loss actually end up changing it along the way. They just can't stay on that diet very long as they don't feel very good on it and they get listless too. I don't honestly know what kind of "diet" they end up on or what resulting biochemical and hormonal adaptations take place when they try some sort of partial Keto diet, but I do know it's probably not overly healthy. Nonetheless, it's probably a bit healthier in the longer term than the stricter Keto diet. My guess is that they're eating more veggies/fruits (both are carbs) than allowed on a strict true Keto diet.

When talking about hormones, people always think about the two sex hormones (estrogen and testosterone), but your body has tons of other equally important hormones. Hormones[184] regulate virtually *everything* your body does, and they're very complex and totally driven by what you eat. Unhealthy diets which don't meet your body's nutritional needs *always* affect your hormones and hormones regulate your metabolism, fertility, pregnancy[185], bone growth, sugar regulation and other important physiological activities. Poor eating habits also have a highly negative affect on your endocrine system, which involves an extremely complex interplay between your glands, *your hormones* and your organs.

Since glucose is your body's preferred go-to fuel, your body will always *store any fats not required*. Obviously, that isn't something you're necessarily aiming for and so this is probably why dieters jump into this diet, a diet that will definitely get rid of body fat. And we know that if you normally have a diet *too high* in carbohydrate (especially processed), your body will store a lot of body fat and you can become obese. On the flip side, if you eat too little carbohydrate, then your body will move into a ketosis state. As I said earlier, this ketosis state is *actually a natural process* used by your body during the breakdown of fats in your liver. The trick is to lower the carbohydrate intake *only slightly*, making your body grab only somebody fat thus creating *only* the necessary ketones to break that fat down in a more natural way.

With the daily Keto diet suggesting *less than 30 grams carbohydrate* and filling the rest of your plate with fat, you're back on Starvation Island. No body balance there! Rather it'll be _body panic._ The only way such a panic can be avoided is to go on the diet while _already having_ *a very highly efficient fat-*

---

[184] Remember that your hormones often work in pairs. Insulin, for example, is a storage hormone that takes excess glucose and stores it as fat and further, *insulin locks the excess fat* and makes it extremely difficult to release. Glucagon (stimulated by dietary protein) is a mobilization hormone, and as such it's the biological opposite of insulin because it *retrieves and then releases stored carbohydrate* (glycogen) as fuel. In essence, one drives your blood sugar down while the other builds it up. Working together, they control your blood sugar levels.

[185] I had a great time hitch-hiking across Europe in the early 70s, although it resulted in a really big scare. I lost my period for about three months – egads. You can imagine my relief to hear the German doctor say, "did you think you were pregnant??" He then explained that the sudden change in my diet might have caused that outcome; recently, I had quit eating all meats and chicken. Phew, close call! I took my pills to West Africa for the two years I was there!!!

burning and calorie-burning ability[186]. Such individuals (e.g., long term bodybuilders) already lift weights, have tons of muscle, a fast metabolism and are very physically fit. They tend to endure such a deprivation diet for only a couple of weeks prior to a stage performance. They'll bulk-up in the gym (lifting heavy weights and eating 1,000s and 1,000s of daily nutritious calories) and then basically starve themselves of carbohydrates just before a stage show. They call is "cutting" and they'll combine it with an increase in cardio exercise. They hate it. It's a hugely tough process on their bodies. But I'll bet that you don't have such a bulked-up body; you're probably a fat-making engine who doesn't lift a lot of weights. If this is you, I'd never suggest the Keto diet.

The Keto diet is an example of a drastic and highly prescriptive diet, bordering on starvation of the carbohydrate nutrient, and causing your body to eat its muscle and its fat for fuel. Better air out that tent out for Starvation Island.

When I plugged in my statistics and the fact that I'm very physically active (downhill skiing, daily gym workouts, etc.), the Keto diet told me to eat about 1,622 daily calories which included 120 grams fat (1080 calories), 22 grams[187] carbohydrate (88 calories), and 113 grams protein (452 calories). Frankly I don't think I could exist with only 22 grams carbohydrate and still feel great. Also, eating that much fat (67% of my diet) and that little protein would be really difficult for me. Normally I would eat almost 7-8 times more daily carbohydrates (a lot of vegetables here, _not_ super-carbohydrate breads or processed foods or sugary stuff) and over 150 grams of protein. I want to retain my protein-eating muscles. This diet would definitely kill my overall energy and subsequently my strength and endurance for the gym. Bye-bye successful muscle-building and weight-training for me! And hello constipation.

---

[186] This is sort of analogous to the use of the treadmill; to be *oxidatively* effective at "cardio" fat-burning, you have to be physically fit in advance of jumping on (otherwise you're eating some of your muscle tissue).

[187] One slice of whole wheat bread has about 10 grams of net carbohydrates (= total carbs less dietary fibre) and 1 cup of chopped raw carrots would be about 12 grams of carbs! And so I'd say that 22 grams sure isn't very much for the day. Good grief, one small banana is 90 calories, 1 medium apple is 95 calories, and ¼ cup of oatmeal is 83 calories. Choose one of those and you're done for the day!!!

Let's spell out the comparison for how I would eat on the *muscle-eating/fat-burning* Keto diet (the current "fad" diet that every obese person is talking about and that is one of the most googled questions) and how I would eat on some of my *muscle-building/fat-burning* diets. See the chart below.

Keep in mind that the more muscle-building you want, then the more weight-training you must and can actually do. When you are eating a surplus of nutritious food, your body will always be able to use that extra caloric energy to train harder and build more beautifully lean toned muscle. That's why bodybuilders can eat a ton of food yet don't get fat. Some of them are eating over 5,000 calories daily and converting it all to muscle!!! Like I've said to some of my clients, "you're not eating enough food to lose fat and gain muscle!"

Diet Used	Total Daily Macro Cals	Carbs @ 4 cals/gm	Fat @ 9cals/gm	Protein @ 4 cals/gm
Advised Keto diet	**About 1620 cals**	**22 gms = 88 cals (about 5%)**	120 gms = 1080 cals (about 67%)	113 gms = 452 cals (about 28%)
My normal maintain diet	About 1650 cals	165 gms = 660 cals (about 40%)	55 gms = 495 cals (about 30%)	124 gms = 495 cals (about 30%)
My lose-overall weight diet.	About 1400 cals[188]	131 gms = 525 cals (about 30%)	52 gms = 465 cals (about 35%)	150 gms = 600 cals (about 35%)
My lose-fat and build-muscle diet	**About 1750 cals** *(my usual diet)*	153 gms = 612 cals (about 35%)	49 gms = 438 cals (about 25%)	**175 gms = 700 cals (about 40%)**

---

[188] My BMR (basal/basic metabolic rate) is about 1200 calories daily just to be alive.

My muscle major bulk-up get-lean diet	About 2000 cals *(only an occasional diet)*	125 gms = 500 cals (about 25%)	67 gms = 600 cals (about 30%)	**225 gms = 900 cals (about 45%)**

Now let's ask what too many body ketones (called *ketoacidosis[189]*) might do to your body's biochemistry[190]. With insufficient insulin to interact with your cells, your liver must *over-produce* ketones. Normally insulin would keep the number of ketones in check, but, with too little insulin, ketone production can go crazy. Ketones are slightly *acidic* and so with too many kicking around your pH level will also be altered and high acidity can result in unhealthy tissue inflammation and a much *slower metabolism*. And acidity always helps you stay in a fat-making mode. It's the enemy of weight- and fat-loss.

Incredibly people still adopt this diet even though they're forewarned about all the negative side-effects in the early days. If a diet is giving you leg cramps or spasms, it's a sign of the lack of minerals including magnesium. When mineral electrolytes are being flushed out, this will include the body's salt[191]. When your electrolyte balance is thrown off, your body will begin to dump potassium as well. That's when your muscles come into action; they'll be broken down in order to supply that potassium and you'll lose lean muscle and develop a negative nitrogen balance as a result. Just the typical metabolic adaptation by your body when vacationing on Starvation Island. And remember what I keep stressing even if you're sick and tired of hearing it, *muscle is your **main** calorie-burning tissue*. You'll also be urinating a lot which means you're losing precious water, hence flirting with dehydration as well as the loss of a whack of micronutrients. Good grief, Keto bodies must be in a major panic mode trying to get back to normal biochemical balance.

---

[189] Heck, if they have a name for it, I guess it must be a potentially serious side effect!

[190] Certainly most Type-1 diabetics (with non-functioning insulin-production) should be cautious with this diet as they don't want their glucose levels severely low. If they do, it should only be under strict medical supervision.

[191] Your body needs salt electrolytes to transmit nerve impulses, contract and relax muscle fibres (think about your heart) as well as maintain a proper biochemical fluid balance.

You already know that all low-carbohydrate diets will slow down your metabolism and that your weight-loss goals can be met over the long-term in a more sustainable way by *only slightly* altering the daily percentage of macronutrients eaten. If you want to gain muscle, then up your protein slightly and lower your carbohydrate slightly. If you want to lose body fat tissue, then lower your dietary carbohydrate and fat intakes slightly. *But keep eating all three macronutrients daily.*

Warning – Yes, I know. I'm repeating myself, but this is so important I just can't help myself! If you go on any of these non-nutritional diets, remember that once your body has experienced a major biochemical hormonal panic mode and you begin to eat more normally (these diets are *never* sustainable), you'll have forced your body to think that it may not get food for a while and so it'll fight like crazy to keep *every calorie* and *every ounce of fat* you eat. In fact, it'll store a lot more body fat because it can usually hang onto that type of tissue longer; and, this will be a lot easier to do because your metabolic calorie-burning rate will have adapted by getting a lot slower.

I could go on analyzing various popular diets but that's not the purpose of this book. When you finish reading the whole book, I hope that you'll understand your body and appreciate its normal biochemical mechanisms a bit better and that you'll agree that there are no short cuts to a beautiful healthy and toned body.

Just another aside. If you're worried about eating after 6pm or 8pm, don't be. Your body doesn't really care when you eat your last daily meal. It only deals with the daily overall intake and whether or not the foods contributing to those intakes are balanced in terms of macronutrients and whether you've chosen nutrient-dense foods or crappy refined, fried, sugary and highly processed calorie-dense foods.

All successful diets share three rules: low-sugar, high-fiber, and only eating fat and carbohydrate with off-setting fiber (not normally seen in refined carbohydrates) and adequate protein to meet your fitness needs.

When you read the diet summary that worked for me, you'll see cottage cheese at night. Why? Because it's very easily digested protein and won't prevent a good sleep as a result. Some people like to eat at night and claim that it makes them sleep better. OK, if that's you then make sure you aren't eating the fattening stuff like refined processed carbohydrates (e.g., packaged cereals), saturated fats, trans-fats and sugary treats. Choose foods with a *nutritiously* high calorie density. Examples include yogurt, cottage cheese, hard cheeses (e.g., cheddar), or a few nuts and seeds.

Having said that, I'll also repeat that it isn't good to get up in the middle of the night to eat! Your body needs its rest on several levels, including digestion and hormonal activity. Remember that your muscle-building and fat-decreasing human growth hormone (HGH), detests sleep deprivation while your waist-fattening cortisol loves a lack of sleep.

And speaking about eating at different times, once I got asked if **shiftwork** alters your ability to lose weight! Obviously, you need to plan for regular day-night sleeping rhythms to maintain an efficient metabolism. And so, even though shift-work can affect your overall weight, it's really only because you *aren't sleeping properly* before or after your shift and you're probably *giving in to your cravings* for high-fat, high-sugar and/or high-calorie quick-to-sugar "simple" carbohydrate foods. These foods will directly affect your cortisol and insulin hormonal balances, your blood acidity level, your fat-making enzymes, your thermogenesis mechanisms *and* your metabolic engine – all resulting in a highly compromised fat-burning ability.

It's simple, you have to eat a healthy *sustainable* diet, get sufficient sleep and you have to exercise. It's good for you on multiple levels.

Practice some patience and quit looking for that unattainable *quick fix that those magazines propose.*

2.28 What the Heck Should I Eat to Lose Weight?

"Learn from yesterday, live for today, hope for tomorrow. The important thing is not to stop questioning." – A.E.

Although the diet I used would probably work for the vast majority of you, I would never suggest that every diet fits every person. Successful diets can depend upon many different factors: carbohydrate-sensitivity, insulin-resistance, lactose-intolerance, diabetes complications, thyroid function (which controls your metabolic rate), toxicity, food allergies, metabolic type, body framework, limited exercise ability (due to permanent physical injury), age, emotional issues, lifestyle habits, stress levels, genetics, and/or other medical conditions.

You'll probably need an integrated and individualized approach to weight-loss that works for you. You need to be honest with yourself as well. You'll need to track yourself over the longer haul to see if the diet plan you chose is actually moving you toward your goals and along a *reasonable* timeline (which would be an average loss of 1% bodyweight weekly). Over time, it'll get a more difficult to lose the same weekly weight as you get closer to your goal. Why? Because the 1% figure gets *smaller* the *more successful* you are.

But with all decisions, you have to take real ownership of the food you put into your mouth. Be food responsible. NO ONE controls what you eat except you![192] Know when enough is enough, know when not to eat, take full responsibility for everything you decide to eat, commit to eating nutritionally superior foods, enjoy your food, take time preparing and eating meals. And most importantly, *quit rushing*. Think about everything you put into your mouth. You won't have to do that forever, but you'll have to do it until you reach your goal. At that point you'll probably have changed how you eat on a permanent level, because you simply won't continue to enjoy the taste of or reaction to bad-for-your-hormones food. Such food can make you feel bloated and a bit sick. That's what happened to me. I'm not currently a perfect eater, like I was while losing that 40 pounds, but I remain a careful and mindful eater most of the time. Once you reach your goal you can relax A BIT.

The classic question is "should I go low-fat or low-carbohydrate?" These are two ends of a very long and often confusing spectrum of choices, but they do provide the extremes and extremes are *never* very good choices. While the low-fat diets usually call for high-carbohydrate intakes, this can be difficult because it can be hard to choose the right kind of carbohydrate for every meal and it's dietary carbohydrates that can make a lot of your body fat, *not* dietary fat. If you choose poorly, it'll lead to fat-storage and reduced rates of body fat breakdown. This sure isn't what you want. On the other side of the choice spectrum, the low-carbohydrate diets do take care of the blood sugar control side of weight-loss; but they can elevate cortisol levels (which facilitates body fat retention) and lower your ability to burn calories by lowering your metabolic rate. This translates into fast weight-loss in the first few weeks, then

---

[192] You probably know that babies will tend to close their mouths or spit out food when they don't want anymore! They still listen to their leptin signalling hormones...don't force feed babies and toddlers. You'll not be doing them any health favours; indeed, you could be moving them toward an obese adulthood. Put a broad variety of nutritious foods on their plates. They'll be just fine! They'll choose what they want and ignore what they don't want, and they won't get over-weight either.

a disheartening plateau, followed by weight-*gain*. And the really extreme no-carbohydrate diets can be extremely hard on your body while it breaks down both muscle and fatty tissues in order to synthesize some glucose fuel for your body's critically needed energy! Such diet approaches are stressful on your organs given all the acidic toxic by-products that must be dealt with in one way or the other.

You should pick a diet that's nutrient-dense yet matches your food preferences (obviously I'm not suggesting chocolate bars), your daily schedules for work, family and exercise. Lower-fat or lower-carb or higher-protein but *balanced* for long-term biochemical and hormonal success. Keep in mind that diets which include very restrictive rules tend to be extremely difficult to endure let alone sustain and they result in feelings of deprivation that can lead to cheating and/or binging as well as a body in major hormonal panic mode.

Once you start eating more protein and more fiber, you'll feel a lot better
and
you'll feel full for longer. You'll then find it'll become easier to make better food choices.
You won't be in such a hurry to guzzle any quickly available food.

If you have no willpower to make reasonable choices and know that you are highly prone to cheating, you may need a very inflexible and rigidly prescriptive diet. But definitely you need a more balanced diet, one that includes all the three macronutrients and fiber in the percentages that reflect your goals. And remember, to be successful at reaching and maintaining your goals over the long haul, your eating plan must be sustainable meaning that you need to be able to follow it for a *long time*. The diet you choose should bring together the metabolic controls of cortisol, insulin, ghrelin, blood sugar and thermogenesis to optimize your overall weight-loss and fat-loss benefits. And it must also be nutrient-dense while avoiding "empty calories" like sugar.

Also, don't overeat, don't eat when you are emotionally upset, depressed or bored. Don't make food a habit or reward and don't let any particular food be addictive. Stop constantly snacking or grazing, don't overindulge in sugar and refined highly processed carbohydrates. Avoid HFCS and all partially hydrogenated oils (i.e., trans-fats). Avoid binge eating, and for heaven's sake, quit drinking your calories. You have the control. Using that control will make you feel wonderfully empowered. Generate your self-worth from within and not via the approval of others. Value yourself for who you are. Don't allow fragile self-esteem or low confidence to define you. You may not be able to self-nurture, thinking that you're a giver and should never be a taker (inherently seen as selfish by many women). Food can become an emotional crutch because you feel guilty putting yourself first and so you overeat to nurture yourself. This will lead to food habits and eventually to food addictions. Stop it! **Habits and addictions are more easily developed then gotten rid of.**

Believe in yourself and love yourself. You deserve to think of yourself first. You're a good person.

The eating plan I subscribed to for about a year is detailed in a subsequent chapter. It's one that should work for most weight-conscious people. I followed it religiously, even when I went to work or went skiing for the day, I took my food with me. Yes, I had to buy a lot of differently shaped plastic containers – some with screw tops for yogurt travel.

I'm not a special person. If I can do it, so can you!

Remember that falling down during your journey-to-fitness might occur, BUT getting up afterwards and carrying on will determine your overall success. TENACITY rules!!!

Use some strategies to control your eating habits. If you tend to snack after dinner while watching TV, then drink a few glasses of water instead. Or have some cottage cheese with fresh fruit. And watch your portions.

Unit 3

The Exercise Challenge

How can exercise change the overall weight picture?

Here are some principles to consider:

- **Weight-training** will increase your metabolic calorie-burning rate.
- **By progressively increasing your weights**, you'll build lean metabolically active calorie-burning tissue
- **Exercise will improve** your insulin hormonal functions, control your blood sugars, keep your cortisol fat-making stress hormones in check and increase your anti-aging growth hormones.
- **Solely using "cardio" equipment** is not the most efficient way to burn body fat.
- **Performing perfect weight-lifting technique and appropriate cardiovascular exercises without a proper diet** will not give you a visibly toned muscular body.

You get what you work for, not what you wish for!!!

3.1 Why Should I Exercise?

"Life is like riding a bicycle. To keep your balance, you must keep moving." – A.E.

Exercise will give you more confidence, better overall health, better posture, a sounder sleep experience, better manage your blood sugar, a lower body fat percentage, a longer life, a more pain-free existence, restore joint and back mobility, and a wonderful frame of mind. You might think that exercise will leave you tired, but actually the opposite is true! It'll also harvest some nice compliments. And you'll be a lot more fun to be with. Why would you avoid it?

If you want to talk timelines, here are some nice expectations once you start lifting weights: <u>after an hour</u> your metabolism stays revved up because your heart is beating faster and you'll have some feel-good serotonin kicking around; <u>after a day</u> you might feel a bit sore as your body repairs its muscle fibers, making them stronger; <u>after a week</u> your mitochondria will start proliferating and you'll have better stamina and sleep better at night; <u>after a month</u> your lungs will be stronger at keeping you oxidative which helps burn more calories and is needed to get rid of body fat; <u>after 6 months</u> you'll begin to look more toned and your clothes will fit better; and finally, <u>after a year</u> you'll be in smaller sized clothes and your bones will be a lot stronger protecting your from injury such as hip fractures. Frankly, you'll have become hooked on exercise and your body will actually become biochemically fitter and look younger than its chronological age!!! It happened to me in my early 60s and it <u>will</u> happen to you regardless of your age.

Although all types of exercise are beneficial, *different types of exercise will deliver different sets of benefits.* If executed properly, aerobic exercises (these use oxygen) such as running, jogging, rowing, cycling and swimming provide cardiovascular, endurance and respiratory benefits. Anaerobic weight-training exercises (these don't use respiratory oxygen) provide benefits for muscular strength, endurance and power, as well as bone health. Both exercise types are valuable for weight and fat-loss[193] and work *together* to improve how sensitive your body is to your fat-making insulin hormone.

---

[193] And I hope you now fully appreciate that the overall loss of weight is not necessarily only the loss of body-fat.

Exercise will give you better posture, a lower body fat percentage,
a longer life, a pain-free existence, more muscle, stronger bones,
increase strength and endurance, improve insulin-sensitivity,
modulate blood sugar and cortisol levels, a beautifully aesthetic healthy
body
and help you lose weight by changing you into a calorie-burning engine.
WOW, sounds great.

A lot of women think that if they jump on the treadmill and sweat a lot, then they're losing fat. Nope, it isn't fat weight you're losing, it's water. To lose fat, you have to be able to burn oxygen – and you have to be physically fit to be oxidative. Sweating is just your body's way of regulating its temperature by removing some heat. Remember that body fat is a storage of triglycerides and a combination of hydrogen and carbon and <u>very little oxygen</u>. This is why you need some oxygen to metabolize it. The chemistry happening is this: respiratory oxygen is added to the hydrogen (H) and carbon (C) bonds in triglycerides. That in turn makes carbon dioxide (CO_2) to breathe out and some water (H_2O). Neat, eh?

And for those of you who get excited about the sauna thinking that you're burning off some body fat, nope, it too is just another form of water-loss in an effort to lose some heat. And it can lead to dehydration. The minute you begin drinking fluids, your level of hydration will return to normal and that pound lost in the sauna will quickly reappear. Dehydration actually *reduces* your capacity to burn calories!

People think that, in addition to better overall health, the main reasons to exercise are to burn tons of calories and to lose weight. But when you finish reading this book, you'll know that these are <u>*not*</u> the key benefits of weight-training. Certainly, cardio machine exercising will burn some calories, but the number simply won't be as high as you probably think and they probably won't match what you see on the machines. That's because those machines are calibrated in a very universal way. I hope that you can now appreciate that *your body* is a very *complex and specific-to-you biochemical unit*; it'll be uniquely different than the other bodies kicking around the gym in terms of its ability to burn calories. Why? Because neither you nor that treadmill know how your metabolic rate compares to the others at the gym, or how comparatively fit you are.

The primary reason to exercise as part of a weight-control plan is because of its ability to *improve* insulin hormonal functions and to *control* your level of blood sugars <u>and</u> circulating cortisol hormones (yeah, exercise reduces stress[194]). Regular exercise can teach your muscles to transport glucose more efficiently and to respond to cortisol more effectively. Exercise will always improve your body's sensitively to <u>both</u> insulin and cortisol, thereby allowing you to get by with *lower* levels of both hormones avoiding the weight-gain that's always associated with elevated levels of one or the other or both.

Exercise will also increase your caloric expenditure and your fat-burning (i.e., thermogenesis). In other words, exercise will, <u>on its own,</u> influence the primary metabolic controls related to your body's weight regulation. Yup, you'll speed up your metabolism <u>and</u> be able to burn more calories. Your current fat-making body will begin to move toward the calorie-burning engine that you want it to be. Exercise also helps to mitigate and even reverse the dreaded age-related weight-gain discussed previously.

Even having said all of the above, the use of exercise to lose weight still remains quite controversial. I always told my heavier clients that weight-training will strengthen and tone their muscles, will burn calories for a couple of days after the gym visit and *will prevent **new** fatty deposits*. I added that it'll give them a strong muscular <u>toned</u> body BUT that unless they changed their eating habits and decisions (which I assumed were poor due to their continuing excess weight), then *no one would SEE that toned body as it would still be well hidden under their remaining bulky fat!*

Regular exercise is also an important tool for the *prevention* of weight regain. It seems counter-intuitive to suggest this; but it's very difficult to promote a significant *negative energy balance* with exercise. When energy intake (calories) is lower than energy expenditure (calorie-burning) then you have a <u>negative</u> energy balance. When energy intake is greater than energy expenditure, you have a <u>positive</u> energy balance. The only ways to achieve negative energy balance include the consumption of fewer *non-nutrient calorie-dense* processed carbohydrates, expend more energy or both. Seems easy but it isn't. Why? Because of a lack of understanding about the *energy*

---

[194] The more you exercise, the fewer stress hormones are needed to control the essential physiological adaptations required by that exercise – with the super great effect of *minimizing the detrimental effects of cortisol* which include the retention of that unattractive abdominal body-fat.

value of different foods and exercises. For example, you might burn 250 calories in an aerobic gym class and then wipe it out by eating just one little slice of pizza. There are many women who go to group gym classes and NEVER lose weight or change their overall shape. I can imagine their frustration. Hmmm, I wonder what they're eating?

With a calorie deficit of 3500 calories needed to lose *just one pound of body fat*, and with the reasonable and healthy goal of losing one to two pounds overall weight per week, this would require a calorie deficit of 500-1000 calories per day. Egads, that's a lot[195]! Rather than carving off that many daily calories, it would mean an hour or two of *really intense* exercise every day of the week. How many of us could stick to one of those plans?

The "cut-calorie" approach would probably move your body into a starvation mode while the "visit-the-gym-daily" approach might prove to be very difficult to continue for many of you – especially if you're working fulltime and/or have young children or are studying at university. With this in mind, I always tried to fit my life around the gym rather than try to fit the gym into my life. And I usually hit the gym floor at least 5 times per week. Before retiring when time was scarcer, I went home after work, walked the dog, got changed and drove to the gym. I got the family dinner ready a bit later than what everyone had been used to it, but it worked fine for us all and after years of putting my family first, I refused to feel guilty about putting my goals first. I awaited the complaints, but there weren't any.

The reason people lose weight and end up with a *smaller version of the same body shape* is because they have employed calorie-restriction with no metabolic intervention such as proper weight-training exercises and balanced macronutrient eating habits. This is simply never good in the longer term as they'll be losing *both* fat *and* muscle during their weight-loss journey. And of course, it's the loss of muscle which is directly related to your metabolic rate.

---

[195] Only a very morbidly obese individual who might normally eat over 3000-5000 daily calories, could shave that many daily calories and it would be solely by moving away from an over-reliance on heavily processed, sugary, fast, fried and saturated fatty foods (all very easy to eat in large quantities, contrary to fibrous foods) in their diet to one of whole nutrient-dense foods and by practicing strict portion-control. It has been estimated that obese individuals eat about 60-70% of their daily calories in the form of overly processed carbohydrates. Carbohydrate intake would normally never be higher than 40% for weight maintenance.

You now know that when you slow down your overall metabolism, you'll need fewer and fewer calories to maintain the same weight.

You must efficiently digest and absorb all the caloric energy you eat. You must affect the energy you use by exercising appropriately (4-6 hours per week minimum), by producing heat during that exercise, by eating lean protein and lots of fresh vegetables (complex starchy slow-to-sugar carbohydrates) at *regular intervals* throughout the day, by incorporating the good inflammation fighting omega-3 fatty-acids, and by sleeping 7-8 hours per night. Eating every 3-4 hours will also help to keep your calorie-burning metabolic engine running at peak performance especially if every meal has protein.

Exercise expands the vascular system in your muscle tissues, opens your blood capillary vessels, causes your blood sugar levels to lower, causes your blood pressure to lower, builds up your lean calorie-eating muscle mass and the directly related strength, endurance and power. Exercise stimulates your fat-burning enzymes, produces more serotonin (an anti-depressant hormone) and endorphins (natural hormonal opiates)[196], increases your joint mobility (always good as you age), strengthens your bones (helping to prevent osteoporosis) and, more generally, increases your hormone production and betters your posture. Along with nutritionally balanced eating, you'll soon discover that exercise *also* benefits the two other main factors which directly affect your weight, specifically chronic stress and sleep deprivation (bye-bye cortisol).

Need I say more positive things about exercise????? Quit waiting for scientists to come up with a magic fat-loss pill. Although I'm not after my youth per say, I still call exercise the "fountain of youth" pill. Exercise can take a body which is 65 years old chronologically and magically transform it into a typical 50-year-old body inside. Nobody believes I'm 72, though I do tell them as I'm very proud of how I look and I want to inspire people to believe it can be done at any age. It took work. It took time. It took weight-training and it took the informed biochemical knowledge-base I am sharing with you via this book.

If your body is not fed properly, it'll always search for amino acids from existing muscle and in effect, cannibalize your muscle tissues to get them. This muscle-wasting is what you'll experience on Starvation Island. This is why

---

[196] One of my clients found that she no longer had to take anti-depressants – now there's an incredible outcome for weightlifting!!!

you need to provide your body with proteins as you age. And it's especially true if you're weight-training in the gym, an anabolic process that will be using the metabolic processes and pathways that *build* the biomolecules which *cause* exercise-induced protein deficiencies and muscle fatigue[197]. You want to be fatigued after weight-training, as it means that you've cycled through your energy reserve capacity.

If you want that gorgeous sexy toned look, if you want to proudly wear sleeveless tank tops in the summer, then weight-training is what you *must* undertake. Because you don't have a lot of male sex hormones, weight-training will never make you look like a bulked-up muscle man. Put simply, weight-training challenges muscles beyond what they're normally used to, creating microscopic *tears* in your muscles. Your body repairs these by making your muscles stronger and denser. But unless you have an unusually high percentage of male testosterone hormones or are on anabolic steroids, you'll *never ever* develop the muscles that a man can. As I said earlier in the book, a man has 40% *more* muscle mass than you do and frankly there's absolutely nothing you can do about that! Quit making excuses borne from ill-informed myths. Work with and build-up what you have.

Exercises are either aerobic (use oxygen) or anaerobic (don't use oxygen). Cardio should be more aerobic, while weight-training is mostly anaerobic.

You want to exercise in order to build-up your calorie-burning muscle. This "hypertrophy" or muscle growth is induced by the release of your DHEA hormone[198] (which has an anabolic growth effect). Unfortunately, *too much*

---

[197] If you supplement with BCAAs (branched chain amino-acids) during your exercising, you'll not suffer as much fatigue. This is because your hardworking muscles don't have to go to your liver to get the amino-acids and this is a super-duper benefit for building that defined and toned muscle you crave. And, of course, a well-deserved breather for your busy liver.

[198] People get mixed up between DHEA (a circulating steroid which is created naturally by your body) and HGH (human growth hormone). HGH is produced by your brain's pituitary gland and it's responsible for muscle-building and healthy organ tissues. Obviously, a growing child has a higher HGH percentage than a fully-grown adult. DHEA is also a growth hormone (**dehydroepiandrosterone**), but it's produced by your adrenal glands, which are sitting on top of your kidneys. It's also used for producing your sex hormones.

strenuous exercise produces the cortisol hormone creating a catabolic metabolic breakdown effect, therefore don't *over-train* your body. Yet again, balance is of primary concern to your body. To over-train, you'd have to be visiting the gym multiple times a day, using poor form with insufficient rest periods for various muscle groups, fatiguing the <u>same</u> muscle groups over and over and over, day after day. Over-training simply means that you've trained beyond your body's natural ability to properly recover. It generally results in a *decrease in strength performance* and/or a lengthy time with frustrating plateauing. This is not to say you can't visit the gym twice a day, you just have to be knowledgeable about what you are doing in order to successfully avoid the over-training syndrome.

Sometimes I exercise twice a day, but I'm very careful. I might do legs in the morning and arms in the afternoon. And then do chest, tris and delts one morning, with back and biceps and traps in the afternoon. I never over-tax/train my muscles by doing the same thing two days in a row. I will give my muscles time off so to speak. Time off to repair themselves, to get stronger and to torch more calories and body fat.

<u>Weight-training results in many body advantages:</u>

- Your <u>appearance</u> can be radically improved, and it masks the appearance of cellulite by smoothing out the lumps and bumps of your skin's under-lying fat.
- It'll boost your <u>metabolism</u>, so that your body is more efficient at burning calories.
- It'll build-up your muscles and lower your <u>body fat percentage</u>; remember that a pound of muscle is much denser than a pound of fat, so you'll sculpt a new body shape by building up lean muscle.
- It'll keep you <u>young</u>; you lose muscle and bone mass as you age, and weight-training can slow such progression as well as help combat osteoporosis.
- It'll keep you tougher and <u>less injury-prone</u> simply due to stronger muscles.
- It <u>reduces anxiety</u> and <u>eases depression and tension</u>.
- It improves your <u>posture</u> allowing you to walk taller and straighter, which I call "walking in a stacked position" (your chin is above your

toes, your shoulders are back and down, you won't be stooped over like some of those older people you see). Imagine walking stooped over all the time, no wonder such poor posture people complain about sore lower backs! Their weight is not over their feet (their base of support). It's too far forward – just try walking like an old person.

- When you walk, push "the girls" out in front of you, you'll look much better, taller and much more powerful (which bodes well for those of you still working fulltime).
- It makes your life so much easier functionally when you can carry your groceries or a grandchild.
- You'll definitely sleep better.

I call weight-training the *anti-aging pill*, the one that has never been created and if a healthy and successful one had been, I suppose it would save a lot of time[199]; but don't hold your breath, just go to the gym and weight-train.

Should you take a supplement while you're exercising?

If you decide to drink a protein mix before, during or after exercising, make sure it isn't full of sugar! Carbohydrate and protein are good during or following a hard workout, obviously non-nutrient sugar isn't.

Protein supplements will reduce fatigue while you're weightlifting. They'll also accelerate muscle tissue recovery and improve your use of fat for workout fuel; but, make certain that your supplement contains branched-chain amino-acids (BCAAs) such as leucine, isoleucine and valine. These three *essential* amino acids make up 35% of those found in your muscle tissues. I drink BCAAs while I exercise not only for the performance benefits, but also because I can work out for longer without feeling tired. BCAAs help to prevent protein breakdown during your weight-training, therein saving your hard-

---

[199] If you're impatient and you want change in a *ridiculously short period* of time, you'll probably end up resorting to those starvation diet promises or to unhealthy diet pills. Do keep in mind that many of these "diet" pills have amphetamines (remember "speed" from the 60s?) which negatively affect many bodily functions, including the potential results of increased heart rate, increased blood pressure, swelling in the legs, increased urination, insomnia, shortness of breath, etc. If this all sounds great to you, in order to lose some weight, well seriously, you've really learned NOTHING while reading this book.

earned calorie-eating muscle. This will give you improved recovery, more muscle rebuilding and increased strength. You can buy powdered BCAAs at any health food store and they come in many delicious flavors. Just find one whose taste you like. They're expensive, so buy only the smallest amounts until you find the perfect brand and your preferred taste. You may like a watermelon taste, I hate it! Do I think the industry actually incorporates real fruit? Probably not, but still I buy it. Mine has "natural flavor" and the synthesized sweetener "sucralose" but I never claimed to be perfect. I use it only when working out at the gym. You can also look for collagen powder in health food stores and you <u>can</u> get this *un*flavored.

If you're "too busy" to exercise, then just accept the fact that you'll *<u>never lose</u>* those extra pounds, because without exercise the metabolic control of your blood sugar and cortisol will *<u>never be optimal.</u>* I think you should invest time in your health, in your body and in yourself. Can you exercise 50-60 minutes daily? Yes! You probably watch TV or spend time on social media for longer periods of time. You read books and the newspaper for longer than that. And I'll bet that you google a lot too. Do you have time to go to a gym? Yes, of course you do. Do you have enough money to join a gym? Yes, you do. You spend lots of money on boots and shoes and clothes and family and friends and restaurant dinners and bars and vacations. Why not put some of that time and money toward a gym membership and, at the outset, a personal trainer?

You ARE worth it!

And, sorry I just have to say this. If you hire a personal trainer, don't be a "whiner" or complain when it's suggested that you lift heavier weights over time. Obviously, <u>pain</u> is a no-go. You should feel muscular tension when lifting weights, but NEVER any acute pain. Body pain is always an indication of a problem. Your trainer will *only* know that you are in pain if you say so. I remember it was actually painful for me to so some of the ab exercises with my trainer, and after I complained he changed the way I was to complete the exercise and I felt fine then. In other cases, a trainer may use a completely different exercise, one that will reap the same muscle group benefits. Complete the exercises the trainer is giving you and do it with proper form. Personal trainers <u>want</u> you to do well. They endeavor to push you a bit more than what you might normally do yourself, all the while moving you to progressively building your muscle strength, cardiovascular endurance and toned skin. And isn't that what you're paying for?

Frankly I just can't say anything negative about exercising.

3.2 How Are Metabolism and Exercise Related?

"Once we accept our limits, we go beyond them." – A.E.

I've been going on and on about your metabolism. Now let's get into even more detail on how it's related to exercise and your body's hormonal balances. By now you must know and appreciate that your metabolic rate or metabolism, your body's engine, is where it's all at!!! You must know by now that you don't want to make it inefficient. You don't want to slow it down with poor nutritional choices. And you most certainly don't want to lose a bunch of your calorie-eating muscle. Remember when we talked about the need to speed up your ability to burn calories, that is, to speed up your metabolism? All of the physical and biochemical activities in your body that convert or use energy/calories are part of your metabolism (e.g., breathing, digesting food, and circulating blood).

I'll bet that you didn't know that your metabolism exists in a combination of two quite distinct metabolic forms. One is catabolism and the other is anabolism. These processes work together *simultaneously* to free up and/or to capture energy in your body. Indeed, your overall metabolic calorie-burning rate will always be some sort of combination of catabolism and anabolism. Together, catabolism (breaking down) and anabolism (building up) are the essential metabolic processes of your life. That said, your health will be determined by the *ratio* of damage (catabolic) to repair (anabolic).

If we compare the ratio of catabolism (how much energy your body *produces*) to anabolism (how much energy your body *uses*), we have these weight-related results:

3. If catabolism is *greater than* anabolism, we have weight-*gain.*
4. If anabolism is *greater than* catabolism, we have weight-*loss.*

Which do you want? I know what I want!

How much of each of these two processes takes place will ultimately determine your overall calorie-burning ability. And so, "do you want to be a fat-making catabolic engine or a calorie-burning anabolic engine???"

Catabolism involves all the metabolic processes that *tear-down or damage biomolecules*[200]. Catabolism is the set of metabolic pathways that breaks down large molecules (e.g., dietary fats) into smaller units which are then *oxidized* to release energy (e.g., fatty acids/triglycerides into water and carbon dioxide). Indeed, and as noted earlier, this is why you need oxygen to burn/release your body fat. Catabolism also provides the biochemical energy necessary for the maintenance and growth of cells and for the creation of the ATP high-energy fuel required to meet your aerobic and anerobic needs. These critically important ATP molecules are constantly being *made* by your body or being *used* by your body (remember that ATM body/bank machine into which you can put calories or from which you can draw out calories). ATP is in every one of your cells; it helps them to create heat/energy to move your muscles (during exercise) and to perform other essential body functions such as pumping your heart.

Other examples of catabolism are of course the eating and breaking down of dietary macronutrients such as protein into amino-acids and carbohydrates into glucose/sugar. When you don't eat enough carbohydrate, your body will then *catabolically* breakdown fat and protein into glucose. And I want to remind you that breaking down protein into glucose energy is a highly inefficient non-preferred biochemical adaptation that'll always result in some serious muscle-wasting. Bon voyage to that toned body you so desperately crave.

Anabolism is the reverse of the destructive or *breakdown* nature of catabolism, as it involves all metabolic processes that *build large biomolecules from small ones.*[201] It's a constructive or *build-up* metabolic process and, contrary to catabolism, its reactions always take place *without the use of cardiorespiratory oxygen.*

Examples of anabolism include bone growth, organ tissue repair and muscle mass increase. Sounds pretty good to me. Some athletes, trying to improve their performance by speeding up the anabolic molecule-building

---

[200] Catabolism involves the following hormones: adrenaline, cortisol, cytokines (secreted by the immune system) and glucagon which of course promotes the *breakdown* of stored glycogen/carbohydrate to glucose in your liver.

[201] Anabolism involves the following hormones: estrogen, insulin, the human growth hormone and testosterone.

process, will use *anabolic* steroids[202]. But there are serious potential health risks with this approach including kidney problems or even failure[203], liver damage, enlarged heart, high blood pressure, increased risk of stroke or heart attack, paranoia, extreme irritability, extreme mood swings, delusions and/or impaired judgement. Frankly it sounds too scary and unhealthy to me!

In order to lose weight,
you want to be more anabolic (build and repair)
than catabolic (tear-down).

Your body will always seek to balance these two metabolic processes but as you age, maybe you aren't helping your body to continue doing that. Maybe you seldom exercise. Maybe you find it especially difficult to resist quick-n-dirty refined, heavily processed, or sugary carbohydrate foods. Maybe your downfall is fried food or lots of saturated dietary fat. Or maybe you're a closet sugar eater like I was.

Now let's look at that anabolic/catabolic *balance* we should seek and the forces of wear and tear on your body. Youthful bodies are anabolic or high in build and repair, but as we age our wear and tear catabolism increases (lowering muscle mass and increasing obesity). We already know that your hormones will affect your body weight and that your hormone balances are largely driven by what you eat. If your metabolism is in a higher anabolic state, it's building and maintaining your muscle mass. That's good. But, if your metabolism is in a higher catabolic state, it's breaking down or losing overall mass, *both muscle and fat*, and you certainly want to avoid losing muscle as much as possible.

Typically, and especially for the physically unfit, catabolism is involved with aerobic or cardiovascular exercises like the treadmill or elliptical.

---

[202] Anabolic steroids are synthetic variations of the male sex hormone testosterone. Earlier I said women lifting heavy weights can _never_ look like men because they simply don't have enough testosterone or basic muscle mass. Well now you know why some women take such steroids; it's the only way to build-up and look like a man! You just can't do it by lifting a ton of heavy weights.

[203] Now you can imagine what probably contributed to Arnold Schwarzenegger (the infamous "Governator") having to endure a kidney transplant in 2003!

Anabolism is involved with weight-training exercises like lifting, pushing or pulling weights. Steer me over to those weights.

With proper exercise, diet and lifestyle you *can* shift your aging catabolic metabolism back towards an anabolic state thereby reducing your chance for obesity and recapturing that super great youthful vitality. If you do a lot of weight-training anabolic workouts, then you'll maintain or even gain muscle as well as shed some body fat. A pound of muscle takes up much less physical space than a pound of fat, so although your body weight[204] and body mass[205] index (BMI)[206] may stay higher with a *leaner* physique, your clothes will sure fit a lot better! I like to call it "body-sculpting." I always tell clients not to worry too much about their overall weight when on a journey to better health, strength and overall fitness, but rather just to check how their clothes are fitting. Clients who believe this and are patient will be much more successful at reaching their fitness goals.

If you must track your overall weight, just do it weekly and do it at the same time on that day – e.g., every Friday morning after getting up in the morning and after visiting the bathroom. Everyone has daily weight fluctuations which are very normal and can be directly attributed to what they've eaten that day, how much they've exercised, how good their sleep was and, of course, how much water they've consumed. You may find that once

---

[204] Most women are overly concerned with their weight. Such a measurement is not always the best indicator of fat-loss.

[205] Basically 99% your body mass is made up of six elements: oxygen, carbon, hydrogen, nitrogen, calcium and phosphorous while the remaining 1% is made up of another five elements: potassium, sulfur, sodium, chlorine and magnesium. You need all 11 elements to support life. Dr. Ashley King, a planetary scientist and stardust expert said that "all the elements in the human body were made in a star and may have come through several supernovas." Remember Joni Mitchell's song that said "we're all made of stardust"? Your body composition is about 35% muscle, 15% bone, 10% skin and a whopping 40% hormones and enzymes (and you know how important these are in terms of body weight and fat accumulation).

[206] BMI is a measure of body-fat based upon your height and your weight. That said, mine looks horrible simply because my height remains the same, and my weight is relatively high given my higher muscle and lower fat content (when compared to some others at the same height). You should use a variety of measurement methods when tracking your changes.

you start eating properly, sufficiently hydrating and exercising daily, you'll more normally have an early morning "poop." Weigh yourself afterwards.

Catabolic workouts may help you shed some weight, reduce stress and strengthen your heart, but they'll work off *both* muscle and fat and you won't change your basic shape. You'll weigh less, but you'll also have a lot less muscle tissue. That's precisely why I don't put unfit clients on those "cardio" machines. I want them to build-up some muscle mass before losing a bunch of it!

3.3 How Should I Exercise?

"Nothing happens until something moves." – A.E.

I'm a really chatty person (yes, I know you've already discerned that fact) and I suppose a bit of a perfectionist when it comes to exercising. But I have to say that I had to quit trying to correct people at the gym. Firstly, it was probably annoying to a bunch of them and secondly it interrupted my own workouts. Suffice it to say that if I got a buck for every time I saw someone doing an exercise or a workout routine incorrectly, I'd be a very rich person indeed. Technique is extremely important as is the *order* in which you do your exercises, the *nature* of your exercises, and the way you change your routines over time.

By now I expect that you appreciate how complicated and complex your body is and how it just wants to maintain homeostasis and balance hormonal reactions and biochemical pathways regardless of how you eat. Well your body is *also* smart enough to figure out what you're doing on the gym floor and it'll adapt pretty fast in an attempt to return to complete balance. We refer to that as a type of workout "plateau." But you can get past that if you know what you're doing!

If you want to experience fast results from weight-training, then you *must* pay extremely close attention to <u>how</u> you're performing your exercises, <u>how much weight</u> you're using, whether you're <u>building that weight progressively</u>, the <u>range-of-motion</u> you're using, the <u>tempo</u> you employ for each repetition (e.g., using slow controlled repetitions) as well as the amount of <u>rest</u> you give yourself between sets of exercises. You also have to alter your training programs periodically to keep your body guessing – every four to eight weeks.

Exercise involves a <u>focused effort</u> and not just movement.

I'd really like to write a book on exercises and how to do them, but I figure you need the knowledge of this book at the outset. This book probably makes you think that food is the most critical issue in weight-loss given the number of chapters devoted to diet-related information; but the proper execution of gym exercises is just as comprehensive for muscle gains and you know that muscle provides most of your calorie-burning tissue. You can't have one without the other. If you want to be successful with *sustainable weight-loss,* muscle growth and its long-term maintenance, as well as efficient fat-loss, then eat carefully and exercise joyfully. Those approaches will also lower your stress levels and help you sleep a heck of a lot better.

Is it complicated to ensure proper weight-training? Absolutely! Is it impossible to learn? No! Knowing that your body is quick to learn is key to achieving great results. If you keep doing exactly the same thing over and over and over and over, not only will you be horribly bored but your body will adapt very quickly and your progress will completely disappear. You have to keep your nervous system on edge, guessing what you're going to do next. As an experienced personal trainer, I always change my exercise tactics every four to nine weeks. I have read that some people have muscles that learn a routine in two weeks, but I believe that's very unusual.

When new to any exercise program, you should start *slowly* and *progressively build the intensity* and duration. The most dramatic results of exercising come with some time, so stick with it. Travel with a notebook of some sort. Track what you do each day on the gym floor in terms of weight used, number of repetitions, and the number of sets for each exercise. Remember what I stressed earlier; it isn't just about heaving heavy weights around; you need *focused effort in order to be successful*. Over time it'll get easier, indeed too easy. That's when you need to increase your weights or the number of repetitions, etc. It means that your body has metabolically adapted and you need to challenge it more in order to continue building your lean muscle mass, burning more body fat and getting past that frustrating plateau.

Generally, I found that clients who changed how they ate and came to the gym at least four to five times weekly began to see a difference in how their clothes fit at about 12 weeks. Did I say this would be easy? Or, fast? NO, never. If you find yourself getting bored, then change up your workout routine or better yet get a workout buddy to meet you at the gym. Working out with someone else will not only get you to the gym at some specified time, it'll inspire you as well. When one of you doesn't feel like going, the other will cajole them into getting there. But still, don't treat your gym workout hour as a social gathering. People are there to work out – a quick "Hey, how's it going?" will suffice as good gym interaction etiquette.

Sometimes it's hard to think about going to the gym. There's always something that might be more fun to do, but when you get there you see all the others there, so it feels like a gang of health-conscious people with similar weight-loss goals. You aren't alone! And it feels extra super great when you're leaving too. You did it!

> ***If you took years to get unhealthy,***
> ***you're certainly not going to undue that in a month.***
> <u>***It takes real dedicated time to retrain a fat-making engine***</u>
> <u>***into a lean calorie-burning engine.***</u>
> ***Be patient as your body metabolically adapts to your workout programs.***

Obviously, there are many different approaches to weight-training exercises. Indeed, there's a wide array of gym equipment from which to choose as well as a dizzying multitude of choices for how to use it.

<u>Some of the equipment types include:</u>

1. Dumbbells – considered "free" weights as they can be raised and lowered in a complete movement, free to move in any direction and in any manner. They'll be rowed up on support racks.
2. Fixed-weight barbells – also considered free weights and they can be moved similarly to dumbbells. They'll be hung from support racks.
3. Circular weight plates – these can be added to various non-fixed-weight barbells.
4. Free weight accessories – free-standing benches (these can be made flat, inclined, declined or into a sit-up chair) and weight benches (these will have non-fixed-barbells, with barbell supports).
5. Cable-pulley machines – machines that move weight with the use of cables.
6. Floor machines[207] – fixed machines dispersed around and bolted to the gym floor, wherein you pick the preferred weight, then follow the posted instructions.

---

[207] I don't recommend these for beginners and be aware that machines are setup for the "average" torso; how many people own one of those? Some machines can be better adapted to different bodies (e.g., limb length, etc.) but of course only to a certain degree so be forewarned; if it doesn't feel right, ***<u>don't use it!!!</u>***

7. Free-weight objects such as medicine balls, kettlebells, elastic bands or tubing – can provide weight resistance for both conventional and unconventional exercises.

8. Stability objects such as exercise balls, BOSU balance trainers and balance boards – will provide unstable support to assist with core and stabilizer muscles.

Some training program examples include:

1. Straight-set[208] training (completing the same exercise, three sets of repetitions in a row).

2. Circuit-set training (doing three different exercises one after the other, then repeating them a second time one after the other and third time in the same order).

3. Super-set training (pairs exercises for agonist[209] and antagonist[210] muscle groups).

4. Compound-set training (similar to super-sets but with two exercises back-to-back for the same muscle group).

5. Giant-set training (similar but incorporates four or more exercises per muscle group) – certainly not recommended for a beginner.

6. Some training-split examples:

(a) upper/lower body split (train upper-body one day, lower-body the next);

---

[208] A "set" is a number of exercise repetitions completed.

[209] Agonist muscles are the targeted muscles for any particular exercise and they'll contract or shorten to complete the movement (e.g., biceps for a bicep dumbbell curl).

[210] Antagonist muscles are the muscles that do the opposite of the agonist muscle. Antagonist muscles will lengthen (or relax) when the agonist muscles are contracting/shortening (e.g., triceps will lengthen while the biceps are contracting to lift a weight and the triceps with contract/shorten while the biceps are lengthening (or relaxing while lowering the weight in the dumbbell curl). This is precisely why it's better to move weight *slowly* so that you can exercise *both* the agonist and antagonist muscles. May as well work those triceps while lowering the weight! This concept is also effective on machines as well. Why let the machine complete the exercise? It doesn't even have muscles; it has gravity as an advantage and it never even paid to join the gym!

(b) three-day training split (an example would be to train legs one day, front of body the next, and back of body the third day); and,

(c) push-pull split (train chest one day with exercises having you <u>push</u> the weight, the back the next day with exercises having you <u>pull</u> the weight).

7. Push-pull training (train the chest with the 1st exercise, then the back with the 2nd exercise, etc.)[211]

8. Whole-body training[212] (single workouts that stress every major muscle group).

9. Extended-set training (doing the same exercise three different ways, for example an incline barbell bench press first – the most difficult, then a flat DB bench press, and finally on a decline DB bench press – the easiest).

10. Twice-a-day training[213] (yep that's right, two gym trips per day and *usually* different muscles each time) – not for those new to exercise or for the faint-hearted or weak, due to potential injury.

11. Unilateral, or one-sided, training (doing the body's right-side on one day and its left-side on another day). This further challenges the stabilizing core/abdominal muscles.

12. Heavy-light training (incorporates heavy weight sets and light weight sets with the same exercise, often a multi-joint one; heavy sets stimulate the fast-twitch muscles, while light sets promote the growth of muscle blood capillaries and induce muscle fatigue).

---

[211] Training this way will make the 2nd muscle group stronger due to the earlier contraction of the antagonist muscle group (e.g., if you do a barbell row and then a bench press, you'll be stronger on the bench press as long as you don't go to failure on the row). Just remember that when you do a bench press your back muscles will inhibit the contraction of your chest muscles a bit. When you do a set of rows before the bench press, this affect will not be as great as you'll already have fatigued them; hence, you can contract your chest muscles more forcefully.

[212] This approach is suggested for beginners as no muscle groups are overly stressed out. I have given a sample 12-week "beginner" workout program in Appendix A.

[213] Only recommended for the more advanced bodybuilders.

13. Drop-set training[214] (after 10-12 repetitions, this involves an immediate 10-20% reduction in weight used in order to complete the next repetitions to failure[215] with no rest period; this can be done for as many sets as you choose but is usually done only for 3-4 weight drops).

14. Small-angle training (multiple variations of angle[216] for a single exercise, for example doing a bicep dumbbell curl but stopping once or twice during the range of movement).

15. 21's training (7 repetitions for first ½ of the movement, 7 repetitions for the last ½ of the movement and finally 7 repetitions for the full range of movement); this is a form of small-angle training which will address any weaknesses in the length of the muscle group fibers.

16. Pyramid training (a stepwise increase and then decrease in weight with each set, starting with a light weight and moving up to the heaviest possible weight and back down again to the lightest weight, usually involving 3-5 weight increases along the way). Not for the beginner, this training approach is wicked!

17. Inverted pyramid training (starting with the heaviest weight, working down to the lowest and then back up to the highest, usually involving 5 sets of repetitions). Really hard!

18. Negative repetition training (resisting the weight and going slow on the eccentric[217], or negative, portion of the exercise)[218].

---

[214] You can push your muscles beyond their limits with this training approach; this translates into more growth hormone.

[215] You simply can't lift more weight with proper control and range-of-motion.

[216] Rarely do muscle fibres run the whole length of the muscle; hence, during an exercise you may have some muscles fibres that simply don't contribute much to the movement and don't get worked much at all. By using different angles, you'll recruit more muscle fibres and stimulate them to grow. This concept also supports the fact that you need to use different exercises to hit all muscle fibres (e.g., triceps dumbbell extensions + reverse grip straight bar cable pushdowns + "assisted" triceps dips + standing triceps cable kickbacks)

[217] When you move a weight, you are either lengthening (eccentrically) or shortening/contracting (concentrically) your muscle(s).

[218] An example would be body-weight chin-ups or pull-ups. Start in the contracted/high position and then let yourself down *extremely* slowly.

19. Isolation training[219] (all exercises that only move one joint).

20. Compound training (all exercises that move more than one joint)[220].

21. Post-exhaustion training (do isolation exercises after compound exercises to make the muscles supporting the multi-joint movement work even harder after being fatigued and get stronger, e.g., squats *and then* leg extensions).

22. Pre-exhaustion training (do isolation exercises before compound exercises to fatigue a muscle making it the weak link in a multi-joint movement e.g., leg curls *before* walking lunges or deadlifts).

23. 5-10-20 training (an advanced type of tri-sets wherein the exercise uses three sets with 5 repetitions, then 10 repetitions, and finally 20 repetitions all with very little rest between sets).

24. 100's training (completing 100 repetitions of *one* exercise, with no rest and only 20-30% of your normal weight – you many look a bit silly in the gym[221] but believe me it's very intense and should only be done for 2-4 weeks maximum)[222] – not for beginners. And remember, there's no room for ego on the gym floor if you really want to build muscle mass!

---

[219] Actually, this is a bit of a misnomer, given that whenever you move a joint you *have to use all muscles attached to that joint – muscles on either side!* That said, isolation exercise machines tend to stress particular muscles with one joint. For example, the leg extension machine is primarily used to workout your quadriceps, but in the background, it's obviously working out your hamstrings and calves albeit *to a much lesser degree.* And it only moves one joint – your knee.

220 An example is the squat which uses your hip, knee and ankle joints. This is why the squat is a great lower-body exercise. Such exercises are referred to as "compound" exercises and they challenge a lot of muscle tissue and eat a lot of calories while doing so. I always find squats interesting in another way; they're one of the first things toddlers learn to do and the first thing adults forget how to do. Why do you think the elderly need higher toilet seat levels?

[221] There's NO room for ego in the gym if your want to succeed in building muscle mass.

[222] This type of training hits the slow-twitch muscle fibres for the first 60-70 repetitions and after that your fast-twitch muscles will kick into action in order to assist the highly fatigued slow-twitchers. If you concentrate, you'll actually feel the transition while it happens!

25. Slow-repetition training (repetitions are performed at an *extremely* slow speed leaving them under tension for longer).

And what about all the body muscles (and I'll just list the main muscles for each "area" along with some *nicknames* for some of them)?

1. Chest (pectorals/*pecs*)
2. Back (laterals/*lats* and rhomboids)
3. Shoulders (deltoids/*delts*)
4. Top of the shoulders (trapezius/*traps*)
5. Back of the arms (triceps/*tris*)
6. Front of the arms (biceps bacchii/*bis*)
7. Lower arms (forearms) – I've always been a pushover for strong forearms on a guy, sooo sexy. But I don't really care about mine.
8. Front of upper legs (quadriceps[223]/*quads*)
9. Back of upper legs (biceps femoris/*hamstrings*[224])
10. Inside of upper legs (adductors)
11. Butt (glutes and abductors[225]/hip extenders)
12. Back of lower legs (gastrocnemius and soleus/*calves*)
13. Front and side of stomach (abdominals[226]/*abs*)

And on top of all the above choice (and please believe me when I say I didn't include it all in those lists), you can also choose to progressively increase your weight load, alter your rest periods and/or your tempo! All of those

---

[223] The "quadricep femoris group" consists of four muscle groups, which contain the rectus femoris, vastus intermedius, vastus lateralis, and the vastus medialis.

[224] Want to know why they're called "*ham*strings"; it's because slaughtered pigs are hung from their strong biceps femoris muscles – sorry, I had to mention that – I'm not a vegan or vegetarian.

[225] There is no actual single "abductor" muscle; rather, the abductors consist of a group of muscles used to move your hips including the gluteus medius, gluteus minimus and tensor facia lata.

[226] Your abs actually have six different muscle groups which include: the rectus abdominus (the infamous "6-pack"), the 2 external (on top) oblique muscles and 2 internal (underneath) oblique muscles (on each side) and the deeply buried transverse abdominis muscle.

choices will change how your muscles are challenged. In other words, you can affect the actual workload volume[227] you make your muscles endure. Always try to progressively increase your workload volume. Be focused with your weights and your movements, travel with a notebook and a pen instead of trying to remember it all – like the big boys.

And now maybe you can see why, in the past, you may not have changed your body, while you see other people *looking like they are doing the same exercises* as you but over time *have changed* their bodies! Maybe they know about total workload volume training[228], so they have progressively built up their workout programs. Maybe they know about full range-of-motion or that they shouldn't rush through the negative[229] part of their exercise or they know about tempo or they know about the different parts of muscles. For example, when you exercise the triceps, you should understand that "tri" means three and so there are three different muscle heads[230] for your triceps. Obviously, you should be hitting all three, hence there are three different approaches or

---

[227] The number of sets you perform is only one of a number of factors that will affect the total workout volume (sets X repetitions X weight) of any exercise you choose to complete.

[228] Total workload training is actually a tracking approach: if you lift 10 pounds, 15 reps for 3 sets then the workload is 450 pounds (10 X 15 X 3). Now if you lift 12 ½ pounds for 15 reps for 3 sets, then you have increased your overall workload for that exercise to 562 ½ pounds (12 ½ X 15 X 3). That's going to be harder on those muscles. Track what you are doing and increase it whenever the load seems too easy.

[229] *The negative* part of the motion is the lengthening of the agonist/main muscle being worked out, and it'll affect the complimentary antagonist muscle (e.g., bicep curls will make the bicep muscles primarily agonist and the triceps muscles primarily antagonist during the movement). Triceps extensions will do the opposite. Now think about this concept for a pull up.

[230] The "head" of any muscle is the muscle's point of origin. Technically it's a "cep" …hence bicep, triceps, quadricep, etc. But, let's take your arm bicep as an example. It has "bi" in the word simply because it has *2 heads* with each one originating from near the shoulder bone and travelling down toward insertion at the elbow. The triceps "muscle" has *3 heads* and the quadriceps "muscle" has *4 heads*. If you only use one exercise for the triceps, you'll probably only be exercising one of its 3 muscle heads. You need to hit <u>all three</u> to get beautifully balanced triceps.

types of exercises that will build-up all three for balanced and strong triceps. Same for the "bi"ceps, which have two heads. How about the shoulder with anterior (front), lateral (side) and posterior (rear) muscle heads? Ensure that you exercise all muscle heads[231].

Yes, there's no doubt that exercising is complicated. It really is a science. If you think that all those people staring at themselves in the mirror are just loving themselves, you might be wrong. Maybe they're checking their form! Believe me, proper form is where it's really at.

And here are some scary questions?

1. Which exercises target which heads of which muscle(s)?[232]
2. In what order should you do the exercises?
3. How many sets should you do?

---

[231] **Ok, I can't help it.**

Here are three good exercises for your triceps and they'll *hit all three heads*:

1-   dumbbell tri extensions (targets your long head),
2-   cable or dumbbell kickbacks (targets your lateral head), and
3-   reverse grip cable pressdowns (targets your medial head).

Here are three good exercises for your delts:

1-   front DB/Barbell raises (anterior head),
2-   lateral dumbbell raises (middle head), and
3-   bent-over dumbbell lateral raises (posterior head)

[232] Here are three for your biceps that will hit both heads as well as the brachialis, located beneath the biceps and something that if worked out will push the biceps out and make them look even more defined:
1 – incline bench curls (long head),
2 – preacher curls (short head); and,
3 – reverse grip barbell curls (brachialis).
There are *many other exercises* for the heads of the different muscles such as the quads, traps, etc. Just do your research. Your body's muscular makeup is really incredibly fascinating. Better yet – check out my IGTV or YouTube "Wanna WorkOut Better?" series/playlist. All major muscle groups are covered.

4. How many repetitions per set should you complete?
5. What is the best rest time between sets?
6. How much resistance/weight should you use?
7. At what speed should you move the weight?
8. Should you use low weight and high reps, or should you use high weight and low reps?

Egads, what to do???

Do what I did. Buy a book or two or three on exercising. Or how about visiting the library – it's free. Read them. Find some comprehensive and *elaborate anatomical pictures* of your muscles. They're beautiful to look at. Try to understand how and why muscles work. There are hundreds of exercise books out there. Such books will describe, with *gloriously detailed pictures*, how your muscles work as well as some tried and true examples of exercises for each of your muscle groups. A really good book will review the different types of training approaches as well, given that all of them will have different goals. If you prefer researching the internet, do ensure that a *detailed description or video of how to properly complete the exercise* is included.

I'm not a huge proponent of DVD, Google or You-tube based workout programs as many are geared to 20-year-olds while others simply don't properly explain form or range-of-motion. You sure don't want to injure yourself trying to do 25 burpees when you're not yet fit!!! That said, I have discovered two Youtube/Google sites that I believe are excellent because they explain the complexities of exercise *and demonstrate* proper form in a clear and concise way. "Fitttle.com" (Geoffrey Verity Schofield, a health consultant and online coach, provides excellent workout tips and demonstrations that are grown from deep knowledge and based in integrity) and "BuiltWithScience.com" (Jeremy Ethier provides extremely thorough science-research-backed training tips and easy to follow demos). Both men do a great job at explaining how to properly execute various exercises as well as goal-oriented nutritional information.

But for me, if I started down this path of detailed workout information, believe me it would constitute a whole other book! Maybe I'll tackle that in a subsequent book.

Suffice it to say that when it comes to training program strategies, you have to decide what your goals are, endurance, strength, or power. And then regardless of the training program, recognize that the *muscles* your workout hits, your *exercise choices*, the *order* in which you perform them, the *weight* you use, and the *rest* periods you allow yourself are extremely <u>critical factors</u> to reaching your goals.

Keep in mind that <u>how</u> you exercise will determine whether you're building your muscles or not. People may appear to be doing the same thing when performing some free-weight exercise or using a fixed-floor machine, but if you look carefully, they probably aren't. If they're using momentum to move a weight, if they're using too little or too much weight for their current strength, if they're not completing a good range-of-motion, if they're only exercising one of the muscle heads in a set of muscles, if they concentrate only on their chest and not incorporate their back as well, then frankly they won't make much of a balanced change in the aesthetic look of their body.

I've had men come up to me on the gym floor, because they knew I was a personal trainer, and ask "I can't seem to build-up my chest. How can I do it better?" Yah, they always want big pectoral muscles. When I look at them, I usually see a guy with rounded shoulders. I tell him he has worked his pectorals way too much to the detriment of his back lats. The result is a very <u>strong chest</u> pulling forward a very <u>weak back</u> through the use of a pair of unaesthetic rounded shoulders. Technically his chest muscles are contracted/shortened and his back muscles are lengthened. Remember it's <u>always easy to lengthen</u> a muscle but it's much more difficult to contract or shorten that muscle. This is why it's more difficult for your biceps to lift a dumbbell (you're shortening the bicep then, just look at the change in the mirror) than to lower it. If you don't complete the curl, then you're not completing the full range-of-motion and simply not contracting the bicep muscle enough to promote much change.

So, my answer to this guy is "Well your chest is great, it's your back that's the real problem. You should concentrate on doing more back exercises for a while. Maybe a ratio of 2:1 for a couple of months so that you do two back or pull[233] exercises for every chest or push exercise." In sum, people need to balance their exercises in order to have a balanced set of agonist/antagonist

---

[233] Whenever you pull a weight toward your body (e.g., a cable row), you'll be exercising the back of your body somewhere. Similarly pushing a weight away would stress the front of your body (e.g., a dumbbell chest press).

muscles. Examples include the following: chest with back, biceps with triceps, quads with hamstrings.

Also, you <u>must</u> exercise at a sufficient intensity to stress your body and in so doing stimulate the necessary muscle adaptation. Lifting little 2 ½ and 5-pound weights week after week after week is simply not enough weight to strengthen your muscles – a bag of groceries weighs more than that! You must weight-train *above* your anaerobic threshold [234] to sufficiently stimulate your body. Training your muscles can be emphasized in three ways: muscle endurance, muscle strength and muscle power.

<u>Endurance</u> involves at least 18-20 repetitions with *very light weights* and a consistent *medium* tempo (1 second eccentric[235]: 1 second pause: 1 second concentric[236]) = **low weight, high repetitions, medium tempo.**

<u>Strength</u> involves between 10-15 repetitions with *medium weights* and a consistent *slow* tempo (3-4 seconds eccentric: 1 second pause: 3-4 seconds concentric) = **medium weight, medium repetitions, slow tempo.**

<u>Power</u> involves only 3-6 repetitions with *very heavy weights* and is most concerned with the amount of work done per unit of time; hence the tempo would be *very fast* on the contraction of the muscle (1-2 seconds eccentric: 1 second pause: less than 1 second concentric) = **high weight, low repetitions, high-velocity tempo.**

Your "workload" is how much force you can exert as you move (push or pull) a weight through a distance (e.g., an object such as a dumbbell moving through a bicep curl or your own body weight as in a push-up). The weight you use coupled with the repetitions you complete and the speed at which you complete them will determine the outcome of the exercise in terms of endurance, strength and power.

---

[234] Your anaerobic threshold is when exercise intensity causes an <u>exponential</u> increase in lactate. This is good because it's the point at which oxygen is low and your body has to breakdown carbohydrate for energy, thereby making the lactate. Remember lactate comes from lactic acid. People say it's bad, but it isn't. It's <u>necessary</u> for muscle growth!

[235] When you extend or lengthen a muscle, that's an "eccentric" movement.

[236] When you contract or shorten a muscle, that's a "concentric" movement. It's always more difficult to shorten a muscle than to lengthen it.

Workload = weight X the number of repetitions

Here are some interesting examples of how the <u>same</u> workload could have <u>different</u> effects on your muscles:

<u>Example #1</u>: 10 lbs. weight X 20 repetitions at a *relaxing medium* speed = 200 lbs. workload on your muscles (increases *endurance*).

<u>Example #2</u>: 20 lbs. weight X 10 repetitions at a *controlled slow* speed = 200 lbs. workload on your muscles (increases *strength*).

<u>Example #3</u>: 40 lbs. weight X 5 repetitions at a *controlled fast* speed = 200 lbs. workload on your muscles (increases *power*).

You'll see a lot of men aiming for the *power* output (maximum force in the shortest time possible), doing very few repetitions with huge weight and trying to do it really quickly. Power always involves the *speed of the force being applied*. Unfortunately, a lot of these men dispense with proper form while completing their repetitions; hence, they're often "cheating." Examples of common cheating include using momentum[237], bouncing, employing "mechanical advantage"[238] and using more joints than necessary to complete the movement. Examples of these problematic approaches include **using**

---

[237] An example is often seen on the reverse-ab crunch machine, the one you stand up on and pull your knees up to your waist. You'll see people swinging their legs back and forth at the bottom of the movement to help get those legs up. Nope, that makes the exercise almost useless for their abs.

[238] Why is it that to lift 40 pounds on one cable machine feels heavier than 40 pounds on another similar-looking cable machine? It's the result of mechanical advantage, which is a measure of the ratio of the output force to the input force. In other words how much force do you need to challenge your muscles in order to overcome the weight force you need to move to complete that particular exercise. Exercise machines will use mechanical advantage to make your work easier, so the higher that advantage, the easier it is to lift or push the stacked weights. Cable machine mechanical advantage is equal to the number of pulleys that support the weight stack. 40 pounds supported by two pulleys is *a lot harder* to lift than 40 pounds supported by 3 or more pulleys. I just like to say the longer the cable (usually using many pulleys), the easier it is, even though technically that's a bit off. Just a bit easier to "calculate" when looking at two different machines that both allow you to perform the very same exercise. Sorry, my physics degree is peeking out.

momentum[239] to start a new repetition or letting the **gym machine assist** with the movement by never resisting the eccentric "return/negative" force (i.e., letting the weight stack fall quickly with little muscle resistance (and it doesn't even have any muscles to build-up!) Or, how about unnecessarily moving a lot of your core or trunk thereby **using too many joints** while completing an exercise (i.e., spreading the dumbbell's weight over a large variety of muscles, hence never stressing out any of them very much – kind of a *weight leakage* issue). Like I said, people complete exercises in many different ways and many may be doing them incorrectly. Quit copying them!!!

Your muscles are designed to work in collaboration with each other to help produce a coordinated movement during any chosen exercise. Do keep in mind that if you're moving weights inappropriately, that is in a fashion that is counter to normal movement patterns or that cause an unnatural unaligned shearing force[240] to your connective tissues, you'll cause damage over the longer term either to your joints or to the muscles that are forced to join the movement in support of the muscle(s) that are being overly burdened. And I'm not talking here about the amount of weight being used, I'm talking about doing some sort of exercise that's not normally going to be handled well by your body. The best example I can detail is when I see someone pull a lat pulldown bar *behind their head* and right down to their shoulders, rather than in front of their chest. It's a nasty assault on the shoulders and a strain on the neck for the vast majority of people, and certainly for older shoulders. I guess they incorporate such an exercise into their workout because they saw someone else doing it! I can't imagine why else they'd be doing it.

---

[239] If a mass is moving then it has momentum, a quantity of motion (in terms of physics momentum = mass X velocity). That means that there is *no* momentum with *no* movement. When you do a bicep curl, rather than swinging your arms in an effort to help get the weight up or "bouncing" with your knees, you should *stop* at the bottom/completion of the movement/repetition for one second *before starting* the next rep. With such proper form, you'll immediately notice that your bicep muscles will be working a lot harder. Like I said, not everyone is doing the same thing in the gym!!!

[240] Shearing occurs when you apply forces to your body tissues and they're in opposite directions. This can produce damaging friction to your muscle tissues. The best analogy is a pair of scissors, where the two "parts" of the scissors are used to cut a piece of paper.

If all of this exercise detail seems too much, then hire a personal trainer even if just for 10-15 paid sessions. Use that trainer only twice per week for 2-3 weeks and then fall down to once a week to stretch out your training/learning sessions. Take some notes when the trainer gives you a rest and do those same exercises on your non-trainer days. Ask questions. Your trainer can be very informative. S/he wants you to get fit. Some personal trainers or gyms will force you to sign up for 3 training sessions per week, but truthfully, if you aren't there, they can't legally charge you (but do read the fine print just in case!) If you work out at least 4 days per week (one of those days with the trainer) and eat a nutritious diet, it'll take you about 12-16 weeks to begin to see a difference in how your clothes fit, so you may as well stretch out those training sessions.

Many people join a gym with great intentions but they often get very discouraged and end up quitting because they simply don't have the know-how. They're overwhelmed. Yes, exercising properly is a very *scientific* endeavor. Many new exercisers end up on the fixed-floor machines (not always the right size for their bodies) or on treadmills (burning muscle like crazy) all out of ignorance, fear of hurting themselves and a major lack of confidence. **I want you to gain confidence through this book.** I want you to understand your biochemical body, how to feed it better and to appreciate its metabolic need for proper weight-training.

If you don't schedule time with a personal trainer or, at least, pre-plan workouts with a buddy, then there will be very minimal or no accountability. Some gyms will allow you and a buddy to share "personal" training and this will keep the hourly cost lower. This approach will work at the outset, but eventually one client will get a lot better more quickly and need to use a different sequence of exercises.

If you're only after a "six-pack" or a "better booty" or "toned arms" and want it in the short-term, you'll be sadly disappointed and probably give up. Quit being seduced by those ludicrous fitness magazines that promise perfect spot-reducing transformations in 8-10 weeks!!! They sell lots of magazines, but they don't really give the best advice for losing inches.

Before you hire a personal trainer, look at them while they're training their clients. Study who seems to be concentrating on their client, not on other gym attendees or friends, looking at themselves in the mirror, or on their cell phone while their client is performing some exercise! You're the paying client and you're paying for their <u>one-on-one</u> time and expertise.

And for heaven's sake don't hire a personal trainer that doesn't appear to be fit! If *they* didn't do it, however will they train *you* to do it??? And a *good* trainer will not be trying to make you fully dependent upon them. They should be explaining to some degree why they're having you complete various exercises and how to properly execute the related movements. If they aren't, then ask for those details. Learn while you're on your coached journey-to-fitness so that you can eventually do it on your own. So empowering.

I used a trainer for 2 years and although I could have stopped after a year as I knew what to do, I just couldn't seem to wean myself off the training! I was lazy, in the sense that I didn't want to have to organize my workout exercises; but rather, just wanted to follow my trainer around the floor! I did eventually get weaned off because he left to go to another gym.

The best and most effective personal trainers are the ones who start working with clients to help them gain physical competence, muscle strength and endurance and then *empower them to do it on their own.* After you've been with your trainer for two to three weeks or so, ask for a training program that you can use while at the gym *in-between personal training sessions*. I did that for my clients, but not right away. I had to be sure that the client could complete a number of exercises for the whole body in proper form.

<u>What about when you're sick.</u> Should you be exercising when you aren't feeling very well? If you have a common cold with no fever and no chest congestion, *moderate* exercise is probably OK but you should wipe down the equipment once you're finished. And be thoughtful, don't be coughing and sneezing over all the gym equipment; other gym goers won't be very appreciative! You should *avoid strenuous* exercise whenever you're sick, so that you don't further stress out your immune system. If you have the flu, extreme fatigue, or swollen lymph glands then you should rest and avoid the gym. Give your muscles a well-deserved rest; they'll just be a bit stronger the next time at the gym. It takes about two weeks for your muscles to begin to weaken and by then you'll already have returned to the gym.

You have to choose the equipment to use, the training program to employ and the muscles you want to build.
Buy an informative exercise book or two or peruse the internet for

appropriate exercise programs[241]; or,
hire a good personal trainer – one that looks lean and healthy!
And for heaven's sake, get the trainer you want;
you don't have to use the trainer suggested by the gym if you want someone
else.
The gym wants your money and you want to get a great body.
Those two "wants" don't have to be mutually exclusive.

OK, for any of you who are "beginners" at weight-training with dumbbells, etc., I've added **Appendix A** which will outline a *beginner program* that will last 12 weeks. At that point you'll have to change your routine in order to keep your muscles guessing. And I know that you'll be completely hooked by then. You'll feel so much better and, if you religiously work through this 12-week program *while* eating nutrient-dense foods, drinking lots of pure water and avoiding junk, sugary, fried and highly processed foods, you'll discover that your clothes will fit differently. You'll also sleep a lot better and feel much less stressed-out. Bye-bye cortisol! Hello HGH!

This beginner workout program has exercises that are easy to learn in terms of proper form. But still, there are many other exercises and training approaches for your various muscle groups. Do what I did; buy an exercise book that takes the time to explain how your muscles work and what exercises stress which muscles. Some books will have fabulous diagrams, and many will give you a choice of training programs that will match the number of weekdays you want to devote to exercise as well as the level of trainee you are – beginner, intermediate, or seasoned.

I would suggest Geoffrey Verity Schofield's book, titled "SWEAT: Special Workouts, Exercises and Advanced Techniques" as an excellent resource as you progress along your physical fitness journey.

The truth of the matter is simple; once you apply some focus to your exercise efforts, you will begin to move your body away from a fat-making

---

[241] Prior to the the publishing of this book, I developed a number of social media sites to assist those interested in performing weight-lifting. This includes Instagram IGTV videos (@calorieburningat72) and a YouTube video channel (are you fat making or calorie burning?). Please subscribe for more information, tips and suggestions regarding your biochemical body and its responses to your decisions on exercise, diet, sleep and stress.

engine and over to a healthy calorie-burning engine. Whoa baby, I know that you'll love that!

3.4. How Do I Know How Hard I'm Exercising?

"Curiosity has its own reason for existing." – A.E.

Don't try to read what those "cardio" machines display. Use a more practical test to figure out your exercise intensity. If you can carry on a conversation while you're exercising (walking, running or on a machine such as a treadmill or elliptical, etc.), then you're using your aerobic system (with oxygen). That's good. If you increase your exercise intensity to the point at which you can hear yourself breathing, then you're using a combination of aerobic and anaerobic (without oxygen) metabolism. If you're exercising so intensely that you can no longer carry on a conversation, you're using mostly your anaerobic metabolism for exercise fuel (i.e., you'll not be oxidative and you'll be wasting some serious muscle tissue). That's not good.

Your body has an amazingly complex system to keep you moving. Depending on the type of exercise you're undertaking and how much oxygen you'll require at that time, your body has a number of different energy-providing systems from which to draw. Your energy circuitry converts food into stored energy which you can access on an as-needed basis. In earlier chapters, I mentioned that this energy can be stored in four quite distinct forms: ATP (in all cells), creatine phosphate (CP – in muscle cells), glycogen (in your liver and muscle tissues) and body fat.

For immediate energy you can just use ATP (adenosine triphosphate) as it's being made constantly by your body. This critically important molecular energy unit is either being made or being used by your body (for such things as muscle contractions, helping with nerve impulses and for the synthesis of chemicals, etc.) That said, you can't store pure ATP in large quantities for very long – *just for a few seconds*! If you need a more continuous effort, then your muscles use a second fuel called CP (creatine phosphate). This is available *after* your ATP fuel is used up. In effect, CP donates a phosphate atom to what is left after ATP is broken down into ADP (a diphosphate) and suddenly you have some more energy to keep you going. But again, this type of fuel-making process is very short-lived, only being available for about *10 seconds*! Gosh, that's still not very long at all.

For the other numerous times, when you need energy for *longer than the 10 seconds covered by your ATP/CP stores*, then glucose and stored glycogen are broken down to help turn more spent ATP into useful fuel for your cells. Lactic acid/lactate is a by-product of the glucose breakdown and, it makes your muscles feel like they are burning when you really push yourself to muscle fatigue at the gym. That soreness is the result of a type of *natural I-know-how-to-deal-with-this* body inflammation. When you experience muscle soreness in the gym, you either have to stop expending energy (stop the exercise) or add some oxygen to the fuel mixture. Remember that weightlifting is mostly anaerobic in nature and not very oxidative. If you really push yourself past your anaerobic limit, then you'll probably be a bit red in the face.

And finally, along this incredible energy continuum, when you need energy for *longer than 2-3 minutes* you must, as noted above, add oxygen to the equation. *This is where your level of fitness or physical conditioning becomes very very important.* A highly conditioned and physically fit person will use oxygen very very efficiently. They'll be able to generate enough energy for long-term, very strenuous high-endurance activities. A perfect example is the long distance Olympic or marathon runner.

When you reach this fitness stage, you're still making ATP, but your muscles must kick in to produce additional long-term energy. And this is where your body fat comes into play. Muscles produce energy by combining oxygen and fatty acids (you want this to happen!) which together produce a sustained source of energy for long-term activities. Your body will move through these various energy formation processes like a dream, and of course, to reach your weight-loss goals, you want to be *burning fuel* and not storing it. To do this, that is to burn your body fat energy stores, you'll definitely need to have an *efficient metabolic rate.* If you're on a "cardio" (aerobic) machine, *low to moderate* intensity exercise is the best way to burn your fat and not dump your muscle. Bet you see many treadmillers running really fast but I'd bet they're not all highly conditioned.[242]

----

[242] Along a side note, when you use a treadmill the idea is to keep your weight over your base of support, your feet. In other words, you would walk or run with your body perpendicular to the moving tread, right? When you decrease the angle then you are supposed to be simulating the walking or running up a hill at some chosen gradient. Why would you hang on to the side or front rails in an attempt to keep your body

I know what you're thinking, and it's very true, the biochemical process for fat-storage is extremely efficient while the process required to burn that body fat is really difficult! It's frustrating but you just can't change those facts. Putting on body fat is a very easy feat. Taking it off is an extremely difficult challenge. If you're an unfit person running fast on the treadmill and heavily restricting your calories, you just ain't gonna get that nice toned muscular lower-fat body *no matter how many hours you devote to the treadmill.*

Why do you see those lean people jumping on those "stair-climber" machines? Are they the best "cardio" equipment choices? You would have to agree that there would be a reasonably strong correlation between stair-climbing and bone density or mass in general and that it should be especially true for older people and for post-menopausal women. It can also improve your leg power which certainly is important in reducing injuries from slips and falls, especially during those icy winter months. Stair-climbing raises your heartbeat immediately thus maximizing your cardiovascular benefits. It's also a great muscle toner. It increases core muscle strength (you have to keep balanced) and engages your body's largest calorie-torching muscle groups (glutes, hamstrings and quadriceps) as well as your calves. As a weight-bearing exercise it helps build bone strength and has a lower impact on your aging knees, contrary to running hard on the treadmill. This I like. Need I say more about the stair-climber as a superior example of cardio equipment, one that works your entire lower body as well as giving you a cardiovascular workout?

If your gym has a stair-climbing machine you should feel lucky, not all do. Try to use it for 10-15 minutes <u>after</u> your weight-training exercises (5 minutes minimum)! If your gym doesn't have a stair-climber machine, go for the rowing machine, stepper-machine or backless stationary bike and then, if need be, choose the easier elliptical-machine (which is good for those of you with

---

perpendicular to that tread, by leaning way back while hanging on for dear life? You may as well just keep it flat! The appropriate way is always to keep your weight over your feet and walk or run just as you would when hiking up a hill. Obviously, you wouldn't be leaning back, in fact you would probably be leaning forward a bit as you climbed that hill! Try it, it's a lot more challenging then hanging on, leaning back and letting the rails hold your weight. Have you ever seen sissy hand bars on a hiking trail or along a marathon run?

aching knees). I'm not against such cardio equipment, I just believe that some cardio machines are much more beneficial than are others.

Why is muscle contraction so important? Muscles are made up of small cylindrical cells called muscle fibers, and these are all bundled together. Although these fibers aren't very thick, they can be *very* long (e.g., 15 cm or almost 6 inches in the biceps/upper front arm)[243]. Muscle fibers are built for contraction (to create joint movement) and they contain complex structures and chemicals in order to complete this work. Muscle fibers have small structures called microfilaments, which can contract with the use of their actin and myosin protein filaments. The thin actin filament slides over the thicker myosin filament and this creates movement; in effect it shortens (or contracts) the full length of your muscle.

When you complete a dumbbell bicep curl, your biceps are contracted to their shortest length when the dumbbells are up at your shoulders. Conversely, your bicep muscles are at their longest when the dumbbells are hanging down near your hips at the completion of the curl. Which requires the greatest effort? Well, it's always more difficult to shorten a muscle than to lengthen it. Just look at your biceps in the mirror while you are performing the curl. You'll see your bicep muscle shorten and lengthen as you move through the curl. You'll notice that it'll be a heck of a lot harder to shorten them as you move those dumbbells up to your shoulder level. When you don't move them all the way up, you aren't completing the movement and you're definitely not challenging your biceps as much as you could be.

Why is *tempo* so very important? When you perform a strength-building/weight-training exercise *slowly and in a controlled manner*, you'll be recruiting all your muscle fibers and you'll be addressing and strengthening various moment angles[244] as well. Additionally, again with the bicep curl

---

[243] Exercise will not, however, change the overall length of your muscle. Some people have gorgeously long biceps or calves, while others have relatively short ones. But you are what you are. Just make your muscles stronger and bigger, which will bring definition or tone to your appearance. And remember that each extra pound of muscle can burn about 50 *additional* calories per day even while resting and this allows you to eat more!

[244] A good example is the slowing down of a bicep curl. When you rush through it, you're not challenging your bicep muscles to the point at which they have to work

example, you'll be exercising both the primary movement *agonist* muscles (biceps) and the secondary movement *antagonist* muscles (triceps). And so maybe now you can see *why* it makes better sense to go slowly and get them all involved.

Also, if you do an exercise you should complete the *full range of movement.* For example, again with the bicep curl, if you only move the dumbbells partially up to your shoulders, then you're not challenging the whole length of your bicep.

There are three different types of muscle fibers,
each with a different energy production system
(e.g., oxidative, non-oxidative or both)
and they all require different combinations of training
as well as fatigue at different rates.

There are a number of muscle fiber "types" or what is sometimes called "myosin heavy chains" (you'll recall that myosin is a muscle protein filament needed for muscle contraction). Each of your muscle fiber types have energy production systems to provide your muscle cells with the required energy.

Your purely slow-twitch Type-I fibers rely only on the aerobic (oxidative) system, helping you run a *long marathon* or complete a triathlon.

―――――――――――――――――

their hardest. Think about it. Once you get those weights up to your shoulders; it's easy and similarly easy at the bottom. The *most difficult point/angle for your bicep muscles* is when the dumbbell is furthest from your body (the joint axis), when your arm is parallel to the floor. It involves the "moment arm" or "lever" arm and it's at its longest half way up. This is the perpendicular distance between the line of action of the force (directed by gravity) and the axis of movement – your joint (M = F x D where moment is M, force/weight is F and distance is D). The *longer* the moment arm (length between the joint axis and line of force), then the more load will be applied to the joint axis via leverage! *Every time you exercise a joint*, there'll be a moment arm involved. Sorry, that's my Physics degree yet again. That said, some machines have very short moment arms. Just take the time to study some of the fixed-floor machine while someone else is using them.

"Oxidative" muscles (these rely on oxygen) – Slow-twitch muscles have a *low-power output* but do remain quite fatigue-resistant. They also have an increased iron[245] level because they need high levels of oxygen for aerobic metabolism and sustained energy outputs. Slow-twitch muscle fibers also contain the most ATP energy producing mitochondria and so they're capable of burning more fat for energy and this is good. Type I muscles are used for low-intensity activities such as walking and low intensity cycling/jogging as well as power-endurance exercise such as running. Over time, as with a long-distance marathon runner, these slow-twitch muscles adapt and become much more efficient at supplying sufficient energy for lengthier duration events. Bet you've never seen a fat triathloner or Olympic marathon runner!

Your hybrid oxidative Type-IIA fibers rely on a combination of aerobic (oxidative) and anaerobic (non-oxidative) glycolic systems, which help you *sprint*.

"Hybrid oxidative-glycolytic[246]" muscles (these are a mixture of slow- and fast-twitch) – These muscles have a *moderate-power output* and some fatigue-resistance for events that might be 1 to 3 minutes long (like running for the bus or dashing up the stairs to catch a runaway toddler). They have more contractile actin/myosin proteins which are used for higher-intensity activities such as jumping and throwing. In general, fast-twitch muscles are the opposite of slow-twitch, because they provide a higher power output, though they do fatigue much more quickly.

And your purely fast-twitch glycolytic Type-IIB fibers rely mostly on the anaerobic (non-oxidative) system and the high energy phosphate ATP system to help with the *high-intensity movements* needed for lifting weights at the gym.

---

[245] Iron is needed to make new red blood cells. You need hemoglobin (the respiratory protein that makes your blood red) to transfer oxygen from your blood to your lungs.
[246] Glycolysis is the metabolic pathway that converts glucose/carbohydrate into lactate. The free energy released during this conversion process is used to make the high-energy ATP phosphate molecules. These chemical reactions are controlled by enzymes.

"Glycolic" muscles (these convert glucose into ATP energy) – These are used for explosive type activities such as jumping, short fast sprints or lifting weights at the gym. These breakdown glucose sugars for energy and they don't need any oxygen to do so. Type IIB muscles burn stored glycogen and, although they can produce a huge amount of power, they can fatigue in as little as 10 seconds. Think of the runners in the 100-meter Olympic sprint. They can't go at that rate for much over 10 seconds. Remember those huge muscles on the shortest-lived (3 days!) gold medalist Olympian Ben Johnston? No sinewy body there.

All of your muscles will have various fast- and slow-twitch combinations, so you should vary your workout program occasionally between low and high weights, high versus low repetitions, and various and sundry combinations. But don't forget that your body learns pretty fast and you have to surprise it every few weeks to prevent the metabolic adaptations that will slow your gains and lead to those dreaded and depressing goal plateaus.

If you're mostly interested in activating your fast-twitch muscles (the ones that burn a lot of glycogen), there are two ways to do that. You can lift *heavier weights,* or you can lift *lighter weights very quickly.* Optimally training your muscles for hypertrophy (or growth) depends on the percentage of slow- or fast-twitch muscles which are present. It may be good to train your slow-twitch muscles with low weights and high repetition sets, and your fast-twitch muscles with high weights and low repetition sets. Your combination Type-IIA slow- and fast-twitch muscles can be trained with a blend of high and low weights and/or repetition sets.

Powerful microscopes have shown that these three muscle fiber types actually run along a continuum with purely slow-twitch at one end and purely fast-twitch at the other end. The hybrid fibers lie in-between. Different body frameworks can have different percentages of each; that is, a given percentage of pure slow-twitch, another percentage with a mixture of slow/fast-twitch and a final percentage of pure fast-twitch. For example, you could have a mixture of muscles that are 40% slow-twitch (Type-I), 30% hybrid combination of slow/fast twitch (Type-IIA), and 30% fast-twitch (Type-IIB).

Can you change those percentages? Yes. But you'll be changing the hybrid Type-IIA only. They're kind of sitting in the middle of the continuum, being able to jump either way. You can actually make them transition to meet your needs. If you decide to weight-train, then a whack of your hybrid fibers will move to fast-twitch and the more strength you build, the higher the percentage of hybrids that'll have transitioned into being fast-twitchers. With a lot of endurance training like marathon running, your hybrids will adapt by moving in the other direction toward the slow-twitch side of the continuum. There isn't really any right or wrong or ideal mix. You have to decide what your long-term goals are. But remember that when you stop all training, your "hybrids" will revert back to their normal sidelines as it were, and they'll do it relatively quickly (2-3 months).

Whenever I return from an extended motorcycle trip (1 – 2 ½ months) I'll be much weaker in the gym for a while. I'll have to get back to practicing patience with my weightlifting again. It'll take me about 3-4 weeks to get back all my strength, that is to make some of my sidelined "hybrids" transfer over to stand in sympathetic solidarity with my fast-twitch ones. This is often referred to as "muscle memory" and the better that memory, the shorter is the period of time after periods of inactivity (vacations, illness, etc.) that it'll take you to regain your muscle mass, strength and calorie-burning ability. This is also because weight-training exercises will have expanded the tight fascia[247] tissues that are wrapped around your muscles, as well as increased your protein synthesizing ability.

Your body's ATM molecular currency involves an intracellular energy transfer by storing and transporting chemical energy within your cells. This is quite complicated because your muscles are comprised of *combinations* of the various fiber types described above. And even within these different fiber types, the three different energy systems (aerobic, anaerobic and high energy ATP phosphate) can all simultaneously work together to make contributions to the final movement. Didn't I say that your biochemical machine is amazingly complex???

When your muscles are required to work harder than they're used to *or* in a different way, there is microscopic damage (small tearing) to your muscle fibers, resulting in soreness or stiffness. Soreness (not acute pain!) is actually a sign of your improving fitness and part of the adaptation process that provides a type of muscle conditioning. That conditioning is called "delayed onset

---

[247] Fascia is a three-tiered layer of tissue that encases and holds in place all of your tissues and organs, sort of like a biological Spanx girdle.

muscle soreness" (DOMS) and it leads to greater muscle strength. You can feel it for up to 2-3 days! That means your fatigued muscles are burning extra calories for 2-3 days *following* completion of the exercise in order to repair themselves! For unfit individuals, that doesn't happen after the treadmill. They'll only burn calories (from both muscle *and* fat) *while* on the treadmill, not after stepping off it. If you're a *highly physically fit* runner or hiker, then you may indeed feel DOMS just like the weightlifters.

To see how all these protein fibers and various energy systems actually work together, let's check out what happens when you run a marathon. Bear with me here. This is complicated but that's because you're a very complex biological and biochemical unit…a unit that can't be tricked or forced by your hopes and desires into doing anything other than what it needs to do in order to stay internally balanced. That's its job, and it's really good at it!

At the beginning of the race, you accelerate up to your speed quickly. To do this you'll use your fast-twitch muscles because they can react quickly and have a high-power output, contracting strongly. To get the necessary fuel, the high energy ATP phosphate (stored in your muscles) is instantly activated for necessary muscle contraction. *But* this stored ATP energy can only last a few *seconds*. The resulting breakdown product is ADP (adenosine di-phosphate) which in turn activates the anaerobic glycolytic energy system which breaks down sugars to produce energy in the form of *glycogen sugar*. This method of energy provision only lasts about *1-3 minutes*, and results in the production of *lactate* which in turn helps to delay muscle fatigue.

NO runner wants to encounter fatigue in the middle of their race and so their running speed must be reduced for sustainability. Hence, to complete the race, the runner needs to maintain a speed rate that relies on both the slow-twitch aerobic (Type-I) and the hybrid slow/fast-twitch (Type-IIA) muscles. Close to the end of the race, the runner will decide when to sprint to the finish. Fast-twitch muscles (Type-IIB) will fatigue within 10 seconds (just like at the outset of the race) and so timing is extremely critical for this decision: start sprinting too early and you'll fatigue too early; start sprinting too late and you'll certainly lose the race.

You've probably seen this in the Tour De France Bicycle races or the Olympic 800-meter races. A front running competitor looks like s/he is definitely going to win the race and may even be way ahead of the others, only to suddenly fall back just before the finish line and come in second, third or worse! Hmmm, now you know…bad timing on fast-twitch application!!!

<u>Muscles and blood flow are also related.</u> When you weight-train[248], you'll reap some great collateral benefits because you'll be *growing more tiny blood capillaries*. These will increase the amount of blood, oxygen and nutrients that can be delivered to your muscles and organ tissues. The opposite occurs with a lack of exercise; that is, decreased capillary size or sometimes blood vessel blockages which can stop the flow of blood to tissues (e.g., leading eventually to a heart attack or stroke).

Your blood capillaries deliver critical nutrients to your muscle fibers by using tiny little blood vessels. They also remove waste products and you'll recall that if you can't get rid of excess toxic waste, you'll be filling up your current fat cells and subsequently creating new body fat cells – yet another biochemical adaptation. You probably know that your red blood cells transport oxygen throughout your body, but did you know that they don't use any of it. It'd be a bit of a conflict of interest if they did! Red blood cells don't have any mitochondria, the major cell-based powerhouses that generate your ATP energy. Indeed, some of your cells have more mitochondria than do others; and this would include your fat cells simply because they have to store *a lot* of energy. Muscle cells have many mitochondria as well and this allows them to respond to any work requirements you may demand from them.

Bottom line: **you should lift weights**. You need more blood capillaries. You need more oxygen and nutrient delivery. You need to get rid of toxic fat-making waste. And you want more ATP energy.

3.5. Is Lactic Acid/Lactate Good or Bad and What Does It Have to Do with Exercise?

"There are only two ways to live your life. One is as though nothing is a miracle. The other is as though everything is a miracle." – A.E.

---

[248] And remember, I only like to see fit and conditioned people on "cardio" equipment. Now, you know why. They need to build-up their oxygen-carrying blood capillaries with weight-training.

Unfortunately, there's a ton of misinformation out there about lactic acid and lactate. Firstly, let's be clear about the labelling. The technical difference between lactic acid and lactate is *purely chemical*. To be able to be called an acid, a substance must be able to donate a hydrogen ion. When "lactic acid" makes this donation, it becomes a base and at that point it's called "lactate." If you were a science keener, you'll recall from your high school chemistry classes that an acid has the ability to donate protons (positively charged) and to accept electrons (negatively charged), while a base has the opposite ability (i.e., accept protons/donate electrons).

Your body produces lactate by the non-oxidative anaerobic glycolysis in muscles. And, contrary to what you may think, rather than being used to improve your exercise performance, muscles actually use lactate for fuel because your liver will recycle it into glucose to help with your fuel-depleted muscle contractions, after which it'll be metabolized back into lactate.

How about this myth? "Following very strenuous weight-lifting exercises, your muscles produce lactic acid as a waste by-product of that anaerobic exercise." Well, muscles don't produce "lactic acid," they produce "lactate" and it's not a toxic waste product at all. Rather, it's an incredibly *important intermediate link* between your anaerobic and aerobic metabolisms.

Another myth that floats around most gym floors is that lactate/lactic acid "causes muscle fatigue" by making the muscles too acidic to contract effectively. This is simply not true. Your muscles will certainly become more acidic during exercise, but lactate is not the cause of that acidity. In fact, the non-acid lactate accumulation in your muscles actually *delays* muscle fatigue! The post-workout soreness you feel is caused by the micro-tearing damage to your muscle fibers and the resulting inflammation (DOMS). Your muscles have to repair themselves and this is what you feel. And they actually get *stronger* as they do it! Where lactate comes into play in this repair time scenario is that lactate makes the adaptation take place by *increasing* the mitochondria inside your muscle cells. Mitochondria have that important role of ATP energy production for your working cells, and so now you know that they're *increased* by lactate. People tend to think of lactate as the enemy, yet it's actually very far from that in terms of calorie-burning muscle growth and skin toning benefits.

And just to be even more technically clear, the reason lactic acid (eventually "lactate") leaves a burning sensation in your muscles[249] is because your glucose is broken down faster than it can be processed by your mitochondria[250] and this causes a lactic acid accumulation. Immediately your intensity ability will weaken. You'll actually feel it when it happens. I'm very physically fit because I've built-up a lot of mitochondria while weight-training and so I just don't get as quickly fatigued as would an unfit person. Mitochondria generate *energy molecules* and these fuel your muscle cells. Obviously the more you can build-up through weight-training exercises, the longer your muscles can respond to your demands. In other words, your *stamina* increases. Usually mitochondria functions decline with age and so exercise is how you can combat the decreasing stamina that often accompanies aging.

Phew! How incredible is your body? And how great is that lactate!

Lactate is the intermediate link between your anaerobic (non-oxidative)
and aerobic (oxidative) metabolisms.
It improves endurance performance and should not be feared.

But it's also important not to have too much lactic acid (lactic acidosis) after extremely intense exercise. You might wonder why highly trained and very fit Olympic athletes with great endurance don't suffer from lactic acidosis. After all, their bodies are like yours in terms of producing lactate. There are theories that they have less lactate in their blood after intense exercise *not* because they produce less but because they use *more as fuel*! Remember it's that intermediate link between your anaerobic and aerobic metabolisms.

Hence if you too are highly conditioned, you may not experience the burning feeling of lactate during weight-training, but this *isn't necessarily*

---

[249] A highly training Olympic athlete will be able to use the aerobic system at such a high rate that although s/he will generate lactic acid/lactate, it'll be used relatively quickly thereby avoiding an overload.

[250] These are the cell parts that help produce energy by using oxygen to turn carbohydrate, fat and protein into chemical energy for use in your body. They're the good guys.

because you've produced less; it's because you've *used or burned more* in your many muscle mitochondria just like those highly trained athletes.

In sum, lactate does not help exercise performance, rather it stimulates the necessary mitochondrial biogenesis <u>after</u> exercise and this improves your muscle endurance in the longer term. Oh yah, bring on that amazing lactate!

3.6 Is Stretching Good for Me?

"All that is valuable in human society depends upon the opportunity for development accorded the individual." – A.E.

Well, stretching is an interesting concept but unfortunately there are many partial truths about it floating around. Let's put it this way – have you ever seen a personal trainer stretching? Probably not! At least those in the know won't be stretching.

But before I put a major bummer on stretching, let's talk about the two quite distinct types of stretching.

There are two types of stretching, dynamic and static.
Static stretching should never involve pain and
should only be done after you've exercised.

One is *dynamic* stretching (always performed with movement) and the other is *static* stretching (always performed without movement). Put simply, dynamic stretching will have you working a number of joints with body movements of some type, while static stretching is simply lengthening a muscle as much you can and it'll be somewhat dependent upon your innate flexibility.

Now of course some of you will swear by yoga classes and that's fine. Yoga combines strength and stretching poses with deep breathing and lots of relaxation. Although yoga can combine both types of stretching it tends to employ *static* stretching the most. I would also say that yoga stretching is strongly focused on the flexibility side of things. This can be great for you as you age, but because older muscles and connective tissues may have lost some flexibility, I would add that you should begin yoga poses very slowly and gently so that you don't hurt yourself.

But I'm writing this book from the muscle-building and weight-training standpoints and not from the yoga-posing perspective. So, keeping that in mind, is stretching even necessary? Which type of stretching is the best, and when is it the best for your body? Or is either type of stretching not very good for your muscles, and when?

Firstly, let's talk about your muscle anatomy. While bones, joints, tendons and ligaments all contribute to your overall flexibility (or *range* of movement), you actually have very little control over those factors. Take me, for example, I am probably the *least flexible* person you'll encounter. I've never been able to touch my toes, even when I was in my 20s! That doesn't mean I'm unhealthy or not strong. It just means my *range-of-motion* might be a bit different than yours for particular exercises.

And frankly the older you get, the more your muscles and joints can become stiffer and tighter as that flexibility diminishes. This is caused by a natural physical degeneration which of course is further exacerbated through physical inactivity. Inevitably and regardless of your hopes and dreams, you'll suffer from the effects of age, but you certainly can improve your decreasing flexibility *to a degree* by increasing your physical activity.

Bones and joints are structured to allow for a *specific range of movement*. The obvious example is your knee joint which will never allow your leg to bend any farther forward then a straight leg. You can try whatever, but you can *never* change this. Obviously, you can't "stretch" a bone or a joint.

Ligaments connect *bone to bone* and they're *joint stabilizers*. Stretching your ligaments is not recommended as it can result in a reduction of joint stability. This in turn can lead to joint weakness and indeed painful injury[251].

Tendons connect *muscle to bone* and they're made up of connective tissue (well gosh, that makes sense!). Although quite elastic, they're extremely strong. Tendons play a major role in *joint stability* as well, but they don't contribute much to your joint's overall flexibility. For this reason, you should never make your tendons the main focus of any stretching.

Skeletal muscles are *fully responsible* for your body's movement. Muscles are very plentiful; you have over 215 pairs of skeletal muscles and they make

---

[251] While first-time snow-boarding with my highly colourful ski instructor's outfit on, I fell awkwardly right under the chair lift (so darn embarrassing) and stretched my ACL knee ligament sufficiently to cause a small tear. I forgot that my feet were no longer independent from one another as they were strapped onto ONE board. It wasn't a great feeling, indeed it reduced me to crutches for awhile and then to an ACL brace for the next 10 years of downhill skiing.

up almost ½ your body weight. Skeletal muscles *are* able to be stretched, that is lengthened.

You really have to assess your goals to decide what type of stretching is best for you. For example, static (or passive) stretching is great for improving your flexibility but certainly *not very useful* for warming up your body for physical activities such as weightlifting. Dynamic stretching, on the other hand, is *great for warming up* your body but it shouldn't be used in the initial stages of rehabilitation after some serious injury (for example a tearing or severing of your ACL – anterior cruciate ligament – a ligament that stabilizes your knee, connecting it to your thigh bone and your shin bone).

Static stretching involves slowly increasing the tension on a set of muscles, by lengthening those muscles. The tension is then held for about 20-30 seconds. I bet you've seen lots of people at the gym doing this before lifting weights or even in-between sets of exercises (really weird to me).

Dynamic stretching involves a swinging or bouncing motion that'll extend your range of movement and flexibility (although the body parts moving are never forced beyond their normal range of movement). Jumping jacks would be a good example.

One of the biggest *myths* about static stretching is that you have to stretch until it's almost painful. Frankly if you do this, your body will resort to a defense mechanism called the "stretch reflex." This occurs whenever your body wants to *prevent* serious muscle, tendon or joint damage by softening its protective response. To do this, it'll actually contract or shorten the muscle (even though you're trying to force it to lengthen!) To avoid this automatic reflex, you should never push a stretch beyond what feels comfortable. Only go to the point of feeling tension, *and not pain*, and then you'll reap the best benefits of static stretching while avoiding unnecessary injury. Any sort of body pain is always an indication of body anger. Weightlifters who adhere to the "no-pain, no-gain" philosophy, are ill-informed at the least. You should never feel pain at the gym, though tension or muscle tightness is OK.

Although stretching is not necessary, the rule I relay to my clients who insist on stretching, is to do dynamic stretching *before* hitting the gym floor weights and do static stretching *after* their workout routine. Even then, static stretching should *only involve the muscles that were worked out that day*!

The reason you should **never** do static stretching before your workout (or *during* your workout) is that it'll always make your *muscles weaker*, hence you simply won't be able to lift as much weight! And this phenomenon can last as long as 24 hours! This is counter to efficiently growing your calorie-eating muscle! Think of your muscles as elastic bands, even though they aren't and we wouldn't want them to be. If you pull out an elastic band as far as you possibly can, without breaking it, and then release it; the elastic will not immediately return to the same size. It'll be longer which of course is the natural reaction to being pulled out or stretched. This will happen to your muscles as well.

What do you think weight- or resistance- or strength-training is? It <u>always</u> involves the lengthening (extending) and shortening (contracting) of your muscles! Lengthening a muscle is easy, shortening it is the more difficult action. Why would you lengthen your muscles <u>before</u> a workout??? Frankly, you'll never be able to contract that muscle as far during the exercise and it's the contraction of the muscle that strengthens it.

Because weightlifting **is** a form of stretching, that's why I don't do any pre-workout stretching. I want to retain my muscle strength at the outset and then fatigue it on the gym floor rather than before the gym floor weightlifting. And I don't do any post-workout stretching, as I already lengthened my muscles during the workout.

3.7 Can I Spot-Reduce?

"Two things are infinite. The universe and human stupidity and I'm not so sure about the universe." – A.E.

As a personal trainer, one of the most frequently asked questions I hear is related to spot-reduction. Spot-reducing is the idea that you can exercise a particular group of muscles (e.g., the abs or the upper arms) and the fat will disappear from that spot *first*. This is a false concept. Your body is a heck of a lot more complex than that idea would allow for.

Here's that famous question: "Can you give me a six-pack (gym lingo for washboard abs)?" Well yes and no. Everybody has a "six-pack" of abdominal muscles (that's why you can bend over, twist, rotate, etc.), but you just can't see them because they're buried under layers of body fat. You'll never see those ab muscles or toned arm muscles unless you remove the fat on top of them. There are <u>no exceptions</u> to this fact.

For those of you who might be wondering if this contradicts my response to the fellow in the earlier chapter, the one who had built up his chest to the detriment of his back, there is no contradiction. For this chap, he was doing lots of complex exercises that emphasized his chest but very few for his back and so he changed his upper body disproportionately. Whenever he was exercising his "chest" he was actually using a broad array of muscles, not just one. I'll bet he was doing a ton of push-ups and these do use the "pectoralis minor" but they *also use* the traps, the front of the shoulders and the back of the upper arms (amongst other more minor working muscles). And he might have been doing a bunch of barbell presses too and these use both the "pectoralis major" and "minor" *as well as* the front of the shoulders (again with some other working muscles thrown in). And so, these exercises are "compound" in nature; that is, they don't isolate one muscle part or one body "spot." They spread the weight over many muscle groups.

OK, so you need to burn fat, sculpt muscle and boost your metabolism. But you just can't direct your body exclusively to one particular problematic site. For this reason, my normal responses to those wanting to spot-reduce include "abs are seen in the kitchen" and "you can't outrun a bad low-fiber diet." These facts don't mean that a personal trainer can't help you strengthen your abs. It means that to *see* them, you must lower your *overall* body fat percentage to about 14-15% for a woman and 9-10% for a man. I have great abs, but I'm not willing to drop my body fat to that level so that you can see my washboard. It's just too difficult to reach and more difficult to maintain. I'm normally at about 22-23% body fat, certainly a healthy percentage for me at my age.

When you see those models in the popular body fitness magazines, the ones with the beautiful abs (supposedly attained in 11 weeks!), believe me they didn't get them by doing 5,000 crunches a day and it took a heck of a lot longer than 11 weeks. They followed good clean eating habits, were never seen on Starvation Island, and they undertook consistent weight-training and cardio/aerobic training. OK, yes – then they starved themselves for a couple of weeks before the photoshoot and followed it up with some airbrushing of the photos. Well yah, we could all look better with airbrushing!!! And remember you can always starve off some water-based inches (which was their plan). Not a great approach over the long haul but for a photo shoot model, what the heck, why not show off some money-making abs!

Everyone's body is different in terms of where it chooses to store extra body fat and from where it chooses to remove that fat. Your body will strip away fatty tissue from wherever it wants to. You can't direct your body to spot reduce your thighs or arms or abs for fat-loss, even with thousands of repetitive exercises specifically directed at those areas!

You'll never see abs by doing 1,000s of daily ab exercises.

Ever see those people doing tons of abdominal crunches, most still have lots of fat laying over their core. You need to burn fat from your *entire* body. Some bodies will remove it from the thighs first, others from the waist first, etc. For me, to my great consternation, my tummy area was the very last to tone up. Certainly very annoying, but I knew that I had to be patient and keep at it.

Tenacity always rules in the gym!!!

3.8 Weight-Training VERSUS Cardio-Training. Which Is Better?

"The legs are the wheels of creativity." – A.E.

Well, when you ask me "which is better," I have to say that it's completely dependent upon your goals. For running sports, there are two extremes. If you want to run a marathon, you need to build-up your slow-twitch muscle endurance and you don't need big muscles. If you want to run the 100-metre dash, you need lots of powerful fast-twitch muscles and don't need much endurance for 9 seconds of effort. And, of course, there are two types of approaches to exercise; weight-training for the dash and cardiovascular (or "cardio") training for the marathon.

Some Benefits of Weight-Training	Some Benefits of Cardiovascular Training

Increased bone/tendon/ligament strength	Improved cardiovascular/respiratory endurance
Helps prevent osteoporosis	Reduced risk of cardiovascular disease
Better muscle coordination and posture	Increased blood volume pumped per heartbeat
Increased metabolic rate and improved insulin sensitivity	Increased amount of hemoglobin
Improves sports performance	Increased stroke volume[252]
Reduces age-related muscle loss	Increased red blood cells
Increased blood capillaries and mitochondria	Lowers blood pressure

Although you probably won't be running the short dash or the long marathon, you still should train with both approaches. *Both* are aerobic *and* anaerobic and both have different benefits for your body. Having said that, *cardio-training should be more* aerobic (uses oxygen) than anaerobic while *weight-training* will always be more anaerobic (doesn't use oxygen) than aerobic. The only time your body is strictly and only aerobic is when you are in a deep REM[253] sleep mode (i.e., *absolutely motionless* when your muscles are completely *immobilized* and your brain activity is very high while it deals with critical and necessary neural connections). And so just take that notion a little further – being aerobic doesn't necessarily mean that you're moving with

---

[252] I just finished watching the 2019 Tour de France (wowie, such incredible endurance). Those athletes have developed a huge "stroke volume/SV," that is they can with every heart beat move a ton of oxygen-carrying blood throughout their hardworking bodies. When you can get more oxygen into your body, your heart just doesn't have to beat as hard. Technically it's the volume of blood pumped from the left heart ventricle per heart beat contraction. Unfit/untrained individuals simply can't increase their SV even though they'll experience a higher heart rate with strenuous exercise.

[253] REM, known as "rapid-eye-movement" sleep, involves dreaming, a faster pulse, quicker breathing and increased brain activity all with absolutely NO muscle movement (other than your eye muscles of course…gotta watch what's happening in your dream even if it's a nightmare, right?)

the use of your muscles. From the hormonal and biochemical perspective, REM is also directly related to your human growth hormone and to the production of tissue-building proteins. HGH kicks in about two hours after falling asleep and those extra proteins aid muscle growth.

Should you do <u>one</u> of these traditional ways of exercising exclusively? NO, absolutely not! You should do both but do them properly. Weight-training will give your muscles the tone you seek, and of course we all know the general benefits of cardiovascular exercise. Just remember that *your heart is a muscle* and the idea of "cardio" exercise is to make your heart muscle stronger, and to increase your overall stamina. Just think about it, you want your heart muscle to be able to efficiently pump your nutrient-carrying blood throughout your body. That said, there are some major pitfalls of "cardio" exercise about which you should be aware.

Excessive "cardio" will increase your catabolic stress hormones (e.g., cortisol and adrenaline). Eventually those hormones will cause the breakdown your muscle tissue for energy and cortisol brings out those fat-storing enzymes. And to exacerbate the problem, it's very keen on storing that excess fat at your waistline. "Cardio" machines were designed for building cardiovascular fitness and training on such equipment at a high heart rate will certainly be great for increasing your heart and lung capacity. That said, they won't necessarily do much for efficiently emptying your fat-storage reserves – and isn't that what you want to do?

But why the heck is this true? OK, we know that *"cardio" "vascular"* exercise is mostly about your heart's arteries and blood vessels (your vascular/vein system) while weight-training exercise is mostly about building calorie-burning lean muscle tissue through the use of resistance forces and weights. Although both approaches are important, they result in completely different biochemical adaptations by your body. "Cardio" is directly related to efficiently using your blood to move oxygen around your body, while weight-training is directly related to your metabolism because gaining or losing muscle will directly alter your calorie-burning rate. Still, why ever would "cardio" create a different fat-burning ability for the physically unfit person when compared to the highly fit person? And what do I mean when I say "cardio" is such an *inefficient* way for unfit bodies to lose body fat?

Let's analyze this fat-burning inefficiency by using the treadmill as an example, because most people new to the gym will pick that piece of equipment first. Afterall, we all know how to walk and how to run, right? And everyone knows that brisk walking is a great overall exercise that can make your heart stronger. And so, it's tempting to just jump on the treadmill when you aren't sure what to do with all that gym equipment. But please don't get me wrong. I'm not against cardiovascular treadmill exercise as long as you do it properly, that is you keep it aerobic! On the flip side, when you're weight-training and using forces against your muscles, your muscles have to work really hard and so they'll get a lot tougher while burning caloric-energy. When you're on the treadmill, there isn't very much force placed against your muscles; indeed, that treadmill was never designed to place extra force on your muscles though of course it'll still burn some caloric energy.

Excessive "cardio" exercise by unfit bodies will cause increased cortisol stress hormones and the breakdown of muscle tissue. Efficient physically fit bodies burn body fat more easily as they have more oxygen carrying blood capillaries and mitochondria throughout their bodies.

And now let's consider the biochemical adaptations that occur within your body with these different exercise approaches. When you lift weights, your body will increase its ability to carry oxygen around your body and increase its mitochondria, the major powerhouses that convert the *food glucose* you eat and the *oxygen* from the air you breathe into ATP energy for your body. Put another way, weight-training puts your blood flow where it's needed *the most* – your muscles. The REAL meaning of being aerobic relates to the _efficiency_ of your vascular system to *absorb* that oxygen and then to *transport it* around your system. Weight-training also increases *myoglobin*, a protein that moves oxygen from your bloodstream into your muscle cells. When you're using respiratory oxygen fuel to burn body fat; that's when you're "oxidative."

When you build-up your blood capillaries and increase your myoglobin and mitochondria through weight-training, you'll _always_ be able to move more oxygen and so you'll stay oxidative for a much longer period of time. Oxygen is fuel and it's needed for the burning of glucose sugar and fatty acids from your cells. When you're oxidative, you'll be able to break up your triglyceride fats and then use them as energy. Over-weight people can have more difficulty breathing deeply and sometimes can experience a shortness of breath; most certainly running on a treadmill isn't going to help them efficiently burn much body fat as they just can't get enough oxygen into their lungs; they're just not oxidative! Whenever you're experiencing labored breathing or coughing, it means that your body is gasping for oxygen.

The success rate when it comes to *permanent* fat-loss by using <u>purely</u> aerobic exercise machines is simply not very high. When at the gym, look at the treadmillers and compare them to the gym floor weight-lifting gals. Bet you don't see too many lean toned bodies spending lots of hours on those treadmills. I'd bet my left bicep that the lean muscular gals are over lifting free weights. You might see them on my favorite stair-climber machine (or possibly a backless stationary bike or seated rowing machine) for a while, but those particular "cardio" machines apply force against your leg or back muscles too.

The myoglobin protein which moves oxygen from your bloodstream into your muscle tissue, is increased through anaerobic weight-lifting exercises.

And while I'm mentioning different "cardio" machines, you may wonder about the elliptical-type machines. I don't believe these are as helpful as the stair-climber at meeting your goals, because when one foot/leg goes up, the other one is *pushing down*. One leg is actually helping the other one due to the simultaneous and alternating push effect. By contrast, in a stair-climbing scenario *you* have to lift and stand up on your right leg as you get it up off the stair platform, <u>without assistance</u> from your left leg. Just think about it, better yet watch someone else on an elliptical machine and study why it might be *easier* to use. Believe me, you'll find the other machines (climber, stepper, backless stationary bike and rower) a heck of a lot harder to do properly and, because you're challenging more muscles by using compound movements, muscles other than those in your legs will be put to work (e.g., your back, arms, traps or shoulders). This is another reason why you'll be torching a lot more calories than just walking on the treadmill.

Whenever and however you work out, your body is forced to work much harder in order to keep your *blood* oxygen levels up and of course this is true for both aerobic and anaerobic types of exercise. And remember that I'm referring to your "blood" oxygen levels and not to your "rate" of breathing.[254] Exercising allows your blood to get oxygen from your lungs and then move that oxygen throughout your body. The longer you work out over time[255], the greater the improvement with your blood flow and oxygen levels (yes blood capillary and mitochondria growth) and the easier it becomes to breathe well throughout your exercise routine[256]. But as soon as you *can't get enough oxygen* from your lungs to support your exercise demands, your body will automatically dip into your muscle tissue glycogen fuel stores. Because fat stores are unlimited, you may be wondering why you'd even worry about replenishing your carbohydrate/glycogen stores. The answer lies in the critically significant fact the oxygen *must be present* to burn your body fat for energy, but it isn't needed at all for the burning of the stored glycogen in your muscle tissues. <u>And therein lies the key problem for the unfit</u>!!!

Doing too much "cardio" when you're physically unfit never works for efficiently lowering your body fat percentage.

Most people on treadmills are in poor condition and they don't know it. They are huffing and puffing, breathing hard through over-exertion, and moving into *quick shallow breathing* in order to get some oxygen into their lungs, but they won't be able to send the air deep enough into their over-worked lungs. Reading the estimated calorie use noted on the machine and believing they're aerobic; they'll think that they're burning a ton of calories and body fat for energy and they'll proudly keep on running. And to make matters worse they can't get their heart beat high enough to deliver more

---

[254] People incorrectly believe that if they are breathing really hard, then they are burning their fat stores. No dice.

[255] And remember what I said earlier; it generally takes at least 12 weeks to see a real difference in your fitness and with how your clothes fit your body. Better start saving some money to buy the new smaller clothing sizes you'll be needing. I even dropped my bra size, no doubt because I lost a lot of the fat on my back and breasts are mostly fat. If you see a really skinny woman with really big perky breasts, she'll probably have had breast implants.

[256] For me, I had to start at level #2 on my gym's stair climber and I'd be lucky to last 1 ½ minutes. I'm now on level #6 and can stay there for an hour. It was a really good improvement and it took me about 4 ½ months to do it. I practiced patience.

oxygen-carrying blood from their lungs to their hardworking muscles. Frankly their bodies simply aren't strong enough to do the required oxidative work and so they'll seek energy to fuel their training from elsewhere – specifically muscle tissue glycogen. That's why you don't see them as "toned." Eventually they may even look "skinny" but it's because they've wasted their muscles and they'll have soft loose skin as well.

Fat can only be broken down for energy if oxygen is available.
When there's insufficient oxygen in your blood,
your body will burn glycogen from your muscle tissues.
That's why you have to be oxidatively fit when running on the treadmill.

All those women on the treadmills would never believe you if you explained the oxidative argument; they'd probably respond "no, this is really good for me...I've lost X pounds!!!" But remember that *losing pounds* does not necessarily mean you're getting a healthier more fit, less fatty and more toned muscular body.

Maybe a good analogy to ponder is an auto trip taken with two different types of cars, both running at the same speed but with different fuel demands. I'll give you two choices to consider:

First, a 3-cylinder 900 cubic inch "SMART" car that gets a whopping 50 miles to a gallon of gas (it doesn't use much gas at all); and,

Second, an 8-cylinder 5.7 liter (5,700 cubic inches) "SUV" that only gets about 20 miles to a gallon of gas (it definitely uses a lot of gas).

Which one is better at running on the treadmill, that is which one is better at burning body fat more efficiently? Whenever I ask a client this question, inevitably they pick the little SMART car and not the SUV. But it's the big honking SUV (the physically fit oxidative individual with tons and tons of lean calorie-burning glycogen-filled muscle) that will burn a lot more fuel (calories and body fat) to keep going. NOT the little, tiny SMART car (light on muscle) which will run the same distance using far less fuel (calories).

A critical factor in training is your overall metabolism. It's made up of two inter-related metabolic rates and these are your "basal" metabolic rate (BMR) and your "resting" metabolic rate (RMR). Your *basal* BMR is the energy it takes *just to be alive*, by supporting organ function, replacing old tissue, transporting oxygen, fixing wounds, and for your beating heart and respiration, etc. Your *resting* RMR includes your BMR *and* the energy needed for any daily workout/mobility activities as well as the thermal energy needed to digest your food. Obviously, you can't do too much about your BMR but you sure can increase your RMR by exercising (*especially by weight-training)* and by not starving yourself. And maybe now you can better appreciate why muscle is so tightly bound with energy consumption (i.e., your calorie-burning and your metabolic rate). And you can better appreciate why insufficient caloric nutrition will always affect your metabolism.

Both your BMR and your RMR are used to measure or estimate the caloric energy requirements to maintain your bodily functions. Your RMR is a measure of the number of calories you will need over a 24-hour period. ***Because your resting RMR is the same as your resting energy <u>expenditure</u>, the higher your RMR, then the more efficient your body is at burning fat for energy 24 hours per day.*** In other words, the higher your RMR then the more calories you'll burn whether you're exercising at the gym, reading a book or even sleeping. Indeed, it's your RMR that burns the most energy. Although age typically decreases your RMR, newly built muscle will *always increase* your RMR. When your RMR is up, your fat-burning is up and your muscle-building is up. Starvation Island, on the other hand, sends your RMR plummeting, your body fat percentage up and your muscle tissue percentage down. Better get moving those gym weights.

If your RMR is about 1650 calories and your BMR is 1200 calories and you want to lose weight, you would lower your carbohydrates slightly and increase your protein slightly always with *nutritionally dense foods* and aim for a daily total being less than the 1650 RMR-related calories – called a "calorie-deficit". That said, you should never let your daily caloric intake fall below 1200 so that your body doesn't think you've moved to Starvation Island. If you want to build more muscle tissue (but not add fatty tissue), you could eat more than 1650 calories, by *significantly increasing* your protein intake[257] in order to feed your muscle growth. Believe it or not, it's actually very difficult to eat enough protein to <u>significantly</u> change your body's muscle tissue percentage. That's why bodybuilders eat chicken at every meal (including breakfast), eat tons of eggs daily, drink lots of protein shakes and

---

[257] Remember that earlier we said that protein is very inefficiently digested. That means that it requires a lot of thermal energy (calories) just to break it down in smaller parts for use by the body. Indeed, this is why you want to eat protein at every meal.

liberally throw protein powder into foods such as cottage cheese and yogurt, etc. They're always eating!

RMR (100%) = BMR (60-70%) + thermal energy needed for digestion (about 10%) + energy needed for daily physical activity (20-30%)

In terms of diet, small regular meals will also increase your RMR while treks to Starvation Island will *definitely* decrease your resting RMR (making it extremely difficult to lose weight and lowering the number of calories burned off in a 24-hour period). The amount of *energy burned by fat-free muscle will not change.* As a metabolically active tissue, muscle has almost 5 times the energy needs than does fat **even while resting**! This is precisely why any loss of muscle will cause poor choice dieters to yo-yo through terribly frustrating fat cycles all the while slowing down their overall RMR rate. In effect they've altered their catabolic (teardown) to anabolic (build-up) metabolism ratio. Looking at these biological facts – facts that you can't alter – guess how bad it is on your body to drop down to a crash diet of 700 calories per day – way below your BMR! *It's always your resting RMR that slows down when you restrict calories* – you'll be burning far fewer calories even while you're sleeping. You simply can't trick your body into any other adaptation. Your biochemical body isn't any different than that of anyone else.[258]

Just remember that MORE muscle means you'll have a higher RMR rate (so you'll definitely need more energy just to exist), you'll burn more calories and you'll have less fatty tissue over time. Sign me up for weight-training! I can eat <u>a lot more food</u>, not feel deprived, build lean muscle <u>and</u> lose body fat.

And before we leave this chapter, let's mention "group" fitness classes. Certainly, these are a lot cheaper than hiring ***personal*** trainers and they tend to attract more women than men. The prevailing theory supporting that last point is that women tend to have a greater desire for affiliation. And finally, let's face it, in the gym it's easier to follow a leader – this is true for weight-training too. When I had a personal trainer, I never had to figure out what to do. I

---

[258] Remember that crash starvation diet woman at the beginning of the book? The one that yo-yoed due to calorie-restrictive eating, losing a ton of weight and then gaining it all back only to look even fatter??? Yup, a much higher body-fat percentage at the end of her journey. A much bigger looking body, even at the very same weight and all because of a much lower RMR!!!

reckoned he had the knowledge and experience and he looked damned good, so I just did what I was told.

Personal trainers will know your fitness goals and be able to recognize specific areas to focus upon in order to improve your overall shape and physical fitness.

I'm not against group fitness classes, but I've noticed that many of the group fitness instructors[259] don't ensure that the individuals in their classes are actually performing an exercise properly. If a group fitness instructor is not going around the class correcting ranges of movement for the exercisers, I can pretty well guarantee that 75% of the attendees will be doing those exercises incorrectly. When an exercise is not performed properly, the related benefits *will always be far fewer*. Also, the weights used in group exercise are usually quite low. I've tried some of these classes to see how I felt and I found that they were more focused on cardiovascular training rather than muscle-building. Again, it just depends on your goals.

Your gym will probably have many group fitness choices including dance fitness, kickboxing, yoga, boot camps, Pilates, cycling, stretching, core training, etc. If you want to build muscle, choose classes that stress any of the following: strength training, barbell training, body pump, body conditioning – all for muscle strength and toning and do pick a variety of weights so that you can strategically *overload your muscles*. If you want to train for a marathon, then pick from the following: treadmill workouts, indoor cycling, core training – all for cardio, endurance, and flexibility.

And so in sum, I'm not just pro weight-lifting and completely against cardio-training, I just want you to be physically fit <u>before</u> doing a lot of "cardio" so that you can oxidatively benefit from your time and efforts,

---

[259] Just remember that "group" instructors are not "personal" trainers. Personal trainers, because they're one-on-one, can plan unique strength-training programs to meet the *specific needs and abilities* of their clients (people arrive at different ages, with varying fitness levels and health issues and a vast array of different goals – for example some muscle training can be related to sports-oriented improvements specific to skiing, hockey or soccer, etc.) When it comes to building a lot of lean calorie-burning muscle, you just can't do it in group classes with no squat BB racks, bench presses or cable machines all of which allow for progressively heavier weights! On the other hand, group classes can give you the motivation and maybe even some excitement during your workout.

whether you're on the treadmill or in a group-based fitness class. Once you've built-up that oxidative ability, your body will become far *more efficient* at burning body fat no matter what kind of exercise you might choose. Yes, <u>now</u> you can hit that treadmill and make it matter in terms of fat-loss.

3.9 How Do I Burn Fat at the Gym?

"An attempt at visualizing the Fourth Dimension: take a point, stretch it into a line, curl it into a circle, twist it into a sphere, and punch through the sphere." – A.E.

There are many confusing ideas on how best to burn fat in the gym. From the earlier chapter I hope that you can now appreciate the importance of building muscle with weight-training and that you must be oxidative to burn body fat during "cardio" exercise. Given the time and dedication it takes to build-up some nice-looking lean muscles, you sure don't want to eat them up for energy because you're on the treadmill and you can't get enough oxygen to burn body fat! You don't need respiratory oxygen to eat muscle for fuel. Your body has biochemically developed fuel alternatives for good reasons. I've never said that attaining your goals for lean muscle and less body fat will be easy. Losing muscle and/or making body fat IS easy; it's making muscle and losing body fat that's really hard!

Often aerobic exercise is paraded around as the best form of physical activity for weight-loss. Some poorly informed personal trainers may even suggest running on the treadmill as the best for fat-loss for their new-to-the-gym clients. Unfortunately, the truth is far from that highly simplistic notion! Yes, you'll lose some fat, but when unfit you'll also lose muscle tissue *and a lot of it*. Saggy arms, get ready, we're running your way!

Your body uses dietary fat calories to meet very specific needs. Let's now consider the types of fatty material that are always required by your body: triglycerides, cholesterol, and phospholipids[260].

---

[260] Phospholipids are lipid molecules that contain fatty-acids, phosphate and a glycerol molecule. They're a major component of the outer layer of all your cell membranes, making a boundary or barrier. They have a water-loving head and a water-fearing tail, hence are critical to your cell's ability to function. Obviously, they line up in particular formations when dealing with the flow of water into or out of your body's cells.

Triglycerides are primarily stored in your body's fat tissues and they're the most involved in *energy production*.

Cholesterol is an *essential structural component* of all cells. Still, when it over-accumulates in your body, it'll collect as a waxy substance on the inner sides of your artery walls. This will cause blood flow vascular issues due to the narrowing of artery widths and that'll hinder oxygen transportation.

Phospholipids are mostly involved in the *clotting of your blood*. They also form a part of the structure of all cell membranes and are critical in brain and nervous system cell membranes.

When you're weight-training, fatty triglycerides provide most of the energy needed. So, that means that weight-training builds muscle *and* burns fat. Great, sign me up!

On the other side of the coin, if you're camped out on Starvation Island and you were to lose 25 pounds of overall weight in 1 month (way too much!), the first 7-10 pounds would be water and the rest would be fat and muscle. You would also loose aerobic power, that is your capacity to *breathe in and process* oxygen would decline and remember that you need oxygen to keep burning body fat! There's also less oxygen to help your muscles burn fat for their workout fuel. You would soon loose overall muscle strength. But the *worst biochemical adaptation* would be the major metabolic slowdown you'd cause which of course means that you just don't have as much use for a lot of caloric fuel.

Your body works as a <u>unit</u>, indeed a biochemical unit that'll always make all necessary adaptations in response to your lifestyle and these will affect everything in terms of fat-loss/gain, muscle-loss/gain and your catabolic to anabolic metabolism calorie-burning rate ratio.

During the initial stages of exercise, oxygen is not available and ATP, that important high energy phosphate compound made by your mitochondria, is used. When you start accelerating on the treadmill, your body must breakdown ATP in order to produce the necessary energy. The muscle's ATP storage is only sufficient for a few seconds and so an instantaneous increase in the rate of oxygen used as a fuel in the muscle allows for the necessary re-synthesis of ATP. If you have poor VO2max (i.e., your **maximal oxygen uptake** through breathing[261]), then you'll have poor cardio/aerobic/oxidative fitness and you'll go anaerobic very quickly on that treadmill. If you're unfit and just can't get enough oxygen fuel you'll have a large and quickly *growing oxygen deficit*, a greater breakdown of muscle tissue and increased concentrations of metabolic by-products such as ADP (an inorganic diphosphate), lactate[262] and hydrogen ions (more acidity) in your contracting/working muscles. Yikes! More succinctly your body will move into muscular fatigue in an effort to give you the important message that it can't get enough energy until it gets more oxygen. Ignore those messages, eat too few nutrient-dense foods and you can get your upper arms ready for those high winds with a long-sleeved loose-fitting blouse or shirt.

Because it could take as much as 40-50 minutes of exercise before my body fat is fully available to act as muscle fuel, I like to devote one weekday to 60 minutes of just climbing on the stair-climber. And I do it at a medium rate, one that has me working but not so hard that I can't comfortably breathe. Another piece of the exercise puzzle is *lipase*, a hormone-sensitive enzyme[263], which promotes the breakdown of fat for energy. Lipase activity is stimulated through weight-training exercises. This is precisely why I do my cardio *after hitting the gym floor* and after completing my weight-training exercise program. I want to get rid of those freed-up fatty-acids.

---

[261] "VO2max" is a measurement of the highest rate of your oxygen intake during increasingly intensive exercise. "V" is for volume, "O2" is for oxygen and "max" is for maximum. It's the very best indicator of cardiovascular fitness and it normally decreases with age (at about 10% per decade). As a measurement of how much oxygen you use when exercising your hardest, you should increase your VO2max. Both cardio (getting your heart rate up) and weight-training (increasing blood volume, as well as capillary and mitochondrial muscle cell densities) exercises will certainly help you do that.

[262] Remember that the more fit you are, then the more lactate you use up as fuel; hence, your muscles simply don't get as fatigued and you don't feel as tired.

[263] Enzymes are always involved in the breakdown of dietary foods. For example, some breakdown fat (lipase), while others breakdown protein (protease) or carbohydrate (amylase). And amylase will *only act in a non-acidic* alkaline pH environment. Most menopausal women have an acidic pH from too much processed and sugary carbs and/or fatty foods and they don't exercise which *means even less amylase* and more body-fat.

But how does this work??? The best analogy is your car. If your car has been running for a while, it's all warmed-up just like your muscles after weight-training. Now if you turn on the car heater, you'll get some nice warm air. When you lift weights you burn up glycogen as energy, creating a glycogen-depleted set of muscles along with the "afterburn" affect (EPOC). This is when your freed up fatty-acids are ready to be burned through cardio-training; in essence, you'll be burning more fat as fuel *after* weight-training rather than before it. Just do it for 10-15 minutes maximum, and don't be panting while doing it or you won't be aerobic. Panting equals muscle-wasting!

Your body must run efficiently, and *your conditioning must be good for you to burn fat as fuel*. This will occur only after *appropriate* anaerobic muscle-building weight-training and proper oxidative aerobic/cardiovascular exercise. Like I've said via this book, you need a good understanding of your biochemical pathways in order to move a fat-making engine into a calorie-burning engine!!!

Cardio exercise is not the most efficient fat-burning activity.
The hormone-sensitive enzyme lipase promotes the breakdown of fat into energy
and it's stimulated through anaerobic weight-training exercise.

Another great thing about proper weight-training exercise is that the more you do it, the less you need worry about calories. Sure, you burn calories *while doing* aerobic exercise but not after completing that exercise. Guess what??? You burn calories *while* weight-training *and for 24-48 hours following that weight-training* as well. In essence, you've raised your metabolic (anabolic) rate while exercising with weights and it stays elevated for several hours while it re-builds the muscles you challenged with progressively heavier weights over time.

Cardio exercise burns calories while you're on the equipment.
Weight-training preserves muscle and burns calories while you're exercising
and for 24-48 hours <u>after</u> the completion of that exercising.

You now know that your overall <u>metabolic rate</u> (or "metabolism") is always some sort of combination of your <u>catabolic (breakdown) rate</u> and your <u>anabolic (build-up) rate</u>.

In order to increase your overall metabolic rate, you must have a higher anabolic rate compared to your catabolic rate. When you're anabolic, you'll need much more energy and that translates into calorie-burning. When you're anabolic, you'll always have weight-loss even though you can eat more food, contrary to the weight-gain that is affiliated with a catabolic state.

Healthy body fat percentages are about 20-24% for women and 15-20% for men. Women's higher body fat percentages reflect one of our genetic differences (we had to give birth to, carry and care for those children, not run around hunting for meat like the guys had to). Serious weight-lifters and professional bodybuilders go to even lower body fat percentages at 10-15% for women and as low as 5-10% for men (that's why you can see those washboard abs so well – they simply have very little fat layered over them). After persistent heavy weight-training, these bodybuilders and magazine models will go on *severe crash diets* for about 2 weeks prior to a show or shoot. It's an awfully challenging process on their bodies, takes incredible focus and dedication, but simply can't be maintained for very long[264]. But remember that the only reason they do have muscle is that they were building it up in the gym *before that two weeks, all the while eating 1,000s and 1,000s of daily calories.* They call it "bulking-up" and they'll do it after a "cutting" stage.

And keep in mind that when someone maintains such a low body fat percentage, they will have sacrificed a lot of muscle strength. This is why I'm stronger on some lifts than are some of those washboard guys! Who'a thought that even possible for a 72-year-old woman???

When you're recovering from strenuous exercise, your body must replenish its depleted fuel/energy stores, repair damaged muscle tissues and initiate training adaptations (yeah, bigger defined/toned shapely arm and shoulder muscles for those nice tank tops). In other words, your body must switch from a predominately catabolic (breakdown) metabolism to a predominantly anabolic (build-up) metabolism. Critical to these metabolic

---

[264] When someone maintains such a low body fat percentage, they will have sacrificed some muscle strength. This is why I am stronger on some weight lifting exercises than are some 6-pack men! Who'da thought that of a 72-year-old woman?

processes are the types, amounts and timing of your nutrient intake. For example, if you want to build muscle, you will have to eat a *higher amount of lean protein* in order to get the amino-acid construction blocks necessary for building cells (and protein enhances the fat-burning glucagon hormone as well).

The efficiency of muscle glycogen storage (to prevent muscle-wasting) can be increased significantly with a protein supplement or meal near your workout time. I drink a protein mixture during my workout and then eat protein after the workout. Protein limits *post-exercise soreness (DOMS)* simply because amino acids with their nitrogen content are the foods used to build-up your muscles.

Many "hardcore" bodybuilders also use a concoction of drugs including anabolic steroids and human growth hormones all of which can cause coronary risks, vision loss, abnormal liver function, severe mood and psychotic disorders and kidney damage (from an *extremely* high-protein intake which causes excessive hyper-filtration of protein waste products leading to the formation of scar tissue). Uh-oh, no thanks! I read that Arnold Schwarzenegger has been rumored to have had heart surgery as well as that kidney transplant. My guess is that, if he did, both were probably related to the mixture of drugs he would have taken to reach and maintain the grotesquely big muscular body he presented when he was labelled Mr. Universe. He did look amazing though and I loved his forearms.

Suffice it to say that when you build active calorie-eating muscle tissue with weight-training exercises, you automatically create a ***different response to the food you eat*** and you become a fat-burning engine which doesn't have to worry about counting calories. And doesn't that just sound glorious!

3.10 Why Should I Worry About My Core?

"Never give up on what you really want to do. The person with big dreams is more powerful than the one with all the facts." – A.E.

Your overall fitness can be better maintained with a strong and flexible "core." People mistakenly think their abdominal muscles *are* their core, but this isn't entirely true. Your core covers your whole torso and includes the muscles of your abdomen and your spine. It's an essential part of every motion you make. It stabilizes you when you sit, stand, walk, run, bend, twist, lift, push, pull and move. Your core directly affects your balance and your overall posture.

When you have good posture, you look taller and you look trimer. Your head should be up, your shoulders back and down (not in a shrug position) and your stomach in. When you have a strong core, you'll walk "stacked" with your weight over your base-of-support, your feet. You won't be stressing out your back and you won't be slumped forward at the shoulders or at the waist. You see this in older people; they have weakened core muscles and bone loss and they begin to walk leaning forward. This hunched over stance further exacerbates their back issues and eventually they have to curve their neck upwards in order to see where they're going.

Just try walking like an old person (or a young person with really bad posture). Stand with your torso leading by bending at the waist and leaning forward. Now walk with your feet trying to catch up to your forward leaning torso. When your feet are behind your torso, gravity forces much of your body's weight straight down to the ground to a spot ahead of your feet; hence, your weight is NOT over your feet[265]. Your feet *should be* where your weight is being supported or carried. When you have poor posture, guess what part of your body takes the brunt of it? Yup, it's always your poor spine. Stand *stacked*: head over waist, waist over feet. Concentrate on making it a habit and soon you'll not have to think about it. You'll look old fast if you walk hunched over, no matter what your age. Pull your shoulders down and back and walk pushing "the girls" out.

When you keep all three curvatures of your spine aligned, you'll be walking with a "neutral" spine; that is, the cervical neck (upper), thoracic (middle) and lumbar (lower) parts of your spine will be nicely aligned. And if you sit at a computer all day, be very careful. Sit with your thoracic area slightly curved in and your shoulders relaxed (down and back). I never lean on the back of a chair when on my computer and I don't let my knees fall below my hips. I keep my head, neck, shoulders, elbows and hips all aligned. Thank

---

[265] In downhill skiing, this is the first skill ski instructors focus on for their students – keeping your weight over your feet and not over the back of your skis. Skiing is a highly dynamic sport, one in which you must quickly adapt to its ever-changing terrain. When your centre of mass is not over your feet, you'll have great difficultly keeping up to your skis and you'll fall. Weight-training will strengthen skiers' cores, resulting in a greatly improved skiing ability.

goodness, because I've been working on this book for nearly two years and still, I'm not finished. My back would have complained otherwise.

Personally, though I do a few, I don't concentrate on doing a lot of isolated repetitive "ab" exercises during my gym floor workout routines. My "core" and "abs" are fatigued during most of the weight-training exercises I perform. Do you think you don't use your core stabilizers while doing lunges, squats, deadlifts, standing bicep curls, chin-ups, push-ups or pull-ups? Wrong!!!

When you perform many full-range-of-motion free-weight movements, you'll be training your stabilizer/core muscles as well. An example of a progression in terms of stabilizers follows:

→ Using a chest press fixed-floor machine will work out your muscles according to that machine and it'll stress your chest over everything else; it'll target specific chest muscles but *not* your core's stabilizing muscles; while,

→ The free weight barbell bench press, with plate weights on the end of a barbell will be great for strengthening/building your pectorals (chest), anterior deltoids (front of shoulders) and triceps (back of upper arms) and will require *some stabilizing* by your core; but,

→ The dumbbell bench press, with a dumbbell in each hand will accomplish what the barbell press did along *with more stabilizing activity* as your arms are completing separate movements, and it'll be better for developing shoulder stability. You can even complete alternating/simultaneous presses (raise one arm up *while the other* is coming down, and then alternate the movement), which will bring in your stabilizers even more.

When you use fixed-floor exercise machines, the weight you're moving will be travelling along *a guided path or along a 2-dimensional plane of motion*. On the other hand, using exercises that have you moving dumbbells or barbells or weight plates, require **you** to *balance the weight yourself* as you're directing the motion path that will be taken by the weight. Basically, you can move in all dimensions (or multi-planes), forward, backward, horizontally and vertically, when dealing will free weights. That's what makes them more challenging for your core.

Your core includes your whole trunk and torso, which includes your abdominals.
Most weight-training exercises involve your core and your stabilizing muscles to some degree.

Whenever you perform an exercise, you'll have "prime" agonist muscle movers and "secondary" antagonist muscles completing the movement, but they never work alone. You also have "stabilizer" muscle movers and though they're not targeted directly, they'll work hard to stabilize your body during the movement. When you're moving in multi-planes, your body must rely upon your abdominal stabilizers.

Torso stability is your ability to stabilize your core. Your stabilizer muscles help to keep you balanced and upright, allowing you to twist and rotate your body when moving. They aren't directly involved in the lifting of weight, but they certainly help to keep your body steady. Stabilizer muscles also allow you to be more powerful, safer and efficient. Don't forget to vary your workouts so that you do challenge them through some type of instability. An example might be to execute lunges with different weights in each hand; or you could do lunges while holding a barbell across your shoulders. This moves the weight higher and causes additional stabilizer stress. Or better yet, how about a barbell across your shoulders/neck with different weight plates at the ends? Yikes say your stabilizing abs!

Fixed-floor machines *do not* stress your stabilizers. But it isn't that these machines are bad and should be avoided. If I do a row on a fixed-floor machine, I'll isolate my back muscles much more and work them harder without taxing the stabilizers as I would do on a cable row or a prone barbell row. For me, a seasoned weightlifter, sometimes I want to isolate one group of muscles and work them out without allowing other more secondary muscles to assist with or share the applied force/weight. No cheat-related weight leakage at all!!!

You have to determine your goals before you decide on a program of attack. Normally, as a personal trainer, I don't tend to use very many floor-mounted machines for beginner clients, though I do incorporate seated leg extension and leg curl fixed-floor machines for beginners in order to better isolate their quadriceps (top of thigh) and hamstrings (back of thigh).

Exercises that use a lot of joints and recruit a greater number of muscles are better for strengthening your stabilizer muscles. For example, when you do a squat (bending at the waist, the knees and the ankles) your body must stabilize itself more than if you were performing seated bicep curls (bending the elbow joint only). Unilateral[266] exercises will also address any muscular imbalances in your physique as well as recruit more stabilizer muscles since you have to stabilizer an uneven load (e.g., single-arm dumbbell rows or single-arm dumbbell shoulder presses).

Free weights (such as dumbbells) will draw upon more core muscles than will fixed-floor machines. Exercises that recruit a large number of muscles and
cause you to move more than one joint will automatically require more core muscles to stabilize the movement (e.g., squats, deadlifts).

The major muscles involved in core *stability* include the following:
-your pelvic floor muscles for assisting with urination and excretion,
-the rectus abdominals between your ribs for flexing your torso and spine (that "six-pack" you want),
-your pelvic bone for flexing your spine,
-your internal/external oblique abdominals on the sides of your rectus abdominals for twisting,
-your transverse abdominals deep under your rectus abdominals and obliques for stabilizing the back and pelvis for limb movements,
-your spine (erector spinae) for side-to-side rotation; and,
-your diaphragm for inhaling and exhaling.

You should be training all of them in some way, either with a variety of multi-joint "compound" weight-training exercises as I do or with some specific "ab" exercises such as forward crunches (using a stabilizer ball will make these more comfortable yet still effective), reverse crunches, various plank exercises, and abdominal rotational exercises.

Because your abs are relatively small muscles, training them daily does not cause the over-training that can happen with your larger muscles. Also, I don't tend to add weights to "ab" exercises. I don't want hugely large abs, as they'll make my waist look wider.

---

[266] A unilateral exercise is performed by only one limb, one arm or one leg, while a bilateral one uses both limbs.

3.11 How Is Food Used in Exercise?

"Education is what remains after one has forgotten what one has learned in school." – A.E.

You know by now that weight-training builds lean calorie-burning muscle tissue. But to build anything, you have to have some *construction* materials. For your body those materials come in the form of the three macronutrients: protein, carbohydrate and fat. The process used by your body to convert those construction materials into building blocks is your metabolism.

Your metabolic rate controls how your body breaks down those three macronutrients in order to generate the energy required for growth and life. Obviously, you want a fast-efficient metabolism, not a slow sluggish one that doesn't want to burn very many calories. During the metabolic process, proteins are broken down into amino acids by an enzyme catalyst called protease. Your cells then use these amino acids to synthesize new proteins. Under any condition of growth, your body manufactures more cells than are lost (e.g., for bone and muscle growth). Your body can manufacture many of the materials needed to build those new cells from stored glycogen and fat; but, to replace and build new protein, your body *must* have protein from the food you consume. Unlike carbohydrate and fat, dietary protein contains <u>nitrogen</u> and this is absolutely necessary to make new protein and for the maintenance, replacement and growth of all of your body tissues. I'm sure you've NEVER seen a diet that says you should eat *less* protein. Even Starvation Island doesn't fly that flag!

Earlier I described the two types of metabolism that are opposite to one another. Anabolism (constructive build-up) and catabolism (destructive tear-down) and that you'll *always* have some combination of the two. These two extremes can be represented by newborn babies (mostly in anabolic constructive metabolism) and the very elderly (mostly in catabolic destructive metabolism). As you age, you must up your exercise-game to keep your body young, that is more anabolic. You want to be in a building and repair state. Hence, I believe weight-training to be the closest thing to a "fountain of youth" pill as it's highly anabolic in nature, and when you're anabolic, you'll find it much easier to lose weight.

Protein drives your anabolic tissue-building growth and that's why it's imperative for building your muscles. When you stress your muscles through weight-training, your muscle cells start making *new* proteins which lead to those more defined and toned muscle tissues. Give your body protein before, during and right after exercise and you'll keep yourself in an anabolic growth state. Carbs before and after a workout will help. But fats are best eaten after a workout.

Eating lean nitrogen-containing protein leads to more fat-releasing enzymes, muscle-building, calorie-burning and fat-burning.

Because protein has such a positive effect on your metabolic engine, you might think simply that if you eat more protein then your body will construct more muscle. But that'd be incorrect. If you eat more protein than what your body can use, the excess will be converted to glucose (to be used for energy) or to body fat (to be stored for future use). That's why fat people who eat a lot of protein and only experience gym drive-byes, never build muscle or lose much weight.

For muscle growth, you must maintain a positive nitrogen balance.[267] This occurs when the total nitrogen excreted by your body is less than the total nitrogen eaten. Nitrogen is primarily lost through your urine and replaced through food. To maintain a positive nitrogen balance, your protein intake must meet your protein requirement. Weight-training will enhance your nitrogen retention and will cause the synthesizing of new muscle tissue. The best way to grow your muscles is to *demand more* from the protein you're eating. Make your body work harder on that gym floor and then your muscles will use more nutrients, including the amino acids from the extra protein you're eating. There are questions regarding the safety of high protein intake on those with kidney disease; however, if you have normal kidney function it shouldn't be harmful.

---

[267] There are many online calculators regarding the amount of protein grams you need to eat per pound/kilogram of body weight in order to gain muscle. Normally you'll see the suggestion of between ½ to 1 gram protein per pound of body weight and, if you're on a fat-loss muscle-building program, **the amount actually climbs**. You'll quickly discover, however, that it's extremely difficult to eat a lot of protein. Indeed, that's why it seems that bodybuilders hardly ever stop eating!

By combining oxygen with nutrients from your food, your cells will generate high energy ATP through one of its three energy systems. As your hardworking muscles are contracted during weight-training, they're directly fueled by that ATP energy. Body fat is also used, but as you now know, body fat can *only* be broken down and released into your blood stream when oxygen is present. Muscle cells *prefer* to burn carbohydrate, want to use protein for growth and repair and to let your body store fat. You sure don't want to accumulate a lot of extra body fat; it really is so darn hard to dump it. And you don't want to lose a bunch of muscle, as it takes a lot of dedicated gym-based effort and time to build-up those muscles. Your body will move seamlessly through *three distinct energy systems*, depending upon what type of exercise demands are being made upon it. You may notice when you're weight-training that sometimes it seems that you just can't do another repetition with that same weight; but, if you take a 5 second rest, voila…suddenly you can do more reps with the same weight.

1.   The phosphagen system rebuilds ATP by supplying a compound called creatine phosphate (CP). Once ATP is used up, it can be replenished with additional food or oxygen. This system is used for short intense bursts of exercise such as heavy weight-training and sprinting to catch a bus but it **lasts only 3-15 seconds** because the ATP and CP in the muscles are rapidly depleted. At that point the ATP and CP *must be replenished* and this is the job of other energy systems in your body.

2.   The glycolytic system makes glucose available to the working muscles by either breaking down digested carbohydrate or by the breakdown of stored muscle and liver glycogen. During this glycolysis process, glycogen is broken down into glucose in the muscles and ultimately converted into more ATP. This system, that is the glycogen reserve in your muscles and liver, only **lasts about 1 – 3 minutes** at a time. This is the system that produces lactate via your hardworking muscles.

3.   The oxidative system helps to fuel aerobic exercise obviously with the use of respiratory oxygen. How long this system lasts is completely dependent on how **physically fit** you are. And although this system can handle the energy needed for *endurance exercises* (e.g., marathons or long-distance bicycling), all three energy systems will be used for endurance activities at some point.

During weight-training, the first two systems dominate and during proper oxidative/aerobic exercise, the third system dominates. Your body's ability to produce energy through one of these three systems can be improved with the right eating plan and a progressive strength-building weight-training exercise program. The result will be a fat-burning, calorie-burning and muscle-building metabolic engine. Yeah, yeah and yeah!

Eating a lot of processed and sugary foods will move your metabolism toward the tear-down catabolic side, while eating lean protein, unsaturated fats and nutritious complex slow-to-sugar/low GI carbohydrates will move it toward the build-up anabolic side. At a high level of performance, you *can* apply some nutrient timing by consuming nutrient-dense carbohydrate within the 30-60 minutes following intense weight-training. It'll replace your muscle glycogen stores and you'll **_never_** have to worry about it being converted into stored body fat.

High intensity interval training (HIIT) with brief periods of rest can help to maximize your anabolic building process as well. HIIT is a training technique during which you give it your all in your workout, like 100% maximum effort. You do quick and intense bursts of exercise and then do a short recovery period, then do the high intensity again[268]. People who adhere to this type of training get their heart rates up and then they'll burn more caloric fuel yet take less time to do so. *If you are physically fit* and you do it properly, you'll not lose precious muscle tissue, you'll lose body fat. Because burning fat always take oxygen, the rest periods built into HIIT training will help you avoid any potential muscle-eating. Sounds great and I can eat more! Sign me up.

Remember those women plugging away daily on those treadmills, eating too little, chugging tons of water, eating muscle and not burning very much body fat. I really feel sad for them. They certainly have commitment and it's admirable that they spent the money to join a gym. It's just unfortunate that they don't comprehend or believe the knowledge that explains the incredible benefits of weight-training coupled with nutrient-dense eating; two things that

---

[268] HIIT examples usually involve "cardio" equipment. An example would be to walk on the treadmill for 2 – 4 minutes (a less intense recovery period) and then run fast for 1 – 2 minutes (a shorter period of high intensity), returning to the walk, then run, alternating on and on. This would force your body to burn fat more efficiently as opposed to muscle glycogen.

will always result in a more efficient and sustained body fat loss. As I've stressed, to lose body fat on the treadmill when you're in poor physical condition is sort of analogous to working for minimum wage and getting little, or no, dividends. You want to be in a strong aerobic/oxidative state rather than be destroying your calorie-burning tissue! And compounding their flaccidity is the reality that when unfit treadmillers are not eating enough, they become metabolically inefficient "skinny-fat" treadmill runners. Yes, they may lose weight and they might begin to look thin (skinny[269]) but they'll be increasing their overall body fat percentage due to the loss of precious lean muscle tissue.

---

[269] I'm terribly insulted in someone calls me "skinny." I'm LEAN, not skinny!!! I worked hard to get my toned muscular body!

Unit 4
Additional Reflections

Other areas of interest and some unusual questions I've been asked.

4.1 Why Do I Want to Eat So Much?

"Common sense is the collection of prejudices acquired by the age of eighteen." – A.E.

In the 1960s, people ate to live. It seems now that we live to eat. What the heck happened? Why do we eat so much? Why do we seem to eat all the time, from morning to night and sometimes in the middle of the night? And just as importantly, why do we choose to eat so many "bad" high-calorie and nutrient-devoid foods?

Even though your body knows what it "needs" nutritionally, you can get tricked into poorly chosen "wants" as replacements. Foods have been manipulated. This develops a problem not centered around calories but, rather, around eating the *wrong* foods for the *wrong* reasons and indeed in the *wrong* portions. Advances in synthetic-making chemistry have contributed to many great tasting albeit unnaturally flavored foods. Unfortunately, these "advances" lead to growing levels of obesity.

Over the years, many things have taken turns taking the blame and being labelled the villain for overweight issues. Some of these rotating villains have included: sugar, saturated fat, high fructose corn syrup (HFCS), trans-fats, carbohydrate, wheat gluten, etc. etc. etc. This has led to many disparate and confusing diet plans. They all take different approaches and suggest eating different foods at different times or sometimes not at all. Examples of some of these diet approaches include: eat no-fat[270], eat no sugar[271], avoid all carbohydrates, eat high-protein, avoid wheat gluten, juice everything in sight, shun red meat, create high ketones, use meal substitutes (usually fiber-free liquids), eat only one meal per day, undertake full-day fasting, alternate between protein (a red-day) and carbohydrate (a green-day) on consecutive days, etc. Do you get the picture? Maybe not, it really is <u>very</u> confusing and terribly frustrating.

OK, now let's think about the actual *act* of eating. Whatever you eat gives off aromatic compounds and vapors which are exhaled from your mouth through the act of chewing and then inhaled into your nose, very conveniently placed right above your mouth. You have about 400 smell receptors that can combine in numerous ways to distinguish a large variety of aromas. Your brain catalogs these smells; hence, you may even remember some earlier experience when tasting a grilled steak, frying bacon or eating chocolate ice cream!

For me, whenever I eat a breakfast of easy-over eggs and fried potatoes (occasionally on a motorcycle vacation road trip with those potatoes as a pure cheat-eat), a very specific and wonderful memory never fails to *immediately* flood back. I was a young only-child at the time, maybe six or seven, and was travelling with my parents to visit my aunt and uncle in a 1953 Chevrolet which at that time constituted a three-to-four-hour car ride. This was a 140-mile trip, and people didn't speed as they do today. At some point I expressed my hunger and my parents stopped at a roadside diner. I can remember sitting between them on a red and black checked swivel stool eating eggs and potatoes at the counter. It was the best food I can remember tasting (and I WAS hungry), a combination I had never eaten up to that point. I even remember that my dad was on my left and my mom on my right, though I can't remember what they were eating or what they were talking about. So, whenever I see fried potatoes

---

[270] Fat can be confusing and there's a whole discussion out there on "good" versus "bad" fats. The fact is that, while there may be some similar components in all fats such as the number of calories per gram, they don't all behave the same way in your body. Different dietary fats have different chemical compositions and different effects on your body-fat, that run from highly helpful to terribly detrimental. For example, synthetic trans-fats are a far different beast that healthy omega-3 fatty-acids.

[271] This approach I wholly support; sugar is *never* necessary for your body. In fact, it's the most useless "food" you can ingest. Calories yes, nutrition no.

and eggs as a menu choice, I just can't avoid them because I love reveling in that memory and I really miss my parents!

But back to eating, the truth is that we really can't blame any one thing for making us fat – I'll eat those potatoes and eggs even if I'm not that hungry. Your body is a complicated entity and it has extremely complex needs. But food is very complicated too. Our genes are the same as they were in the 1960s and so what is it that has changed? What has made the average North American so much heavier than their 1960 counterpart?

The "wanting" and the "needing" of food are quite different concepts.
The food industry tinkers with salt, fat, sugar, crunch and
artificial/synthetic flavorings
to create strong food desires and addictions which are difficult to avoid.

How does your body know what it wants or what it needs? The "wanting" and the "needing" of food are quite different; but it's the "wanting" that's the real problem. Certain dietary foods and additives make us *want* them more: sugar, high fructose corn syrup, fat, simple carbohydrates; while other things (like memories) also have something to do with the "want" obsession we experience with foods. And, of course, the food industry is well aware of that.

Good nutrients don't cause your food "want" problem. Sure, we now know that your body turns all the excess heavily refined carbohydrate foods you eat into body fat, that's what your body is supposed to do with that kind of food. But the problem is even more simple, people eat *far too much food*. They can't resist the *desire* to eat. They can't resist the *lure* of the food. And they sure don't practice much portion-control. But what is it about food that has changed enough to cause such crazy reactions in us?

Well actually, it's the "flavor" of food. It's the high palatability of the food; food that gives your palate high satisfaction and a super great taste reward. Indeed, food palatability is actually quite complicated, and it can have a built-in memory like my eggs-and-potatoes story. Your palate separates your nose and mouth cavities and it's highly sophisticated and quite selective. The food industry uses this fact and it has evolved to be really good at chemical manipulation, legally accepted yet deceptive labelling and succulent hard-to-resist tastes.

306

In reality, food tastes quite different now than it did in the 1960s. Junk-food in particular will tinker with various combinations of salt, fat, sugar, crunch and synthetic "fake" flavorings to create in you an irresistible desire for more. I'm certain you will have experienced this. Is it that we've lost the ability to taste simple whole food? Food that should stand on its own as tasting as good as it did in the 1960s. Hmmm, maybe artificial flavoring is the real offender.

Years ago, foods all had their own specific flavors. Popcorn and corn chips tasted like corn and potato chips tasted like potatoes. But now, you can buy potato chips that taste like bacon and tortilla chips that taste like limes. And you can drink a bottle of lemonade that tastes like freshly squeezed lemonade although it contains absolutely no lemons in any form whatsoever. And what about the explosion of different cracker tastes? In the 1960s crackers were very plain. They were just a simple treat to put pate or cheese on. But then herbs were added, and it made them tastier on their own. This has now progressed into rows upon rows of differently flavored crackers on your grocery store shelves. No one even has to add cheese, or olives or pickles or whatever. These crackers stand on their own and people snack on these irresistible albeit *highly processed carbohydrate* foods by the handful.

You must have noticed that the idea of *multi-mix flavoring* has moved into everything, whether it's normally whole nutritious food that used to stand on its own (do we really need pre-packaged mustard/maple sugar Atlantic salmon?) or junk-food such as honey/Dijon potato chips. There are even TV contests asking for potential flavor mixes that the industry will make if enough people vote for them. They've moved us into their marketing meetings and we don't even get paid to work there!

And remember that all flavor mixes will have lots of fat, salt and/or sugar – the holy grails for conjuring up *tasty irresistible* processed foods. Some of the dreamed-up flavor results just for potato chips have included: dill pickle, ketchup, smoky bacon, pizza flavor, taco flavor, sweet onion, rotisserie chicken (what the heck?), crab spice (good grief), and Thai sweet chili. Surely you can't believe that they've put a whole bunch of real cheddar into that package of "grilled cheese" potato chips! There are rows upon rows upon rows of different choices on your grocery store shelves; the food industry can make *whatever you dream up*! Such wide-choice *fake* flavoring has recently begun to hit the popcorn bags (e.g., salted caramel bourbon and Texas toast) and even

M&Ms too. In the States, you can buy English Toffee, Thai Coconut and Mexican Jalapeno M&Ms! Sort of ridiculous wouldn't you say. And, if you want to believe that the industry is using real (non-synthesized) flavorings, I bet I could sell you some more of my prime swampland in Florida.

Flavoring is often marketed as "natural flavoring" because it conjures up thoughts of wholesomeness to the buyer. But any flavoring engineered by the food industry is really "synthetic" flavoring only. Flavor found in plants and animals should be called "natural" flavoring. How can the blending of chemicals in some laboratory, maybe used to flavor a granola bar or instant porridge, be legally allowed to be called "natural flavoring" when it was synthesized in a laboratory? Why are they allowed to call it "natural"?

Are you confused? The food industry calls flavorings "natural" simply because the *process* used to make them was indeed natural (e.g., by using *natural* enzymes or a *natural* healing process). But if the industry used a "non-natural" way, say with petrochemicals and industrial chemistry, then they'd have to list them as "artificial flavorings." So maybe you're beginning to get the overall picture now: that is, the word "natural" refers to the *process* and not necessarily to the actual "flavoring" you're eating. Consider what you buy, thinking it IS wholesome, because it might say "natural" flavoring. Some examples can include the following: chocolate chips, salad dressings, deli meats, canned baked beans, sausages, curry sauce, frozen pizza, instant oatmeal, and the list goes on and on. Scary, eh?

Another reality about the good ol' 1960s (sorry I'm a baby-boomer[272]), is that an acre of farming land in those days was producing *far fewer* potatoes and/or corn than it does now[273]. I can certainly remember when corn had a

---

[272] Baby boomers were born within 10 years after World War II...me in 1947 when you were lucky to have a TV. It was black and white and you had to get up to change the channel (with only three choices!) Yup, every aspect of our lives involved a lot more exercise than today's youth with their remote controls, smart tablets and cell phones.

[273] With the use of *non-manure* cost-effective fertilizers, crops grow faster and bigger so that the crop yield is increased significantly. Indeed, in some cases, farmers can get two and sometimes three (!) annual crops from the same soil acreage through the use of fertilizers that provide the essential chemicals needed for growth (especially nitrogen). But what happens to the soil by over-planting annually? I wonder; does the taste potency and maybe even the nutritive value of the food get diminished and we simply don't notice because of our flavouring decadence?

richer corn taste than what I eat these days. Blander tastes can be countered with the addition of artificial flavorings and this helps the food industry sell their products. The industry has taken <u>real appetizing food</u> and made it into <u>a junk-food that's highly appetizing</u> only because it's slathered in non-nutritive calories, dipped in sugary sauces, and sprinkled with synthetic flavors. Yuk for your weight-loss hopes.

Synthetically flavored food is never the same to your body as *naturally flavorful* food. Your body possesses a very complex flavor sensing ability, and even though you may like the taste of some industrially produced food, your body simply isn't adapted for the resulting non-nutritive calories and synthetic flavoring trickery. And your body will always adapt biochemically in terms of your fat-burning ability.

Food industry laboratories have also learned how to manipulate foods so that a highly processed food tastes and smells *exactly* like the original one. One example is vanilla. If I gave you a taste or smell of both "imitation" vanilla and "pure" vanilla, you wouldn't be able to tell the difference between them. Real vanilla extract is made from pure vanilla beans, whereas imitation vanilla is made from *vanillin*, a *chemically synthetic concoction* made from about 30 compounds from the petrochemicals and by-products from the paper industry! And guess what? The real deal will cost you a heck of a lot more money than the synthetic stuff and that's why the food industry uses an imitation. It knows you want to be economically frugal when grocery shopping. Unfortunately, when you shop for the cheaper version; not only your wallet, but your body will know the difference (even though to your taste buds and to your nose you may not notice any difference at all.) As I like to say about every type of purchase, food or otherwise, "Ya get what ya pay for!"

One of my previous clients was very committed, meeting me five times a week to weight-train. Her strength improved dramatically; nevertheless, she remained extremely heavy. Her beautifully muscular body was cloaked in a body of fat, albeit 35 pounds less than at the outset of her journey to health. She finally went to a therapist and was told, after some analysis, that she was addicted to food, specifically highly refined carbohydrate/sugary foods, yes foods created by the big very powerful I-really-don't-care-about-your-body fat food industry. Taken from an alternate perspective, you could say that the food industry is proficiently creating food addictions and then supplying the resulting demands!

Food-addicted brains are never very happy brains. Sugar, trans-fat and salt are the often-hidden villains lurking in your foods and they can and will cause obesity. The food industry knows this, and it has been playing around with all three to entice us to eat more and more, to drive up their profits more and more. They don't really care much about the overall health or weight of their buyers. They don't mind that you eat too much. They know exactly how much sugar is perfect. They know how to shape the salt molecules so that they burst in your mouth perfectly. And they know the perfect "mouth feel" of fat that you tend to prefer. They've done a ton of detailed and expensive research on willing subjects to know these things and they have the big profits that allow them to continue figuring out how to get us to buy more and more of their products.

On another note, the Canadian Food Guide has just been changed in an effort to address the types of poor food choices people are making. But before we compare the 2019 version to the dated 2007 one, consider these realities:

1. The 2007 version was put together by a 12-member advisory committee, of which *almost 25%* of the members were representatives of *big corporation* food industries (e.g., the dairy lobbyists and the oilseed producers for safflower, sunflower and corn – all with tons of those inflammation-causing omega-6 fatty-acids)

2. The 2007 food guide *promotes* the consumption of 2-3 glasses of milk daily, includes fruit juice (terribly high in sugar with no fiber) in the "fruits and vegetables" section, and downplays the trans-fats (artificially created saturated fats) that are such an assault on your liver.

3. Big food industries will inevitably *win big or lose big* depending on what a food guide recommends and they know that.

4. The beef producers and the milk industry *lobby groups* (especially the dairy farmers) are already up in arms because the 2019 guide downplays the importance of both meat consumption and drinking milk. Yep, that sure got their undivided attention.

I believe that any national food guide should be completely free of the commercially motivated and biased interests of all food industry-based lobbyists. Obviously, their profits depend upon us buying lots of their products so it sure seems like a major conflict of interest to me.

The new 2019 Canadian Food Guide de-emphasizes animal proteins and dairy products and it's very straightforward and easy to understand. It endorses a <u>mostly plant-based diet</u> and <u>warns against excessive sugar, salt and saturated fats</u>. The guide recommends that you:

—   *Abandon quantities and measurements*, and instead fill up your plate with ½ vegetables and fruits, ¼ with alternate protein choices such as tofu, legumes, chickpeas, nuts and seeds rather than meats and poultry, and ¼ of your plate with whole grains including quinoa and brown rice.

- *Drink more water.*
- *Eat whole foods.*
- *Buy only lower fat milk, yogurt and cheese products*
- *Avoid junk, processed, fried and sugary foods, including fruit juices*
- *Eat at home more.* Covid19 has helped us here.
- *Monitor the amount of alcohol consumed* (due to the inherent calories and other deleterious effects). Covid19 has hindered many of us here.

Do I agree with everything suggested? Most of it, but not all of it. I would never lump fruits with vegetables as they react differently in your body. I don't have an issue with full-fat dairy products in the correct quantities as many alternatives have a lot of added sugar. And I believe that nuts should fall into the dietary fat category, but then again, this version is not based solely on a macronutrient approach. It does however want Canadians to make healthier food choices. All of this is great because the guide puts the onus on the individual to figure out how to eat and to really think about food. It even devotes some of its time to cooking skills and recipes. Certainly a nice touch; people *should* eat more at home. Then they know what they're actually eating and they can avoid all the hidden and fake additives.

Already the beef industry is up in arms stating that the new Guide will cause more people to become obese. They cite that a palm-sized steak will provide 26 grams of protein and 104 calories, whereas getting 26 grams of protein from beans would mean that you'd have to eat an entire large can – which would also provide 4 times the calories at 420. I don't know what type of beans or what sized can they are referring to, but I know that a 540 ml can

311

of dark red kidney beans provides 15 grams of protein and 250 calories. Personally, I could never eat a whole can of beans, so I'd not get as much protein as that steak would provide. And get ready for the cereal makers and the energy sports drink lobbyists to start screaming too!

Remember what I said at the outset. You need clean nutrient-dense eating, weight training and a real commitment to be sustainably successful in the long-term…all combined with good doses of portion control, stress control and sufficient sleep.

But, while we're on this issue of eating too much, it's OK to have a cheat-day when you're trying to lose weight. I know that it may sound contradictory to other suggestions in this book, but we're still looking at LONG-TERM weight- and fat-loss. Sometimes you need a nice break, almost like a weekly reward to look forward to. Decide what day of the week is normally the most difficult for you to stick to perfect eating and call it your *cheat-day*. For me, it's normally Saturdays. I usually still have a good breakfast, but I relax for the other meals and just eat whatever I want in whatever quantities. The next day I'm back on the wagon.

If you can't wait until some specified cheat-day, you can also follow a nutrient-dense diet for 90% of the week and *still lose weight*. An example for me was when I ate 6 meals/snacks daily. This translated into 42 per week. If I adhered to 90% diet perfection then I could have about 4 "cheats" per week. That might be an alcoholic drink, a piece of pizza, some pasta, a "bad" work lunch with colleagues, or whatever else I would normally avoid.

# of Daily Meals	# of Weekly Meals	90% on Diet	10% "Cheats" Allowed
6	42	38	4
5	35	32	3
4	28	25	3
3	21	19	2

But, sorry, to be brutally honest, I must stress that if you're _never_ disciplined with your food choices or with your portion-control and you just go with the industry flow, your body doesn't really stand much of a chance to get healthier and you'll fail at reaching your weight- and body fat goals.

Be aware of your eating habits and any behaviors that can lead to over-eating.
You're the only one in control.

4.2 Is It True That My Blood Type Can Affect My Metabolism?

"All religions, arts and sciences are branches of the same tree." – A.E.
Your blood type was completely determined by your genetics. You inherited your genes from your parents, one set from your Mother and one set from your Father. You can do nothing about this. But blood type versus metabolic type? A genetically-generated blood type that can be connected to your metabolic ability to burn calories? Hmmm...an interesting twist to consider, though I haven't seen any real science-based proof of this idea.

Still I've been asked about this concept a number of times and, as strange as it may sound, there are studies regarding the metabolic types of different people. In 1996, Dr. Peter D'Adamo, a naturopathic doctor, published a book about this. He claims that people can live longer, be healthier and be able to attain and maintain a more ideal body weight if they eat according to their blood type. Can your blood type affect which diet is best for you and which diets might cause some health issues? I can't find any extensive supporting scientific evidence (based on large sample groups) that correlates blood genetic profiles in terms of weight management and food choices.

That said, there are a number of books out there that describe differences in blood type chemistries that can determine what foods are *optimally digested*. In all honesty I'm not a big proponent of these theories but of course you never know. And if you know me a bit better by now, you know that I sure don't want to suggest that I know everything about the body! Who does? And medical research is an ever-moving creature. In any case, what harm is there in food exploration? As I said earlier, knowledge is very powerful in helping inform your nutritional decisions so I'll note some of the suggestions made by blood-type believers; and, it never hurts to try a new way of eating as long as you get your three macronutrients daily.

OK, here we go…and remember that these sorts of blood type studies are usually talking about cancer and not weight-gain or -loss, but they do explain how many different factors could possibly contribute to the diet most biochemically optimal for you.

If you have a weaker digestion, which usually means you have lower levels of gut probiotics, you'll probably tend to be healthier on a lower animal protein diet, and one that is higher in both 100% whole grains and fresh vegetables as well as fermented foods like sauerkraut and yogurt. If you have a stronger digestion, which usually means you have lots of digestive get-the-job-done enzymes, you can eat more protein though you may have to avoid eating a lot of grains.

Blood types and metabolic types can be related to lectins, which are carbohydrate/sugar-binding plant-based proteins somewhat resistant to human digestion. Corn is one of the highest lectin foods and that's why the kernels can reach the toilet almost whole!

Blood type analysis has also led some to the conclusion that the lectins[274] that differentiate the four main[275] blood types (O, A, B, AB) interact differently with foods. These lectins occur on your blood cells, body cells, organs (such as your liver), bacteria and on bacterial microbes and apparently, according to these analyses, they can attach themselves according to the blood groups in many different ways.

Blood type O +/- (about 44% of the North American population) stems from the "hunter-gatherer" ancestral phase (low-fat low-glycemic) – ever see

---

[274] Lectins are a type of protein found in carbohydrates. They are able to bind to the membranes of cells; and they're carbohydrate-binding (especially sugar).

[275] There are eight basic types of blood, all based upon a combination of the "ABO" and "Rh-positive/Rh-negative" typing systems. Obviously, *ABO* deals with the O, A, B and AB blood types you're familiar with. The *Rh factor* is a "self-antigen" found on your red blood cell membranes. In general, *self*-antigens are ignored by your immune system, while antigens are foreign substances that are attacked by your immune system's antibodies. If your cells have self-antigens, then they're labelled Rh-positive. With no such self-antigens, they're Rh-negative.

refined processed foods when chasing wild game or picking up wild fresh food from the ground??? So the best diet for these people is higher protein (from hunting and fishing) with vegetables, nuts, and fruits (from gathering). O-types have stronger digestion, hence more stomach acidity problems and strong intestinal reactions when eating the wrong foods. Grains are the product of relatively recent farming[276] and they weren't available in the hunter-gatherer days. Apparently, O-types are poorly adapted to these foods. Some Os even complain of indigestion after eating a *small amount of wheat* (i.e., wheat gluten). They also produce more insulin to store nutrients; this ability would have helped the hunter-gatherer get through long periods when food simply wasn't easily available. Unfortunately, higher insulin levels can also cause an increased risk of diabetes. Wheat and corn contain lectins that *block insulin* receptors and bind with sugars. For O-type cells this can lead to insulin-resistance which in turn can prevent the Os from losing weight and getting their blood sugar levels under control.

Occurring much later in our evolutionary development, the blood type A (about 42%) became much more adapted to a grain-based and meat-free diet. With a weaker digestion, they find animal proteins harder to digest and can suffer from various lectin interactions. They often feel better after adhering to a vegetarian diet and actually do very poorly with excessive dairy and animal products. They do really well with fruits, vegetables, beans, legumes and 100% whole grains. I guess under this theory, type-As would find the 2019 Canadian food guide right up their eating alley!

Blood types B +/- and AB +/- are actually much much rarer types with their own unique dietary needs. Blood type B +/- (about 10%) is adapted to eating green vegetables, eggs, some meats and low-fat dairy. Blood type AB +/- (only about 4%), with low stomach acid, generally does better with tofu, seafood, dairy and green vegetables.

---

[276] Yes, I say 3,500 BC is relatively recent. It may be a long time ago to you, but to your biochemical body it isn't at all, given the difficulty for your body to permanently adapt to diet changes (e.g., farming of ancient wheat grain).

I haven't seen anything in too much detail regarding how the self-antigen Rh-factors of the four blood types (e.g., AB-negative[277]) might affect your optimal diet, but you can certainly research it if you feel so motivated.

Again, if you've never experienced abdominal pain of any sort after eating, then you can probably write this off as utter nonsense. If you have had abdominal pain, then jump into this approach wholeheartedly. You never know, maybe it'll work for you and you can devise a workable eating plan. For me (someone who prefers to try an approach out on myself before suggesting it to others), as an O-positive blood type, I find that I do occasionally get gut pain and I that *I do better* when I refrain from a lot of grain-based eating. Hmmm, fascinating indeed!

Gut pain is very unpleasant especially if you're on vacation, as happened to me in Florida. I wasted a full day lying in bed *in one position* to keep the sharp pains at bay. When I got home, I went to our local drugstore and took a very comprehensive blood test; one that allegedly isolated food intolerances that I had somehow developed. The test reported on about 400 different foods and additives, categorizing them as "acceptable" or as showing a "moderate sensitivity/intolerance" or a "severe sensitivity/intolerance." Actually, I have to give credit to my wonderful cousin Catherine Morrissey, who'd also taken the same test and recommended it to me at a family reunion.

This test suggested that a food intolerance, although similar, is actually quite a different biochemical *process* than that of a food allergy. The classic food allergy is an immediate reaction to some food, while an intolerance is an irritation of tissues (i.e., inflammation) caused by a food allergen. With an intolerance, there is a time-lag between the time of consumption and the resulting reaction. This is why food *intolerances* are not always easily recognized.

When I got my results back, I was really surprised; I had the weirdest list of "intolerance" foods. Some of the "severe" ones included almonds, cashews (walnuts were OK), coffee, peanuts, banana, lamb, pork, maple syrup, squid,

---

[277] In terms of blood types, O-positive is generally considered to be the most common North American blood type at 37% (and a "universal" donor"), while AB-negative is considered the most rare at only ½ %. If you have AB-negative blood, you will be majorly loved by the blood banks (as is our middle son).

beef liver (I love "greasy-spoon restaurant" liver!), molasses[278], eggs and veal. While my list of "moderate intolerance" ones included limes (lemons were acceptable!), oranges, grapefruit, white potato, chamomile tea, sugar beet, cinnamon flounder, blue cheese, vanilla, tuna, pinto beans (red kidney beans were OK), trout and wheat flour (corn flour was acceptable). Obviously, I'm not listing everything…they tested 400!

But I did follow the rules. I avoided the "severe" group of foods for about 12 months and the "moderate" group of foods for about 10-12 weeks. And when I reintroduced them into my diet, I did so very gradually. They also suggested not combining the "severe" or "moderate" foods during the reintroduction period. In any case, it *completely cleared up my gut pains* for about 4 years. If they ever threaten, I just get out my trusty list and stick to the rules. I'm an O+ blood type and so maybe there is something to this blood type analysis for diet and weight-control. Just sayin'…

4.3 Should I Exercise Differently Depending upon the "Body Type" That I Have?

Instead of Einstein, let me say something! Quit being down on yourself. Love yourself and commit to a body transformation that is just for you; one that will make you feel wonderful. You can "get into shape" and you can _stay that way for the rest of your life_ if you commit to changing your lifestyle in terms of diet, exercise, sleep and stress. Your biochemistry will thank you in multiple ways.

There are three main "body types": ectomorph, mesomorph and endomorph. I like to call them body "frameworks." That said, your body could actually be a mixture of these.

An ectomorph tends to be more naturally lean (although some are skinny), having a small frame, a light bone structure, small joints, a taller body with relatively long limbs, thin shoulders, narrow waist and often a flat chest. With the *highest metabolism*, ectomorphs usually have very little fat and not a lot of

---

[278] I told the nurse who returned the test results that I never eat molasses and only seldom have maple syrup, but she said these two additives are included in many foods and that I just didn't know how much I was eating! Hmmm…

extra muscle. An ectomorph can lose weight easily but will have *much more difficulty* gaining lean muscle mass. Think here of an endurance athlete like a marathoner. They are thyroid-dependent, and the thyroid regulates energy use. It's almost as though their bodies put all their energy into growing tall and not round!

A mesomorph appears athletic with a muscular and fairly well-built body. Mesomorphs have a *comparatively fast metabolism*, large bones and muscles, with slim hips and wider waists. They tend to be more naturally strong and have responsive muscle cells and very good endurance. A mesomorph has a rectangular-shaped trunk (due to those slim hips and wider waist); but they'll be able to alter their weight *much more easily* than the others. They are growth-hormone dependent and this stimulates muscle growth. Quit worrying about it or wishing it was you. Just accept that some people were born a bit lucky.

An endomorph has a shorter stocky more plump and thick build and a solid, but usually soft and round body. They have thick short limbs and strong large legs; although, they have *under*developed muscles especially in the upper half of their bodies. With a *relatively slow metabolism*, they tend to have high body fat especially in the lower half of their bodies. Although possible, weight-loss can be a lot *more difficult* for an endomorph. They are insulin-dependent leading to a lower carbohydrate tolerance making it more difficult to lose body fat.

Nevertheless, *whatever* body type or combination of types you might have, please don't be discouraged! Although you'll be somewhat bound to your body's "framework," you *can* still change the overall "shape" of your body. Even though the innate tendencies[279] of your particular body framework will never change, you *can* move your body along different aesthetic directions with proper nutrition and appropriate exercise. I like to think of this as "body-sculpting."

Sometimes you'll hear bodies described as "apple-shaped"[280] which translates into being top heavy (i.e., broad shoulders, large chest, a full bust, wider waist than shoulders, slim hips and legs, with a thick full upper back) or "pear-shaped" (i.e., smaller bust, flatter stomach, wider hips than shoulders

---

[279] For example, an endomorph will usually have a greater tendency toward storing body fat.

[280] Usually men and post-menopausal women due to hormonal changes and little physical exercise.

and backside, with a larger lower body). You *can* re-sculpt these shapes with hard, dedicated and appropriate workouts, nutritious eating plans, less stress and more sleep.

And what was I? I believe I was *apple-shaped with a mostly mesomorph framework*. When I lost the 40 pounds, I was no longer apple-shaped, but was more of a rectangle. Is it my favorite framework and shape? NO. I'd rather be more like a muscular feminine-shaped endomorph but you have to deal with reality, right? I also lost two bra sizes…which seems right as breasts are mostly fat and I was carrying around a lot of fat on my back. You can see it on the front cover in my "before" picture.

And so similarly if you're pear-shaped, regardless of your fat-loss success, you'll retain the voluptuousness of such a body (I'm always jealous of this shape – it looks a lot more feminine than my rectangular one – think of Marilyn Monroe here). Humph; I still remember my Dad saying to me, "women are supposed to have shapely hips!" Nonetheless, exercise and proper nutrition will give your hips and thighs a trim, toned and healthy look and isn't that what you really want? Also, if you have a pear-shaped body it's normally healthier than an apple-shaped body. That's because the body fat deposited on your hips (as opposed to your waist like me) is less likely to travel around your body and organs causing far less risk of cardiovascular disease and possible stroke.

Ok, so the next question is *what the heck can you do*?

You can change the look of your body with exercise and, remember, this takes a lot of time and serious knowledgeable effort. You can lose large amounts of fat and you can build beautifully lean toned muscle with exercise. But remember, changing your body shape also requires that you eat a proper daily macronutrient-dense diet.

How should an **ectomorph** exercise and eat?

- Do *minimum* cardio-machine exercises.
- Push/pull routines are good (e.g., push-ups, pull-ups, cable rows, lat pulldowns).
- Use free-weight routines (i.e., not fixed-floor machines).

- Focus on big compound exercises (exercises that use many joints, such as deadlifts, squats[281] and lunges).
- Use "progressive overload"[282] training (track yourself over time).
- Vary the repetition ranges for exercise sets (e.g., 5-8, 8-12, 12-15, 20+).
- Don't do full-body training (unless new to the gym floor); split body muscles up over different days (e.g., do legs and abs one day, do chest and back another day, arms another day – which would include shoulders).
- Rest times between sets can be 2-3 minutes.
- Abdominal/core exercises should be done only at the end of a workout routine and can be done daily if you want; other muscle groups should not be done on consecutive days in order to give your muscles a rest (e.g., legs, chest, back, arms, etc.)
- Eat all three macronutrients and ensure daily fiber; eat unprocessed, 100% whole grain carbohydrate and starchy vegetables (e.g., sweet potatoes) and eat lean protein with every meal.
- Eat many small meals throughout the day (e.g., every 3-4 hours).
- Eat at least 40% daily calories from carbohydrates.

How should a **mesomorph** exercise and eat?

- Should train with *heavy weights* (progressively build-up to these of course).
- Rest times can be 1 – 2 minutes (between sets).

---

[281] Ectomorphs with very long limbs have to be careful with squats simply because of the length of their femur/thigh bone. The longer that bone, the more difficult it is to keep the weight balanced over their feet (the base of support). When you have to lean way over to get down, then you can stress your lower back by losing the ability to keep a neutral back while in the lower squatting position. Split squats (with one foot ahead and the other foot behind, with the weight dropping in-between) might be a better choice.

[282] Progressive overload requires a gradual increase in volume (number of repetitions X number of sets X the weight used), intensity, frequency, tempo, rest periods or even by changing your training program. It's the *gradual* increase of stress placed upon your muscles and joints during an exercise.

- Try to go to muscle fatigue/failure (i.e., you simply can't do one more repetition in good form).
- No need to do heavy cardio-machine exercises but can if good body conditioning is present (maybe 10-15 minutes maximum) on a workout weight-lifting day and up to 60 minutes at a slow-to-medium steady rate on non-workout days.
- Abdominal/core exercises should be done only at the end of a workout routine and can be done daily if you want (do not add any weights).
- Eat a macronutrient-dense diet with all three: lean protein, complex carbohydrate and unsaturated fat (with daily fiber).
- Eat about 35% daily calories from carbohydrates.

How should an **endomorph** exercise and eat?

- Do at least eight sets or more per body part(s) being exercised.
- The majority of sets should have a 12-15 repetition range, 3-5 sets per exercise.
- *Rest times should be at as short as is possible* (maybe only ½ – 1 minute between sets).
- Compound or multi-joint exercises with a higher muscle recruitment[283] are best done first, with isolation exercises following (e.g., lunges and then leg extensions).
- Training 4-6 days a week is best (without overtraining[284]).
- Train with a mixture of steady-state and high-intensity cardio intervals[285] (3-4 times weekly and *only after* completing your weight-training workout routine).
- Abdominal/core exercises should be done only at the end of a workout routine and can be done daily if you want.

---

[283] The biggest muscle groups reside in your lower body: quads, glutes, calves and hamstrings. They constitute about 73% of your body's musculature.

[284] Over-training results from too little rest to allow your muscles to rejuvenate after increased training volume and/or intensity. This in turn results in a diminished performance. You need sufficient muscle recovery to build endurance and strength.

[285] Interval training (HIIT) involves doing 2-4 minutes slow, followed by 1-2 minutes fast, etc.

- Eat all three macronutrients; but still, super-carbohydrates should *always* be avoided (e.g., bread, rice, white potatoes, pasta, sugar and cereals).
- Be <u>extremely</u> careful with the glycemic index/load of foods.
- Eat no more than 30% daily calories from carbohydrates and ensure that they are "complex" slow-2-sugar/low GI carbs, not "super-carbs".

***Regardless of your body type or shape, you should strive
to build bigger muscles as they're metabolically active tissues.***

4.4 Should I Take Vitamin or Mineral Supplements?

"Everyone is a genius. But if you judge a fish by its ability to climb a tree, it will live its whole life believing that it is stupid." – A.E.

Personally, I have to be honest and admit that I take daily supplements and have done so for many years *even though I'm a good nutrient-dense eater* and get a sufficiently healthy and more natural mix of macro/micronutrients from my diet. It may sound like a contradiction leading you to think "well, if she's eating so well, why the heck does she need any vitamin or mineral supplements?" When I got into my 50's I developed osteopenia, a precursor to the brittle bones of osteoporosis. My doctor recommended daily calcium and magnesium pills to counter that and it has really helped. I've never developed osteoporosis, then again I started weight-training in my early 60's and that included lots of lower body exercises that stress those large leg muscles and build great bone strength too (e.g., squats, lunges, deadlifts and leg presses).

My supplement regimen includes the following and you'll see the main rationale for why I take each of these, though most of these supplements will also accomplish other benefits for my body:

- vitamin C – a very strong antioxidant which can reduce blood uric acid levels as well as lower my risk for common infections such a cold
- vitamin D3 – can lower body inflammation
- vitamin E – great at reducing the effects of UV skin damage
- calcium* citrate – to build and maintain strong non-brittle bones

- magnesium* citrate – for strong bone formation and as a calcium *associate* it's also needed by your body in order to help your ATP provide energy; it can also normalize insulin levels
- potassium* – to enhance electrolytic functions
- selenium* – another powerful antioxidant that can reduce triglyceride fats
- omega-3 oil – a great anti-inflammatory to counter the highly inflammatory omega-6 found in many foods; it normalizes insulin levels and counters pH acidity
- cod liver oil – another healthy omega-3 source
- milk thistle – great for my liver, a hardworking organ I want to help out as much as I can
- garlic – an antioxidant that can lower bad cholesterol
- glucosamine-chondroitin – to improve joint mobility and help slow any cartilage deterioration[286]

these are alkaline-forming minerals which will lower my body acidity

Clear all choices and dosages with your medical doctor.

We all know that calcium helps strengthen bones. But I also take calcium supplements because higher calcium intake with associated magnesium can result in a higher rate of both calorie expenditure and fat metabolism. On the flip side, low calcium levels can increase cortisol levels and add body fat. But how does this happen? When your body is calcium deficient, in addition to raiding your bones, it'll also resort to stealing calcium from your fat cells out of sheer necessity. This in turn leads directly to the production of cortisol in those fat cells, which of course ultimately leads to the accumulation of yet more abdominal fat. Another cycle you want to avoid.

---

[286] When our aging Shetland Sheepdog Schroddy, named after the Nobel prize-winning physicist Erwin Schrodinger, started limping, we began feeding him non-canine drug-store bought glucosamine pills (a lot cheaper than the canine ones!) and voila, he'd be spry again in about three days. When our daughter, a competitive swimmer with aching knees, ran out of her glucosamine pills I'd just swipe Schroddy's and low-and-behold, she'd be fine and he'd be limping again *in about 3 days*! Yup, they definitely work for better mobility.

Now of course you should always check with your doctor to see if you need to take any vitamin or mineral supplements and if you do, what they should be and at what dosage, especially if you're taking any prescription medications. That said, you could be taking something that's detrimental for you individually. When my doctor told me calcium and magnesium were good for my bones, I got a little carried away with the magnesium. I was taking double the daily magnesium recommended and ended up with a bad case of diarrhea, though I had no idea what was causing it.

I didn't know that magnesium salts needed to be broken down by my stomach for absorption further down in my intestines. My stomach acid was breaking the magnesium I was taking into an ionic form which in turn caused a change in the *pressure* of my gut. Due to osmosis, the process by which water passes through a cell membrane from a low (more water) to a high (less water) concentration solution on each side of that membrane, water will be drawn into your intestines to equalize the concentration on both sides. Well, guess what? The high amount of magnesium in me caused a huge difference in concentration and a large intake of water through the intestinal membrane causing really unpleasant diarrhea.

If you decide to buy magnesium supplements, be careful which ones you purchase. Magnesium *citrate* (derived from citrus acid) has an excellent 90% bioavailability which means it's very efficiently absorbed and used by your body. Magnesium *oxide* is far less bioavailable at only 4% and is used in cheap supplements. May as well not waste your money. Calcium is another example. Again go for easily absorbed calcium "citrate" and not the cheaper calcium "oxide" or "carbonate."

Here's another example of my ill-informed foolishness. A nurse who happened to be one of my clients said I should be taking B12 supplements, stating that older women usually don't have enough or don't absorb enough B12. Not checking with my doctor, I was keen and bought them, guzzling them according to the bottle's prescribed dosage – after all she WAS a nurse! It happened that shortly afterwards I was due for some blood work. Within a few days, I got a call from my doctor asking if I was taking B12 supplements. After proudly responding "yes!" she told me I was *seriously overdosed* on B12 and should stop taking those supplements! Indeed, it seems that contrary to other vitamin Bs, excess vitamin B12 is stored in your liver. Oh no, yet another reason to feel sorry for my busy 3 ½ – pound liver.

A couple of the other symptoms of chronically high B12 levels include constipation, higher blood pressure, poorer cardiovascular health and *weight-loss*. Now you might decide to take a bunch of B12s based upon that last symptom. In fact, it's my understanding that some obese people are encouraged to take very high doses of B12 specifically to boost both weight-loss and a higher metabolic rate – some even tolerate injections that are extremely high in B12. Does it work? I don't know, but I guess many obese people want to take the quickest and easiest path to overall weight-loss. Do I think it would be as healthy as eating a nutrient-dense diet and exercising at the gym with weights? NO BL**DY WAY.

Like I said at the book's outset, it took me almost two years to get the body I wanted. How many people do you know who have gone to lose-it-quick clinics, some of which follow the B12 route, take off a whack of weight only to pack it back on shortly afterwards? Most of them is my guess. Like I said, your body is a biochemical beast and you just can't change that in any way. Unhealthy short-cuts will always bring on hormonal reactions, biochemical adaptations and metabolic alterations not conducive to healthy and sustainable muscle-building and fat-burning.

Chromium acts as an insulin transport mechanism and enables your insulin to work more quickly and efficiently to maintain lean muscle mass, help your body burn fat, control your appetite and regulate your cravings. I've not read *anything* negative about it. I don't take this particular supplement, but you can get it from health food stores. But always check with your medical doctor as I have actually seen a wide array of recommended doses. Do keep in mind that if your doctor told you that you are pre-diabetic, excessive doses of chromium might *worsen* your insulin-sensitivity.

But don't forget about <u>good ol' Mother Nature</u>.
Eating a healthy nutrient-dense diet, drinking lots of pure water
and avoiding the salt, fat and sugar in processed foods
will go a long way in terms of vitamins and mineral consumption.

4.5 What Is the Microbiome and What Are Prebiotics and Probiotics?

"Great spirits have always encountered violent opposition from mediocre minds." – A.E.

We have to consider our microbiome when thinking about pre- and probiotics. Your microbiome is the collection of all of the microorganisms that inhabit your body. They're your digestive-tract microbes and these "bugs" are made up of more than a 1,000 different species of bacteria, plus some smaller populations of yeasts and viruses, fungi and other single-celled organisms. They all call your body "home sweet home." You may be saying "yuck," but they're heavily involved in both your health and potential disease. Indeed, your body's microbiome is host to billions and billions of these microbes. Your gut microbes are so plentiful that they can weigh as much as 5 pounds, or about 2 kilograms. That's like the weight of your brain! Wow better keep them happy.

What is a healthy microbiome and how might it become unhealthy? Well, guess what? Food doesn't just boss around all of your hormones, it's also the major factor contributing to the health, diversity and sickness of your microbiome. Remember that expression – "you are what you eat"? Yup, you just can't change the fact that food really does matter. In addition to your hormones, your gut bacteria are <u>directly related</u> to what you eat. How can you not believe that?

Your intestinal *probiotics* are living hence, just like you, they too need to eat and that's where *prebiotics* come in. Prebiotics are non-living, non-digestible forms of *fiber* that provide your living probiotic intestinal bacteria with the food they need to multiply and be healthy. You can get probiotics *and* prebiotics through foods, but if you're eating a lot of processed, refined, fried, high-sugar and low-fiber foods, you won't get enough to help the bacteria in your digestive system.

If you're relying heavily or solely upon yogurt to provide probiotics, it may be that you're *not* getting enough to prevent the growth of disease-causing bacteria or to regulate your bowel movements. Not all yogurts are made with the bacteria recognized by Health Canada as probiotic. To be called a *probiotic* food, yogurt must contain *at least one billion* live colony-forming units (e.g., active probiotic cultures) of a recognized probiotic species *per serving*. Read food labels very carefully and always get a yogurt which contains "active bacterial cultures."

If you buy yogurt in order to get your probiotics, don't get one with sugar.
Buy plain yogurt and then, if you want it sweetened,
add some fresh fruit or some honey.
And while you're at it, throw in some ground/powdered flax seed.

Even so, you'd have to eat a heck of a lot of yogurt to get enough (probably over 15 *or more* servings!) You could make your own yogurt. It's a fairly easy process and you can buy an electric yogurt maker that'll make it even easier. Also, you could add kefir, a fermented milk drink made from kefir grains, to your regular diet. It's usually sold as a probiotic beverage and it has many rich and diverse types of bacteria and yeasts. Just another aside; all excited to assist my digestive tract, I bought some kefir. Ugh! I found it disgusting and threw it out but, to each their own as they say.

And fermentation can actually create probiotic-rich foods. Read labels very carefully because modern day industrialized food processing could easily have killed the probiotics you may think are there.

<u>Examples of non-dairy probiotic-rich foods include the following:</u>

- Sauerkraut (fermented cabbage) – Buy brands that say "<u>uncooked</u>."
- Miso (fermented Japanese seasoning made from beans and grains) – <u>Don't cook with it</u> as heat will destroy the probiotics; add it <u>after</u> you have cooked the food.
- Pickles (fermented cucumbers) – <u>Don't get "pasteurized"</u> pickles as that process kills probiotics.
- Eggplant (fermented) – There are <u>online recipes</u> on how to ferment eggplants.

<u>Prebiotic rich foods</u> include oats, barley, legumes, beans, artichokes, asparagus, leeks, *ground* flax seeds, plantain, banana, garlic, soybeans and onions. All of these contain "inulins" (also found in psyllium), which are naturally occurring polysaccharides (a type of non-digestible dietary fiber).

Now of course, we have to talk about the effect of *antibiotics* on your probiotic and prebiotic microbiome. Let's start with the word itself. The word means "against" (anti) "life" (biotic) and so it can't be the best for your biotics, can it??? Antibiotics work by affecting things that bacterial cells have but human cells don't. An example would be cell walls. Bacterial cells have *walls*, human cells don't. They have *membranes* and these thin sheets of boundary tissue are made up of lipids (i.e., fats[287]) and proteins. The antibiotic penicillin, for example, works by keeping a bacterium from building a cell wall.

The problem with antibiotics lies in what else is killed along the way. If you're on antibiotics for a long time, guess what else gets killed along the way? Yup, they're "anti" killers to your probiotics and prebiotics because these don't have any fortifying walls, they have *permeable* membranes. Antibiotics can upset your sensitive gut biotics very quickly and these support your immunity along with the proper digestion of food. Please ensure that you eat a diet high in pro- and prebiotics if you're on an antibiotic regimen and for a while afterwards too. And don't get me going on the fact that some people always bug[288] their doctors, whenever they're sick, for antibiotics even when they don't have a bacterial infection, rather they have a viral infection. Viruses are not affected in the least by any antibiotic! You won't be treating the virus, but you'll be killing your gut biotics for no good reason at all. Not a very good path to take.

Of course, antibiotics are sometimes necessary for non-common infections such as "strep throat" (a serious streptococcus bacterial infection causing throat pain, painful swallowing, and swollen tonsils) and your doctor will probably prescribe a lengthy dose of antibiotics. The main rationale supporting this is that the antibiotic will kill the bacteria or at least prevent them from multiplying. And strep throat, if left untreated, can lead to very serious illnesses such as kidney inflammation, rheumatic fever and heart damage.

Before we move on to the next chapter, I would like to mention something normally ignored, specifically the act of passing gas. Of course, it goes without saying that "tooting" in public is a no-no, but passing gas is actually a sign of good health and it's quite normal. Intestinal gas indicates that you have healthy gut bacteria. Some people are methane producers, while others are hydrogen

---

[287] Didn't I say that eating unsaturated fats is good for you and that when portion-controlled they don't make you fat!!!

[288] Do pardon the pun!

sulfide producers (that's the stinky rotten-egg gas). You guessed right; it's completely related to what you eat. If you eat a lot of foods with sulfur then hydrogen sulfide gas results from your body breaking them down via bacterial fermentation.

Examples of such foods include the cruciferous vegetables (cabbage, broccoli, cauliflower, kale, brussels sprouts, turnip and radishes) as well as beans/legumes. Just remember that when you eat food, you do have to digest it as well and gas forms as your bacteria ferment the foods passing through your colon.

Unfortunately, I have to add that gas can be symptomatic of an unhealthy digestive system as well. This can result in bloating, constipation, diarrhea and heartburn. Such unhealthy gas can be caused by many things including high-sugar diets, sleep disturbances, and various and sundry food intolerances.

Often you hear about people who helped control their weight
by drinking apple cider vinegar.
Well, it's made by fermenting apple juice and it does lower blood cholesterol
and blood sugar, as well as help with glucose-resistance issues.
And so, as with other fermented probiotic-friendly food products,
it'll support weight-loss programs.

4.6 What Are the Causes of Inflammation and Why Should I Avoid It?

"I speak to everyone the same way, whether he is the garbage man or the president of the university." – A.E.

Inflammation itself isn't normally bad. It's a natural body reaction. It's the process by which your body's white blood cells, and substances that they produce, protect you from infection from foreign organisms such as undesirable bacteria and those unwelcome viruses. That's all good!

Inflammation is a part of your body's very complex biological protection mechanism. It's the natural healing response of your body's tissues to any harmful stimulus such as an infection, an injury or a toxin. It involves your immune cells (antibodies) and your blood vessels. Chemicals from your white blood cells are released into your bloodstream and into your affected tissues to

329

protect them from further injury (think of a heel blister from the rubbing of a shoe on your skin's surface). With _acute_ inflammation caused by some injury, there's an increase in blood flow to the injured area and this results in redness, warmth, pain and swelling. Think of a broken wrist.

The problem with inflammation only occurs when your body's defense system triggers an inflammatory response when there _aren't any foreign invaders_ to fight off. You may wonder why your body would ever do this, but it can and there's an explanation. You must know by now that there's always an explanation in the form of a biochemical adaptation for anything and everything your body does. For our weight-loss purposes, we'll talk about toxic waste by-products as examples of invaders that will cause body inflammation.

With _chronic_ inflammation, your body's reaction is a bit subtler. Chronic inflammation can result from poor unhealthy eating habits, not exercising enough and eating too many high-calorie low-nutrient foods. When you grow fat cells you can expect weight gain, and you'll always make more fat cells when your body has to get rid of a bunch of toxic waste by-products caused by refined carbohydrates and high acid-forming foods (e.g., junk-foods, processed foods and sweets). When you gain weight, your body fat cells are expanded to their capacity while they're still trying to store the extra unnecessary calories and to keep the toxic waste away from healthy cells. Whenever this happens your body, always your savior, will just create more fat cells to get more storage capacity. It'll also develop an unnatural inflammation over time. When left untreated, chronic inflammation can result in autoimmune illnesses[289]. Such illnesses can end up affecting your lungs (asthma), joints (rheumatoid arthritis), skin (psoriasis), organs (e.g., the pancreas for diabetics), intestines (irritable bowel disease) or in some cases, the whole body (lupus and multiple sclerosis). Some doctors even add high blood pressure and Parkinson's disease to the list. There's a lot of research out there on autoimmune diseases, it's really a hugely intriguing and _ongoing_ field of study.

The typical North American diet is filled with high-fat, high-sugar, highly processed refined and fried foods. These foods are all very directly linked to fat cell creation, high body acidity and to chronic inflammation. The medical

---

[289] Autoimmune diseases or disorders occur when your healthy tissue is being attacked by your body because the healthy tissue just isn't recognized as being healthy by your immune system.

world is always keen on studying inflammatory autoimmune diseases with the hope of eradicating some of them.

Some of the foods which will cause inflammation include[290]:

- Sugar and HFCS (high fructose corn syrup)
- Artificial trans-fats
- Some vegetable and seed oils (hydrogenated and partially hydrogenated)
- Refined carbohydrates such as bread, pasta and pastries
- Excessive alcohol (oh no!)
- Processed meats (full of sodium nitrates which accelerate cellular aging)
- French fries and other fried foods
- Carbonated soda pop drinks
- Margarine, shortening and lard

Some of the foods considered to be anti-inflammatory include:

- Tomatoes
- Extra virgin olive oil (high in omega-9 fatty-acids)
- Green leafy vegetables (especially spinach)
- Almonds and walnuts
- Fatty fish such as salmon, tuna and sardines[291]
- Fruits such as strawberries, blueberries, cherries, pineapples and oranges

---

[290] In general, many inflammatory foods contain omega-6 fatty-acids (leading to high acidity) as well as high amounts of the plant-based lectin protein, both of which inhibit the loss of body-fat.

[291] So, back to the cat and me, from my recollected story earlier, we were eating good omega-3 fats that were *also* anti-inflammatory. I never got sick in Nigeria, although I did get malaria once, and I flew off my motorcycle once (but I had a trusty first-aid kit with me). But unfortunately, I gained a ton of weight, which I suspect was due to eating too much pounded yam, eating too much bread and drinking too much warm beer!!! Gimme a break, it was really hot over there near the equator!

- Broccoli
- Fermented foods
- Onions
- Garlic and ginger

Eating a diet filled with high-fat, high-sugar,
highly processed refined and fried foods, fast foods,
and carbohydrates with lots of omega-6 fatty-acids
is directly linked to an acidic body, inflammation and obesity.

4.7 What Is Cholesterol and Why Do I Have to Worry About It?

"Never memorize something you can look up." – A.E.

Cholesterol is an organic molecule that's a type of fatty lipid. Your body cells manufacture cholesterol because it's an *essential* component of all cell membranes. It maintains the structural integrity of your cell membranes and even allows cells to change shape if need be (e.g., blood cells have to change their shape to improve their motion as they move through narrower blood vessels). And remember, membranes are not simple impermeable "walls." They're continually interacting with their environments, both inside and outside your cells in a determined effort to maintain biochemical balance. Via osmosis, cell membranes are able to allow nutrients, enzymes and fluids to pass between the inside of your cells and their outside environment.

Cholesterol fat is a waxy solid that comes in two forms, one is in your blood, while the other is found in food. Your body can make its own required cholesterol and so you really don't need to eat any from food. In fact, the cholesterol you eat <u>doesn't even become</u> the cholesterol in your bloodstream. Why then, should you *limit* the amount of saturated animal fat you eat. It's because your liver manufactures *extra* blood cholesterol from any saturated fat you eat. It's a simple equation: the more saturated fat you eat, the more extra blood cholesterol you'll create.

<u>Excess</u> waxy solid cholesterol will collect on your inner artery walls. This waxy accumulation is called plaque and you probably already know that it narrows the width of your arteries and can cause heart attacks because your blood flow has been slowed down. And remember that blood carries oxygen,

332

hormones and nutrients throughout your body. Do you really want to slow it down? I think not. Slow blood flow sure isn't going to help you stay oxidative and so it'll quickly compromise your fat-burning ability regardless of what kind of exercising you do.

You've probably heard of LDL (low density lipoprotein) and HDL (high density lipoprotein) cholesterol. But what are these designations? LDL contains more cholesterol than HDL and is known as the "bad" cholesterol, while HDL contains less cholesterol and is known as the "good" cholesterol. When your doctor does blood work on you, s/he wants to see a higher "good" HDL count in your blood compared to the "bad" LDL. HDL's job is to remove cholesterol from your artery's cell membranes and transport it back to your liver for reprocessing or for removal as waste. Yup, back to your busy liver. If you eat a lot of saturated fat, your liver will be working extra hard to get rid of all that additional cholesterol. With higher HDL to LDL ratios, your overall HDL no longer has too much LDL to effectively deal with.

Now, think back to your high school chemistry classes yet again; fat and water simply don't mix together, right? Blood and bodily fluids are mostly water. So how *does* your body move lipids (i.e., fat lipids and cholesterol wax) around your body when it has to use your blood? Well, your body uses *both* the LDLs and HDLs as transport proteins and the higher the density of your lipoproteins, the healthier it is for you. Transport proteins sort of make a tunnel across your cell membranes and this helps bring various molecules into your cells. As stated above, HDLs are better than LDLs mainly because they can transport more lipids/fats and leave fewer stuck to your artery walls. But you still need both types of cholesterol lipoproteins.

4.8 What's the Difference Between Subcutaneous Fat and Visceral Fat?

"A clever person solves a problem. A wise person avoids it." – A.E.

There are the two main types of fat in your body: subcutaneous fat and visceral fat. Subcutaneous fat is just under your skin and medical doctors say it's relatively harmless. Visceral fat is wrapped around your abdomen, your liver, your intestines and other organs and it's believed by most doctors to be a major health risk. It's also not aesthetically pleasing to have a big belly of fat supported by a couple of skinny legs![292]

If you're carrying around excess fat, your genetics have probably determined whether it's mostly subcutaneous or visceral fat. But don't be discouraged, you *can lose both* types of fat if you eat nutrient-dense foods, exercise with weights, commit to better sleeping patterns and better control your reaction to stress triggers. Also, it'll be a nice surprise for you to know that the most dangerous fat, the visceral kind, is actually the easiest to lose! You might wonder why, but it's a proximity issue coupled with the fact that visceral fat is much more metabolically active than is subcutaneous fat. Unless you've developed a bad case of insulin-resistance (making your metabolism less efficient and more catabolic), your visceral fat is closer to your liver and so it's usually easier to burn.

High amounts of sugar have been associated with increased visceral belly fat and linked to medical issues such as metabolic syndrome. You will recall that metabolic syndrome is actually a *cluster of conditions* such as increased blood pressure, high blood sugar, excess abdominal fat, and abnormal cholesterol or triglycerides. In turn, these conditions can lead to heart disease, stroke and Type-2 diabetes. This is what my doctor told me I had at the age of 60. It scared me and that's a major reason why I joined a gym, hired a personal trainer and chose to eat differently; I'm fine now. I found my waist at the age of 62 and I got to dump a whack of prescriptions too.

The accumulation of both kinds of body fat is also related to the way your body deals with fructose and by now you know that fructose is hidden in many foods and drinks. Fructose, bypassing your intestines when eaten as HFCS, is made into fatty-acids and triglycerides by your liver and these ultimately enter your bloodstream. These triglycerides can also bunch together in your body fat tissues. The fattening of your liver can also lead to insulin-resistance leaving even *more* sugar in your bloodstream. When your insulin levels are very high, *only the glucose in your bloodstream* is used for energy while the rest of the fat remains in your body fat cells. And you thought fat made fat. A bit surprising, eh?

Some people can appear thin but actually can be quite fat. This is because they can have a lot of visceral fat *around* their organs and that can be more

---

[292] Lots of guys at the gym, while concentrating heavily on their upper body, often ignore their legs. Just look at them and you'll see what I call "chicken-legs."

difficult to see. In effect, they are thin on the outside and fat on the inside. We call these people "skinny-fat" people. Compared to how they appear, they'll have a surprisingly high body fat percentage measurement and that's never very healthy.

4.9 What About the Color of Foods?

"Everything is energy and that's all there is to it. Match the frequency of the reality you want and you cannot help but get that reality. It can be no other way. This is not philosophy. This is physics." – A.E.

Mother nature has produced whole natural foods with different colors based upon the types of nutritious properties in them. You can ensure that you get a healthy broad range of essential nutrients if you eat a variety of differently colored foods daily. Eating a daily "rainbow" of foods will significantly broaden the mix of nutrients you'll be eating. Food colors are an indication of different pigments and these include carotenoids (orange and yellow), flavonoids (blue, red and cream) and chlorophyll (green).

RED foods indicate the presence of lycopene and anthocyanins, both of which help maintain a healthy heart, good memory and keep your urinary tract healthy. Some examples include strawberries, cherries, cranberries, raspberries, red grapefruit, watermelon, red apples, red peppers, pomegranates, beets, radishes, red cabbage, rhubarb and tomatoes.

YELLOW and ORANGE foods indicate the presence of carotenoids, which help keep your immune system strong, maintain sharp vision, and lower your risk of heart disease. Some examples include apricots, cantaloupe, grapefruit, mango, papaya, peaches, oranges, pineapples, lemons, tangerines, yellow peppers, pumpkin, butternut squash, acorn squash, yellow summer squash, carrots and sweet potatoes.

GREEN foods contain lutein and indoles (a type of phytochemical believed by some to fight cancer) and key minerals; all of which keep your vision sharp and maintain strong bones and teeth. Some examples include green apples, deep green vegetables, honeydew melon, green grapes, kiwi, limes, pears, avocado, asparagus, arugula, artichokes, broccoli, kale, green peppers, green beans, lettuce, cucumbers, spinach, zucchini and green cabbage.

BLUE and PURPLE foods have anthocyanins and phenolics, which may have anti-aging benefits. Some examples include blackberries, blueberries, plums, grapes, raisins, eggplant, purple potatoes and purple asparagus.

Some CREAM and BROWN foods have antimicrobial properties which can stop the growth of antibacterial microorganisms, and some contain allicin which may prevent some diseases such as heart disease as well as help lower bad cholesterol levels.[293] Some examples include bananas, dates, cauliflower, garlic, onion, mushrooms, ginger, parsnips, shallots and turnips. Notice that I didn't list "white" bread here. That's because the food industry has made that bread white, not mother nature. The darker and heavier a bread, the slower it'll make blood glucose!

4.10 How Should I Read Food Labels and Ingredient Listings?

"The measure of intelligence is the ability to change." – A.E.

If you want to know what you're eating, you MUST learn how to read food labels and ingredient listings [294]. Having said that you'll soon discover that it isn't an easy task to educate and empower yourself on the food industry's many misleading statements. The industry uses chemically processed additives and processed ingredients to make food more appealing in terms of visual effect, flavor and, of course, convenience. Obviously, some ingredients, such as salt and sugar, create problems when used excessively. And you do want to avoid empty/non-nutritive calories and harmful chemicals.

Many grocery store products boast that they're "free" of something. Some examples are: "fat-free," "wheat-free," "sugar-free" and "dairy-free." But the *more important question* might be "what's actually in it???" rather than what *isn't* in it. You may buy something that's labelled a non-fat sugar-free dessert topping because you want something healthier than real whipped cream, but that "topping" may just be a laboratory blend of synthesized chemicals that are actually far *worse* for you than eating the real whipped cream even with its saturated fat.

---

[293] www.ncbi.nlm.nin.gov

[294] To put this another way, you simply can't automatically believe the food industry's packaging.

Sugars provide one of the best examples of the difficulty in reading and understanding food labels. If you've ever listened to some of the elite chefs, like Jamie Oliver, you'll hear about "honest" and "dishonest" sugars. When we know we're eating sugars, we'll label them "honest" like those in a chocolate bar. But hidden or "dishonest" sugars can be disguised, and they can be in foods in which you might *never expect* to find sugar (e.g., canned soups, barbecue sauces, ketchup, flavored <u>non-fat</u> yogurts, lasagna, milk, gluten-free and low-fat foods).

Many fat-free food concoctions have so much added sugar that they end up having the same number of calories as the full-fat choice! And fat is a heck of a lot better for your body than is sugar. Fat has the ability to slow the arrival of bloodstream glucose sugar (less insulin hormone), to lower bad LDL cholesterol levels, to give you some added energy (remember that 9 calories/gram) and to support cell growth among many other capabilities. Fat-free foods can also contain artificial ingredients which can interfere with your body's biochemistry including your calorie-burning metabolic rate. Who'd have guessed that?

Compare the levels of sugar in some fat-free yogurts with those in a full-fat yogurt. Bet you'll be surprised! If you're monitoring the TOTAL amount of daily sugars you eat, then you must understand from where they come and whether they're dangerous or not. For example, the "lactose" sugar in milk doesn't promote metabolic disorders such as diabetes, but it *still is a sugar*. Sugar molecules, such as glucose, fructose and sucrose (a combination of glucose and fructose molecules), are played with by the food industry. It knows you want to avoid sugar, and so it manipulates food labels to mislead you as best it can within federal guidelines and legal regulations. It knows sugar makes food taste good, especially if one of the current food villains is salt or fat, and that sugar will entice you to eat more – great yet again for the industry, you buy and eat more, and they increase their profits via your growing waistline.

When you read labels, also be careful with the "serving size." Measure it out. You may think a glass of juice is 250 ml/8 oz (1 cup) as suggested on their label; but you may normally be drinking twice that by filling one of your own glasses with fruit juice simply because your glass holds a lot more than 1 cup.

Ok, now for the infamous labelling issue. Don't be fooled by the "no added sugars" label; many food items already have so much inherent sugar that the food industry simply doesn't need to add any more sweetness. If a small glass of orange juice is the equivalent of 5 spoons of sugar, then you sure don't have to *add* any, right? The food industry can just say "no added sugar" and you believe that that is great! That said, if you insist on drinking fruit juice, at least get the kind that has some pulpy fiber in it! Still it's just sugar to your body, but at least with a bit of fiber it moves to blood sugar *a tiny bit* more slowly, though not by much. *I never drink my calories – except for booze once in a while.*

Now let's talk about those "added" sugars. It's easier to read the total amount of sugar in a processed food because the law now forces the food industry to list the number of grams of sugar on the label. Unfortunately, you don't necessarily know the *type* of sugar added. Not all sugar is biochemically harmful with natural milk lactose as a prime example. Similarly, the natural sugars in fresh *whole fruit* are not harmful due to the simultaneously consumed fiber. This doesn't mean you shouldn't count these sugars within daily sugar counts during weight-loss regimes but rather, that these aren't the most harmful sugars to your body.[295]

You do want to monitor the amount of glucose, fructose and sucrose daily. If you look at "Christie Wheat Thins" with "37% less fat" then their "original" wheat thin crackers, you'll see 2 grams of sugar (for 13 crackers) in the "nutrition facts" list. But, in the "ingredients" listing you'll read "sugar" and "glucose-fructose" with NO indication of how much of each. So, you don't know how much of the feared HFCS fructose you're actually ingesting. Just an aside, different crackers are different sizes too. So, when you see sugar or calories *per cracker*, it's almost impossible to compare the labels on different boxes of crackers. You won't know the *actual size* of the crackers in the box and obviously the size will impact the number of crackers (and resultant calories) you might decide to consume.

The food industry plays with salt, fat and sugar to make processed foods taste good.
If a food is "free" of one of these three you can be certain that it'll be high in one or both of the other two.

---

[295] A diabetic still must count the milk's lactose as ingested sugar when tallying how much insulin to inject.

You really need to appreciate and understand that it just doesn't matter to your body whether sugar is white, brown, raw, molasses or fruit juice concentrate, it all has *a bad effect* on your health. Because the food industry knows you want to avoid eating too much sugar, it'll use many many different names for it.

<u>Some</u> of the many different words in ingredients listings that *always* translate into "added" sugar include the following 52, yes, I said fifty-two!!! And I'll wager that you didn't even know some of them were sugar. Indeed, a bunch of them even sound "healthy."

- agave nectar*[296] (made from the bulb of the agave plant; 90% fructose)
- beet sugar (a sucrose)
- blackstrap molasses
- brown sugar (basically this is sucrose coated with molasses made simply by cutting short the refining process so that the sugar retains some of the molasses; or, made fraudulently by adding brown caramel coloring to white sugar)
- cane sugar (less refined than beet sugar, and typically used as table sugar)
- cane syrup
- caster sugar
- coconut sugar (made from the flower buds of coconut palms; 70-79% sucrose)
- concentrated fruit juice
- corn maltodextrin
- corn-starch (glucose derived from corn)
- corn syrup**[297] (glucose and water)
- crystalline dextrose**
- crystalline fructose

---

[296] Those marked with an * are sometimes put into "sugar-free" foods because they're supposedly healthier sugar alternatives. <u>Don't be fooled,</u> they're *still some form of sugar*! And they still have bad affects on your body! Diabetics should beware (especially of HFCS).

[297] Have you ever wondered why the heck there are so many corn fields? They seem to be everywhere. More than ½ the cornstarch milled in North America is converted into corn sugar or syrups by use of hydrolysis with heat and acids or enzymes. Some of the usual suspects are noted ** in the list.

- dextrose** (sucrose is sometimes called dextrose)
- evaporated cane syrup/juice
- fancy molasses (made from sugar cane juice)
- fig juice concentrate (a nutritionally void liquid)
- fructose (usually HFCS and not necessarily fruit derived as you might think)**
- fruit juice (most of the fiber has been removed)
- fruit juice concentrate
- fruit puree
- fruit sugar (basically fructose)
- glucose**
- glucose solids**
- glucose syrup**
- glucose-fructose syrup**
- grape sugar
- guar gum
- high fructose corn syrup (made from turning the glucose molecules in corn into fructose; resulting with between 42-90% fructose concentration using enzyme applications; the abundant use of HFCS has allowed the corn industry to become the number one sweetener supplier; in the early 1980s, gene-splicing technology was applied to HFCS processing and suddenly corn syrup could actually produce 100% fructose!**)
- honey*
- hydrolyzed starch (e.g., corn, soy, wheat)
- invert sugar (can be 100% fructose)**
- inverted sugar (can be 100% fructose)**
- isoglucose (just another trick as another name of HFCS, and "ose" *always* denotes sugar)
- liquid corn sugar**
- lump sugar**
- maltodextrin
- maltose (a glucose)
- malt sugar
- maple sugar (66% sucrose)
- maple syrup* (from the sap of the maple tree)
- molasses

- organic palm sugar
- palm sugar (is not coconut sugar; it comes from the sap of the date palm)
- raw organic cane sugar
- rice malt syrup (made from brown rice starch and has glucose and maltose, but no fructose; it has a very high glycemic index)
- sucrose (made from either sugar cane or sugar beet; 50% glucose and 50% fructose; this is the most dramatic in terms of insulin release because the glucose/fructose bond is very easily broken, releasing a quick surge of bloodstream sugar)
- sugar (a glucose and fructose combination)
- syrup
- turbinado sugar
- xanthan gum

Now, why don't you pull some foods out of your cupboards and check the labels to see if any bad or "dishonest" sugars have been added. How about looking at mayonnaise, ketchup, dried soups, canned soups, canned vegetables, canned meats, BBQ sauce, basil pesto sauce, tomato sauce, chicken or beef broth, taco seasoning mix, crackers, "stove-top" stuffing mix, relishes, Worcestershire sauce, some peanut butters, and almost every breakfast food or health bar, etc. I bet you had absolutely no idea that these items contained "added" sugars. Why do you think kids put so much ketchup on their foods! They're not looking for the taste of healthy tomatoes. They love the big sugar rush! And now you see that you may have been getting fatter and *it wasn't entirely your fault*!

There are many ways to read labels depending upon your goals. You can compare the number of calories, salt content, protein content, fiber content, sugar content, fat content, trans-fat content, etc. etc.

Look at the sugar content listed on a food label and recall that 4 grams of sugar is the equivalent of 1 teaspoon of sugar or about 16 calories. That can add up quickly over the day. Yes, sugar is virtually 100% pure *but in calories only* with absolutely nothing else to offer your body in terms of healthy nutrients. If you're trying to lose weight and you cut out any other food, you are cutting nutrients as well as calories. Not true for sugar. If you stop eating sugar, you're *only* cutting calories and the fewer nutritionally empty calories you eat the better your overall weight-loss will be.

When I looked at an artificial version of real whipped cream, I was horrified at the ingredients and even though I knew it was a fully processed food, it proved to be an industrially processed product example at its best, one that I actually found to be a bit scary!

Get ready, here are the listed "ingredients": "water, glucose-fructose, 22% hydrogenated coconut and palm kernel oil, sodium caseinate (from milk), polysorbate 60, natural and artificial flavor, sorbitan monostearate, xanthan gum, guar gum, color."

Now let's try to figure out this product:

1   Ok "water" is good and it's listed *first*, wow maybe this is a good product. Remember that the higher on the ingredient list, the higher the % of that item in the food product.

2   Now that I know the different names for added sugars, I know that "glucose-fructose" (the second ingredient listed) is probably HFCS, and that "xanthan gum" and "guar gum" are both sugars so now I'm realizing that maybe this product has far too much sugar in it.

3   What happens when ingredients are "hydrogenated"? Let's just summarize for clarity; oils that are hydrogenated are treated by forcing hydrogen into the oil at high temperatures via a chemical reaction (making that food unnatural). Oils that are fully hydrogenated are turned into solid fat (and remember an oil is not normally solid at any temperature and that's why it's better at travelling through the body without clogging up your arteries). When oils are fully hydrogenated, their more natural omega-based fatty-acids have been transformed into saturated-fats. Oils only *partially hydrogenated* are even *worse* because they contain trans-fatty acids[298] (or the dreaded trans-fats). Oils in processed foods are generally hydrogenated, just like this product's "hydrogenated coconut and palm kernel oil." Ok, so that's a really bad ingredient (and it's *third* on the ingredients list). Oh dear, we're going downhill fast!

4   Casein and whey are the two types of protein naturally found in milk. "Sodium caseinate" contains extracted casein protein and is usually used as an emulsifier additive (a food stabilizer to keep parts of the

---

[298] Trans-fatty-acids will always disrupt the functioning of your cells resulting in more body-fat.

food from separating). I guess processed foods need such an item simply because they're processed and not natural. Hmmm, maybe I shouldn't eat much of that.

5   And what the heck is "polysorbate 60"? It's yet another emulsifying stabilizer created by adding a steric acid molecule (a solid saturated fatty-acid) to sorbitol (a synthetic sweet-tasting crystalline compound). In reality it's a waxy substance that can make foods not taste so greasy. Well, in my mind, I'm thinking maybe the food industry used this so that we don't notice how bad the mouth feel might be for this highly manufactured product! I'm not going to call it "food" as that should be associated with nutrition.

6   Ok, let's move on to the ubiquitous "natural and artificial flavor." Good grief, what the heck is that? It sounds OK, but we simply don't know what it is. In food processing, both natural and artificial flavors contain chemicals! The only distinction between the two is the source of those chemicals. "Natural" ones come from anything that can be eaten (e.g., vegetables, tree bark, fruits, meats, eggs, etc.) even if heavily processed in a laboratory, while artificial (non-natural or "fake") flavors come from anything inedible (e.g., petroleum) that can be processed to create flavor chemicals. That said, "natural" flavoring may sound better, but it too can be processed in a laboratory and be mixed with other chemicals to make it *imitate* real flavors. Sometimes the term "natural" is only referring to the process used to create the "flavoring" (e.g., "heat" is a completely "natural" process). Your best bet is not to buy any processed flavored foods.

7   Ever wanted to eat synthetic wax? Ok "sorbitan monostearate" is your answer; yet another emulsifier. Good Lord, why does this stuff need so many emulsifiers?

8   Food "color" is a dye or pigment additive. But why do they have to make this product white. What color was it before having to be dyed?

Well at least we had some water, though how much we don't know. And don't forget, this product also prides itself on having no cholesterol and being able to live in the refrigerator for two weeks! Why don't you just whip up some real heavy cream into whipped cream? It's a lot healthier even with its saturated fat and cholesterol. You'll be avoiding all those emulsifiers, sugars and synthetic trans-fats and it tastes a heck of a lot better too.

Then I thought, why not look at something that should be better per normal common sense. I chose the "fig balsamic" olive oil dressing and marinade I happen to have in my cupboard.

OK, for this product the ingredients list stated the following: "water, vinegar, vegetable oils (extra virgin olive oil, canola oil and soybean oil), sugar, fig juice concentrate, balsamic vinegar, honey, salt, garlic, spices, xanthan gum (thickener), potassium sorbate (maintains quality,) poppy seeds, calcium disodium edta (maintains flavor), acetylated monoglycerides (prevents oil separation)."

Let's have a go at this product; it should be a lot better, right?

1 "Water." Super great and it's the first thing listed.

2 "Vinegar." OK.

3 "Vegetable oils." Extra virgin olive, canola and soybean oils are all good for you as healthy fats. But are these those really bad *partially hydrogenated* ones? It doesn't say and so we don't know if there are hidden trans-fats.

4 "Sugar." Oh no, and we don't even know what kind of sugar is used in this product, though I'd be willing to bet big that it's the HFCS villain.

5 "Fig juice concentrate." Yes, yet another sugar product.

6 "Balsamic vinegar." Well that certainly makes sense although we don't know how the "balsamic" flavor got created! Is it the filtered juice from crushed Modenese grapes (true balsamic)? Or something concocted in a laboratory? I'll betcha it's a lab concoction of some sort!!!

7 "Honey." Another sugar albeit one of the better ones (if it's real).

8 "Salt." OK if you haven't been told by your doctor to avoid it. That said, I doubt there's very much in the product, at least not enough to worry about.

9 "Garlic." Again, not an issue.

10 "Spices." Hmmm, I wonder what these are and why can't we know? The food industry often categorizes non-specific additives as *spices* or

flavorings making it very difficult to fully determine what you're actually eating.

11 "Xanthan gum." Well the industry of course wants you to feel better about this product in case you're label-reading, so they say they need this as a "thickener" (and I'm sure that's true). But sorry, it's still a sugar.

12 "Potassium sorbate" is a quality maintainer. But what really is it? It's a chemical compound and is the potassium salt version of sorbic acid; a white salt which is very soluble in water and a polyunsaturated fat that has been created synthetically. It's actual use in this product is as a food preservative.

13 "Poppy seeds." OK by me; but still, why are they even included??? Must be taste-oriented.

14 "Calcium bisodium edta." What the heck is that? "EDTA" or "ethylenediaminetetraaceyic acid" is a chemical salt used to separate heavy metals from dyes and other substances. In the food production world, one of its forms is called "calcium bisodium EDTA" and it's used to prevent air from spoiling the food by introducing oxygen into the product's molecular structures. To the food industry it's a preservative which also prevents color and flavor deterioration and inhibits disagreeable odors and decomposing oils in this dressing, as well as sauces, mayonnaise, pickled cabbage, canned beans, canned mushrooms, and canned crabmeat. The industry likes to say that this chemical salt "maintains flavor" but in fact its jobs are much much more.

15 "Acetylated monoglycerides." These are emulsifiers that help stabilize and extend the shelf-life of the fat system in a food. Remember that monoglycerides are glycerides which are composed of a molecule of glycerol linked to or bonded with a fatty acid. They're just like partially hydrogenated oils and do contain those very dangerous trans-fats. Monoglycerides have one fatty-acid, while diglycerides have two fatty-acids. Nope, I don't like this food additive, one which hides the trans-fat composition. The food industry advertises that it just wants to "prevent separation." Yah, it's going to prevent separation of my artery walls too!

Hmmm, I think I'll just whip up some homemade dressing with balsamic vinegar, extra virgin olive oil, black pepper and some sea salt[299]. I could even get fancy with crushed garlic and basil. It's a simple recipe, keeps nicely in the refrigerator and I don't really need any more sugar or salt, or poppy seeds or weird chemical food additives, stabilizers and emulsifiers.

And regarding the also much maligned carbohydrate, when you're looking at nutritional labels you'll see a "total carbohydrate" number of grams. Rather, you should really calculate how much "net" carbohydrate you're eating, as that's the measurement of what your body will actually use. To get that number simply take the "total" carbohydrate grams and subtract the total number of fiber grams. Labels have to include these gram counts.

When you're comparing the nutrition labels on various foods, be cognizant of how the package is presented. Here are three *processed* cracker examples that you might be comparing while shopping for your charcuterie board presentation. This chart will depict the difficulty in deciding which one has the least bioavailable carbohydrates per cracker (though we don't know how big any of the crackers are and that will probably affect how many you and your guests eat).

Nutrition Label	Box #1	Box #2	Box #3
# of Crackers Listed on the Package's Ingredients' Listing	4	6	12
Total Carbs	8	18	20
Dietary Fiber	0	3	2
"Net" Bioavailable Carbs (carbs less fiber)	4 crackers Have 8 carbs $(8 - 0 = 8)$	6 crackers have 15 carbs $(18 - 3 = 15)$	12 crackers Have 18 carbs $(20 - 2 = 18)$
Net Carbs for 1 cracker	**2 carbs/cracker**	**2 ½ carbs/cracker**	**1 ½ carbs/cracker**

---

[299] Use 1:3 ratio of vinegar to oil and shake up.

Comments	You may have picked this one, simply because you saw the *lowest total carbs* and you also never considered the *number of crackers* being counted.	You may have picked this one during comparison because you saw a *higher fiber count.*	You may have avoided this one, simply because it stated the *highest total carbs* compared to the other two! ***This one is the best choice in terms of lower NET carbohydrates from a processed food.***

For another example, here's what's listed on most peanut butter ingredient nutrition facts:

- Roasted peanuts
- soybean oil (has 51% omega-6 inflammation and acidity causing fatty-acids)
- corn maltodextrin (another useless sugar)
- sugar (but what kind? – not that any sugar is good, just that some types are far worse)
- salt
- hydrogenated vegetable oil (terrible synthetic saturated trans-fats)
- mono- and diglycerides (emulsifiers to keep the processed peanut butter as one consistency – if you buy non-preservative peanut butter, you'll soon find the oil floating to the top – that's what it's supposed to do and that's exactly what my Nigerian *absolutely pure* peanut butter always did!!!) Just store it upside down.

If you're reading food ingredient listings, here are some general rules:

1. Higher non-digestible fiber is generally better.
2. More protein is better.
3. Less sugar is *always* better.
4. Fewer ingredients is better – go for labels that only have 5 or 6 recognizable ingredients.

5. More vitamins and minerals is better.
6. Hydrogenated- or trans- anything is very bad.
7. Anything you can't pronounce is *probably* bad.
8. Ingredients are listed with the biggest contributor first, the second biggest second, etc.
9. Concentrate on the first 3-4 ingredients as they'll probably make up over 50% of the calories.

But if you want to be a better food buyer, remember that real/whole nutrient-dense food doesn't need to have a nutrition label or an ingredient listing. This is why shopping on the outside aisles of your grocery store is always better for your waistline. That's where you'll find the fruits, vegetables, cheeses, eggs, yogurts, meats, poultry and fish, etc. They don't put the packaged and canned processed stuff there, it's all in the center aisles.

Ever see one of those people handing out free little bits of "food." I can guarantee they'll be near one of those aisles and they'll be pushing some processed item with a lengthy ingredient list. Sure it's free for your tasting, but don't stop to eat that sample! Keep pushing your cart past them. Look the other way if you have to. Don't listen to their pitch for a little taste. Your body won't like the resulting biochemical adaptations it'll be forced to undertake in an effort to get hormonally re-balanced.

Do be very careful with the serving sizes noted on labels.
Rely on your own measuring in terms of portion size.
And remember that every 4 grams of sugar
on those ingredient labels is the equivalent of 1 teaspoon of sugar
which is about 16 calories to your body – completely useless calories.

4.11 How Can Food Be "Fake"?

"Don't wait for miracles, your whole life is a miracle." – A.E.

This is a huge subject. But I have to say that it's extremely important in terms of selecting the nutrient-dense foods that'll support calorie-burning. Suffice it to say that when you're knowledgeable about food ingredient labels, they can be very interesting. They can be used by the food industry to *intentionally* encourage buyers into believing their products are better than

348

those of some of their competitors. Indeed, some food definitions have no *legal* definition and so the industry can use lots of imagination.

Another take on foods involves the *marketing or advertising* side of the game. Labels can be confusing and often a bit ridiculous. Usually food labelling reflects whatever the current "in" or "bad" food trend is at the time. A current example is "gluten-free." Well look out! Read that label and you'll more than likely see tons of added sugar. You'll even see "gluten-free" on margarine labels or mustard labels. Good grief, though these examples *never* had any wheat flour to begin with, food manufacturers are desperate to jump onto the current gluten-is-bad-for-you bandwagon too! Again, anything that might translate into more consumers.

I could go on forever on this topic but won't. I'll just give some examples of oddly misleading labels – labels that depict a food that seems to be nutritious from some perspective.

Let's say you want to give some kids coming to your BBQ a higher quality hot dogs and you see "<u>100 percent pure beef</u>" to describe a hot dog. Well sure, the beef may be 100% beef but most certainly there are other ingredients in that hot dog! Would you believe corn syrup solids (sugar), modified corn starch (sugar), potassium lactate, sodium phosphate, sodium diacetate, dextrose (sugar), sodium erythorbate, garlic power (Ok, I know what that is), spice extractives (what are those?), sodium nitrite and smoke! Bottom line, lots of corn (a relatively cheap carbohydrate additive) and sugar (yet another carbohydrate) in those hot dogs, and so those hot dogs are certainly are <u>not</u> 100% beef, indeed they're probably less than 45% beef although the beef itself IS 100% beef! I'm certain you don't necessarily believe hot dogs are a nutritious food, but you might be more inclined to buy this product because of the "100% beef" label on the front of the package.

How about when you buy "<u>100 percent grated parmesan cheese</u>." This term is also a bit misleading because although it describes a tin of grated "parmesan" cheese, the "100%" actually refers to the "grated" and not to the actual "cheese" content! Just look at the list of ingredients and you'll see more than cheese. And when you scrutinize the ingredients listing, what the heck are "<u>modified milk ingredients</u>"? Well, I'll tell you; this is a term used for a group of milk products that have an *altered chemical state* from that which is naturally found in milk. The percentage of such modified products used will vary, but sometimes they're used to *entirely replace* the milk in a product!!!

Yup, "100% grated" is definitely true. Although a lot more expensive, I prefer to buy a small block of real parmesan cheese and grate it at home. It tastes wonderful and it lasts in the refrigerator for quite a while.

Another good example is olive oil labelling; labelling that causes you to buy oil that's *not* primarily the healthy olive oil you may think it is and indeed may not even have as many omega-9 fatty-acids as you think.

"*Pure* olive oil" is thought by many to be only olive oil and to be the very best olive oil to buy. In reality it's NOT the highest quality to buy; indeed, it's the lowest quality and it's not "virgin" at all. The word "pure" means it's a mixture of various types of olives and *other* lower-grade vegetable oils (these may have high omega-6 fatty-acids, the bad ones!) Weird, eh?

"*Light* olive oil" does NOT mean fewer calories, as you might assume when the word "light" is used. It means less quality, less nutrition and a very neutral taste. It's cheaper to manufacture and it sells because people think it's better for their waistlines (check the amount of fat on "light" vs another olive oil…nope, not maybe what you thought). In the restaurant industry it's known as "light in flavor." You'd never find it in culinary TV superstar Gordon Ramsay's "Hell's Kitchen" restaurant. He'd be screaming for sure!

You want those omega-9 fatty-acids so still buy olive oil but get the kind that says, "extra virgin." It may not be the real Italian deal, but without that label, you can be guaranteed you're buying an inferior and relatively tasteless olive oil. Olive oil is "virgin" when it's the product of *one pure pressed* olive crop (no vegetable oils), giving it the highest quality and the best flavor. In sum, don't buy olive oils that say "premium," "super," "light," "extra light," "olive oil blend," "Mediterranean blend," "pure," "virgin" or simply "olive oil."

Other labels used to entice buyers can include "natural" and "organic." If you don't want to be misled your best route is to eat more whole[300] food that can't be adulterated by the food industry. You must shop more carefully and you should cook more at home. This will certainly give you much better

---

[300] Whole foods are natural, unprocessed, and unrefined before being consumed. These foods still have their natural features. A "whole food" diet would include the following: vegetables, fruits, nuts, seeds, eggs, meat, fish and poultry. These foods provide all the necessary nutrients for optimal health.

control over what you're eating if you cook it yourself than if you buy it already made or if you eat out at restaurants a lot.[301]

When you make your own 6-ounce "100%" beef patty hamburgers and grill them on the BBQ, they'll significantly reduce in diameter/size. Wow now put some of those store-bought burgers on your BBQ. NO such issue. The added "fillers" keep those frozen factory-produced burgers nice and big (after BBQing) for your equally big super-carbohydrate processed hamburger buns.

Read all ingredient labels very carefully. Heavily processed foods have *huge lists* of ingredients. You've seen them, and you don't even know what they are let alone how to pronounce them. If you read an ingredient label and it goes on forever, *just don't buy that product*. I don't like to buy anything with more than 5 or 6 ingredients. I also try to recognize those ingredients. As soon as I spot an ingredient that I don't know, I just don't buy that food item. And remember, the food industry is mandated to list all ingredients from the top percentage down. If sugar is within the first 3 ingredients, look out for some fat-making.

We know that highly processed foods are high in added sugar and/or fat and/or salt and that they're usually low in or completely devoid of fiber. The food industry knows that you're becoming more aware of labelling and that you may even have started perusing ingredient lists. This is why they hide some of the chemically synthesized components in their highly processed foods and these will add many unnecessary chemicals to the food you swallow. One way they do this is by listing, *within* the overall food's ingredient list, more complex *multi-ingredient* foods which are not legally required to be broken down into their separate ingredient percentages. Examples include BBQ and pesto sauces with their *tomato paste or puree* (high in salt and added sugars) and pancake syrups which list *corn syrup* (high in fructose sugar). Even though you might not know exactly what you're eating, your biochemical body always will and it'll have to adapt in some way that won't help you move toward your fat-burning goal.

---

[301] Another distant memory. My Mom lived in Wichita Kansas and she told me about an American acquaintance of hers – and this is incredibly hard to forget – who was building a house <u>without a kitchen</u>! Apparently, she and her husband <u>never</u> ate at home – and you just can't make this stuff up. All I can say is "OMG!"

Legally, all ingredients for any food must be listed from the highest
to the lowest inclusion percentage. If sugar is in the top 2 or 3 ingredients,
you can bet that there's a very high percentage of it.
The food industry will try to call it something else or bury it in a more
complex
"multi-ingredient" food so that it's either not listed or it gets noted further
down
the ingredients' listing making you believe it's less prominent.

Big food companies are aware of current food trends and they gear their labelling and marketing accordingly. One of the really great examples is margarine, though it isn't a "fake" food, it's a food that purports to be something that is "in" at the time. Margarine can be cloaked many ways; indeed, we could even call it a *super-cloaker*. A tub of margarine might say any of the following: gluten-free, made with olive or avocado oil (the oils currently touted as healthy), 50% calories of regular (for the calorie-counters), heart healthy (no animal-based saturated fat), salt-free (for the high blood pressure buyers), trans-fat-free, vegan, buttery taste (hmmm, that "taste" must have been industrially created), etc. Do you see the timely *cloaking issue*? It seems that margarine will always reflect a lack of the current food-related villain or an inclusion of some food hero. I don't think there ever was wheat gluten[302] in margarine, but I do feel like I'm with James T. Kirk's Enterprise trying to find a Klingon ship that has activated its cloaking device. Only Star Trek fans will understand this analogy.

Just remember, margarine is still margarine! It's a *non-dairy artificial product created simply as a butter substitute.* Its primary ingredients are oils, water, salt, and emulsifiers (substances used in food manufacturing which help

---

[302] *Unfortunately, gluten, as with fructose,* is hidden in many foods, despite the gluten-free bandwagon people have jumped on. Can you believe it's in the following items? Ice cream, milkshakes, malt vinegar, most pastas, baked foods, cereals, granola, breading/coating mixes, most noodles, pancakes, most sauces/gravies, processed luncheon meats, tortilla chips, salad dressings, marinades, soy sauce, and some restaurant/hotel scrambled eggs. Is it any wonder so much gluten-intolerance and so many allergies have moved to the forefront? If you grow sensitive to one of the gluten proteins (glutenins or gliadins) you can experience inflammation and damaged tissues as your body tries valiantly to get everything under control.

to combine liquids of different thicknesses, keeping them from separating – something that they *naturally want to do*). Butter is made from the butterfat/cream of milk, while margarine is made mainly from refined wholly or partially hydrogenated vegetable oil. Both butter and margarine contain the same amount of *total* dietary fat though of course margarines can contain those bad saturated trans-fats which are far worse for you than are natural non-synthetic saturated fats (e.g., from butter or that delicious grilled steak). Solid margarine sticks usually have more trans-fat than soft tub or liquid margarines (remember all the spaces will be filled with hydrogen). So if you want to move away from fat-storage, maybe you should avoid both butter and margarine, using butter only if necessary and <u>always</u> avoiding margarine. Of course, for those of you who are lactose-intolerant, butter is a no-no and so you may need to occasionally use some margarine.

Another example of hydrogenated oil is the widespread use of relatively cheap "modified palm oil."[303] Did you know that in parts of some rain forests, fires are started **intentionally** so that the land can be cleared for the planting of oil palm trees? Think of Indonesia and, more recently, Brazil! You'll see palm oil in many processed foods including candy, pastries and *cheap* chocolate such as the usual Easter chocolate that you probably buy. The term "modified" in front of any oil will mean that that oil is hydrogenated or partially hydrogenated (i.e., saturated trans-fats with a high percentage of omega-6 fatty-acids). That means more body acidity and far less fat-burning as a direct result. So you've been forewarned.

Another funny advertisement I heard recently on the radio was for "gluten-free wine." Think about it, wine is made from grapes and grapes certainly don't contain any gluten and so wine *should always be* gluten free. I began to check it out and it turns out that wine companies which advertise "gluten-free" do so simply because they don't seal their barrels with wheat paste (apparently done at some wineries). Frankly I don't care what sealant they use on the barrel as I expect not much wine contacts that sealant. Celiac sufferers have been told they *can drink any* wine, but that most beers would be problematic due of

---

[303] Palm oil is taken from date palm and coconut palm trees, but when I lived in Nigeria that palm tree sap was also fermented into a very sweet "palm-wine." The locals loved the 4% alcoholic drink, one that was a thick goopy white liquid. I wasn't a huge fan so I stuck to warm beer (not too many refrigerators in the small Gboko town where I lived!) and I wasn't into healthy eating at the time so beer sugar sufficed.

course to their grain base. The wine industry is just getting on the we-want-to-sell-more-so-let's-get-on-the-gluten-free bandwagon. Yet another successful marketing meeting over and done.

If you want to better control your nutrition
and body fat, eat more meals at home.
Read all food labels very carefully and avoid those with
extensive lists of ingredients.

Many fast-food places and even some hotels with their scrambled eggs, are advertising breakfast sandwiches of some sort. Most will say they are made with "100% real eggs" and this is definitely true. But there's a bit of deception here – in the form of another very clever marketing tactic. Most of those sandwiches have an "egg mixture" (to which water is added before cooking) which will include many of the following ingredients: whole eggs (OK great), xanthan gum (a sugar), citric acid, triglycerides (fats), cornstarch (carbohydrate) and powdered cellulose (tiny powdered pieces of non-digestible wood pulp or other plant fibers)[304]!

When I first started writing this book (2 years ago), the ONLY fast-food joint that actually used freshly cracked eggs (i.e., not a powdered or precooked mixture) in their breakfast sandwiches was…are you ready for this? McDonalds. Bet you're surprised! Many others still don't crack fresh eggs at their franchisees, unless it's a plate with actual easy-over eggs and bacon, as you'd see at home! You really can't slip a powdered mixture onto that plate.

Do you now understand that you can't blindly believe all ads? You may be eating a lot of fake stuff that will hamper your progression from fat-making to calorie-burning. Do your own thinking and don't rely on front-face package wording or ingredient listings or TV marketing ads or even what you're looking at to tell you what's in or not in a particular "food." Good nutritious foods don't need labels and ingredient listings.

---

[304] Wood pulp cellulose is loved by the food industry because it's cheap and it stabilizes food. You can usually find it in pre-shredded cheese as well because it repels moisture. It's a fibre, so it's not horrible for you but why not just shred some cheese yourself?

4.12 How Can I Cope with Restaurant Menus?

**"The best way to cheer yourself up is to cheer somebody else up." –
A.E.**

The best approach to controlling what you eat is to eat at home. Then you know what you're eating. This may sound like an odd statement, but restaurant foods can look the same as your home cooked food but often be heavily laced with one or more of fat, sugar or salt. Why? Well frankly it makes the food taste better. We all know this.

Not only is cooking at home better for you than eating out in a restaurant, it's less expensive and as the chef, you won't be slipping duck fat, tallow (beef fat), lard (pig fat), chicken fat or bacon grease into your meal. Have you ever read the book "Kitchen Confidential: Adventures in the Culinary Underbelly" by the late Anthony Bourdain? Wow, upper end restaurants use a lot of tasty bad-for-you-fat and there can be a lot of unplanned sex, drugs and booze in the wings! I'm not suggesting this happens in all expensive restaurants but the book was certainly an eye-opener. A real fun read indeed!

Another trick is to not arrive at the restaurant overly hungry (also true for grocery shopping)! Your eyes will be bigger than your stomach for sure! Do you really need an appetizer, the whole bread bowl, a main course and that dessert? Surely you wouldn't be eating all of those courses at home.

I'll share one of my restaurant experiences with you. I went to a high-end burger restaurant (yes there are such beasts!) and ordered a "100% lean beef" one. It was absolutely delicious. But for two days after I had terrible gut pains eventually ending with bad diarrhea. One of our nieces worked at that restaurant and told me afterwards that they loaded up the "100% lean" meat with gobs of butter before making it into a patty and then grilling it with more butter! No wonder it was so delicious, though it was something I would never have guessed in a million years.

The only way you can really completely know what you're eating is to cook at home.

Still, we'll all be eating in restaurants while travelling or celebrating and certainly during special occasions. When at a restaurant just eat slowly until you're full and then ask for a "take-out" box. It takes about 15-20 minutes for your stomach to tell your brain that it doesn't want any more food; that's your leptin signaling in action.

If you don't go to restaurants on a daily basis, and you want to cheat when at one (don't we all?), just be a healthy eater the rest of the week. Drop the guilt about it. Look forward, not backward. You're on an extended health journey. Falling off the wagon the odd time is fine. Just don't make a habit of it. Food addictions and bad eating habits can creep back on you. You can even be careful at a "fast-food" establishment. Ask for no "cheese"[305] and remember, they have salads too! It's hard to taint a garden salad with saturated fats or processed carbohydrates (unless you decide to add creamy salad dressings or tortilla chips or seasoned bread croutons).

<u>Here are some general tips for dining out:</u>

1. Pick a good restaurant, one that has healthy nutritive-dense food choices.
2. Choose foods with less fat and avoid fried, crispy (just another word for fried), battered, creamy or cheesy menu choices.
3. Avoid the entrée sauces.
4. Avoid "set" menus (which encourage you to eat a ton of food).
5. Don't be afraid to make special requests such as sauces and dressings on the side or ask for "no cheese" (you can claim to be lactose-intolerant – that'll force them to be extremely careful – they don't want to be sued) or "no butter" or a "salad substitute" for French fries.
6. Beware of big portions. Do you really need to eat the whole darn thing??? Eat only until you feel satiated, no matter what you paid for the meal! Options could be to take some home or to split the entrée with your partner (especially in the United States where the portions are *ridiculously* large – probably made for the already obese big eater).
7. You could choose just to order a couple of appetizers which tend to be a more reasonable size and also can be more interesting to eat as well but do avoid the more fatty or sugary appetizers.
8. If you're a sucker for bread, then ask that no breadbasket be brought to the table.

---

[305] Fast-food restaurants usually use processed cheese slices.

9. Drink a couple of glasses of lemon water (not sweetened lemonade) while awaiting your meal.
10. Eat only ½ the sandwich lunch bun and eliminate the mayonnaise.
11. Start your meal with a low-fat choice such as a garden salad (with an oil and vinegar or a balsamic dressing) or maybe a shrimp cocktail to address your appetite.
12. Always order your salads with dressings on the side.
13. Avoid Caesar's salad (one of the *most fattening salads with as many as 450 calories!*)
14. Skip the cream soups, fried vegetables and the cheese sticks.
15. Choose tomato or vegetable sauces rather than cream-based sauces such as Alfredo or Hollandaise.
16. Order grilled or poached or braised but *not fried*.
17. Skip the French fries and go for a *naked* baked potato (or better yet a baked sweet potato).
18. Eat slowly, savor your food choices and enjoy the company you're dining with. Isn't that what special outside-the-house meals are supposed to be about.
19. Skip the dessert. If you must have a dessert, then make it a little bit of fresh fruit or share a dessert with your partner.
20. If you're sharing a traditional dessert, then just have 2 or 3 bites, eat slowly and put the fork down in-between each bite. You don't have to eat half if your partner is racing to eat most of it, that's just fine for your fat-loss goal.

4.13 What Are Some Quick Energy and/or Travelling Snacks?

"I am thankful for all those who said NO to me. It's because of them I'm doing it myself." – A.E.

- Small apple with real cheese (1-2 ounces)

- Turkey/chicken[306] (2 slices real, non-processed) and tomato (1-2 slices)
- Low-fat plain cottage cheese (1/2 cup) and a piece of whole fruit
- One fresh fruit
- Almonds (8-10) and walnuts (8-10)
- Plain hummus (1/4 cup) and baby carrots and/or celery (1/2 cup)
- Plain yogurt (2/3 cup) with fresh berries (1/3 cup)
- Reduced fat cheddar or mozzarella cheese (1 ½ ounces) with celery sticks (any amount)
- Hard-boiled egg (1 or 2)
- Raw veggies with guacamole or hummus – homemade won't have any nasty additives (1/3 cup)
- Low sugar beef jerky (one or two strips)
- Protein bars (look for high protein, high fiber, and low sucrose; some will have sugar alcohol)
- Nuts and seeds (small handful only)
- A bottle of plain water

Do you see any processed foods above?
Do you see any fried or junk-foods above?
Do you see any sugary foods above?
Do you see any fruit juices above?
Do you see any soda pop above, sweetened or unsweetened?

4.14 Why Do People Wear Those 5-Toed Shoes at the Gym?

I just can't envision Albert Einstein standing at the blackboard in those shoes, can you?

Should you wear those five-toed shoes that you see on some of the gym attendees? Or should you just stick with regular running shoes? This remains an ongoing controversy. Five-toed shoes are trying to replicate a bare-footed stance while padded and supported running shoes are attempting to make

---

[306] If you're in a hurry, just buy one of the pre-roasted chickens at your grocery store. You can slice it up, freeze it in little packets. It's a quick and nutritious protein.

walking and running more comfortable. You'll see both in the gym. I've been wearing 5-toed shoes for about 10 years and I absolutely love them.

5-toed shoes are quite different for your feet and indeed your knees and legs; they move *with* your feet and not against them. When people run in 5-toed shoes they'll not be landing on their heels, as do most who wear regular heal padded "running" shoes. They'll be landing on the balls of their feet. If you look at a barefoot runner, you'll see that the heel never wholly touches the ground. A prime example is the bare-footed Kenyan long-distance runner using long strides and landing on the ball of his/her foot. Indeed Abebe Bikila, an Ethiopian *barefoot* marathon runner, won Olympic medals in both 1960 and 1964. On the other hand, most people you see on the treadmills will be pounding their heavily cushioned heels into the treadmill first. Why? *Because they can,* and it doesn't hurt at all.

The big debate centers around whether it's good for your lower leg to be pounding down on your heel first. When you run without any shoes on, you'll quickly discover that you'll tend to lower your center of gravity more than when you're running with shoes on. You'll also not be planting your heels first – it'll hurt too much. A lower stance actually reduces the stress on your legs when your foot strikes the ground. It sort of allows a bit more bounciness and makes you less prone to injury. When you run with cushioned soles and use a hard heel strike, you can put a force that's up to *3 times your body weight* and this can lead to stress fractures.

Also, keep in mind that the primary weight-bearing joints in your body are your hips, knees and ankles. These are extremely susceptible to excess body weight because of the mechanical force placed on them. Haven't you noticed that most of the people applying for hip and knee replacement surgeries are excessively overweight. A reality is that walking on level ground will put a force on your knees that is the equivalent of *1 ½ times your body weight.* Think about it. At 165 pounds, my poor knees were dealing with about 250 pounds with *every step*! For every pound of weight lost, there'll always be a resultant reduction in knee stress or load. At 125 pounds of body weight, my knees loved the smaller 190 pounds of force. Hmmm, I think your knees would appreciatively thank you when you lose overall weight – I know mine did.

If you discover that 5-toed shoes are difficult to find[307], some companies like Nike and Puma, do have *gym "training" shoes* that have soft pliable soles (i.e., bendably flexible). They too are great for full foot movement – something you'll enjoy on "leg days" for lunges and squats, when you want to track what your heel and the ball of your foot are doing in relation to the floor. For example, when I execute a squat, I always want to ensure that I don't raise either the front or the back of my feet off the floor. Wearing 5-toed or soft pliable shoes will help me feel my feet without having to look at them.

4.15 What Is Epigenetics and Should I Be Concerned About It?

"In the middle of difficulty lies opportunity." – A.E.

I went to an academic[308] seminar on this, given to personal trainers, and really found the idea quite fascinating. Epigenetics, an emerging field of enquiry, discusses differences in gene expressions. Basically, it's the study of changes in bodies caused by the modification of genes. Could this include the propensity toward inflammation, big appetites and glucose tolerance? Possibly. Can your epigenetics create an imbalance between your energy intake (calories) and your energy expenditure (exercise)? Maybe. Can your epigenetics prevent some enzymes from optimally breaking down the foods you eat? Perhaps. Can your epigenetics predispose you to obesity? These are all very interesting questions.

Epigenetics considers potential *hereditary changes* in gene functions, specifically ones that *do not involve changes* in your genetic chromosome sequence. It studies how your body switches genes off and on. Basically, it marks how genes are read by your cells. In essence, epigenetic gene modifications control your genes by *either silencing them or activating them*. Wow, such an intriguing concept.

---

[307] My preference is Vibram 5-toed training shoes and I have about 6 pairs. They're washable, come in an assortment of designs and colors and last many years.

[308] Yes, *academic* because it was given by a University of Montreal professor, not some person trying to sell something. It was actually at a Fitness Conference in Toronto and I was captivated by his developing research.

360

Ever wonder why some people have extremely pale skin or hate the taste of slimy foods? That's me – I don't like anything slimy in my mouth, like okra or oysters or avocados[309]? These examples are all observable differences. They represent different combinations of genes being turned on or off, and of course this makes everyone very unique. The seminar I attended even suggested that some epigenetic changes could be inherited through *multiple generations*. That said, and contrary to the genes inherited from our parental chromosomal sequence, epigenetic changes are passed along through a different mechanism, one which uses various *spontaneous* epigenetic modifications.

I have to add that the scientific world doesn't completely understand such epigenetic modifications in terms of normal and abnormal biochemical processes. Epigenetic researchers hope that their continued research will shed some light on these modifications and eventually reveal non-environmental biological contributions to disease as well as any potential environmental influences.

But what does this mean for your weight-control and how do we move between genetics and epigenetics regarding weight-gain or fat-loss? Well, there's a lot of new research on these questions especially related to morbidly obese individuals and if interested you should delve into it[310]. You'll see that some studies suggest that you can backtrack some abnormal epigenetic regulations such as morbid weight-gain with diet and exercise. This book just isn't long enough to go into every weight-control topic out there.

I was labelled "clinically obese" when I began my weight-loss journey. I didn't decide to blame my epigenetics for it and to give up; I just assumed that I was eating wrong and not exercising enough. I didn't want to look for excuses and you shouldn't either. Believe me, the actual percentage of North Americans who can ***never*** lose weight regardless of what they do is infinitesimal.

Do you really think you're one of them??? I really doubt it.

---

[309] When I was a teenager suffering through the acne years, I was told that eating avocados would help yet still I just couldn't eat them.

[310] "Individuality and epigenetics in obesity," J. Campion, F.I. Milagro, J.A. Martinez, 2009.

Unit 5

Tips for Success

Some rules approach and measurements for success with fat-loss and weight-control. The main problem for most people who decide to control their ballooning weight and the amount of body fat they're carrying is that they just don't have the ***stick-to-it-ness*** required. We all know that it isn't easy to *always* do the right thing in terms of controlling your eating, exercising, sleep patterns or high stress. **But you have to ask yourself four very serious questions.**

1. How important is the weight-loss goal you've set for yourself?
2. Are you prepared to sacrifice some poor-choice and maybe additive foods?
3. Will you be able to devote some of your valuable time in order to exercise?
4. Are you willing to fully dedicate <u>at least six months</u> to testing out the information presented in this book?

**And you have to believe that your body will
biochemically respond to your choices.
Do you live to eat, or do you eat to live???
Pretend that I'm sitting on your shoulder every time you
consider putting something into your mouth.
Given the knowledge you gained from reading this book,
would I agree with your choice?
I know that sounds ridiculous and maybe even a little pretentious,
but I want you to succeed. I'm not so gullible that I believe everyone
reading this book will follow the advice and be successful.
That said, I DO want YOU to be one of the ones who**

DOES take these suggestions seriously and
DOES become a calorie-burning machine.

5.1 Some Foundational Rules/Approaches to Fat-Loss and Weight-Control.

"Only one who devotes himself to a cause with his whole strength and soul can be a true master. For this reason, mastery demands all of a person." – A.E.

OK, some of you will have jumped to this Unit right away. Gotcha!!! I would have done the very same thing. As I said earlier, lots of concepts regarding exercise and weight and diet make total sense and are what you would expect but read on, and then go back and read the *entire book* to fully appreciate these rules.

It's my hope that if you fully understand why you should do something, then you'll want to do it. Education never fails to empower!

Your health is much more than achieving an ideal weight; it's really about achieving your very best LEAN body mass and physical fitness. This book should have you convinced not to focus on *calories*. Rather, you should focus on *food quality* and your *biology*. Rather than calories alone, it's the nutritional and hormonal impact of calories that matter the most. Suffice it to say, that every time you eat, you're influencing your hormone balance and affecting your biochemical adaptations. You lose power over your body *as soon as you swallow any food*. If you want to lose overall weight and body fat in a fully sustainable way, then you must make healthier choices!!!

Even though there are references to calories in the rules below, you should consider the following reality as a way of reminding yourself that calories are never the best measurement for food intake and overall weight is not the best indication of physical fitness and good health.

An obese 5'3" woman (wearing a size 16 dress) may weigh 135 pounds, while a lean muscular woman who is 5'3" (wearing a size 4 dress) **also** weighs 135 pounds. Why do they look so different? Why does the obese woman find it difficult to believe that the scales read the very same for both of them – scales that don't lie? How can the significantly smaller woman weigh exactly the same??? It's simply because one pound of body fat tissue is a heck of a lot more bulky than one pound of lean muscle tissue!

If you're eating something as a snack with only 100 calories, a number that the food industry thinks will sell as a good in-between and "healthy" snack simply because it isn't terribly high in calories, still check the ingredients. What about the high fructose corn syrup? Refined flour? Trans-fats? Synthetic sugars? "Hidden" sugars, especially fructose which has multiple names? Hydrogenated oils? And other junky stuff that's needed to maintain a low production cost and a long shelf-life? Stuff that supports big bellies and poor fitness.

Please keep in mind that *all foods* that are rich in low-quality/non-nutritive high-calorie carbohydrates and saturated fats create inflammation in your body and that inflammation will injure the neurons in your hypothalamus – the organ that controls your metabolic calorie-burning rate and is the most affected by high-calorie foods. Yup, when your hypothalamus' neurons can *no longer read the leptin hormone signals that normally help you feel satiated or full,* you'll just keep eating more and more thinking that you're still hungry.

Also horrifyingly true is the fact that when you have a bunch of unhealthy toxins and other negative waste by-products kicking around your body, resulting from eating a lot of bad foods, your body must store them in fat cells because it simply can't deal with it all in an efficient manner. And it doesn't want any of those acidic toxins bothering healthy cells. Yikes, who'd have thought that???

And remember, your incredible body can *always* deal with toxic waste by-products with its normal processes by sweating, urinating or defecating them out or putting them into your existing fat cells. Only when you have too many toxins to deal with through these natural outlets, does it need to make new fat cells into which it can store all that excessive acidic goop. Get to the gym, eat better and you can dump a lot of toxic waste instead of storing it as fat!!!

Sure, it's true that many of the rules listed below will *already be known by you* and they're sort of obvious. The others you'll have learned by reading this book. The book's main focus is to give you **the means to be an informed individual,** one who will no longer be deluded by the profit-oriented food industry. One who will appreciate the incredible effects of a good night's sleep, controlled reactions to stress triggers, nutritious foods, proper weight-training and the use of 'cardio' gym equipment on your highly complex biochemical body.

1 <u>Eat enough to lose weight and don't starve yourself.</u> You want to up your anabolic/build-up metabolic state. You want to build calorie-burning muscle tissue. If you don't eat enough then your body will give up burning calories (simply because there isn't enough of them to burn!) and it'll move into a catabolic/teardown metabolic state. Don't eat and you make fat and loose muscle. Eat the right stuff and you lose fat and make muscle.

2 <u>Don't sit around all day.</u> This will lead to muscle stiffness, poor balance and less mobility. It can also contribute to lower-back, neck and/or hip pains. This is directly related to changes in your connective tissues. They cover your muscles and if you're constantly in a seated position much of the day, they'll get "set" into that position. Connective tissues are in different positions in relation to your core/trunk when standing versus when sitting (or bent over). Makes sense! When sitting your hip flexor muscles have to be slightly contracted or shortened. For good overall posture, you need strong hip flexors in order to walk tall and stacked over your feet and not walk with that back-breaking forward lean you see with many older people.

3 <u>Eat mindfully!</u> Don't be in a big rush. Don't be distracted. When you eat "mindfully," it means that you're aware of *what* you're putting into your mouth and *how much* you're putting in your mouth. Remember that once you swallow that food, your body and its hormones take over. You'll have given control of your metabolic engine to your body.

4 <u>Once you find the right eating plan for you, quit making exceptions to it.</u> If I had a buck for every client that changed their diet plan to reflect their eating preferences and then complained that they were either staying at the same weight or, God forbid, gaining weight, I'd be a lot richer. We're looking for a long-term and sustainable change in eating behavior – that infamous lifestyle change.

5 <u>Try not to eat too much at one sitting.</u> Do you really need that second helping of food? I read that "we dig our graves with our teeth." Practice portion-control at every meal and with every snack.

6 <u>Don't heap the food on your plate.</u> After waiting 10 minutes, if you're still hungry you can always go back for "seconds" (within reason of course). And remember that, unless you're on the Keto diet, you can eat as many daily complex vegetables as you want, the ones that you would find in a green salad. They're fibrous and very filling.

7   Try using a smaller plate. Surprisingly, it can trick your mind into thinking you are eating more. Yes, it does seem silly, but if it works, why not try it? I always give myself a slightly smaller plate when I'm entertaining and no one has ever noticed…mind you, I have a set of matching dishes with multiple-sized plates, so mine looks the same as those of my guests – and I am short one larger plate, so it works on another level too.

8   If you really don't enjoy eating some particular food (even if it's a healthy one), then don't eat it. You'll have more room for the nutrient-dense foods that you do enjoy and that your body wants.

9   Buy the smallest packages of food available. You'll waste less too.

10   Food should never be elevated to some sort of reward. That can just be a throwback to some childhood memory. Don't let food control you. Be strong. You can control your food choices.

11   STOP procrastinating and STOP making excuses!!! I really doubt that being obese has anything to do with your genes, your epigenetics, your bone size, your culture, your income, the fact that you have kids, that you are a stay-at-home mom, that you work too many hours, that you're too tired, that you have no time, that you have grandchildren, that you work shift-work, that you're a hardworking student, that you're depressed, or that your body isn't very flexible[311], or whatever the heck else you can come up with. I've heard it all. Give me a bl**dy break!

12   Stop skipping meals or going more than 4 hours without eating. Doing these things will cause your blood sugar to plunge and you'll soon want to eat again and you'll be craving high-sugar foods. Eat every 3-4 hours which includes healthy nutritious snacks. I would suggest eating 5-6 times daily to keep your metabolic calorie-burning engine properly fueled. Kind of like filling up your car's gas tank. When you're really low on gas (calories), your engine (metabolism) starts sputtering.

13   Eat fresh/raw and whole foods when you can (they take more energy to breakdown). They'll slow the arrival of sugar/glucose into your bloodstream, translating to fewer fat-storing insulin hormones kicking around and you'll avoid the development of insulin-resistance.

---

[311] Flexibility is highly over-rated in my opinion. I'm one of the least flexible people you'll meet. I've never been able to touch my toes! And frankly, I don't care. My lack of good flexibility doesn't affect how lean I am, how much muscle or fat I have, how physically fit I am or how much I weigh.

14   Eat alkaline-forming foods. These will lower the glycemic effect of foods and can include sourdough, lemon (squeeze some into your water glass) and vinegar (slows the absorption of carbohydrates), all of which will slow down the emptying of your stomach into your intestines. Yeah, sooo nice for your hardworking liver.

15   Avoid acid-forming omega-6 foods. When your body is too acidic, it's more prone to fat-storage and to inflammation. Examples include smoked meats, sugar, sunflower and safflower oils.

16   Quit drinking your calories. Give up fruit juice, energy drinks and flavored vitamin water. Liquid sugars move to blood glucose too quickly for your body to cope with.

17   Don't drink any carbonated soda pop. Many are the equivalent of a bag of candies or an average chocolate bar in terms of sugar. They're all just liquid candy. Artificially sweetened soda pop is almost worse for you because of the clearing of blood glucose and then subsequent dumping of the insulin hormone into your bloodstream. Also, carbonation has a terrible tendency to steal bone calcium and dump a bunch of synthetic chemicals into your system!

18   Alter your diet so that you don't eat a lot of grain-based high-glycemic super-carbohydrates (e.g., bread and pasta). Replacing those "simple" quick-to-sugar carbohydrates with low-calorie "complex" starch carbohydrates (slow to make blood sugar) that are very rich in water and nutrients, such as vegetables, can also help outmaneuver your hunger because of their fibrous roughage (good for your probiotics).

19   Fill up on vegetables (complex low-sugar carbohydrates with fiber). They can be fresh, cooked or raw. The deeper the color and the bigger the variety of colors you consume the better. Vegetables have a lot of fiber and water, and no useless calories. Good for constipation too. They make you fill fuller and take longer to eat, without all the added "empty" non-nutritious calories. Women should aim for about 25 grams daily fiber, men 38.

20   Avoid all sugary foods and refined/processed carbohydrates. They cause your blood sugar to spike quickly and then to fall again. This affects your overall energy level and makes you feel hungry soon after, causing the eating cycle to hit you again. Like I said in the book, good fat choices don't make you fat; bad carbohydrate choices do.

21   Don't eat fried foods or unnatural synthetic trans-fats. This is such an obvious rule; it should not need further explaining! Just remember that trans-

fat is one of the top two body-fitness enemies along with high fructose corn syrup (HFCS).

22 Avoid all foods and drinks that contain sugar. The *only* "food" (and I use that word loosely) that adds NO nutrients and always makes you fat is sugar. Stop eating all those industrially placed "hidden" sugars too; read the ingredient labels religiously. Remember that anything ending in "ose" (a sugar) or "ol" (a synthetic sweetener) may be adding useless carbohydrates too, ones without any fiber or vitamins.

23 Know *all of the names* used by the food industry for the dreaded "fructose" ingredient. Conscientiously *avoid all foods with fructose.* HFCS fructose is the most pervasive toxin ever created by the food industry. It loves to make fat cells and body fat cells *hate* to be empty.

24 If you really NEED to eat something sweet, just have a fresh fruit. And remember that fruit juice is not fruit, it's just liquid sugar to your body and liver. Keep in mind that pineapples, watermelon and dates (all of which taste so great) are relatively high in calories and have easily absorbed sugars (especially poor choices for diabetics). Dried fruits (high sugar GI count) and avocados (high fat, albeit good fat) should be eaten in moderation. Berries are fantastic fruits, high in antioxidants[312] as well as having much less fructose than most other fruits.

25 Avoid too much alcohol. It counts as 7 calories per gram and it goes straight to your liver to be processed into fatty acids. This will halt your fat-burning for the full day. Beer is particularly bad with its maltose sugar *and* grains.

26 Don't store bad food choices in your home, for the times when "you need them." Get rid of all temptations, especially the key potentially addictive foods that satisfy *your* cravings. Make failure much harder to attain. Clear out your cupboards. You'll feel so much better about yourself, yup I'm talking about your self-esteem here.

27 Make your life easier by having some nutritious back-up snacks handy. Prepare and keep some rinsed ready-to-eat veggies/fruits in your refrigerator; add a bit of fresh (non-canned) fruit with their skins to your salad; add chopped celery, onion and bell peppers to your tuna or salmon salad; make a batch of broth-based vegetable soup; buy pre-washed greens for a quick salad

---

[312] Vitamin C and E or beta-carotene are antioxidants that fight against disease-causing free radicals.

base. I hate cutting up leafy greens, so to ensure I eat a lot of them I do buy the expensive pre-cut stuff. I know, lazy, but for me, effective. Carry some almonds, walnuts, beef jerky and *home-made* non-sugar granola in your car.

28 Avoid fake, fast, processed and refined foods. Shop the outside corridors of your grocery store and steer clear of fast-food joints. Most bad foods are a combination of highly processed carbohydrate and really bad omega-6 fats. Actually, that's what makes them taste great *and* what can cause food addictions for some people! When you eat "fast" "cheap" food, you get a lot of calories at a much lower price/calorie; that is, a bigger bang for your food buck. This can be very appealing for those on a strict budget. But they'll be concentrated non-nutritional calories. People need knowledge, good strategies and time in order to eat well and keep within their budget. Don't be lazy!!!

29 Avoid all canned foods. Canned sausages and vegetables have very high salt contents and a lack of nutrients, and canned fruits are just fructose with no fiber at all. If you do buy them, rinse them with clear water before using. That will get rid of most of the preservatives and salt. *Eating canned fish, such as wild salmon, herring and sardines, is healthy given the omega-3 fatty-acids (which are anti-inflammatory).*

30 If you tend to eat a lot, then try starting your meal with a broth-based soup, especially a vegetable non-creamy soup. Broths are easily made at home. Use left-over veggies (not potatoes or pasta). [313]

31 Quit making "weight-adding" decisions. Don't eat food that you wouldn't be eating at that time of the day (e.g., office meeting freebie treats). Quit buying a cookie with your lunch. Stop having second helpings just because your hostess suggested it. Don't eat your kids' leftover food just so that it isn't wasted (well I guess it isn't wasted …it's going into your fat-storage because you already ate what your body needed).

---

[313] Way back in my crazy European hitchhiking days in the early 70s (nobody hitchhikes anymore), I needed some additional travel money so I got a job in an Austrian youth hostel in Salzburg (jeepers, I can't believe I never went skiing). Guess how they created their thick creamy soups? They put all the day's unused potatoes and pasta and whatever other vegetable dish was leftover into the food blender and used it as a base for the next day's creamy soups. That's all I can imagine when I see thick white restaurant soups. Really tasty but lots of *super-carbohydrates* for a quick sugar rush.

32 Eat more at home rather than in restaurants. Here are some good ingredient substitutions for your recipes: use mashed avocados for butter or oil in baking; use plain Greek yogurt for mayonnaise or sour cream; use mashed bananas for sugar or fats; use applesauce for sugar in baking recipes; use rolled oats for bread crumbs; use nuts in salads in place of bread croutons; and, use spaghetti squash for pasta. And remember that vinegar can do the same thing for a recipe as can salt. It can heighten the flavor of a recipe.

33 Avoid large fatty meals. They'll leave you feeling sluggish and your body has to work really hard to digest them, leading it to send a lot of extra energy (AKA calories) to body fat storage. Fat clicks in at 9 calories of energy per gram, much higher than either carbohydrate (at 4) or protein (at 4). But this doesn't mean you shouldn't eat fat. Just remember that the only way dietary fat makes you fat is by eating way too much of it and way too much of the bad saturated and/or artificial industrially created trans-fats found in most non-whole processed refined foods.

34 Eat protein with breakfast (1st meal of the day that "breaks" your "fast") and lunch and dinner. To lose weight, you should increase your daily protein intake slightly and decrease your daily carbohydrate intake slightly. This will not surprise your body into some sort of reactive biochemical adaptation as it will not have experienced any hormonal imbalance.

35 It happens! If you cheat on your healthy eating diet, move on, don't look back, look forward and don't get depressed. For you to gain a pound of body fat, you would have to consume almost 3500 calories in excess of your body's energy needs. I'm not saying to cheat, do avoid a lot of cheating, just don't throw the towel in because you went off the rails for some big family-outing dinner.

36 Multiply your weight in pounds by 10 and then add your weight. The resulting number is about the number of calories you need in order to maintain your current weight. Subtract 500 to lose 1 pound per week, 1,000 to lose 2 pounds per week. But do NOT allow your caloric intake to fall below 1,200 calories per day. Losing 1% of your bodyweight per week is considered healthy. Losing more than 1-2 pounds per week will cause physiological changes to your body such as damaging your metabolism and screwing up your hormone balances. Just believe me, you'll not become a calorie-burning engine doing that, you'll remain a really strong fat-making engine.

37 <u>You can determine/count your calories by managing your macronutrients</u>. Remember that lean protein (4 calories/gram), complex carbohydrates (4 calories/gram) and poly- or monounsaturated fats (9 calories/gram) are all nutrient-dense choices. But, if you habitually provide your body with more daily calories[314] than it can burn that day, you'll gain weight and body fat. You have to exercise if you want to eat a lot of food and you must include protein at every meal!

38 <u>Cover 1/3 of your plate with *nutrient-dense* protein</u>. Remember that a diet high in protein, as well as fiber, can regulate your ghrelin "I'm hungry" hormone thereby decreasing your overall appetite. Protein also triggers the release of the fat-burning glucagon hormone, along with some fat-releasing enzymes. And the nitrogen in protein is needed by your body in order to synthesize more protein and to build-up your muscle tissues.

39 <u>Cover 1/6 of your plate with whole-food unsaturated fats such as nuts and seeds.</u>

40 <u>Cover 1/2 of your plate with fresh or frozen vegetables</u>[315].

41 <u>If you want to eat fresh fruits (i.e., simple high-sugar carbohydrates with a bit of fiber), cover no more than 1/6 of your plate (i.e., 1/3 of the vegetable half of your plate)</u>. As with vegetables, fruits can be frozen as well. They're just as good as fresh and sometimes more convenient and less expensive (if not normally available that time of the year).

Rather than counting calories and weighing your food selections, set up your plate as follows:

---

[314] Yes, it's true not all calories are treated the same by your very complex biochemical body. I'm really getting at quantity here and at the fact that people eat way too many processed high-calorie and low-nutrient foods.

[315] Frozen vegetables have normally been *flash frozen* (a relatively new way to freeze fresh produce which causes less damage to their cell membranes) very near to the time of their picking; hence, they have *all their nutrients* (contrary to vegetables that have travelled long distances over time).

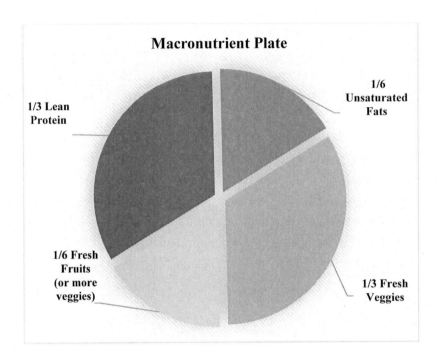

Macronutrient Plate

1/6 Unsaturated Fats

1/3 Lean Protein

1/6 Fresh Fruits (or more veggies)

1/3 Fresh Veggies

42   When you're grocery shopping, base your decisions on these four very basic rules: low/no-sugar, high-fiber, low omega-6 fatty-acids (highly acidic), low/no-trans-fats (synthetic).

43   Exercise smart. You can do 5,000 crunches every day and you'll never ever see that abdominal six-pack. I like to say that "*visible* abs are built in the kitchen." You need to lose fat *all over your entire body* before you'll ever see those abdominal muscles. Multi-joint exercises such as squats, leg presses, prone barbell rows, chest presses, pull-downs and -ups, overhead presses and deadlifts work the most and the largest muscles hence burn the most calories. Use as much weight as you can with proper range-of-motion and good exercise form and go to complete fatigue/failure (i.e., you can't lift any more or add more resistance/weight *while* still maintaining good form).

44   If you want to grow your calorie-burning muscle, then you must challenge your muscles with *progressively more weight.* They'll never adapt by growing bigger otherwise. Gradually increase your training volume using this equation:

TOTAL TRAINING VOLUME = # of sets X # of repetitions/set X weight used *Increasing <u>any one</u> of these three <u>will</u> increase the volume or intensity of the training completed.*

45   <u>Plan to lift weights four-five times a week minimum.</u> This is strength- or resistance- or weight-training and it should be progressive in nature with a linear increase in training volume. Balance front and back, for example for every "push" exercise you do (e.g., push-up, shoulder press, bench/dumbbell press), do a "pull" exercise (e.g., cable row or lat pulldown). For every "bicep" exercise (e.g., dumbbell curls), do a "triceps" exercise (e.g., triceps dumbbell extension). *Always* track your progress to ensure that your muscles are getting stronger and bigger. And you'll even look cool carrying a notebook around the gym, just like the big boys.

46   <u>Use both anaerobic/weight-lifting and aerobic/cardio exercises.</u> Do your weightlifting first and your cardio-training last, as cardio can burn those fatty-acids that have been brought to the forefront by your weightlifting. Be careful not to overdo your cardio time, until you're more physically fit with a healthy oxidative fitness (meaning that you can provide the oxygen needed to release excess body fat).

47   <u>Always keep your body's water content **over** 50% (it should be closer to 60-65%) and your urine clear and uncloudy.</u> Drink at least 8 glasses of pure water daily. It'll help with body acidity and inflammation, both of which compromise your fat-burning ability.

48   <u>If you're feeling down about something, instead of eating a dessert or some junk-food, go out to the mall and buy yourself something (no…not edible!).</u> Even something small and not too expensive will help, and you'll be walking too. Better yet why not visit the gym?

49   <u>Quit thinking that you should have complete success at reaching your goals within a few weeks or even a few months.</u> Rapid weight-loss is never good, and it certainly isn't from losing body fat! It'll be mostly water for sure along with a bunch of calorie-burning muscle tissue.

If you're serious, you'll be patient and you'll devote
1-2 years to your fitness journey.
It's a journey that pays wonderful benefits.
But it takes real dedicated time and a committed effort

to shift your biochemical body
from enduring an inefficient fat-making metabolism
into enjoying a wonderfully efficient calorie-burning metabolism.

5.2 The Sweet-16 Commandments for Consistent Long-Term Fat-Burning Success.

"The important thing is to not stop questioning. Curiosity has its own reason for existing." – A.E.

1. Eat all three macronutrients daily (lean protein, complex carbohydrates and unsaturated fats).
2. Avoid all sugar and sugar-laced foods, including artificially sweetened foods.
3. Avoid all highly refined, processed, fast and fried foods.
4. Never drink your calories (including fruit juice).
5. Avoid "super"- carbohydrates such as breads and pastas.
6. Increase your daily vegetable and fiber[316] intakes.
7. Decrease your daily fruit intake (no more than two fruits, wherein one large banana = 2).
8. Manage your stress.
9. Get more sleep.
10. Increase your pure water intake.
11. Decrease your alcohol intake.
12. Take up progressive weight-training exercises.
13. Reduce your "cardio" exercising (e.g., treadmill running).
14. Increase your Omega-3 and decrease your Omega-6 fatty-acid intakes.
15. Increase your alkaline-forming food intake.
16. Become an informed food-label/ingredient reader.

Marcus Arelius, a Roman Emperor during the 2nd Century, was a stoic philosopher. If you watched Russel Crowe's Gladiator film, Marcus Arelius was the father of Commodus, the young emperor who succeeded his father

---

[316] You can only get your daily fibre from dietary carbohydrate such as vegetables and fruits; not from protein or from fat.

only to be killed in the Coliseum by Crowe. This film was based a lot on actual history, though the story enjoyed some Hollywood liberties as well.

Here is one of Marcus Arelius' famous quotes and it's a good one for us all to think about in terms of food addictions and portion-control.

"You have power over your mind – not outside events.
Realize this, and you will find strength."

5.3 How Can I Measure My Success?

"Technological progress is like an axe in the hands of a pathological criminal." – A.E.

There are many ways and of course it's dependent upon your goals. Typically, someone wants either to lose weight, build muscle, lose fat, get healthy, lower blood pressure or cholesterol and on and on. There are many books and online sites that list ideal measurements/goals for particular heights, age, gender, etc.

Depending on your goal(s), you might use one or more of the following methods to track your success on a chart and please practice some patience. It may take 3-4 months to see measurable success. And your friends and work colleagues will begin to notice as well. I never told people at work what I was doing. I just didn't want people mentioning it all the time. Still, they sure did notice it. They'd say, "Have you lost weight???" and I'd respond, "No, I don't think so, but thanks." When it became more obvious, I had to own up to it, and then guess what? They were trying to sabotage me by offering homemade goodies. I'd have to say no. For the ones who expressed visible frustration, I would agree to take the homemade cake or whatever and then when they left my office, I'd pitch it into the garbage. I was really determined.

Here are some tracking methods, not listed in any particular order:

Weigh yourself either daily or weekly

This is the easiest method although it doesn't really give the detailed information you might be after[317]. For example, are you burning up muscle

---

[317] Remember that gym acquaintance who couldn't believe she weighed the same 135 pounds as me. She was a huge water drinker and a very light eater. Indeed, she was

instead of fat? Also, weigh yourself in the morning as soon as you get up and, if possible, after your morning constitutional and before your first coffee. Note that measuring daily can be disappointing as there are many factors that can intertwine to move your weight up or down. I find weekly at the outset is better, and once you have achieved good success you can move to daily weigh-ins just to stay on track. If you're losing weight in a sustainable healthy way, you may lose less weight than you think yet find that your clothes are fitting better (I like to call this body sculpting). This is because a pound of body fat takes up a heck of a lot more space (inches) than does a pound of dense lean muscle tissue.

Measure your body fat percentage

You'll need a hand-held body fat device to measure this. Your gym will have one you can borrow for a few minutes, or you can buy one at a fitness store or order one online. These too are not perfectly reliable, but at least they'll track relative changes. And remember that the higher your body fat percentage, then the less lean muscle mass you possess and the less fit you are. Normal fitness level body fat percentages usually range between 20-24% for women and between 15-20% for men. Your body normally prefers to maintain about 10-13% <u>essential</u> fat; men 2-5%. Athletes tend to have a body fat percentage that lies somewhere between the "essential" and the "fitness" levels. You can do it too but it's really hard, it takes time and you have to be incredibly disciplined with both diet and exercise. ***AND NOW FOR MY VERY FAVORITE MEASUREMENT***

Check how your clothes fit you

Pick out something of yours that's a bit tight and see if you can make it looser over 12 weeks.

Calculate your body mass index (BMI)

---

continually obsessed with her weight. It was the only measurement she concerned herself with. It's true that she looked like she weighed about 180 and maybe I looked more like 110; but I don't carry around a lot of body-fat, while she doesn't have much muscle tissue. Remember that one pound of fat takes up a lot more physical space than one pound of lean muscle tissue. It was obvious to me that she was *not eating enough* to turn her body's metabolism away from its fat-making catabolic mode into an efficient muscle-building/calorie-burning anabolic mode. She was probably a regular Starvation Island vacationer! Indeed, I think she purchased a condo there.

BMI considers both your weight and your height. The ideal BMI is between 18-25. Go to a BMI web site and put in your statistics (weight and height). It'll give you an answer although it too isn't a perfect measure as a lean healthy person with a lot of muscle will score a high BMI although they have very little body fat.

Take body measurements

At the outset of your diet and workout programs and for a benchmark to track your progress, measure and record each of your thighs at the widest part, your hips at the widest part, your waist 1" above your naval, each upper arm at the widest part, and chest at the nipples (with the same bra on) and re-measure all on the *first day* of every month. Be careful to continue measuring in the same spots. And remember to be reasonably patient!!!

Track your waist-to-height ratio

Measure your waist 1" above your naval and compare it to your height. Generally, your waist should not be more than half your height.

Track your waist-to-hip ratio

Measure your waist 1" above the naval and your hips at the widest part. Ideally, a woman should be below .80 and not higher than .85 (e.g., if your hips are 40", then your waist should be no bigger than 34"). You always want your waist to be smaller than your hips.

Visit your medical doctor

Have your blood pressure and cholesterol checked periodically by your medical doctor. This would probably be once a year at the least, although every 6 months would be more interesting to track. You can also get your blood acidity checked.

None of the above measurement approaches are perfect methods, hence you should adopt a combination of a few of the above as change indicators. ***Don't obsess with daily changes***. Be in the game for the longer run. Your body will adapt and it'll adapt at its own pace, and that pace may be different than that of your friend. So what???

Be honest with your measurements.

5.4 How Did I Eat, While Weight-Training, to Lose 40 Pounds?

"I never think of the future. It comes soon enough." – A.E.

Now that you've read this book you should appreciate that, when you *commit to modifying your daily diet, getting more sleep, controlling your reaction to stressful situations <u>and</u> hitting weight-lifting in the gym*, you'll be able to develop a body that reacts differently to the food you swallow. You'll also be eating foods that help your body maintain its preferred homeostasis, respond to food properly and avoid unnecessary fat-storage. Of course, inside your body, by eating correctly you're actually altering your biochemistry, and this will include the following positive outcomes: lowering both your bloodstream sugar levels and triglyceride fats; balancing your hormones; and, increasing your calorie-burning ability (your anabolic metabolic rate).

When you can control your body's blood chemistry,
your weight will also be under better control.
This will involve monitoring and controlling all four factors:
diet, exercise, sleep and stress.

Ok, in terms of my diet, I did the following and it worked for me. My personal trainer told me I wasn't eating enough to lose weight. I thought that sounded really weird. It was about the only thing I hadn't tried in order to lose weight, so I thought "What do I know? What the heck! Why not get off Starvation Island? He probably knows more than me…and he looks really great!"

But don't forget that I was <u>also weight-training</u> at least 4-5 days weekly and drinking BCAAs while training. You'll recall from an earlier chapter that BCAAs are branched chain amino-acid proteins that help your muscles recover. Recently I've added some powdered collagen (a highly bioavailable amino acid) to my workout drink as well for enhanced joint and muscle recovery.

Breakfast   - two whole eggs (or just the egg whites), 1/3 – 1/2 a bell pepper, 1 oz. low-fat mozzarella cheese (this mixture can be fried in a tiny bit of olive or canola oil or it can be microwaved)

= ***protein, low-sugar/GI complex carbs, fat, fibre***

Optional Snack - one whole fruit (only if I exercised in the early morning and ate breakfast before exercising – normally I eat breakfast after exercising and don't have this snack)

= ***high-sugar simple carbs with fibre***

Lunch   a large spinach/lettuce/kale salad with any number of raw veggies I had in the refrigerator, a few walnuts (5-7) and almonds[318] (5-7), along with a fistful of lean protein (e.g., leftover chicken, or a drained can of albacore tuna or red salmon) with 2 tbsps. balsamic vinaigrette.

= ***protein, low-sugar/GI complex carbs, fat, fibre***

Snack   2/3 cup of plain (which is low-fat by definition[319]) yogurt (can be Greek) with ½ cup of berries (such as blueberries, strawberries, raspberries and/or blackberries - frozen or fresh), and 1/3 cup of "Original Fibre-1" cereal[320] (I'd mix the cereal in later if at work and the frozen berries sitting on top of the yogurt kept the yogurt cool even without using a refrigerator); you can also add

---

[318] Walnuts and almonds are both great for essential fatty acids, good protein and fibre. Walnuts offer anti-inflammatory omega-3 fatty acids, while almonds also offer magnesium and vitamin E.

[319] This does *not contravene* my argument to avoid no-fat or low-fat foods. Plain yogurt is just that, plain and with no added fat. If I buy a *no-fat flavoured* yogurt, it'll always have added sugar. I'd rather add real fruit to the plain yogurt, rather than let the industry do it for me (with that nasty fructose syrup).

[320] In the book I have tried to avoid the names of actual products but in this case, I wanted you to know what cereal I used. Most cereals are so incredibly high in sugars you may as well just spoon some table sugar into your mouth.

1-2 tbsp. ground flax seed to the mixture if you want some extra fibre

= *protein, high-sugar carbs with fibre, fat*

Dinner - lean protein (about the size of a clenched fist), any amount of cooked or fresh veggies and/or salad, and a *naked* baked sweet potato or brown rice or wild rice (a grass) or unrefined grain such as quinoa (again fist size)[321]

= *protein, higher sugar/GIcarbs, fat, fibre*

Snack ¾ - 1 cup of 2% plain cottage cheese which is very easily digested overnight, (and again you can add ground flax seed and/or 1/3 cup fruit if you want)

= *protein, fat, (carbs, fibre)*

And, of course I drank my daily water ration and tried to avoid alcohol as much as I could. Remember that alcohol, although a carbohydrate, rings in at a whopping 7 calories per gram and it puts your body's fat-releasing ability on hold.

Also notice that in addition to *no sugar*, there is *no bread, no white rice* and *no pasta of any type,* all are super-carbohydrates. Sometimes at dinner for some variety, I did eat some super-carbohydrate white potato or rice (usually Basmati but it has a lower glycemic load than many other types of rice.) Yup, I wasn't always perfect! But I didn't beat myself up about it, I just carried on looking long-term for results.

Interestingly *you won't find any foods that contain BOTH fat AND higher GI carbohydrate combinations.* Why is this? Well, it's closer to nature. Most foods contain fat OR carbohydrate but not both! Vegetables and fruits have carbohydrates and fiber, but no fat. Meats have fat, but no carbohydrates. Some fruits like avocados have fat, but only *very little* carbohydrate. Cow milk is an exception as it has both, though our ancestors normally didn't drink milk after being weaned off breast milk. I don't think we should be drinking a ton of milk

---

[321] Eating the higher glycemic starchy-type carbs later in the day, contrary to what you might think, is better for you as it regulates your blood sugar levels while you're getting those valuable anti-cortisol 7 hours of sleep.

or eating fats and low-fiber carbohydrates in the same food, and guess what some of the typical such fat/low-fiber/carb examples are? Yup, junk-food, processed food, chocolate milk, sweets, pastries, etc. Like I've been saying throughout this book, *it's not how much food you eat, it's what kinds of food you choose to eat.*

You can follow this diet as well and you can do it at work (as I did) and you can follow it at a restaurant for dinner too. If you don't like either cottage cheese or yogurt, substitute one for the other. And remember your macronutrient percentages and the fact that you don't want to shock your biochemical unit, your very responsive body, into a crazy adaptation that slows down your calorie-burning anabolic metabolism. You can tweak this eating plan by altering your carbohydrate percentage <u>slightly</u> or your protein percentage <u>slightly</u> or your fat percentage <u>slightly</u>, all dependent upon your goals. If you want, you can gradually alter those percentages a second or third time as your body gets used to your new eating plans. If you're lactose-intolerant or a vegetarian, you'll obviously have to make some adjustments.

And this diet can be followed 90% of the time and still do wonders.

Hence, if you're eating five meals a day, that's 35 meals in one week and you can have three "cheats"; but, guess what, a "cheat" on this diet includes MISSING one of the daily meals! Remember I said that you have to eat to lose weight! Other cheats can include alcohol, desserts, bread, pasta, white potato, junk/fast food, etc.

This diet also has some built in nutrient-timing[322] and can be applied to a time-restricted intermittent-fasting eating plan too (e.g., eating only between 10 am and 6 pm). Eating frequent smaller meals will give you a timed release of energy while lowering the total amount of fiber eaten at any one meal. It'll also aid with appetite control. This is because protein is consumed at all meals and it always triggers the "I'm full" leptin signal. You're probably surprised to see the starchy, albeit medium-GI carbs, eaten at dinner time. This helped my body to restore its glycogen and regulate my blood sugar levels while I slept.

---

[322] Nutrient-timing involves eating foods at strategic times, all dependent upon your goals of course. For example, if you want to grow serious body builder muscle, you'll need to have protein before, during and after your workout; carbs before and after your workout; and, fat only after your workout. My diet wasn't as strict.

Bodies need constant fuel, even while sleeping and it'll also help to burn fat the next day due to the overnight glycogen depletion.

If you're into counting calories, make them *nutrient-dense* ones. A quick-n-dirty calculation is to multiply your current weight by 10, then add your weight to that number. This'll give you the approximate daily calories you'll need in order to *maintain your current weight <u>with no exercise</u>.*

For example, if you weigh 130 pounds, then you can eat about <u>1,300 (130 X 10) + 130 = 1,430 calories</u> daily and not change your overall weight. If you eat *more*, you'll need to complete anabolic exercises (weightlifting) in order to burn the extra calories and stay at the same weight. If while you're exercising, you also increase your *lean* protein intake a bit, and lower your carbohydrate intake a bit (avoiding *simple* carbohydrates), then you'll begin to lose body fat and gain calorie-burning muscle tissue. Sign me up!

5.5 Book Synopsis

What have you learned in all of the above chapters in terms of weight-gain or weight-loss?

Hopefully you've come to an important understanding of why all those typically known rules for losing weight work, and how your food choices and your exercise patterns interact with your biochemical and hormonal balances.

Now that you've read the whole book (and I hope you have!), I've amalgamated the book's material concerning your body's adaptive responses into a concise summative chart.

Whenever you eat a food, whenever you exercise, whether you get enough sleep to rejuvenate your body, and how well you manage your stress levels will force <u>hormonal reactions</u> that will cause <u>biochemical adaptations and metabolic rate alterations</u>. And, to make matters even more complicated, hormones impact upon one another. Like the song, "the leg bone is connected to the hip bone which is connected to the...," the endocrine system connects everything too. For this reason, when your body must process an excess of one hormone there'll be a balancing drop in some other paired or opposing hormone.

This is why I said earlier that the expression "you are what you eat" should be "your *hormones* are what you eat" and why I've been stressing that you **must** undertake progressive weight-lifting in order to build-up your calorie-burning muscle tissue (while you implement better eating habits to deal with your extra body fat)!

Only YOU can control your overall weight and the comparative percentages of your <u>fatty tissue and muscular tissue</u>.

<u>Only YOU</u> can change your metabolic calorie-burning rate.
<u>Only YOU</u> can move that rate
from *catabolic fat-making* to *anabolic calorie-burning/muscle-building*.

Certainly, this book has given you the rationale supporting the various guidelines for loosing overall weight and for lowering your body fat percentage, and more importantly the reasons why they work. Read the chart on the next page very carefully. I worked really hard at figuring out a nice little synopsis that would visually depict the unbelievable control your biochemical body always has after you make any decision on diet, exercise, sleep or stress control. Enjoy!

<u>Only YOU can move your fat-making body into a calorie-burning body</u>.
Do it for yourself. Never look back.
I wrote this book for you. I want you to succeed.
I want you to like yourself again.
I want you to feel strong and empowered.

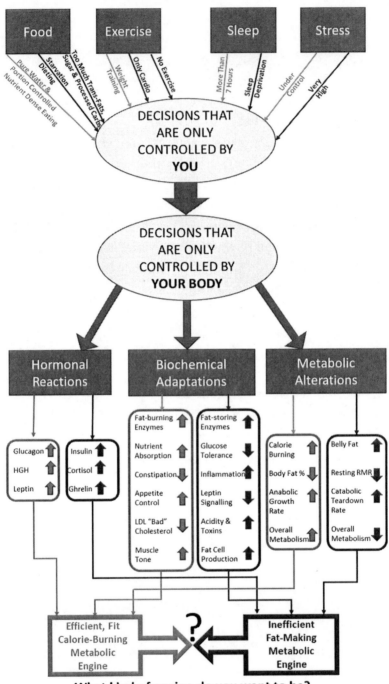

What kind of engine do you want to be?
The choice is YOURS to make!

In general what we see in this chart is that with poor non-nutritional eating habits, little exercise, sleep deprivation and chronic stress, you'll always compromise the loss of body fat and the building of muscle due to higher inflammation, higher body acidity, more body toxins, newly produced fat cells to deal with those toxins, increased leptin-resistance, increased insulin-resistance, decreased insulin efficiency, decreased fat-burning enzymes, increased fat-storing enzymes, poorer appetite control, higher carbohydrate cravings, poorer muscle tissue repair, and a really fast blood sugar release leading to extreme insulin highs and lows. All of these biochemical results will lead to many adaptations including a more catabolic slower metabolism, a compromised ability to burn fat, decreased muscle tone, increased belly fat deposits, decreased calorie-burning, increased weight gain and poorer muscle repair and building.

If you can't change or refuse to change your eating habits, your exercise level, your stress level and develop good sleeping habits then your body cannot move its metabolic rate from being predominantly fat-making to becoming efficiently calorie-burning; and, you will *always be doomed* to be overweight and depressed about it.

Just try to eat "complex" fiber-filled carbohydrates, avoid trans-fatty, fried and sugary foods, drink a lot of plain water, get more sleep, avoid chronic stress (or learn to better cope with it), to never visit Starvation Island, and exercise by lifting progressively heavier weights. Do it for SIX months minimum. You'll be really surprised at how your clothes fit and how great you feel. You'll become hooked and you'll want to continue eating well and exercising wisely. That's what happened to me!

Once you get lean, you'll be able to have eat-cheats, but of course you should save them for special occasions.

And the best gift of all is when you love yourself again. And that makes it easier for others to love you!

"He who can no longer pause to wonder and stand rapt in awe, is as good as dead; his eyes are closed." – A.E.

Yes, we must agree with Mr. "Smarty-Pants." Our bodies really are truly remarkable.

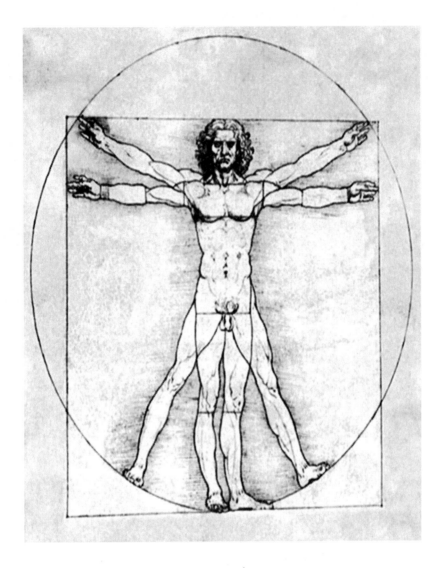

The **Vitruvian Man** is a famous 15th century Renaissance drawing by Leonardo da Vinci. As a blend of art and science, the drawing is da Vinci's exploration of the ideal human proportions of a male body per architect Vitruvius Pollio. The diagram demonstrates the geometry of perfect proportions, by having the extended hands and feet simultaneously inscribed within a circle *and* a square. Indeed, the feat of equating a circle's area with a square's area in a single mathematical formula, called "squaring the circle," was attempted but never accomplished. The Vitruvian Man was the only way to connect the two. Vitruvius believed that there was a divine connection between the human form and the universe and that an architect should focus on three themes when considering a design: <u>strength, functionality and beauty</u>.

<u>Yes, your biochemical body is truly a beautiful system!</u> For you to cultivate a beautifully lean Vitruvian body with muscle *strength*, biochemical *functionality* and the *beauty* of loving yourself, you need to be committed to wholesome foods and weight-bearing exercises. Just imagine drawing the 21st century **Food Industry Man,** the one who incessantly encounters synthetic trans-fats, HFCS, heavily refined carbohydrates, hidden sugars and fake-foods. I don't think da Vinci would be inspired to pick up his pen!

Appendix A

12-Week Beginner Workout Program

When you decide to undertake a workout program, don't try to work your program around your life. You have to work your life AROUND your program. A paradigm shift.

All workouts should take a maximum of about an hour of your time, not any longer. This program is geared toward the first time-to-weights individual and I've used exercises that are not too difficult to learn without a personal trainer.

The workout below is for a "beginner", one who has been lifting weights only for 0-12 months. An "intermediate" would be 1-6 years, and "advanced" for more than 6 years. There are many other more challenging exercises that can be taken on over time.

Weeks 1 through 4 = whole body training
(such training will stress *every* major muscle group[323] *every* training day)

- **3 days/week** (with at least 1 rest day between each workout day)
Example = Monday, Wednesday and Friday
Or
Tuesday, Thursday and one weekend day

---

[323] The major muscle groups include quadriceps, hamstrings, glutes, calves, chest, back, arms, shoulders, trapezius and abdominals. And remember that the lower half of your body constitutes two third's of your skeletal muscle content. This is why deadlift, squat and lunge variations burn so many calories!!!

Weeks 5 through 8 = 2-day training split

(such training will stress *all muscle groups* over 2 days *only*)

\-   **4 days/week** (with 2 consecutive workout days and at least 1 rest day between each pair)

Example = Monday/Tuesday and Thursday/Friday (Wednesday = rest day)
Or
Tuesday/Wednesday and Friday/Saturday (Thursday = rest day)
Or
Wednesday/Thursday and Saturday/Sunday (Friday = rest day)

Weeks 9 through 12 = 5-day training split

(these weeks will involve training *different muscle groups on different days* which allows longer rest periods for the worked muscles to recover and thereby get stronger); in effect, you can increase the *intensity* of the training as well as the *total workout volume* on any of the major muscle groups)

\-   **5 days/week** (you choose the 5 workout days; don't worry about when you incorporate your 2 rest days)

I'll detail each 4-week sub-program and add some tips at the end. You must track yourself as you'll find that the amount of weight you move will eventually become too easy as your muscle strength improves. That's when you have to use incrementally higher weights. This is why I suggest carrying around a notebook and pen. I'll show you how to write down your sets and reps and weights with sample sheets. You can photocopy them. Again, I have to stress how excited you'll be as you experience personal improvement. Yes, you'll be hooked on weight-training and the benefits you'll reap from your dedication.

And I do profusely apologize for the small font and for the fact that some workouts are spread out over two pages, but I wanted it to be set up more easily for photocopying. You can enlarge it at that point if you wish to avoid the use of bifocals on the gym floor.

Weeks 1 through 4 (do this work out every day at the gym)

Exercise (every day)	# of Sets	# of Reps	Week 1 Weight[324]	Week 2 Weight	Week 3 Weight	Week 4 Weight
LEG PRESS MACHINE[325] (keep your knees in line with your feet)	3	8-10				
INCLINE BENCH DB CHEST PRESS	3	8-10				
SEATED CABLE ROW (elbows and shoulders are only moving joints)	3	8-10				
SEATED DB SHOULDER PRESS (straight arms at top of movement)	3	8-10				
STANDING DB BICEP CURL	3	10-12				

---

[324] Write your weights in the empty columns. You can see the suggested sets and repetitions. As you increase weight over the weeks, you may be writing 5-5-5 at the outset, then 7 ½ – 5-5, then 7 ½ – 7 ½ – 5 (e.g., you increase the weight but fatigue before the final set) and eventually 7 ½ – 7 ½ – 7 ½ by the completion of the 4th week. Just ensure that you get the *proper number of sets and reps completed* even if you end up lowering the weight as you continue. Fatigue is what is important. Rest for a minute or so between each set of reps. Always maintain good form and range of motion (per your flexibility).

[325] If a machine is in use, go to another exercise and return later. This is the advantage of "straight" sets. Given that you use a machine for 3 sets in a row, you can flip the order as needed.

STANDING TRICEP ROPE PRESSDOWN (don't allow shoulder joint to move)	3	10-12				
FORWARD BALL CRUNCH or glute bridges	3	12-15				
STAIR-CLIMBER *"cardio" machine – use a "stepper" machine or box if no "climber" at gym.*	1	5-10 mins				

Weeks 5 through 8 (do this work out only on day #1 of each week)

Exercise (day #1)	# of Sets	# of Reps	WEEK 5 Weight	WEEK 6 Weight	WEEK 7 Weight	WEEK 8 Weight
BB DEADLIFTS (keep neutral spine, go slow)	3	10-12				
SEATED DB SHOULDER PRESS	3	8-10				
SPLIT LEG BB SQUATS (each side) (back knee should almost touch floor)	2	10-12				
STANDING DB LATERAL RAISE (arms should only go to parallel to floor, not higher)	3	8-10				

Exercise	# of Sets	# of Reps				
MACHINE SEATED LEG CURL (keep knees at pivot line)	3	10-12				
MACHINE SEATED LEG EXTENSION (keep knees at pivot line)	3	10-12				
CABLE "SHRUGS" (put chin down during movement)	2	10-12				
FORWARD BALL CRUNCH or reverse crunches	3	12-15				
STAIR-CLIMBER (don't lean forward) or rowing machine	1	5-10 mins				

Weeks 5 through 8 (do this work out only on day #2 of each week)

Exercise (day #2)	# of Sets	# of Reps	Week 5 Weight	Week 6 Weight	Week 7 Weight	Week 8 Weight
INCLINE DB CHEST PRESS	3	10-12				
SEATED CABLE ROW (lock your trunk and only move at the elbow and shoulder)	3	10-12				

PUSH-UPS (hands higher than feet on a squat machine BB)	2	8-10	Track the position of the bar. Lower is harder.			
LAT PULLDOWN (don't move at your hips)	3	10-12				
STANDING DB BICEP CURLS	3	10-12				
STANDING TRICEP ROPE PRESSDOWN (concentrate on pushing handles out as you go down)	3	10-12				
STANDING DB HAMMER CURLS	3	8-10				
LYING DB TRICEP EXTENSIONS (only bend at elbow and not shoulder)	3	10-12				
STAIR-CLIMBER or stationary bike	1	5-10 mins				

Weeks 9 through 12 (do this work out only on day #1 of each week)

Exercise (LEG AND ABS DAY)	# of Sets	# of Reps	Week 9 day#1 Weight	Week 10 day#1 Weight	Week 11 day#1 Weight	Week 12– day#1 Weight
BB BACK SQUAT	3	12-15				
MACHINE LEG EXTENSION (ensure your knees are at the pivot line)	3	12-15				
WALKING LUNGES WITH DBs (keep your trunk upright)	3	20				
MACHINE LEG CURL (ensure your knees are at the pivot line)	3	12-15				
FORWARD BALL CRUNCH	3	12-15				
PLANKS (keep your body perfectly straight)	3	12-15				
MACHINE LYING LEG CURL (keep your knees off the bench)	2	10-12				

Exercise	# of Sets	# of Reps				
BALL "V" TOSS (ensure that you lift your head/shoulders off the floor too)	2	10-12				
STAIR-CLIMBER	1	5-10 mins				

Weeks 9 through 12 (do this work out only on day #2 of each week)

Exercise (CHEST AND TRICEPS DAY)	# of Sets	# of Reps	Week 9 day#2 Weight	Week 10 day#2 Weight	Week 11 day#2 Weight	Week 12 day#2 Weight
INCLINE DB CHEST PRESS	3	12-15				
LYING DB TRICEPS EXTENSION	3	12-15				
PEC FLYE MACHINE (try to hug-a-bear, keep shoulders back)	3	12-15				
ASSISTED MACHINE TRICEP DIPS (put knees on back of pad)	3	12-15				
BB BENCH (CHEST) PRESS (hands wider than shoulders)	3	8-10				

Exercise	# of Sets	# of Reps					
REVERSE GRIP CABLE PRESSDOWN (use an EZ bar, bend only at elbows)	3	8-10					
STANDING TRICEP ROPE PRESSDOWN	2	12-15					
HANGING LEG RAISE (keep lower spine off backrest if possible)	2	8-10					
ROWING MACHINE	1	5-10 mins					

Weeks 9 through 12 (do this work out only on day #3 of each week)

Exercise (BACK AND BICEPS DAY)	# of Sets	# of Reps	Week 9 day#3 Weight	Week 10 day#3 Weight	Week 11 day#3 Weight	Week 12 day#3 Weight
LAT PULLDOWNS	3	12-15				
STANDING DB BICEP CURLS	3	12-15				
SEATED CABLE ROWS	3	12-15				
STANDING DB HAMMER CURLS	3	12-15				
ASSISTED MACHINE PULL-UPS (finish the movement right up to the top)	3	12-15				

INCLINE BENCH DB CURLS	3	12-15					
STRAIGHT BAR CABLE PRESSDOWN	2	12-15					
REVERSE CRUNCH	2	10-12					
STAIR-CLIMBER	1	5-10 mins					

Weeks 9 through 12 (do this work out only on day #4 of each week)

Exercise (LEGS AND DELTS DAY)	# of Sets	# of Reps	Week 9 day#4 Weight	Week 10 day#4 Weight	Week 11 day#4 Weight	Week 12 day#4 Weight
PRONE "SMITH MACHINE" BB ROWS (keep back almost parallel to floor)	2	10-12				
BB DEADLIFTS	3	12-15				
SEATED DB SHOULDER PRESS	3	12-15				
MACHINE LEG CURL	3	12-15				

Exercise						
DELT DB LATERAL RAISE	3	12-15				
MACHINE LEG EXTENSION	3	12-15				
DELT DB FRONT RAISES	2	10-12				
MOUNTAIN CLIMBER PLANKS	2	16-20 (one leg = a count of 1)				
STAIR-CLIMBER or stationary bike	1	5-10 mins				

Weeks 9 through 12 (do this work out only on day #5 of each week)

Exercise (PUSH/PULL AND TRAPS DAY)	# of Sets	# of Reps	Week 9 day#5 Weight	Week 10 day#5 Weight	Week 11 day#5 Weight	Week 12 day#5 Weight
PUSH-UPS (lower the BB support over time)	2	10-12				
ASSISTED MACHINE PULL-UPS	3	12-15				
PEC FLYE MACHINE (shoulders back)	3	12-15				
LAT PULLDOWN (shoulders down)	3	12-15				

INCLINE BB BENCH PRESS	2	10-12				
SEATED CABLE ROWS	3	12-15				
CABLE "SHRUGS"	3	8-10				
BALL "V" TOSS	2	10-12				
STAIR-CLIMBER	1	5-10 mins				

Please remember the following:

- -It may feel boring doing the same thing over and over, but it's the best way to *develop muscle strength and perfect good form.* You have to build-up your exercise *repertoire* gradually.

- -Google the names of the exercises listed on the pages above BEFORE you go to the gym to see *how best to perform* them. In my next book or via Instagram or YouTube videos, I'll detail exercise approaches in greater detail.

- -The above are all *"straight"* sets; that is, you do the same exercise on the same machine for 3 sets.

- -Move only the joints necessary to complete the full *range-of-motion* for each of the exercises.

- -Maintain *good form* throughout all exercises, use the mirrors to help study and correct your form. Reduce the weight used if unable to lift properly, but complete all required reps.

- -Be careful with your shoulders; usually you have to ensure they're held down and back during weight-lifting movements.

- -Always employ a *slow tempo* on all exercise movements; don't use any swinging momentum. Don't be in a hurry!

- -*If hurried*, shorten (or skip) stair-climber time. If you have extra time, stay on the stair-climber longer than 10-15 minutes.

Index of Key Terms and Concepts

lactose-intolerance, 202
large intestine, 40
LDL (low density lipoprotein), 333
LDL cholesterol, 337
lead acetate, 136
lean protein, 64, 88, 89, 90, 98, 105, 107, 108, 115, 120, 122, 138, 139, 234, 294, 302, 321, 371, 374, 379, 380, 382
lectins, 113, 314, 315
lemon juice, 150, 162, 180, 183
Leonardo da Vinci, 386
leptin, 45, 57
leptin hormones, 45, 138
leptin-resistance, 45, 57, 100, 135, 385
leucine, 110, 112, 237
ligaments, 60, 73, 104, 143, 275
lipase, 39, 291, 292
lipogenic enzymes, 43
lipolytic enzymes, 43
lumbar, 295
lutein, 139, 335
lycopene, 335
lymphatic system, 72

M

magazine models, 293
magnesium, 56, 62, 86, 144, 145, 147, 152, 158, 159, 223, 242, 323, 324
manganese, 158
marathon runners, 133, 153, 175
Marcus Arelius, 374, 375
maximal oxygen uptake, 290
Mediterranean diet, 98
menopausal women, 159, 264, 291, 318
menopause, 19, 37, 51, 52, 53, 59, 60, 61, 66, 71
Menopause, 51

mercury, 96
mesomorph, 317, 318, 319, 320
metabolic adaptations, 268
metabolic disease, 191
metabolic hormones, 59, 61
metabolic rate, 39, 47, 63, 121, 149, 167, 174, 231, 233, 239, 263, 280, 293, 299, 325, 337, 378, 382, 385
metabolic syndrome, 198, 334
metabolism, 26, 239
metabolites, 130
methane producers, 328
microbes, 314, 326
microbiome, 156, 326, 328
Microbiome, 326
microfilaments, 265
micronutrients, 86, 215, 223, 322
milk thistle, 323
mitochondria, 230, 267, 271, 272, 273, 274, 280, 282, 284, 290
moment angles, 265
moment arm, 266
momentum, 255, 257, 258, 399
monoglycerides, 344, 345
monosaccharide, 201, 203
monosodium glutamate, 160
monounsaturated fat, 93, 99
MSG, 160, 190
multi-joint exercises, 250, 321
muscle contraction, 265, 266, 270
muscle endurance, 164, 256, 274, 279
muscle fatigue, 235, 248, 263, 270, 272, 321
muscle heads, 253, 255
muscle mass, 36, 49, 61, 65, 73, 82, 88, 106, 108, 122, 172, 217, 234, 235, 240, 241, 243, 245, 269, 318, 325
muscle memory, 269
muscle power, 256

muscle strength, 159, 238, 256, 260, 264, 270, 277, 288, 290, 387, 389, 399

muscle tissue percentage, 26, 73, 286

muscle-building, 37, 49, 106, 107, 121, 185, 214, 221, 222, 225, 235, 275, 286, 288, 292, 300, 302, 325, 376, 383

muscle-eating, 187, 222, 294, 302, 303

muscle-loss, 49, 173, 290

muscle-wasting, 36, 187, 234, 240, 292

myoglobin, 282, 283

myosin, 73, 265, 266, 267

N

natural flavoring, 308

negative energy balance, 232

net carbohydrates, 126, 221

neurons, 364

neurotransmitter, 209

nitrates, 331

nitrogen, 64, 106, 110, 153, 242, 294, 299, 300, 308, 371

non-hydrogenated oils, 70

nutrient-timing, 381

nutritional electrolyte minerals, 152

nutritional labels, 346

O

obese, 15

oil lipids, 92

omega-3 fatty-acids, 56, 93, 94, 95, 96, 100, 101, 102, 123, 130, 142, 169, 234, 305, 369

omega-6 fatty-acids, 56, 93, 94, 96, 97, 102, 139, 160, 310, 331, 332, 350, 353

omega-9 fatty-acids, 93, 94, 96, 350

opposing hormones, 35, 79

optimal calorie consumption, 26

osmosis, 324, 332

osteopenia, 19, 62, 322

osteoporosis, 62, 146, 234, 236, 280

over-training, 104, 236, 298, 321

over-worked liver, 152, 163, 164, 180, 196

oxidation, 128, 140

oxidative, 74, 102, 175, 189, 231, 262, 263, 266, 267, 272, 273, 282, 285, 289, 291, 292, 301, 302, 303, 333, 373

P

palatability, 114, 306

palm oil, 353

pancreas, 32, 35, 43, 50, 54, 101, 107, 118, 121, 170, 198, 207, 218, 330

panting, 292

partially hydrogenated oils, 56, 70, 97, 227, 345

penicillin, 328

personal trainer, 7, 16, 18, 19, 20, 21, 186, 238, 245, 255, 259, 260, 261, 274, 277, 278, 287, 297, 334, 378

pH, 85, 157, 158, 159, 160, 162, 163, 197, 223, 291

Ph, 157

phenolics, 336

phosphate, 116, 152, 262, 267, 269, 270, 289, 290, 301, 349

phospholipids, 289

phosphorus/phosphoric acid, 158

phytoestrogen, 133

pituitary gland, 61, 235

plant-based meat alternatives, 113

Bibliography

Action Plan for Menopause (2005), Barbara Bushman and Anice Clark Young, American College of Sports Medicine.

The Addictocarb Diet (2015), Bruce Roseman, Benbella Books, Inc.

Alkalize or Die (1991), Theodore A. Baroody, Holographic Health Press.

The BioChemical Machine: Empowering Your Body Chemistry (2004), Eleonora De Lennart, Big Apple Vision Publishing, Inc.

Brain Maker (2015), David Perlmutter, Hachette Book Club.

The Calorie Myth (2014), Jonathan Bailor, Harper-Collins Publisher.

The Cortisol Connection Diet (2004), Shawn Talbot, Hunter House Inc.

The Dorito Effect: The Surprising New Truth About Food and Flavor (2015), Mark Schatzker, Simon & Schuster.

Eat Yourself Thin (1999), Michel Montignac, Michel-Ange Publishing.

The 8 Hour Diet (2013), David Zinczenko, New York, Rodale Inc.

Encyclopedia of Muscle & Strength (2006), Jim Stoppani, Human Kinetics.

Enter the Zone (1995), Barry Spears, Harper Collins Publishers.

Fat and Furious: Overcome your body's resistance to weight loss now (2004), Loree Taylor Jordan, Madison Publishing.

Fat Chance: Beating the Odds Against Sugar, Processed Food, Obesity, and Disease (2013), Robert H. Lustig, Hudson Street Press.

Fat Wars: 45 Days to Transform Your Body (2000), Brad J. King, Macmillan Canada.

Got Milked? (2015), Alissa Hamilton, Harper Collins Publishers.

Gut: The Inside Story of Our Body's Most Underrated Organ (2015), Giulia Enders, Greystone Books Ltd.

Hardwired For Fitness (2011), Robert Portman and John Ivy, Basis Health Publications, Inc.

How Food Works (2017), Dr. Sarah Brewer (Editorial Consultant), Penquin Random House.

Just the Rules! (2011), Tosca Reno, Robert Kennedy Publishing.

Ketogenic Mediterranean Diet (2017), Robert Santos-Prowse, Ulysses Press.

Make Over Your Metabolism (2006), Robert Reames, Meredith Books.

Power Eating (2014), Susan Kleiner, Human Kinetics.

Probiotics for Dummies (2012), Shekhar K. Challa, John Wiley and Sons, Inc.

Pure, White and Deadly (2016), John Yudkin, Penquin Life.

Quit Digging Your Grave with a Knife and Fork (2005), Mike Huckabee, Time Warner Book Club.

Real Food Fake Food (2016), Larry Olmsted, Algonquin Books of Chapel Hill.

Salt Sugar Fat: How the Food Giants Hooked Us (2013), Michael Moss, McClelland & Stewart Ltd.

Small Changes, Big Results (2005), Ellie Krieger, Clarkson Potter/Publishers.

The South Beach Diet (2003), Arthur Agatston, Rodelle Inc.

Sugar Counter for Health – The Smart Person's Guide to Hidden Sugars (2016), Elizabeth Roberts, Souvenir Press Ltd., London.

Superbodies: Peak Performance Secrets from the World's Best Athletes (2012), Greg Wells, HarperCollins Publishers.

The Sweetener Trap & How to Avoid It (2008), Beatrice Trum Hunter, Houghton Mifflin.

That Sugar Book (2015), Damon Gameau, Macmillan.

Totally Toned Arms (2010), Rylan Duggan, New York, Grand Central Publishing.

Wheat Belly (2011), William Davis, New York, Rodale Inc.

You're Not Sick, You're Thirsty! (2003), Fereydoon Batmanghelidj, Hachette Book Group.

Recommended Reading:

Atomic Habits: An Easy and Proven Way to Build Good Habits and Break Bad Ones (2018), James Clear, Penquin Random House.

SWEAT: Special Workouts, Exercises and Advanced Techniques (2020), Geoffrey Verity Schofield, Independently Published.

The Plant Paradox: The Hidden Dangers in "Healthy" Foods That Cause Disease and Weight Gain (2017), Steven Gundry, Harper Collins.